Download Forms on Nolo.com

You can download the forms in this book at:

 www.nolo.com/back-of-book/LICE.html

We'll also post updates whenever there's an important change to the law affecting this book—as well as articles and other related materials.

More Resources from Nolo.com

 Legal Forms, Books, & Software
Hundreds of do-it-yourself products—all written in plain English, approved, and updated by our in-house legal editors.

 Legal Articles
Get informed with thousands of free articles on everyday legal topics. Our articles are accurate, up to date, and reader friendly.

Find a Lawyer
Want to talk to a lawyer? Use Nolo to find a lawyer who can help you with your case.

⚖ NOLO **The Trusted Name**
(but don't take our word for it)

"In Nolo you can trust."
THE NEW YORK TIMES

"Nolo is always there in a jam as the nation's premier publisher of do-it-yourself legal books."
NEWSWEEK

"Nolo publications...guide people simply through the how, when, where and why of the law."
THE WASHINGTON POST

"[Nolo's]...material is developed by experienced attorneys who have a knack for making complicated material accessible."
LIBRARY JOURNAL

"When it comes to self-help legal stuff, nobody does a better job than Nolo..."
USA TODAY

"The most prominent U.S. publisher of self-help legal aids."
TIME MAGAZINE

"Nolo is a pioneer in both consumer and business self-help books and software."
LOS ANGELES TIMES

10th Edition

Profit From Your Idea

How to Make Smart Licensing Deals

Attorney Richard Stim

Riverhead Free Library
330 Court Street
Riverhead NY 11901

TENTH EDITION	AUGUST 2020
Editor	REBECCA PIRIUS
Cover Design	SUSAN PUTNEY
Production	SUSAN PUTNEY
Proofreading	SUSAN CARLSON GREENE
Index	VICTORIA BAKER
Printing	BANG PRINTING

Names: Stim, Richard, author.
Title: Profit from your idea : how to make smart licensing deals / Attorney
  Richard Stim.
Description: 10th edition. | Berkeley : NOLO, 2020. | Includes index.
Identifiers: LCCN 2020007202 (print) | LCCN 2020007203 (ebook) | ISBN
  9781413327915 (paperback) | ISBN 9781413327922 (ebook)
Subjects: LCSH: License agreements--United States--Popular works. | Patent
  licenses--United States--Popular works.
Classification: LCC KF3145 .S75 2020 (print) | LCC KF3145 (ebook) | DDC
  346.7304/86--dc23
LC record available at https://lccn.loc.gov/2020007202
LC ebook record available at https://lccn.loc.gov/2020007203

This book covers only United States law, unless it specifically states otherwise.

Please note

We know that accurate, plain-English legal information can help you solve many of your own legal problems. But this text is not a substitute for personalized advice from a knowledgeable lawyer. If you want the help of a trained professional—and we'll always point out situations in which we think that's a good idea—consult an attorney licensed to practice in your state.

Dedication

This book is dedicated to Andrew Bergman.

About the Author

Rich Stim is the author of several Nolo books including *Music Law: How to Run Your Band's Business*; *Patent, Copyright & Trademark: An Intellectual Property Desk Reference*; and *Patent Pending in 24 Hours*. He writes the Dear Rich blog (http://dearrichblog.com) where he answers questions regarding intellectual property.

Table of Contents

Your Legal Companion 1

1 Gearing Up to License Your Invention 3

Licenses 5

Assignments 9

The Licensing Process 10

Avoiding Conflicts Among Multiple Agreements 12

Challenges to Your Ownership 18

Transferring Ownership of Your Invention to Your Business 20

Disclosing Information About Your Invention 32

Keeping Your Records 34

No False Hopes! Reviewing Your Invention's Commercial Potential 36

2 Intellectual Property Protection 43

General Rules for Legal Protection of Inventions 45

Utility Patents 47

Trade Secrets 55

Trademarks 61

Design Patents 63

Copyright Law 65

Sorting Out Nonfunctional Features: Design Patents, Product
    Configurations, and Copyright 66

3 Ownership Issues for Inventor Employees 69

What Type of Intellectual Property Is Involved? 70

Employer/Employee: Patent and Trade Secret Ownership 71

Inventions Covered by Copyright 79

Special Employment Situations 79

Working Out Ownership Issues With Your Employer 84

4 Invention Financing and Joint Ownership 89

How Much Money Do You Need to License Your Idea? 91

Sources of Funding 94

Joint Ownership 103

How Income, Loans, or Investments Can Create Joint Ownership 106

The Joint Ownership Agreement 108

5 Licensing Agents and Representatives 115

Agents 116

Completing the Agent Agreement 119

Attorneys as Agents 126

Invention Marketing Scams 128

6 Soliciting Potential Licensees 133

Before You Begin Your Search 135

How to Find Potential Licensees 137

How to Overcome a Licensee's Bias Against Submissions 140

What's the Best Way to Solicit a Potential Licensee? 142

Product Presentations 146

Should You Solicit Foreign Licensees? 147

7 Protecting Confidential Information 155

Confidential Information and Nondisclosure Agreements 156

Proceeding Without an Agreement 168

Waiver Agreements... 170

When You Have Sufficient Bargaining Power... 172

Disclosing to Employees and Contractors 174

Disclosing to an Attorney 175

8 The Key Elements of Your Agreement.. 177

From Handshake to License... 178

Identifying the Parties... 179

Describing Your Invention and the Licensed Products................................ 180

Specifying Which Rights Are Granted.. 185

Defining the Territory 192

Setting the Length (Term) of the Agreement 194

9 Money: It Matters 205

Some Basic Royalty Definitions... 207

Ways to Get Paid 209

The Mysteries of Net Sales and Deductions... 214

How Much Do You Get?.. 216

Royalty Provisions... 220

10 Negotiating Your Agreement... 231

What, Me Negotiate?... 232

Documenting the Important Contract Elements... 235

Letter of Intent... 238

Option Agreements... 244

What If the Licensee Wants to Proceed Without a Written License
  Agreement?... 252

11 **Sample Agreement**...253

License Agreement 255

Optional License Agreement Provisions...290

Modifying the Sample Agreement for Your Needs...........................297

12 **Warranties, Indemnification, and Proprietary Rights Provisions**...........299

Promises, Promises ... Warranties, Representations, and Covenants...........300

Indemnity: The "Hold Harmless" Provision 303

Licensee Warranties and Indemnity...310

Proprietary Rights 312

Commercialization and Exploitation...316

Samples and Quality Control...317

Insurance...317

13 **Termination and Posttermination** 321

Termination and Posttermination... 322

Termination Based Upon a Fixed Term... 323

Termination at Will...324

Termination Based on Contract Problems 324

Termination and Bankruptcy... 326

Posttermination: What Happens Afterwards?...........................327

Survival of the Fittest... 329

14 **Boilerplate and Standard Provisions**... 331

Paying the Lawyer's Bills... 333

Dispute Resolution 335

Governing Law 337

Jurisdiction 338

Waiver... 339

Severability...340

Entire Understanding 340

Attachments and Exhibits 341

Notices 341

No Joint Venture 342

Assignments 342

Force Majeure 344

Headings 344

Establishing Escrow Accounts 345

15 Service Provisions 351

Service Provisions Versus Separate Service Agreements 352

Training the Licensee's Personnel 354

Installation of Equipment 355

Technical Support for the Licensee or for End Users 356

Improving, Modifying, and Delivering the Invention 357

16 Handling the Licensee's Agreement 365

Dealing With Suggested Changes 366

Evaluating an Agreement Presented to You 368

Evaluating the Provisions and Suggesting Changes 369

The Cover Letter 379

17 After You Sign the Agreement 381

Create Your Contract Calendar 383

Dealing With Royalty Statements 385

Resolving Licensing Disputes 388

Avoiding Patent Misuse and Illegal Agreements 390

The Taxman Cometh 394

Quality Control 395

18 Help Beyond This Book...397

Licensing and Intellectual Property Resources.................................398

Working With an Attorney 402

Appendixes

How to Use the Downloadable Forms on the Nolo Website...................407

Editing RTFs...408

List of Forms and Interviews..409

Index...411

Your Legal Companion

If you're like most inventors, you know how hard it is to design and patent a great idea. Guess what? Earning money from that great idea is even harder. For every successful patented invention, there are thousands and thousands of financially unsuccessful ventures.

What can you do to minimize your risks and maximize your chances of earning a profit from your invention? The most successful approach is to license your great idea. A license is an agreement that allows someone else (usually a company) to use or sell your invention for a limited period of time. In return, you receive either a one-time payment or continuing payments called royalties.

How do you find a company to license your invention? And then, how do you negotiate and enter into a fair agreement with that company without spending all your profits on attorneys' fees?

This book can help. By streamlining the licensing process and offering a layperson's guide to licensing deals, it will enable you to make a smooth transition from inventor to licensor.

This book has three parts:

- **Ownership rights.** Chapters 1 through 4 are geared at sorting out your ownership rights under patent, trade secret, or copyright laws.
- **Soliciting licensees.** Chapters 5 through 7 explain how to deal with licensing agents, how to find and solicit prospective companies, and how to protect your trade secrets.
- **The license agreement.** Chapters 8 through 15 provide information about the license agreement, from the key elements (including royalties, geographic boundaries, and length) to the boilerplate (or more secondary) terms. Chapter 16 shows you how to deal with changes to your agreement (or how to deal with a company's proposed agreement). Chapter 17 discusses issues that may arise after you sign the license agreement.

This Book Isn't for You If...

This book is not for people who wish to manufacture and market their inventions themselves—for example, if you invented a new mousetrap and created a company to make and sell your product.

1

Gearing Up to License Your Invention

Licenses 5

    When You License, You Are Leasing Your Legal Rights 6

    Licenses Can Be Flexible 7

    Licenses Can Be Written or Oral 9

Assignments 9

The Licensing Process 10

    Meet and Greet the Potential Licensee 10

    Negotiating the License 12

    Execution and Monitoring 12

Avoiding Conflicts Among Multiple Agreements 12

    Agreements That Can Affect Licensing 15

    Keeping Track of Agreements 18

Challenges to Your Ownership 18

    Types of Ownership Challenges 20

    Dealing With Ownership Challenges 20

Transferring Ownership of Your Invention to Your Business 20

    Sole Proprietorships 21

    General Partnerships 22

    Limited Partnerships 23

    Corporations 23

    How Do You Transfer Ownership of Your Invention to Your Business? 25

Disclosing Information About Your Invention 32

Keeping Your Records... 34

   Keep an Inventor's Notebook 34

   Use Nondisclosure Agreements... 34

   Maintain a Business Notebook and Files 34

   Insist on Written Agreements 35

No False Hopes! Reviewing Your Invention's Commercial Potential 36

   The SBA's Four Tests for Commercial Potential...37

   The Innovation Center's Factors for Commercial Potential...............................37

   The *Patent It Yourself* Factors for Commercial Potential....................................39

   Testing the Waters Yourself.. 40

   Getting an Expert Opinion...41

   What If There Is No Commercial Potential? 41

E ureka! You've developed an invention and believe it has commercial potential. What's next? For many inventors, the best way to profit from an invention is to have someone else—usually a company that already specializes in similar products—develop, manufacture, or market the invention. However, since an inventor holds ownership rights (sometimes called title) in an invention, another company cannot do these things unless the inventor gives permission. Broadly speaking, this permission is called a license.

This chapter will give you an overview of the licensing process and help you screen out potential problems that could hinder your ability to license your invention. Review this chapter if you answer "yes" to any of the following questions:

- Would you like an explanation of the difference between a license and an assignment?
- Do you want a brief description of the legal rights related to your invention?
- Have you signed any documents regarding your invention?
- Would you like an understanding of who might own your invention besides yourself?
- Have you shown your invention to—or discussed it with—anyone?
- Do you want some help in keeping track of your business transactions?

- Would you like information about how to assess the potential value of your invention in the marketplace?

What We Mean by an Invention

The term "invention" as used throughout this book refers to any innovation, device, or process that can be commercially used or developed. Although the strongest form of protection for your invention is a patent, this book does not deal solely with patented or patentable inventions. Many inventions might not qualify for patent protection but can be protected under some other legal principle, such as trade secret or copyright. If your invention has commercial potential and is protectable under some form of intellectual property law, you can use this book to help you license it to others. See Chapter 2 for an overview of the different ways your invention may be protected.

Licenses

A license is an agreement in which you let someone else use, develop, or reproduce your invention for a period of time. In return, you receive compensation—either a onetime payment or continuing payments called royalties. Your power to make this kind of agreement is based on the premise that you control the right to make and sell your invention—which, in turn, depends upon whether your invention is protected under intellectual property laws. (See Chapter 2.) If your invention cannot be protected under intellectual property laws, it's unlikely you will license your invention. Why? Because, if your invention is not protected, anyone can make and sell it. So, why should they pay you?

If your invention is protectable, you can stop others from making or selling it. In other words, a company can make and sell a "protected" invention only if you give them permission. By negotiating a license, a company can make, sell, or use your invention without fear of a lawsuit, as long as it abides by the terms of the license. Basically, a license gives the company a right to do something it would otherwise be prohibited from doing.

**Voice Alert System for Use on Bicycles
No. 6,317,036**

You Are the Licensor, They Are the Licensee

For purposes of this book, you—as owner of the invention—will always be the licensor, and the company using or reproducing your invention is called the licensee.

According to legal practice, the person who is the source of the activity gets an "er" or "or" suffix (such as employer, lessor, discloser). The person who is the recipient of the activity gets an "ee" (such as employee or lessee).

When You License, You Are Leasing Your Legal Rights

A license for an invention is similar to a lease for a house or an apartment. A tenant makes periodic payments to an owner of property for the right to use it. If the tenant fails to honor the terms of the lease or rental agreement, the owner can reclaim possession and make the tenant leave. Similarly, a licensee pays you royalties (similar to rent) for the right to manufacture, sell, or use your invention for a period of time. If the licensee fails to pay you or otherwise breaches your agreement, the agreement may terminate and, provided the license is drafted properly, you can license your invention to someone else.

It's also important to realize that you do not license the invention itself. Rather, you license your legal rights to the invention. This distinction causes confusion for some inventors. Legal rights —patent, copyright, trademark, or trade secret rights—are what give you title or ownership of the invention, much like a deed to a house gives you title to the property. When you license your invention, what you are really transferring to the licensee are your legal rights, such as your rights to manufacture, sell, and use the invention. These legal rights will be explained in more detail in Chapter 2. It's beyond the scope of this book to assist you in securing intellectual property protection. In Chapter 18, "Help Beyond This Book," we refer you to other resources for protecting intellectual property.

For now, keep in mind that the primary goals in licensing are to:

- determine what legal rights you have
- acquire the appropriate protection for those rights, and
- license those rights to others who can pay you for the privilege.

Licenses Can Be Flexible

A license agreement can be drafted according to the specific needs of the licensor or licensee. For example, you can limit the license of your invention for a period of time, such as one year. You can limit the license to a certain area, such as Canada. You can even license your invention to more than one manufacturer at one time.

> **EXAMPLE:** Joe invented a patented flotation device. Two companies are interested in it: a toy company and a company that makes boating products. Joe can sign two license agreements and earn royalties for both uses.

Because a license can be as flexible as the parties wish it to be, the task of drafting a license typically involves much more than simply agreeing to standardized language often found in legal agreements. That is what this book is all about—teaching you how to draft a license agreement that is just right for you. Drafting a license agreement is covered thoroughly in Chapter 8.

Frictionless Noncontact Engaging Drive Skate & Skateboard
No. 6,007,074

Forms of Intellectual Property

Because licensing basically involves lending your legal rights to someone else, it's crucial that you know precisely which legal rights are associated with your invention. These rights are sometimes referred to as "proprietary rights" or "intellectual property rights." Below are the intellectual property rights associated with inventions. Chapter 2 provides more information on intellectual property.

Utility patents protect inventions (functional devices and processes) that are new and unique. When you have a utility patent, you can stop others from making, selling, or using your invention. You must apply for and receive a patent from the federal government before you have patent rights in the United States.

Design patents protect decorative designs that are used on functional devices. You must acquire a design patent from the federal government before you have design patent rights. As with utility patents, you can't stop illegal copying of your design until your design patent has been issued.

Trade secret law protects confidential information that gives you an advantage over competitors. You must treat the information with secrecy and disclose it only to those who agree to keep it secret. No registration is necessary, as registration would defeat the confidentiality requirement. A trade secret is sometimes an alternative or complement to patent protection, particularly for inventors who don't wish to make their methods or processes public. An inventor can also use trade secrets as a form of protection during the period between applying for and getting a patent.

Copyright protects the artistic expression contained in writing, software, art, music, dance, architecture, and movies. Copyright does not protect functional objects, such as clothing or furniture; it protects only the artistic elements, such as fabric designs or ornamental furniture legs. You have copyright protection under the law as soon as you create the work. You don't have to register your work to get copyright protection, but we advise doing so to strengthen your rights

Trademark law is part of a family of laws known as "unfair competition" (see below) and protects your right to exclusively use a name or symbol to signify your goods or services. Trademark law also protects certain designs or features of your goods, such as the uniquely shaped Absolut vodka bottle. You have trademark rights once you use the trademark in commerce (that is, once you sell the goods to consumers). You don't have to register your work to get trademark protection, but we advise doing so to strengthen your rights.

Unfair competition law protects the way you sell your product. A number of state and federal laws prohibit business practices that unfairly hinder marketplace rivalries, such as making fraudulent (false) claims about a competitor's invention. However, with the exception of rules about trademarks, unfair competition generally doesn't pertain to the rights that you are licensing.

More information on the different forms of intellectual property protection is provided in Chapter 2.

Licenses Can Be Written or Oral

Most licenses are written. But, a license doesn't have to be written to be valid. An oral license can be enforceable under contract law principles. However, you should be aware of the limits on oral agreements. For example, in most states, an oral agreement is only valid for one year.

Due to their limitations and because proving an oral agreement is usually more difficult than proving one set out in writing, we strongly recommend against relying on an oral licensing agreement.

Assignments

Unlike a license, an assignment is a permanent transfer of ownership rights. When you assign your invention, you are the assignor and whoever purchases the rights is the assignee. An assignment is like the sale of a house, after which the seller no longer has any rights over the property. As the assignor, you might receive a lump sum payment or periodic royalty payments.

Even though they have different legal meanings, the terms assignment and license are sometimes used inter-changeably. Indeed, these two types of agreements sometimes seem to have the exact same effect. This is true in the case of an unlimited exclusive license, in which a licensee obtains the sole right to market

---

Assignments, Licenses, Termination, and Reversions

If someone hands you an agreement and tells you it's a license, the key to determining whether it *really* is a license—regardless of the title—is whether you get the rights back to your innovation once the agreement terminates. (This return of ownership is sometimes referred to as a "reversion" or "reversionary rights.") Most likely you're holding a license and the company retains exclusive rights for only a limited period of time, if the agreement provides for you to get the rights back in any of the following events:

- The agreement terminates.
- The company stops selling your work for a fixed period of time.
- The company doesn't start selling your product by a certain date.
- The company materially breaches the agreement.

This issue—whether rights are returned to you—is crucial to licensing, so if you are in doubt as to your rights under an agreement, contact an intellectual property attorney for advice.

---

the invention for an unlimited period of time. In this situation, the license really has the same effect as an assignment, because the licensor is not keeping any rights that could be made the subject of another license.

Because the two terms—assignment and license—can overlap in effect, it's important to examine the specific conditions and obligations of each agreement, rather than simply to rely on terms such as assignment and license.

See "Assignments, Licenses, Termination, and Reversions," above. The categorization can affect tax treatment of income from the agreement. See Chapter 17 for more information on taxes and licensing agreements.

The Licensing Process

Licensing is a union between the inventor (the licensor) and the company that licenses the right to manufacture or distribute your invention (the licensee).

The process begins with a meeting and disclosure period followed by a proposal and negotiation stage. If you agree on the major principles, the two of you can create a formal relationship. After entering into the agreement (often called executing the agreement), each party should periodically monitor the other to determine adherence to the agreement. If either party breaches (fails to honor) the agreement, the agreement may be terminated.

The following sections describe the various stages in the licensing process.

Should You Manufacture and Market Your Invention Instead of Licensing It?

Before considering licensing, it's important for an inventor to consider the two other basic options to licensing: assigning your rights or manufacturing and selling the invention by yourself. Although a license allows you to retain ownership of the invention, some inventors prefer to assign all rights in return for a large onetime payment. As for manufacturing and selling the invention yourself (referred to as a venture), most inventors do not have the funds or experience to create ventures or to market their own products. Manufacturing and marketing require money, knowledge about an industry, connections with distributors, and a lot of hard, hard work. In addition, many inventors cannot afford the significant expense of pursuing infringers. For this reason, most inventors choose licensing instead of ventures. However, if you are inclined to sell your invention on your own, we provide some resources for venturers in Chapter 18, "Help Beyond This Book."

Meet and Greet the Potential Licensee

The most difficult step you will face is finding a company to license your

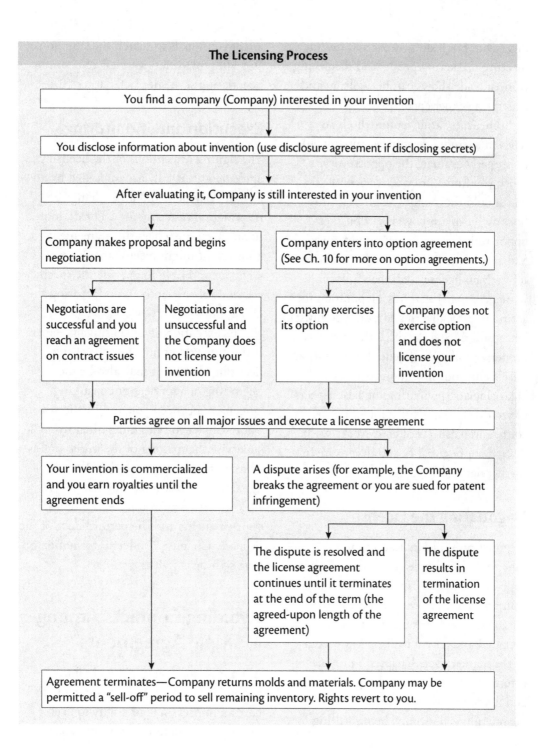

The Licensing Process

You find a company (Company) interested in your invention

You disclose information about invention (use disclosure agreement if disclosing secrets)

After evaluating it, Company is still interested in your invention

Company makes proposal and begins negotiation

Company enters into option agreement (See Ch. 10 for more on option agreements.)

Negotiations are successful and you reach an agreement on contract issues

Negotiations are unsuccessful and the Company does not license your invention

Company exercises its option

Company does not exercise option and does not license your invention

Parties agree on all major issues and execute a license agreement

Your invention is commercialized and you earn royalties until the agreement ends

A dispute arises (for example, the Company breaks the agreement or you are sued for patent infringement)

The dispute is resolved and the license agreement continues until it terminates at the end of the term (the agreed-upon length of the agreement)

The dispute results in termination of the license agreement

Agreement terminates—Company returns molds and materials. Company may be permitted a "sell-off" period to sell remaining inventory. Rights revert to you.

invention. For a shy, introverted inventor, meeting marketing people and displaying work at trade shows can be a jolting and frustrating experience.

Sometimes, an inventor who is so relieved to find a receptive company fails to properly evaluate the opportunity. Once you find a prospective licensee, you should thoroughly research it; this book will explain how. Every business opportunity is not a great opportunity. Sad as it may seem, you might be better off with no license at all than a license with a company that has a reputation for acting unethically. In addition, you must be careful during the disclosure process to properly protect confidential information. Disclosing your invention requires a balancing act: presenting the best aspects of your invention while protecting the confidential aspects of your work. We'll discuss confidentiality and disclosure in further detail in Chapter 7.

Negotiating the License

Negotiation skills are learned, not inherited. The simple rule is that the best approach to negotiating your licensing contract is to educate yourself and to set goals. Good negotiators are well prepared and have a realistic knowledge of the marketplace. Chapter 6 provides information about researching industries and markets. Also important in any negotiation is flexibility, being willing to

adapt your goals to match the situation. We will provide an overview of common negotiating strategies in Chapter 10.

Execution and Monitoring

The signing (execution) of the licensing agreement is usually accompanied by an advance payment and an exchange of information or technology. For example, upon executing a licensing agreement, an inventor might receive an advance payment and have to provide the specific methods of efficiently manufacturing the invention.

The execution of a licensing agreement is the climax, but not the end, of the licensing process. It may also be the beginning of a services or consulting agreement between you and the licensee. For example, you might be hired to supervise the making of the initial molds or manufacturing prototypes. Service agreements are covered in Chapter 15. Plus, as a licensor you have to monitor your payments and the performance of the licensee. Chapter 17 offers information on post-signing activities.

Avoiding Conflicts Among Multiple Agreements

As an inventor, you might enter into various agreements, each of which might have an impact on your ability to license in the future. Before you license your

The Real World: How One Inventor Had a Good Hair Day

Many inventors have used this book for licensing, and one of the most interesting examples is David Silva, founder of Localoc, Inc. (pronounced lock a lock), a company specializing in hair accessory products. David invented and received two patents for his Vidal Sassoon Twist 'n' Clip Headband—a plastic headband combined with hair clips aligned along its top. His invention allows women to easily twist small sections of hair into rows. Before his device, women had to twist sections of hair into rows around their face and fasten them with a clip, a process that, according to Silva, required "ten hands." Below is the story of Silva's licensing odyssey.

Question: *How did you find Helen of Troy, the company to which you licensed your products?*
Silva: Helen of Troy is one of the leading manufacturers of hair appliances and hair accessories in the world and owns many popular trademarks, such as Vidal Sassoon and Revlon. When I invented the Twist 'n' Clip Headband, I went to the hair aisles of the major retailers and looked at the back of the popular hair accessory packages to see who the distributors and owners of the popular hair accessories were.

Question: *What was it like pitching your products? Any tips you can give others about making a product pitch?*
Silva: Pitching something you believe in and worked hard to create is always nerve-racking. My advice is to not only prepare exactly how you will present the invention, making sure it can be understood in a short period of time (a few minutes or forget it), but to also learn the history of the company you are pitching to, including the names of the people who run it, and the industry itself (in my case, hairstyling and hair products).

The difference between sending the item in the mail (which usually results in an immediate rejection) and pitching in person would amaze you. Something about putting a face to the product that makes all the difference. The "twisting-rows" hairstyle was popular when I invented the Twist 'n' Clip Headband; however, it took a lot of persistence to convince Helen of Troy that I invented an easier way to create a popular hairstyle. I would send them magazine photos of models wearing the style, articles mentioning it, and made sure they understood just how complicated the popular style was to create without my product.

The Real World: How One Inventor Had a Good Hair Day (continued)

The company you're pitching to really needs to sense that you know what you're talking about. Also, the old saying "Don't take no for an answer" is true. If they do say no, continue to come up with reasons why they are wrong.

Question: *What about negotiations? Did they furnish an agreement? Did you use an attorney at any point? Did the other side have an attorney?*

Silva: Negotiations were a challenge. The first thing [the company] did was decide on a royalty. I've learned that when telling a company the royalty you want, you should always start high. I knew that the average royalty for inventors was 5% and that I wanted 8%. So I told Helen of Troy I wouldn't take anything under 12%. They said they usually never give anything over 5% but came back with 6%. I then explained that 6% was just a little above average and my product was so new and innovative, with huge sales potential, that I would only be willing to go to 10% (you have to act confident). They adamantly said no, but when I eventually asked if they would be willing to give me 6% for the first 250,000 units sold and 8% thereafter, they agreed (this was a typical royalty negotiation). Once we agreed on a royalty amount, their corporate attorney furnished me with their agreement. Their agreement allowed for so many deductions that the agreed-upon 8%

royalty would have really been around 1.5%. It even had a clause that would essentially give them the rights to any future inventions I came up with.

At this point, I had a few choices: One was to spend a fortune hiring an attorney to negotiate their agreement, spend a fortune hiring an attorney to write my own agreement, or write my own agreement. I took a trip to the local bookstore and found *License Your Invention* (the previous title of this book). I filled in the blanks of the [model agreement] in *License Your Invention*, and the rest is history. The best advice I can give about negotiations is that an inventor should never be so excited that a company is interested in their invention that they can't walk away from the negotiations. As they say, the one that is willing to walk is the one with the upper hand.

Question: *Were there any disappointments or setbacks in the process? If so, could you avoid them in the future?*

Silva: Although the product is a success, it took [Helen of Troy] around two years to really start selling it. Companies with many products like to say they move quickly to market, but quick to them seems like an eternity to an inventor.

The first few payments were late, but because there was a late payment clause in the agreement, a letter threatening to terminate took care of the problem.

The Real World: How One Inventor Had a Good Hair Day (continued)

I had also licensed a couple other items to Helen of Troy after the first, but they didn't sell well. I found that when licensing an invention to a large corporation, it helps if the product sells itself, because most companies test the items in small quantities in stores to see if they will sell at all. They almost never advertise them at first, so if the product doesn't sell itself, it won't pass its test, and they won't continue selling it.

The Twist 'n' Clip passed its test because it sold itself. I took a popular style and made it easier to create. The customer could tell exactly what it did the second they saw it. The other products I had licensed needed more explanation and never really did that well. If I ever licensed another product it would always be a simple item that sells itself.

Question: *What's it like to walk into a store and see your products on the shelf?*

Silva: I have to say it never gets old seeing my products on the shelf. The first time seeing them was really exciting. I'm sure it's a lot like a singer hearing her song on the radio for the first time. But what tops seeing my products on the shelf is seeing someone walk by wearing one. I recently saw a character on a television sitcom wearing one—it doesn't get better than that.

---

invention, review your current signed commitments to make sure that none of them conflict with your ability to license. The easiest way to manage this review is to create and maintain a record of all signed documents. For the most part, you should be concerned with documents that affect your ownership, financial interest, or control over the rights to your invention.

Agreements That Can Affect Licensing

When examining other agreements, first determine what kind of agreement it is. The name of the document will probably help you classify it (although titles are not always conclusive proof). If you're not sure of the type of document, the first or second paragraph often describes the document's purpose. If you're still not sure, try comparing the document's provisions with the provisions of the sample agreements in this book.

Below is a brief description of some common documents an inventor may execute and the effect they may have on the inventor's ability to license an invention.

Co-Ownership or Joint Inventor Agreements

A co-ownership or joint inventor agreement is executed between the owners—usually the creators—of an invention. It establishes the rights and obligations of each party in respect to the invention.

Impact on Licensing: A co-ownership agreement may establish which owner has the right to enter into licensing agreements and may require a mutual decision when it's time to decide upon a licensee. See Chapter 4 for more information.

Corporate and Stock Agreements

Have you created a corporation to exploit your invention? Corporate agreements are executed as part of each state's incorporation process. Stock agreements formalize sales of corporate stock to investors.

Impact on Licensing: Corporate and stock agreements establish who makes decisions about licensing or whether such decisions require a vote of the board of directors (the group that is elected by stockholders to make the important corporate decisions). See Chapter 4 for more information.

Employment Agreements

Employment agreements define your employment obligations and responsibilities.

Impact on Licensing: An employment agreement may limit your rights to inventions created during your employment. See Chapter 3 for more information.

Loan Agreements

A loan agreement is an agreement to lend money, services, or supplies in exchange for a promise of repayment, usually with interest.

Impact on Licensing: If a loan agreement uses your legal rights to an invention as collateral to secure repayment of the loan, it may prevent you from licensing the invention. See Chapter 4 for more information.

Nondisclosure Agreements

Under a nondisclosure agreement, certain information identified in the agreement must be kept confidential.

Impact on Licensing: An improperly drafted nondisclosure agreement could result in your loss of the right to consider your invention a trade secret—which could, in turn, affect your ability to license the invention (especially if the licensee considers trade secret protection an important part of the transaction). See Chapter 7 for more information.

Option Agreements

An option agreement gives one party the right to enter into a license (or another type of agreement) at a later date. Typically, in return for a nonrefundable payment, the licensee gets an exclusive period of time to decide whether to enter into a license.

Impact on Licensing: An option agreement may establish terms (such as length of agreement, royalties, territory, and so forth) to be used in a license and may prevent you from licensing to anyone other than the option owner. See Chapter 10 for more information.

Evaluation Agreements

An evaluation agreement is a mixture of a nondisclosure and an option agreement. With an evaluation agreement, a company acquires the right to evaluate an invention and then, if desired, to enter into a license agreement.

Impact on Licensing: An evaluation agreement with one company may prevent you from signing a licensing agreement with a different company. See Chapter 10 for more information.

Outsourcing or Manufacturing Agreements

An outsourcing or manufacturing agreement authorizes a company to manufacture—but not necessarily sell—goods embodying your invention.

Impact on Licensing: Your failure to include a confidentiality provision in an outsourcing or manufacturing agreement may result in the loss of trade secret rights, which could have an impact on your ability to license. See Chapter 7 for more information.

Partnership Agreements

In a partnership agreement, two or more persons join together in an enterprise. The partnership agreement establishes the contributions, liabilities, and shares of profit for each contributing partner.

**Movable Shelter
No. 6,295,765**

Impact on Licensing: Your partnership agreement may define which partner can execute a license, and it may require participation by all partners in the negotiation process. See Chapter 4 for more information.

Representation Agreements

A representation agreement (sometimes referred to as a rep agreement or an agency agreement) is an arrangement with an agent or a representative who will attempt to license your invention for you. In return, an agent usually seeks a portion of the profits or royalties.

Impact on Licensing: A rep agreement may require you to pay the rep percentages for a license which the rep did not even negotiate. See Chapter 5 for more information.

Keeping Track of Agreements

After you identify your agreements, make sure you have copies for your records. Then list each agreement along with any appropriate dates for activity (for example, due dates for loan payments) on a worksheet (we provide a sample below). If you believe that one of these agreements will have an impact on your ability to license, it's important to identify these potential obstacles now, before the licensing process begins.

We suggest you use the worksheet on the following page to keep track of each agreement. Some agreements terminate by a certain event or date. Some agreements can be renewed on a specific date. You should review your agreements for the relevant information and plug it in your worksheet. You should also keep your worksheets and other important documents—including the copies of the agreements themselves—in a special notebook. We discuss record keeping later in this chapter.

Challenges to Your Ownership

Is anyone likely to challenge your claim to ownership of your invention? Of course, if someone has already asserted an ownership claim, then the answer to this question is yes. But, even if no one has made an actual assertion, an informal conversation might have alerted you to this possibility. The ownership issue might have been raised in several different contexts:

- You worked with someone who believes that he or she is entitled to be considered one of the inventors.
- Another inventor has already alerted you to the possibility that your invention infringes a previous invention that is protected by a patent or some other intellectual property device.
- You know about an active (in force) patent that describes an invention very similar to yours.

A Licensee Can Challenge Your Patent

Don't presume that a licensee can't challenge your patent. Just because a company is paying you to use your invention doesn't prevent that company from challenging the validity (and your ownership rights) of your patent. Under a Supreme Court ruling in January 2007, a licensee can challenge the validity of the patents it has licensed without having to break the license agreement. In addition, the Supreme Court did not limit this holding to patents—indicating that perhaps a trademark or copyright licensee can also challenge the validity of a title. (*MedImmune v. Genentech*, 549 U.S. 118 (2007).)

Agreement Worksheet

Title of agreement: _____

Category (select one):

    ☐ co-ownership   ☐ corporate   ☐ employment   ☐ nondisclosure

    ☐ evaluation   ☐ option   ☐ outsourcing   ☐ loan or financial

    ☐ representation   ☐ partnership   ☐ other: _____

Date of agreement: _____

Parties to agreement: _____

_____

Is there a termination date?   ☐ Yes ☐ No   If yes, list date: _____

Is there a renewal date?   ☐ Yes ☐ No   If yes, list date: _____

Where is the agreement located or filed? _____

Ownership notes: _____

_____

_____

_____

_____

_____

_____

_____

_____

_____

_____

_____

Types of Ownership Challenges

The first type of ownership claim usually occurs when a former employer, employee, or coworker claims rights to your invention (that is, "I worked for/with you, or you worked for/with me, and I own part or all of that invention"). If you are not familiar with principles such as joint ownership, joint authorship, work for hire, or shop right rules, read Chapters 3 and 4.

The second and third types of potential challenges to your rights are based on a doctrine known as patent infringement. Patent infringement claims are usually brought by inventors who believe your invention is the same as theirs (that is, "I patented this invention first and you ripped me off"). Under patent law, an infringement may be exactly the same invention or it may be a similar or "equivalent" invention.

Dealing With Ownership Challenges

You might have difficulty licensing your invention in any of these situations. Because a potential licensee will want to make sure that you own the rights you are licensing, the agreement will inevitably contain a warranty clause, which guarantees that you do, in fact, have the right to license. Many licensees will also insist on an indemnity clause, which basically holds you financially responsible for damages suffered by the licensee if

your warranty proves false. If you don't have ownership rights or if those rights are challenged in a lawsuit, you might have to pay to defend yourself and the licensee.

What should you do if there is an ownership issue? You'll need to determine if the challenge is valid. It's best to consult an intellectual property attorney experienced in your type of intellectual property, because you'll likely need an expert legal opinion regarding the validity of the challenge. See Chapter 2 for more information about types of intellectual property.

When Others Infringe Your Invention

If you think that someone might have ripped off your invention, review your rights under intellectual property laws. You might not have been "ripped off" in a legal sense. If you're unsure, consult an intellectual property attorney. (See Chapter 18, "Help Beyond This Book.")

Transferring Ownership of Your Invention to Your Business

Every business has a structure (sometimes known as a "business form"). There are five common business forms:
- sole proprietorship
- general partnership

- limited partnership
- limited liability company, and
- corporation.

For legal or tax reasons, you might decide to form a business to exploit your invention. For example, suppose you and several investors form a corporation to license your invention. Why form a corporation? Perhaps your accountant recognized a tax advantage, or perhaps the investors wanted a corporate business form to shield them from any personal liability.

Often, if you form a business to exploit your invention, you must share ownership of your invention (for example, in the case of a partnership, you may share it with your partners), or you must assign invention rights to the business (for example, you form a corporation and assign your rights to the corporation, which then becomes the owner). If you assign all rights to your business, then that business, not you, will enter into the license agreement with the licensee.

Descriptions of the common types of business forms follow.

Sole Proprietorships

If you are the sole inventor and owner of your invention, you are probably a sole proprietor. A sole proprietorship is an unincorporated business owned by one person. You, as sole proprietor, make all business decisions.

The advantages of a sole proprietorship are freedom to make decisions (no pesky partners to contradict you) and simplicity (no filings with the state government; no double taxation of income). The main disadvantage is that sole proprietors are personally liable for all business debts. This means that if your business gets into financial hot water, for reasons such as poor sales or an expensive lawsuit, your creditors can sue you and go after not only your business assets but your personal assets as well (such as your house). If you have personal assets that you want to protect from liability, you may want to incorporate. Unlike sole proprietors, owners of corporations are usually not personally liable for business obligations.

Fictitious Business Names

If you operate your sole proprietorship under a fictitious name, you're required under most state laws to file a fictitious business name statement with your county government. This filing does not create your business; it only provides a public record of the names of the individuals who own the business. Many sole proprietors don't bother with this filing until they begin receiving revenue under the fictitious business name, at which point the bank will require the filing before cashing company checks.

As a sole proprietor, you may create a name for your business and do business under that name. For example, if Joan Smith operates a sole proprietorship under the name SmittyCo, she would execute a license agreement as "Joan Smith, an individual doing business as SmittyCo."

General Partnerships

A general partnership is basically a sole proprietorship with more than one owner. If you're in business with one or more other people and haven't incorporated, you're engaged in a partnership.

Each partner contributes something to the partnership, and each receives a percentage of the profits. You don't have to go through a formal procedure or even a written agreement to start a partnership. In fact, partnerships are often created by the actions of the parties. For example, say a friend offers to help you promote an invention. You agree to give him a percentage of the profits, and in return, he agrees to devote 20 hours a week to promoting your invention. He's contributing services and will be receiving a share of the profits. He's now your partner or joint venturer. (There's no difference between a partnership and a joint venture except that joint ventures are usually limited to two partners.)

The advantage of a partnership is simplicity. It's not necessary to register a partnership with the state government,

although your partnership must file a partnership tax form. The partnership's income is not taxed until it is distributed to the partners, who declare this income on their personal tax returns. The disadvantage of a partnership is that partners are personally liable for business debts. In addition, each individual partner can be liable for the entire debt of the business. That is, a person who sues the partnership can recover all of the damages from any one partner's personal assets. This rule cannot be altered by the partnership agreement (although the agreement can obligate partners to repay such debts). To protect your personal assets from partnership debts, you should incorporate or form a limited liability company, discussed below.

Accepting money from someone does not necessarily create a partnership. As explained in this chapter, some payments may be characterized as loans, some as gifts, and some as investments. However,

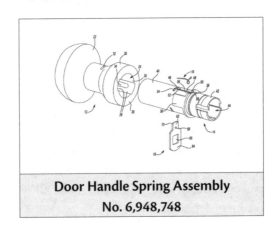

**Door Handle Spring Assembly
No. 6,948,748**

if someone gives you cash or property with the understanding that it buys a share in the profits and ownership of the business, then you have formed a partnership. For example, suppose you invented a fruit slicer and a friend agreed to contribute $25,000 to help manufacture prototypes, with the understanding that she would share in the profits. You and your friend are partners.

What Is Your Relationship With an Agent?

When you enter into an agreement with a product agent or anyone else who will represent you to a licensee, you are entering into an agency relationship, not a partnership. An agency relationship is similar to hiring an independent contractor to perform services for you. You are the principal and the agent's job is to act on your behalf. In return for performing the services, you agree to pay the agent a percentage of the profits. For more information on product reps and agents, review Chapter 5.

Limited Partnerships

A limited partnership is a partnership with one or more general partners and one or more limited partners. The general partners manage the business, make contributions or perform services, and share in the profits. Limited partners, however, do not participate in business management; they only invest money. In return for giving up any say in management, their liability is limited to the amount of their investments.

The advantage of a limited partnership is that limited partners are not personally liable for business debts. Using this system, you can obtain investment income from a limited partner who doesn't have to worry about being personally liable.

However, a few disadvantages exist. You must abide by legal formalities, such as filing with the state government, and you must also have a written partnership agreement, as required by your state law. Also, limited partners cannot contribute to the business decisions and general partners can be personally liable for all business debts.

Corporations

A business corporation is a legal entity, created by law, which has an existence separate from its owners. Unlike other business forms, it can exist perpetually— that is, it does not end with the death of the investors or owners. In order to obtain capital (money), you sell shares in the corporation. Purchasers of these shares are called shareholders. These shares create an ownership interest for the shareholders. The shareholders invest in the hopes that the invention will become successful and the shares become more valuable. Shareholders generally acquire voting rights and use their votes to influence decisions about licensing. Those shareholders who maintain a controlling interest (that is, they have the most shares) will have control over what happens to the licensing of the invention.

Shareholders in a corporation are not personally liable for debts of the corporation. For example, if a corporation licensed an invention and that invention injured someone, the injured person could sue the corporation to the extent of the corporation's assets—but not the personal assets of the shareholders. A few exceptions to this rule exist, however. One example, a legal doctrine known as "piercing the corporate veil," lifts the protective shield (or veil) of the corporation form and allows shareholders to be held personally liable. This usually happens when a corporation is insufficiently capitalized or if the shareholders act in violation of the law.

Corporations can be advantageous because they offer limited liability for shareholders. But corporations also come with formalities and expenses. A corporation must file documents with the state government to receive a certificate of incorporation. Forming a corporation is a big step, particularly in states like California, where the formation fees can exceed $1,000. Certain legal formalities must be observed on a regular basis, such as creating a board of directors, establishing bylaws, and issuing shares of stock.

Dear Rich: Can a Nonprofit Be an Invention Licensor?

Dear Rich: I have invented a very useful tool and have a patent pending. Also, I have an arrangement with a nonprofit and some principals. The nonprofit will operate the business of selling the tool to generate revenue. The principals provide funding and agree to use their retail outlets for the sales. Can we license a manufacturer to manufacture only and license the nonprofit to sell the product?

The short answer to your question is that more information is needed and, most likely, you'll need the assistance of an attorney. For example, we're concerned about both maintaining your nonprofit tax benefits *and* the value of your patent pending status. We're also not sure what you mean when you say you want to "license a manufacturer to manufacture only"? Do you mean versus manufacturing and selling? Finally, we're not sure who controls the rights to the invention, you or the principals? All of these questions must be answered before you can proceed with your plans. In a situation like this—when you're mixing issues like investors, inventions, and 501(c) tax status—you're best off bringing an attorney to the table.

How Do You Transfer Ownership of Your Invention to Your Business?

If you are the sole inventor and owner of your invention and you operate as a sole proprietor, you don't need to do anything. If you have formed a corporation, general partnership, limited partnership, or limited liability company for the purpose of licensing, you will probably assign your invention rights to the business. In that case, the business—not you—owns the invention and any licenses are granted by the business (not you). All assignments should be in writing. If the invention is patented, any such assignment must be recorded with the U.S. Patent and Trademark Office (USPTO). In order to record it, you must send a copy of the signed assignment with a cover sheet and fee to the USPTO. If you assign invention rights before filing a patent, you can record the assignment by sending it in with your patent application. (For more information on recording an assignment, visit the USPTO website or see the patent resources in Chapter 18, "Help Beyond This Book.")

Three sample assignments are provided below. The first is for the assignment of an invention for which a patent has been issued. The second assignment should be used if a patent application has been filed. The third assignment can be used if no patent application has been filed.

 CAUTION

Never assign your invention for the "promise" of future payments. Always get the money before signing the assignment. That's because if the assignee (the person who owes you the money) fails to pay you, you will be trapped in litigation, fighting to get your patent back. If the assignee insists on a series of payments, there are several solutions, such as establishing an escrow account, transferring partial assignments per payment, or setting up a license agreement that allows for ownership transfer after the final payment. You should consult with an attorney to best protect your interests.

Having a Spouse Sign an Assignment

If you conceived of your invention during the time you were married, your spouse may claim a portion of your invention income. To make sure your assignment is complete and your spouse will not later dispute the assignment, you might want to include a provision in your assignment similar to the one below. This provision protects the assignee (person acquiring the rights to the invention) from later being sued by the spouse of the inventor. This provision is not required in license agreements. When used in assignments, it usually appears below the signature line for the inventor.

DOWNLOAD FORMS
You can download this form
(and all other forms in this book) from
this book's companion page on Nolo.com;
see the appendix for the link.

Sample Provision for Spousal Assignment

I am the spouse of Assignor and I acknowledge that I have read and understand this Assignment agreement. I am aware that my spouse agrees to assign [*choose one*] his/her interest in the Invention, including any community property interest or other equitable property interest that I may have in it. I consent to the assignment and agree that my interest, if any, in the Invention is subject to the provisions of this Agreement. I will take no action to hinder the Agreement or the underlying assignment of rights.

_____

Spouse's signature

Assignment of Rights: Patent

[*Insert name of person or company assigning rights*] ("Assignor") is owner of U.S. Patent Number: _____ , dated _____ , titled [*insert name of invention*] (the "Patent"). [*Insert name of person or company to whom rights will be assigned*] ("Assignee") desires to acquire rights in and to the Patent.

Therefore, for valuable consideration, the receipt of which is acknowledged, Assignor assigns to Assignee [*insert percentage of interest that is being assigned—it can be less than 100%, but it cannot be more than 100%*]% of Assignor's right, title, and interest in the invention and Patent to Assignee for the entire term of the Patent and any reissues or extensions and for the entire terms of any patents, reissues, or extensions that may issue from foreign applications, divisions, continuations in whole or part, or substitute applications filed claiming the benefit of the Patent as well as any priority rights resulting from patent application filings. The right, title, and interest conveyed in this Assignment is to be held and enjoyed by Assignee and Assignee's successors as fully and exclusively as it would have been held and enjoyed by Assignor had this assignment not been made.

Assignor further agrees to (a) cooperate with Assignee in the protection of the patent rights and prosecution and protection of foreign counterparts; (b) execute, verify, acknowledge, and deliver all such further papers, including patent applications and instruments of transfer; and (c) perform such other acts as Assignee lawfully may request to obtain or maintain the Patent and any and all applications and registrations for the invention in any and all countries.

Assignor: _____ Date: _____

[*To be completed by notary public*]

On this _____ day of _____ , before me, _____ _____ , the undersigned Notary Public, personally appeared _____ , ASSIGNOR, personally known to me (or proved to me on the basis of satisfactory evidence) to be the person whose name is subscribed to the within instrument, and acknowledged to me executing the same. WITNESS my hand and official seal in _____ County of _____ on the date set forth in this certificate.

_____
Notary Public

[*In California, include the following statement.*] I certify UNDER PENALTY OF PERJURY under the laws of the State of California that the foregoing is true and correct.

Assignment of Rights: Patent Application

[*Insert name of person or company assigning rights*] ("Assignor") is owner of [*insert name of invention*] as described in the U.S. Patent Application signed by Assignor on [*insert date application was signed*], U.S. Patent and Trademark Office Serial Number: _____ , filed [*insert filing date*], (the "Patent Application"). [*Insert name of person or company to whom rights will be assigned*] ("Assignee") desires to acquire all rights in and to the Patent Application and the patent (and any reissues or extensions that may be granted).

Therefore, for valuable consideration, the receipt of which is acknowledged, Assignor assigns to Assignee [*insert percentage of interest that is being assigned—it can be less than 100%, but it cannot be more than 100%*]% of Assignor's right, title, and interest in the invention and Patent Application (as well as such rights in any divisions, continuations in whole or part, or substitute applications) to Assignee for the entire term of the issued Patent and any reissues or extensions that may be granted and for the entire terms of any and all foreign patents that may issue from foreign applications (as well as divisions, continuations in whole or part, or substitute applications) filed claiming the benefit of the Patent Application and any priority rights resulting from the Patent Application.

Assignor authorizes the United States Patent and Trademark Office to issue any Patents resulting from the Patent Application to Assignee according to the percentage interest indicated in this assignment. The right, title, and interest is to be held and enjoyed by Assignee and Assignee's successors and assigns as fully and exclusively as it would have been held and enjoyed by Assignor had this assignment not been made.

Assignor further agrees to: (a) cooperate with Assignee in the prosecution of the Application and foreign counterparts; (b) execute, verify, acknowledge, and deliver all such further papers, including patent applications and instruments of transfer; and (c) perform such other acts as Assignee lawfully may request to obtain or maintain the Patent for the invention in any and all countries.

Assignor: _____ Date: _____

[*To be completed by notary public*]

On this _____ day of _____ , before me, _____

_____ , the undersigned Notary Public, personally appeared

_____ , ASSIGNOR, personally known to me (or proved

to me on the basis of satisfactory evidence) to be the person whose name is subscribed to

the within instrument, and acknowledged to me executing the same. WITNESS my hand and

official seal in _____ County of _____

on the date set forth in this certificate.

_____
Notary Public

[*In California, include the following statement.*] I certify UNDER PENALTY OF PERJURY under the laws of the State of California that the foregoing is true and correct.

Assignment of Rights: No Patent Issued or Application Filed

[*Insert name of person or company assigning rights*] ("Assignor") is the owner of all proprietary and intellectual property rights, including copyrights and patents, in the concepts and technologies known as [*insert name of invention*] and more specifically described in Attachment A [*attach a description of the invention to the Assignment and label it "Attachment A"*] to this Assignment (and referred to collectively as the "Invention") and the right to registrations to the Invention; and [*insert name of person or company to whom rights will be assigned*] ("Assignee") desires to acquire the ownership of all proprietary rights, including, but not limited to, the copyrights, trade secrets, trademarks, and associated goodwill and patent rights in the Invention and the registrations to the Invention.

Therefore, for valuable consideration, the receipt of which is acknowledged, Assignor hereby assigns to Assignee [*insert percentage of interest that is being assigned—it can be less than 100%, but it cannot be more than 100%*]% of all right, title, and interest in the Invention, including:

(1) all copyrights, trade secrets, trademarks, and associated goodwill and all patents which may be granted on the Invention;

(2) all applications for patents (including divisions, continuations in whole or part, or substitute applications) in the United States or any foreign countries whose duty it is to issue such patents;

(3) any reissues and extensions of such patents; and

(4) all priority rights under the International Convention for the Protection of Industrial Property for every member country.

Assignor warrants: (a) that Assignor is the legal owner of all right, title, and interest in the Invention; (b) that such rights have not been previously licensed, pledged, assigned, or encumbered; and (c) that this Assignment does not infringe on the rights of any person. Assignor agrees to cooperate with Assignee and to execute and deliver all papers, instruments, and assignments as may be necessary to vest all right, title, and interest in and to the intellectual property rights to the Invention in Assignee. Assignor further agrees to testify in any legal proceeding, sign all lawful papers and applications, and make all rightful oaths and generally do everything possible to aid Assignee to obtain and enforce proper protection for the Invention in all countries.

Assignor: _____ Date: _____

[*To be completed by notary public*]

On this _____ day of _____ , before me, _____
_____ , the undersigned Notary Public, personally appeared
_____ , ASSIGNOR, personally known to me (or proved
to me on the basis of satisfactory evidence) to be the person whose name is subscribed to
the within instrument, and acknowledged to me executing the same. WITNESS my hand and
official seal in _____ County of _____
on the date set forth in this certificate.

_____
Notary Public

[*In California, include the following statement.*] I certify UNDER PENALTY OF PERJURY
under the laws of the State of California that the foregoing is true and correct.

Disclosing Information About Your Invention

If you invented something new and exciting, then you have a natural desire to share your discovery. Unfortunately, sharing your invention without proper precautions may cost you your legal rights. For example, public disclosures prior to filing a utility patent application will likely prevent you from obtaining a patent. (There are exceptions if the inventor makes the disclosure; see the section on prior art in Chapter 2.) Public disclosure will also prevent you from obtaining trade secret protection, because any authorized public disclosure ends trade secret protection. A trade secret is confidential information which gives you a competitive advantage over other inventors or their licensees. Trade secrets are valuable because they are not known to the public. Trade secret laws will protect your invention so long as you do not disclose information about it indiscriminately. Unrestricted disclosures about an invention protected by trade secret will usually terminate the protection.

Trade secret protection isn't a concern for all inventions, however. An invention that has received a patent no longer needs trade secret protection. Disclosures about a patented invention will not affect your patent rights. But, as explained below, if you've applied for a patent that has not yet been issued, the only protection you

might have is trade secret protection. In that situation, you should not disclose confidential information about your invention. Finally, if you have trade secrets that complement the patent but are not part of the patent (for example, an efficient way to construct the invention), you must treat this information with confidentiality, as well.

Summing up, there are four major concerns regarding disclosing information about your invention:

- If you have not applied for a patent, the disclosure might prevent you from obtaining a patent. (See Chapter 2.)
- A disclosure might affect your claim of trade secret rights.
- A disclosure might affect your ability to compete, because the information could become available to makers of similar or related inventions.
- A disclosure might affect your ability to contract, because a company may not want to enter into an agreement if the information is available to competitors.

If you have made disclosures regarding your invention to anyone, you should determine how trade secret law might affect your situation. If you disclosed information about your invention in printed materials, such as journals, financial agreements (such as loan documents), or advertisements, you will also need

Dear Rich:
Should I Reveal My Invention to My Attorney?

Dear Rich: I have a series of inventions, but for right now my only focus is one and it is one of rather strong global consequence. I am going to an I.P. lawyer tomorrow and the intimidation factor is quite strong. I know enough to inquire of the attorney's engineering background, patent experience, to obtain a full quote as well as what payment arrangements would be expected, and to ask for a reasonable expectation of a timeline. I do not really intend to reveal what my invention is. Is that okay?

We know that many inventors see attorneys and manufacturers as wolves in corporate clothing, and although we don't agree, we understand the paranoia. We're reminded of David Mamet's 1992 movie, *The Water Engine*, in which the creator of a machine that ran on water was double-crossed by crooked patent attorneys.

Invention = disclosure. At some point every inventor who wants to commercialize an invention must make disclosures. These disclosures may be to the patent office, to business partners, to attorneys, or to manufacturers. Even if you seek to protect your invention under trade secrecy law, you will need to disclose it to others under the protection of a nondisclosure agreement.

Attorneys and disclosures. There is no reason you must disclose your invention at your preliminary meeting with your patent attorney. But if you retain this attorney,

you will have to disclose your invention. Otherwise the attorney cannot properly assess its value and the protection it requires. Your communications with the attorney are privileged, meaning that unless you authorize publication, the attorney cannot disclose what you say. One situation in which you must make a public disclosure is if a patent application is filed. Unless you do not plan on filing foreign applications, your U.S. patent application will be published 18 months after you file. Alternatively, if the patent is granted, it will also be published.

The trick with disclosures ... We believe that proper precautions should be taken when making invention disclosures. Maintain your information with secrecy and only disclose it under the protection of privilege, or nondisclosure agreements. But, perhaps more importantly, try to use personal radar to determine whether you can trust those to whom you have made disclosures. For example, prolific inventor Maurice Kanbar had a strong 35-year relationship with his patent attorney, Mike Ebert. In his book, *Secrets from an Inventor's Notebook*, Kanbar wrote:

"Most basically, you need to be able to communicate with your attorney. I can call Mike on the phone, describe my idea and detail its mechanics and Mike will 'get it' instantly and start writing it up. If an attorney has a different understanding of your invention, or if he or she doesn't quickly get your drift, go elsewhere."

to determine if the timing or disclosure will affect your ability to obtain patent protection. (See Chapter 2.) If you entered into a disclosure or confidentiality agreement, you should compare its provisions with those in the sample agreements in Chapter 7.

 CAUTION

Beware that your patent rights will be lost if you file your application after public disclosure of the invention. This may include publications in journals or even on the Internet. (While an exception exists for certain disclosures made by an inventor within a year of the patent application filing date, patent practitioners generally discourage prefiling public disclosures by inventors. See section on prior art in Chapter 2.)

Keeping Your Records

A Chinese proverb says the palest ink is better than the best memory. This is certainly true in law and science, where a written document is the best way to authenticate facts. Although agreements and scientific claims can be based upon oral conversations or implied by the actions of the parties, as a general rule: GET IT IN WRITING! The best legal and scientific protection is documentation. This rule is repeated throughout this book and should be immediately applied in the following ways.

Keep an Inventor's Notebook

Every inventor should keep a notebook documenting the creative process. This notebook is necessary to record the steps involved in creating the work and to deflect claims by others that they are the true inventors.

Use Nondisclosure Agreements

If someone wants to learn technical details about your invention, review Chapter 7 to determine if a written nondisclosure agreement or similar document is necessary. It probably is. Information about your invention should be disclosed only on a need-to-know basis and under a guarantee of secrecy. This includes disclosures to coworkers, contractors, suppliers, and persons who evaluate your work.

Maintain a Business Notebook and Files

Poor record keeping is a roadblock to success. You must maintain a central depository—such as a notebook or binder—of files for all paperwork. Besides maintaining your signed agreements and other records, you should document business discussions, including phone calls and business-related conversations. Your file should have a section for contacts, a log of meetings and phone calls, a method of tracking money, and a listing of business documents. This is also a good place to store registration certificates or any proofs of ownership.

Insist on Written Agreements

If you're in a discussion regarding licensing—even if you are positive about the deal—you should preface your comments with a disclaimer such as, "This sounds fine, but I can't commit until I see a written agreement." Make it a part of your business vocabulary, and avoid taking actions that are contrary. For example, don't claim you need a written agreement and then subsequently permit someone to invest money or begin production of your invention without something in writing. Similarly, don't contract for design of a prototype or model without a signed contractor's or outsourcing agreement. Even a one-page signed summary of the contract terms is better than nothing at all. See Chapter 10 for information about letters of intent and contract summary sheets.

Dear Rich:
My Inventor's Notebook—Is it Tamperproof?

Dear Rich: After reading Nolo's *Patent It Yourself*, I learned of the importance of keeping a notebook to record and track the progress of an invention I'm working on. I went out and bought a spiral notebook at an office store to use as my inventor's notebook, and have entered ten pages to date. Lately I've been reading that a spiral notebook is not "tamper-proof" enough as compared to sewn or glue-bound notebooks. What are your thoughts? I plan on keeping the original notebook no matter what I decide to do.

The short answer is that your notebook is fine for your purposes, especially if it includes signed, dated, and witnessed entries that detail the creation of your invention. We spoke with David Pressman, one of the authors of *Patent It Yourself*, who said, "It's just about impossible to remove and reinsert a page in a spiral-bound notebook. The signatures and the witnesses in chronological order are powerful proof of authenticity."

What's an inventor's notebook do? An inventor's notebook (sometimes called a "lab notebook") documents the development of an invention and can be used to assess commercial potential, make improvements, and keep track of contacts and notes. Inventor's notebooks are sometimes used to resolve disputes about inventorship.

Dear Rich:
When Can I Start Deducting Invention Expenses?

Dear Rich: I've been working on a "green" invention for a few years but I haven't been deducting my invention expenses because I was told I had to wait until I start making the product. Is that right?

The general rule is that you can begin making these tax deductions once your inventing business begins using its assets to produce products for sale. However, it's not necessary that the product be completed or sales be made. Thus, for example, courts have held that a writer's business begins when he or she starts working on a writing project. The act of production itself is "carrying on" the trade or business of writing. Similarly, courts have found that inventors who worked on inventions—but never completed or patented them—were carrying on a business. Under the logic of these court decisions, your inventing business begins for tax purposes on the day you actually begin developing an invention. Thinking or dreaming about an invention

is not sufficient. You must do real work on it—but it is not necessary for you to finish it, patent it, or make money from it. A thorough and complete inventor's notebook documenting your work is the best evidence you can have to prove when you started working on your invention.

Start-up expenses. Start-up expenses are a whole different topic. Unlike business operating expenses, start-up expenses cannot all be deducted in a single year. This is because the money you spend to start an inventing (or any other) business is a capital expense—a cost that will benefit you for more than one year. Normally, you can't deduct these types of capital expenses until you sell or otherwise dispose of the business. However, a special tax rule allows you to deduct up to $5,000 in start-up expenses the first year you are in business, and then deduct the remainder, if any, in equal amounts over the next 15 years. (IRC Sec. 195.)

No False Hopes! Reviewing Your Invention's Commercial Potential

For many inventors, the process of pitching an invention can be heartbreaking and fruitless. After thousands of hours of work on an invention and hundreds more

attempting to license it, an inventor might sadly conclude that no market for this product exists.

One way to avoid this problem is to make an effort to determine how marketable your product is before attempting licensing or even beginning the patent process. Two or three out of every 100 new inventions succeed in the marketplace. What good is investing thousands of dollars and weeks of work into the patent or licensing process without some expectation of a return? Although there is no foolproof method of determining commercial potential, you can use the following tests to help figure your odds of success and act accordingly.

The SBA's Four Tests for Commercial Potential

The U.S. Small Business Administration (SBA) poses four tests for an invention to pass to show that it will have commercial potential. These are:

- **Is it original, or has someone else already come up with it?** You might be surprised to learn that someone else has already thought up something similar to your invention, and that the invention has already been rejected in the marketplace. You can get a rough notion of whether your invention has already been tried by checking trade directories or Internet services, or by performing an abstract search of the USPTO at its website—all of which are free and are explained in Chapter 18.
- **Can I find a likely distributor?** As you will learn (or might have already learned), very large companies are generally not interested in unsolicited ideas from outsiders. It's difficult to penetrate these companies and convince them to take a chance on manufacturing and distributing your product. Smaller or midsized companies may be more receptive, but they will still view your invention from a bottom-line mentality.
- **Is it a moneymaker?** This is the most difficult question to answer. Start by asking, "What's the cost to make it, and what is the likely return?" If the profit margin is small, it will be difficult to convince anyone to take a chance. Below, we suggest some methods of testing the marketability of your invention.
- **Does your invention qualify for legal protection?** Unless you have some legally protectable invention, you won't be able to stop others from copying it. Without legal protection you can rely only on the forces of strong marketing to gain a position in the marketplace.

The Innovation Center's Factors for Commercial Potential

Many years ago, the University of Oregon's Innovation Center developed a list of 33 areas and factors that inventors should consider when determining the commercial potential of an invention. These factors are:

- **Legality.** Will there be legal problems commercializing your invention?

- **Safety.** Are there safety issues (for example, a potential for consumer injuries) that may scare away licensing companies?
- **Environmental impact.** Will your invention have a positive or negative effect on the environment, and how will this affect the commercial potential?
- **Societal impact.** Will your invention have a positive or negative effect on society, and how will this affect the commercial potential?
- **Potential market.** Who will buy your invention?
- **Product life cycle.** Does your invention's usefulness diminish over time?
- **Usage learning.** How long does it take to learn how to use your invention?
- **Product visibility.** Will your product have a distinctiveness so as to stand out in the marketplace?
- **Service.** Will your product provide a valuable service?
- **Durability.** How sturdy is your invention? Will it require frequent maintenance?
- **New competition.** What is the likelihood of new competitors appearing once your invention is commercialized?
- **Functional feasibility.** How workable are the functional aspects of your invention?
- **Production feasibility.** How practicable is it to produce your invention for sale?

- **Stability of demand.** Will the demand for your invention die off?
- **Consumer/user compatibility.** Will consumers find that your invention is compatible with their needs or lifestyles?
- **Marketing research.** What does marketing research indicate?
- **Distribution.** How can your invention reach consumers? What types of distribution are available?
- **Perceived function.** What do you perceive as the invention's primary function? Will consumers perceive this as its function as well?
- **Existing competition.** What competition exists now?
- **Potential sales.** Have you any way of estimating the potential sales?
- **Development status.** In what stage of development is your invention?
- **Investment costs.** What type of start-up expenses do you anticipate in order to manufacture the device?
- **Trend of demand.** What do consumer trends indicate for the demand for your invention?
- **Product line potential.** Is there a potential to expand your invention into a line of products?
- **Need.** Is there a need for your invention?
- **Promotion.** What type of promotion is needed to sell your invention?
- **Appearance.** Does your invention's appearance add to its commercial appeal?

- **Price.** Is your invention affordable to the relevant market?
- **Protection.** What forms of legal protection are available for your invention?
- **Payback period.** How long will it take to receive a payback on your invention?
- **Profitability.** What is the margin between the cost and the sale price?
- **Product interdependence.** Is your invention dependent on or related to another device or product?
- **Research and development.** Is further research and development necessary before you sell the invention?

It may be difficult for you to assess each factor, particularly at the beginning of the invention process. In addition, the importance of each factor may vary. However, it becomes obvious when you view all of the factors cumulatively that the brilliance of your invention may pale under the light of commercial scrutiny. For example, an invention that has fluctuating demand, an unfeasible production system, and a slow payback period will be very difficult to license.

The *Patent It Yourself* Factors for Commercial Potential

In the book *Patent It Yourself*, by David Pressman and David E. Blau (Nolo), the authors provide 55 positive and negative factors that can help you determine whether your invention has commercial potential.

The Bag of Parts Analysis

One successful toy representative explained that when presented with a prospective toy idea, the first thing he does is isolate the parts and imagine the parts were in a bag. How much would this bag of parts cost? He then multiplies the cost of the parts by five to get an idea of the retail price (referred to as the "price point"). Finally, he compares the potential retail price with the competition. If the price point is above the range of competing toy items, the rep will not handle the toy. No matter how brilliant the toy idea, the rep believes that it will be too difficult to convince companies and stores to handle an item that is not priced competitively. The same is true for most industries. The buying public is price conscious and will forgo a brilliant invention if its price is prohibitive.

Cost is an easy starting point. How much will it cost to make your invention? How much will the parts cost? How much will the assembly of the parts cost? How much will the packaging cost?

Other factors that might be equally important include:

- **Competition.** Are opposing products firmly entrenched? Is the field crowded with competition? Is the market too small to merit the promotional effort?

- **Ease of use.** How easy is it to obtain results from your device?
- **Demand.** Is there a need for your device?

As to the final factor—demand—you might wish to pursue your own research with family and friends, as described below.

Testing the Waters Yourself

One of the simplest methods of determining marketability is to conduct your own personal market research by performing focus group research. This is a system in which you present your invention to groups of people and get their responses. Conducting such a market survey may reveal whether potential consumers will have any interest in the device.

This type of research requires organization. You will need to prepare your presentation. If you don't have a prototype, you'll need to find some way of showing or describing your creation so that the viewers can evaluate it. You will also need to pinpoint the right questions to ask (for example, "Would you buy it? What is the most you would pay?") and be able to compile the responses. Even if the research convinces you not to proceed, this method is excellent practice for making presentations to licensees or potential business partners.

Because you might be disclosing certain information that should be maintained as a trade secret, you might need to take precautions. Rather than have each guest sign a nondisclosure agreement (an unfriendly method of getting opinions), use a logbook or a page in the inventor's notebook that evaluators can sign which states something such as:

> The following understand, have witnessed, and agree not to disclose any confidential information regarding the invention known as [*insert the name of your invention—for example, "the Purple Plunger"*] on the dates indicated below.

Although this logbook method is not as protective as a disclosure agreement, it puts the evaluator on notice that the invention is confidential.

 CAUTION

Testing your idea on friends or family. Using friends or family for opinions can create uncomfortable situations. You might be offended by their comments. They may be hesitant to tell you the truth. Here are four tips to help deal with this issue:

- Create an atmosphere where your viewers are comfortable expressing their opinions.
- Avoid taking criticism personally. It's hard, but it will help you in business.
- Do not interrupt or argue when others are making criticisms.
- Don't disclose your invention to someone if you don't trust them.

Getting an Expert Opinion

The opinions of a test group might be helpful, but they might not be sufficient. Perhaps they are not the item's intended consumers, or perhaps they lack the proper industry perspective to determine potential success. You might need an expert opinion.

Who counts as an expert? Generally, anyone involved in the chain of distribution is an expert to a certain degree, from inventor to manufacturer to supplier to distributor to salesperson to consumer. If you have an auto accessories product, for example, you might solicit the opinion of a mechanic, a driver, the owner of an accessories store, or even a gas station attendant.

Being an expert doesn't require a college education, only experience, knowledge, or expertise in the appropriate marketplace.

Local inventor groups may provide expert assistance for evaluation, or they may lead you to organizations that assess marketability. Objective evaluations are performed by some companies, often for a fee. For more information, check the resources in Chapter 18, "Help Beyond This Book."

If you hire an expert to evaluate your invention, you'll need a prototype (or some model or mock-up) of your invention in order to obtain an expert evaluation. For information about prototypes and presentations, see Chapter 6.

CAUTION

Beware of scam invention marketing firms! If you have contacted an invention marketing firm and their so-called experts told you that your invention will be a success and sell millions, you're in trouble! Hopefully, you haven't paid for this opinion. If you have, you should not pay any more. Although legitimate companies exist that will evaluate your product's commercial potential, the majority of the invention marketing firms are scam operations. If you are not sure what an invention marketing firm is, or if you are considering making a payment to a company that proposes to help you patent your invention or get you a licensing deal, review Chapter 5 before proceeding.

What If There Is No Commercial Potential?

Trying to market a new product is like gambling, and as in any game of chance, you have to know when to quit. This might be the most difficult decision for an inventor to face. Because of this, you must have a realistic view and avoid the false hopes that come with the excitement of inventing. It is important to remember that the invention embodies only one aspect of your creative ability, and if you were able to create one invention, there is more intellectual property in your brain waiting to be mined. Don't be discouraged! You can still achieve your goal of commercial success, but perhaps with a different invention. Remember: It is the ability to invent, not the invention itself, that is rewarded.

Dear Rich:
My Great Idea: Somebody Had It First!

Dear Rich: I had this great idea for "something." I researched it online and found something that accomplishes the same thing but in a different way. It has a trademark but doesn't seem to be patented. I am so upset because I thought this was a terrific idea and now I'm not sure if I can patent it. Can you help me?

The short answer is that you can patent a device that accomplishes the same result as an existing invention provided that the manner in which it accomplishes that result is novel and not obvious to others in the field. For example, there are many ways to hold hair in place and no shortage of patents. An attorney would need to advise you about your particular situation since there's not enough information in your letter for us to provide much guidance.

Search on Your Own. You can certainly search the patent database to see if someone has registered a similar idea—we prefer Google's patent searching system over the USPTO database. And you can review the trademark database—lately, we like Trademarkia.com more than the USPTO (although they each have searching idiosyncrasies).

Great Ideas R Us. We respect you for coming up with one great idea and hope you come up with more. But keep in mind, there's a reason for Thomas Edison's inspiration/perspiration equation. As Edison himself acknowledged, his success was primarily attributable to being a "hustler" rather than to any of the great ideas he instigated, cajoled for, or "borrowed." In other words, coming up with great ideas is not the hard part; the challenge is in selling your brainstorm.

Intellectual Property Protection

General Rules for Legal Protection of Inventions 45

  Functional Versus Nonfunctional 45

  The Component Approach 46

Utility Patents 47

  Types of Inventions Qualifying for a Utility Patent........................... 48

  Useful, Novel, and Nonobvious.. 48

  Deadlines and Length of Patent Protection (Patent Term) 50

  Patent Pending..51

  The Patent Application Process..52

  The Provisional Patent Application: Shortcut or Detour? 53

  The U.S. Patent and Trademark Office 54

Trade Secrets..55

  Protection for Functional and Nonfunctional Features.................... 56

  Protection of Know-How 57

  Patents and Trade Secrets: A Comparison..57

  Managing Your Trade Secrets 60

Trademarks 61

  You Must Have "Trade" to Have a Trademark 62

  Length of Protection..62

  Federal Registration..62

  Intent-to-Use Registrations 63

  The Application Process..63

Design Patents..63

    Standard for Obtaining a Design Patent 64

    Deadlines and Length of Protection... 64

    Registration 65

Copyright Law 65

    What Copyright Won't Protect...65

    Length of Protection...65

Sorting Out Nonfunctional Features: Design Patents, Product

    Configurations, and Copyright.. 66

    Not All Designs Qualify for All Forms of Protection 66

    Not All Forms of Design Protection Cost the Same 66

    Stopping Infringers: Trademarks, Copyrights, and Design Patents.................67

ntellectual property includes the legal rights associated with patents, trade secrets, trademarks, and copyrights. Each type of intellectual property gives you certain rights. For example, if a patent is issued for your invention, you have the exclusive right to make, use, and sell the invention. If the name of your invention qualifies as a trademark, you have the exclusive right to use the name on certain products. It is these rights that are the subject of a license: When you license your invention, you are actually licensing your rights to it under intellectual property laws.

Because licensing your invention involves a transfer of your rights to someone else, you should not license your invention until you know what intellectual property rights you have. If you haven't already figured this out, you'll need to do so before proceeding.

Obtaining intellectual property protection is a little like getting a bank loan—some inventions qualify and some don't. Because legal protection can enhance the value of your invention, we suggest you evaluate every aspect of your creation in order to acquire the broadest possible protection.

 SKIP AHEAD

If you already own a patent for your invention or if you understand the type of intellectual property that you own in your invention, you can skip this chapter and go to Chapter 3, which discusses ownership rights.

General Rules for Legal Protection of Inventions

A basic rule of intellectual property law is that various features of the same invention may be protected by different types of intellectual property. In general:

- The *functional* features of your invention (how it works and what it does) may be protectable under:
  - utility patent laws, and
  - trade secret laws.
- The *nonfunctional* features (the decorative appearance, artistic expression, or packaging) may be protectable under:
  - trademark laws
  - design patent laws, and
  - copyright laws.

The Public Domain

When an invention, artwork, or a symbol used on a product is not protected by intellectual property law, it's considered to be in the public domain. A work that is in the public domain is free for all to use and may be copied. Inventions that are not protected by intellectual property laws are in the public domain.

Functional Versus Nonfunctional

Intellectual property rights are often divided between functional elements (protected by utility patents and trade secrets) and nonfunctional elements (protected by trademarks, copyrights, and design patents). How can you determine whether a feature is functional or nonfunctional? Ask the question: "Does this feature make the invention work better or is it done primarily for aesthetic reasons?"

For example, the unique V-shape of an electric guitar is not necessary for the guitar to function. It's primarily a decorative or nonfunctional element. Similarly, the unique shape of a maple syrup bottle isn't necessary for the bottle to hold liquid; it's primarily aesthetic and nonfunctional because it serves to distinguish the product's appearance. On the other hand, a uniquely shaped hook used on a hanger could be primarily functional if it prevents the hanger from snagging on clothing.

The Component Approach

Because the various types of intellectual property protection overlap, you should review your product in terms of its components. To identify each component, try separating the functional and nonfunctional features of your invention.

> **EXAMPLE:** In 2001, Apple Computer released the "iPod," a small, stylish device that weighed 6.5 ounces and held approximately 1,000 songs.

The iPod didn't really do anything new—other devices already allowed users to store and play back digital music. And, the iPod was expensive —$400. At the time, $400 seemed an unthinkable amount to pay within the industry. But the iPod went on to dominate its category in sales numbers and revenue, because it was the first device to combine three elements important to consumers: small size, large storage capacity, and a classy design. Also, a novel feature distinguished the iPod from its competitors: the "scroll wheel," a circular switch that appeared submerged within the body of the iPod. Using this innovation, users could maneuver through song lists, choose songs, or adjust volume. The functional components of the iPod included the player, storage device, and scroll wheel. The nonfunctional components consisted of the name "iPod," the Apple logo, the design/appearance of the scroll wheel, and the total appearance of the exterior. Although Apple abandoned the scroll wheel in favor of the touch screen, the groundbreaking functional and nonfunctional aspects of the first generation iPod evolved into Apple's most profitable product—the iPhone.

Once you've broken down your invention into components, categorize which laws protect which components. For example, the iPod's design (or the appearance of the scroll wheel) could be protectable under design patent law. The technology that connects the scroll wheel to the player might be protectable under utility patent law. And the name "iPod" is protectable under trademark law. Once you've determined which types of intellectual property protection apply to the various components of your invention, pursue the legal protection for each component.

EXAMPLE: Jay Sorensen, a real estate broker, was accidentally burned by a cup of takeout coffee. Instead of suing the store for the coffee burn, Mr. Sorensen invented the Java Jacket: a cup holder assembled from pressed paper pulp. Unlike other coffee cup holders, the Java Jacket is manufactured in a flat sheet and the user assembles it by interlocking the ends and slipping the coffee cup into it. The Java Jacket is a functional device that prevents coffee drinkers from being burned. Since the device is functional, Mr. Sorensen applied for and received a utility patent (5,425,497) for his creation. One nonfunctional feature

of the Java Jacket is also protectable— its name. The term "Java Jacket" meets the standards for federal trademark registration. Mr. Sorenson registered it as a federal trademark in 1995 (Serial #74-553168).

Utility Patents

For purposes of invention licensing, a utility patent is the strongest protection available. If you can obtain a patent for your invention and your invention has commercial potential, you will be in the best position to license it.

A utility patent is a federal grant to an inventor who has created a new and useful invention. It allows an inventor the exclusive right to make, use, and sell the invention—and the right to prevent others from doing so with a similar (or infringing) invention. Some patent practitioners refer to the utility patent as a "hunting license," because it gives the inventor the right to hunt infringers and obtain damages and other legal remedies.

To obtain a utility patent, you need to file a patent application with the U.S. Patent and Trademark Office (USPTO) that meets the standards of the agency's examiners and pay the appropriate filing, issuance, and maintenance fees.

Types of Inventions Qualifying for a Utility Patent

A utility patent can be issued for any new and useful:

- process—a method of accomplishing a result through a series of steps (for example, a process for sterilizing surgical equipment)
- machine—a device that accomplishes a result by the interaction of its parts (for example, a gear shift in a rowing machine)
- article of manufacture—a single object without movable parts (such as a pencil or a garden rake) or an object with movable parts that are incidental (such as a folding chair or an ironing board)
- composition of matter—any combination of chemical or other materials (for example, Teflon or WD-40), or
- improvement on an already-existing invention (for example, an improvement upon a household plunger), unless the underlying invention is still protected under patent law and you don't have authorization from the patent owner.

The USPTO interprets these categories very broadly, and it's possible that your invention may overlap various classes.

 INTELLECTUAL PROPERTY MYTH

The First Person to Create Something Always Acquires Protection

Don't presume that, because you were the first to create something, you automatically have priority over other inventors. Generally, creators are not rewarded for being first under intellectual property laws. For example, under patent law, the inventor who is first to file (not to invent) receives the patent. In copyright law, all that matters is whether the creation is original to the author (and not copied from another source). Trademark law doesn't reward the first to create a trademark; rather, the trademark registration goes to the company that first uses it in commerce.

Useful, Novel, and Nonobvious

To qualify for a utility patent, your invention must also be: (1) useful, (2) novel, and (3) nonobvious.

Usefulness

An invention must have a use or purpose and must work (that is, be capable of performing its intended purpose). The USPTO may reject an application if the use has not been established or the only use would be illegal or deceptive. For example, an invention to counterfeit one-hundred-dollar bills wouldn't be eligible for patent protection unless the inventor could demonstrate some alternative legal use of the device.

Novelty

To be novel, an invention must differ in some way from "prior art," which is any other invention publicly known at that time or considered existing knowledge in the field (see "What Is Prior Art?" on the next page). The USPTO will not issue a patent if the invention was known or used by others in this country, or patented or described in a printed publication in this or a foreign country, before the filing date of the patent application.

Nonobviousness

All inventions must meet a standard of nonobviousness, which is an inquiry into whether persons working in the field of the invention would consider the invention unexpected and surprising (nonobvious), rather than evident or apparent (obvious). Many inventions—the safety pin, the ironing board, the sewing machine, the collapsible tube, and the cylinder lock—seem obvious now, but that wasn't the case when they were invented. This is one of the paradoxes of great inventions: Once created, they seem obvious.

1 + 1 Must Equal 3

In 2007, the U.S. Supreme Court tweaked the obviousness rule as to "combination inventions"—innovations in which two or more functioning devices are combined (for example, combining a flashlight and an emergency siren). The Supreme Court ruled that when elements, techniques, items, or devices are combined, united, or arranged, and when, in combination, each item performs the function it was designed to perform, the resulting combination—something the court called "ordinary innovation"—is not patentable. For example, if you combine eyeglasses with earpieces, the invention will be considered obvious (and unpatentable) if the eyeglasses and headphones function as they normally would. What is patentable is a synergistic result—that is, the sum of the resulting combination is greater than its whole and altered in its functionality. (*KSR v. Teleflex*, 550 U.S. 398 (2007).)

In addition to being unexpected, factors that bear on whether an invention is nonobvious are:

- whether the invention has enjoyed commercial success
- whether a need exists in the industry for the invention
- whether others have tried but failed to achieve the same result

What Is Prior Art?

Prior art is the existing technical information against which your invention is judged. That is, in order to determine if your invention is novel and nonobvious enough to acquire patent protection, the patent examiner looks at the existing information related to your invention. If the prior art demonstrates that your invention wasn't novel or that your invention was obvious, the patent will not be issued. The patent examiner (or federal courts) will consider the following types of information as prior art:

- anything in public use or on sale in the world before the filing date of the patent application
- prior patents that issued before the filing date of the patent
- prior publications dated before the filing date of the patent

- anything that was publicly known or used by others before the filing date, and
- anything that was made or built by another person before the filing date.

An important exception exists: Any disclosure made by the inventor within a year prior to the patent application filing date is not considered prior art as to that patent application, but is considered prior art as to other inventors.

The USPTO considers the patent application filed on the date it receives all of the required elements of the patent application. However, if the inventor had previously filed a provisional patent application and within one year files a utility patent application, the effective filing date reverts back to the date the provisional application was filed.

- whether the inventor did what others said could not be done
- whether others have copied the invention, and
- whether the invention has been praised by others in the field.

Deadlines and Length of Patent Protection (Patent Term)

Under U.S. patent law, like rest of the world, the first inventor to file a patent

application (or "first to file") is granted protection, regardless of who was first to create the invention.

A utility patent lasts 20 years from the date of filing, provided that fees necessary to keep the patent in force (maintenance fees) are paid.

Under certain circumstances, the patent period may be extended if the commercial marketing of the product is delayed by government regulations or review. For example, the patent term

What Are Patent Claims?

As mentioned above, a utility patent grants you the right to stop others from making, selling, or using your invention during the term of the patent. The extent of these rights depends largely upon the scope and boundaries of your invention. Patent claims —which essentially define the scope of your invention—are the heart of your invention and what makes it attractive to licensees. These claims are located in your patent application. The claims define the boundaries of the invention in the same way that a deed establishes the boundaries of real property. Drafting patent claims is a specialized skill (as you will no doubt see from the example claim for a toy glider airplane below) that often, but not always, requires the expertise of a patent attorney. For more information about drafting patent claims, see the patent resources in Chapter 18, "Help Beyond This Book."

EXAMPLE: Patent claims for a toy glider airplane: a model airplane or toy glider having a wing adapted to be assembled with a complex, three-dimensional, folded fuselage constructed of semirigid scorable and foldable material, said fuselage having generally symmetrical left and right half portions joined along less than the length of said fuselage, said fuselage in unassembled unfolded condition being generally V-shaped, said folded fuselage being attached to said wing via elastic band.

for certain human and animal drugs can be extended for up to five years to compensate for lengthy government safety tests. In an attempt to guarantee at least 17 years of patent protection, Congress amended the patent laws in 1999 requiring the USPTO to issue (or reject) a patent within three years after its actual filing date. Under this law, the term of a patent will be extended if the USPTO failed to issue a patent within three years from filing due to its own delays. The patent term will not be extended, however, if the applicant caused the delay, for example, by filing a continuation application.

After the patent expires, the invention falls into the public domain. (See "The Public Domain" at the beginning of this chapter.)

Patent Pending

Patent rights don't begin until the patent is issued. Years can pass between when a patent application is filed and the patent issues. This period of time is known as the pendency or patent pending period. The owner of a patent can't prevent any infringing activity that occurs during the pendency period, but can stop infringing activity that continues after the patent is issued.

EXAMPLE: Say an inventor developed a can capable of dispensing food. The invention permitted snack foods to be sold in machines originally manufactured to sell only beverages. During the period when the patent was pending, a snack food company test marketed the same idea. The inventor was awarded a patent on December 28, 2019, and filed an infringement lawsuit against the snack food company on the same day. If the inventor can prove infringement of the patent, the court may order the snack food company to stop selling the device and award the inventor any profits resulting from infringements occurring after December 28, 2019.

There is one occasion in which the patent owner can receive compensation for infringement during the pendency period. The USPTO publishes all pending applications, for public view, 18 months after the earliest effective filing date. An inventor, whose application is published, may seek infringement damages from the date of the publication, provided a patent is later issued and the infringer had actual notice of the published application.

EXAMPLE: Sally applied for a patent for a new type of fogless, night-vision swimming goggles on January 1, 2019. Swimco, a swimming products company, manufactured an identical pair of goggles starting in January 2020. Sally sent Swimco a copy of the patent application after it was published in June 2020. The USPTO issues Sally's patent in December 2020. Once the patent issues, Sally can sue to stop Swimco from further manufacturing its goggles and seek Swimco's profits for sales after June 2020 (the date Swimco had actual notice of Sally's published application).

Compensation for pendency infringements is not available if the inventor seeks only domestic and not international patent rights, *and* if the inventor prevents publication of the application by filing a "Nonpublication Request."

The Patent Application Process

The process of obtaining a patent is often referred to as "prosecution of the patent application." The patent prosecution process is beyond the scope of this book. However, if you wish to pursue a patent, check out *Patent It Yourself,* by David Pressman and David E. Blau (Nolo). If you're not comfortable preparing your own application, contact a patent attorney. You can locate a patent attorney through your local bar association or via an Internet search. (Chapter 18, "Help Beyond This Book," offers information on finding and working with attorneys.) If you decide not to handle your own patent application, the entire process—including attorneys' fees, filing fees, and fees for searching the patent database—can cost thousands of dollars. The application process often lasts 18 months to three years (or longer). There are legal deadlines for filing patent applications. Failure to meet these deadlines can prevent you from obtaining patent protection.

 INTELLECTUAL PROPERTY MYTH

The Government Will Enforce Intellectual Property Rights

Although some intellectual property laws provide for government enforcement, that type of government action is rarely taken. When it is, it is because a business has already investigated the claim on its own and has the political clout to convince the local U.S. Attorney or Customs Office to go after the infringers. In other words, the government will not pursue infringers on its own.

Nolo Provides Assistance for Provisional Patent Application (PPA) Filing

Nolo (www.nolo.com), the publisher of this book, offers assistance in the electronic filing of PPAs. Get the details at store.nolo.com/products/online-Provisional-Patent-application-nnppa.html.

The Provisional Patent Application: Shortcut or Detour?

The Provisional Patent Application (PPA) permits an inventor to file an abbreviated patent application that can be used to establish a filing date. If a regular patent application is filed within one year of filing the PPA, the inventor can use the PPA's filing date for the legal purposes of deciding whether prior art is relevant and, in the event an interference exists, who is entitled to the patent. (Note: The PPA is not available for design patents.)

The PPA must contain a description of the invention and drawings if necessary to understand the description. The invention's description must clearly explain how to make and use the invention. If the invention has several versions or modes of operation, the best mode or version must be disclosed. Claims, formal drawings, and other elements of the regular patent application may be included if the inventor wishes, but they are not required.

The advantages of filing a PPA compared to a patent application include: It saves thousands of dollars (if you decide not to file for a regular patent), doesn't require witnesses, saves the expense of building and testing, and is much simpler to complete. Also, if a PPA is filed, the inventor can publish, sell, or show the invention to others without fear of theft or loss of any U.S. patent rights, because anyone who sees and steals the invention would have a later (and inferior) filing date.

However, if the inventor doesn't file a regular patent application within a year of the PPA, the PPA is abandoned and no longer provides a filing date for purposes of prior art. The PPA is also worthless if the inventor changes the invention so that it no longer matches the PPA description. Also, the filing of a PPA can affect an inventor's foreign rights. As with a regular U.S. application, an inventor must pursue foreign patent applications within one year of the PPA's filing date.

EXAMPLE: Sam invented an expandable picture frame, a device made from a flexible plastic that can adjust to fit different-sized snapshots. He files a PPA on July 1, 2018. On May 1, 2019, he files a regular patent application. His patent issues on January 10, 2020.

If anyone contests Sam's right to his invention, Sam will have proof that his invention predated any similar invention as of July 1, 2018. If Sam had waited more than a year after filing his PPA to file his regular patent application, he wouldn't be able to claim the 2018 filing date.

You Can License Before Receiving a Patent

If you proceed with the patent application process, you can license your invention before the patent is issued. Sometimes, a licensee may condition the license upon the granting of the patent. That is, if the patent doesn't issue, the license is canceled or the royalties are reduced to reflect only the nonpatentable aspects that have been licensed. Some inventors prefer to wait for the issuance of the patent because they feel more secure with patent protection when disclosing and licensing their inventions.

The U.S. Patent and Trademark Office

The United States Patent and Trademark Office (USPTO)—a division of the Department of Commerce—is responsible for the federal registration of patents (www.uspto.gov). Correspondence to the USPTO should be mailed to the

Dear Rich:
Manufacturer Wants Invention, But Not the Patent

Dear Rich: I created an invention that involves snowmobiles, and it's currently patent pending in the U.S. and Canada. I proposed a deal whereby the manufacturer would advance me $7,000, most of it for patent prosecution costs, and a 7% royalty. However, the manufacturer responded that they do not see the value in a patent, so they don't want to pay the $7,000.

Question 1: Can I legally make a contract without having patent pending (or other forms of intellectual property) to offer them?
It helps to be able to point to a patent or a trademark registration when licensing, but not having a government registration doesn't preclude you from licensing an idea. The idea may involve trade secrets or know-how, or some other product of the mind, and the fact that a licensee is willing to pay for it indicates that it has value.

Ideas are commonly licensed in the toy and entertainment industry.

Question 2: Let's assume we do license the "idea," and the manufacturer sells a bunch of units. And let's say our patents do not issue because the idea has already been patented by a third party. Can that third party sue us directly for having sold an "idea" that we do not own to a manufacturer?
If a second inventor is claiming the same invention as you, and you disclosed it or offered it for sale prior to the second inventor's filing for the patent, you would prevail in a lawsuit. If the second inventor's patent was filed before your disclosure or offer for sale, you would not prevail. If the latter is a possibility, you could try to request that the manufacturer indemnify you if you are sued for infringement.

Commissioner of Patents, P.O. Box 1450, Alexandria, VA 22313-1450. Rules and regulations for USPTO activities are established in the Code of Federal Regulations (known as the C.F.R.) and in special USPTO publications, such as the *Manual of Patent Examining Procedure* (MPEP). For more information about the USPTO, see Chapter 18, "Help Beyond This Book."

Trade Secrets

A trade secret is any confidential information used in your business that gives you an advantage over competitors who do not know it or use it. In order to maintain ownership rights over a trade secret, you must treat the information with secrecy. Any public disclosure will end trade secrecy status for the information, and anyone will be free to use it.

The Defend Trade Secrets Act (DTSA)

The federal Defend Trade Secrets Act (DTSA) provides a procedure for trade secret owners to file civil lawsuits in federal court. Any company possessing a trade secret that is "related to a product or service used in, or intended for use in, interstate or foreign commerce" can take advantage of the provisions of the DTSA. Prior to the DTSA, trade secret owners could only bring civil lawsuits in state courts, under state laws based on the Uniform Trade Secrets Act (UTSA). (Except for New York, every state has adopted some version of the UTSA.) In many important ways the DTSA and state laws based on the UTSA are similar—for example, the definitions of trade secrets and misappropriation are the same, as are the statute of limitations (three years) and the remedies for theft (injunctive relief, compensatory damages). But the DTSA can be more favorable to trade secret owners because it provides access to federal courts and the option of seizing trade secrets without giving any notice to the defendant—an unprecedented leap from the notice requirements of state laws based on the UTSA.

To determine if material might qualify as a trade secret, ask yourself: Would your business be damaged if a competitor acquired the information? For example, if you've devised a new method of testing the life of a lightbulb, you would want to keep that information secret in order to have an edge on your competitors. Information that appears to give your business an advantage over competitors should be kept secret until you've determined how to protect it (by either trade secret or patent protection).

As the owner of a trade secret, you can prevent anyone who has obtained the secret by improper means from using it. "Improper means" refers to misappropriation and generally occurs through theft by former employees, bribery (the thief pays someone in your company in order to get the secret), misrepresentation (the thief poses as someone else to get the secret), or breach of a promise not to disclose the information (someone such as an ex-employee promises not to disclose it but tells the secret anyway).

However, you cannot prevent someone from using the secret if they acquired it by legitimate means, such as reverse engineering or independent invention (see below).

Protection for Functional and Nonfunctional Features

As we indicated above in our rules of intellectual property, trade secrets generally protect your invention's functional features. In other words, trade secrets usually protect secret features of your invention that make it perform unlike other inventions. For example, the secret lubricant that your company uses might make your gear shift superior to other gear shift inventions. It is this valuable trade secret aspect of your invention that makes it licensable.

Trade secrets can also protect information that is nonfunctional—for example, your design of a new logo or name for your invention. (Be aware, though, once you use the new name or logo in commerce or show your new design to the public, it loses its trade secrecy status.)

Protection of Know-How

In addition to licensing your patented invention, a licensee might want to license your know-how. Sometimes the term "know-how" is used as a synonym for trade secrets. That is, the licensee might want to license both your patent and any related trade secrets.

However, know-how does not always refer to secret information. Know-how sometimes refers to a particular kind of technical knowledge needed to accomplish some task. For example, your know-how might be necessary to train the licensee's employees how to make or use your invention. Think of know-how as a combination of secret and nonsecret information that has value because it's needed to commercialize your invention.

**Non-Fogging Shower Mirror
No. 5,953,157**

Know-how can also be the subject of a separate services agreement. For example, the licensee wants you to train employees using your knowledge of the invention and the industry. As a general rule, you should assume know-how is protectable as a trade secret and treat it as such. To that extent, if you are disclosing know-how to a licensee's employees or contractors, use a disclosure agreement. See Chapter 7 for more information about disclosure agreements.

Patents and Trade Secrets: A Comparison

Some inventors choose to protect their inventions under trade secret law rather than under patent law. Compared to a patent, trade secret protection involves minimal cost and does not involve a public disclosure program (such as that used by the USPTO). But a downside to choosing trade secret protection is you risk losing the secret through reverse engineering (see below). Therefore, inventors must carefully weigh the methods of protection they choose. Below, we outline some of the differences between trade secrets and patents.

Stopping Infringers

In general, the protection afforded by a patent makes it easier to stop an infringer, because you need only prove that the competitor is making, using, or selling your invention or an equivalent invention. It's not necessary to prove the competitor intended to infringe upon your rights (although that might influence the amount of damages). And you don't have to prove how the competitor acquired the information. Many patent owners use their patents to earn more money suing infringers than from selling the inventions. To stop infringement of your trade secret, you must demonstrate that (a) you have treated the secret with confidentiality, and (b) the infringer acquired the secret through improper means. If the competitor can show that you disclosed the information without confidentiality—even to someone other than the infringer—or the information was legitimately reverse engineered or independently developed, you will not able to stop the competitor.

 INTELLECTUAL PROPERTY MYTH

Legal Rights Equate With Commercial Success

Acquiring patent or other intellectual property rights does not create value. It only enhances or preserves the inherent value, if any, of your invention. Intellectual property protection is like title to land. It guarantees your rights to the property, but it doesn't guarantee the value of the property.

Length of Protection

Trade secret protection will last as long as the secret is kept confidential. Patent protection lasts for 20 years from the date of filing, provided that the maintenance fees are paid.

Reverse Engineering and Independent Invention

For some inventors, a downside of trade secret protection is that the protection ends once someone obtains the secret legitimately—at which point, the inventor cannot prevent the use of the information and any competitor is free to use the trade secret.

This principle is not true for patents. No matter how the competitor obtained information about your invention, patent law prohibits the competitor from making, using, or selling your invention.

So how can a competitor obtain your trade secret legitimately? The two most common methods of obtaining a secret legitimately are by (a) reverse engineering and (b) independent development of the technology.

Reverse Engineering

It's not a violation of trade secret law to disassemble and examine a product that is available to the public. For example, you may purchase Coca-Cola and analyze the chemical formula, which is protected by trade secret. You are free to manufacture a similar cola based on your analysis of ingredients (although trademark laws prohibit you from calling it a name similar to Coca-Cola).

Reverse engineering must be done legitimately. That is, the person doing the reverse engineering must obtain the invention rightfully. For example, you can't reverse engineer from a stolen computer program. It's also not enough for someone accused of trade secret infringement to state that she could have reverse engineered the invention and obtained the same information. The accused infringer must have actually reverse engineered it.

Independent Development—The Clean Room

If you independently develop an invention, you can use or sell it even if it is similar or identical to someone else's trade secret. For example, if you invent a unique method of sorting coins, you can use it even if it is identical to a method protected under trade secret law. This independent development rule doesn't apply for patented inventions.

To demonstrate that you independently developed an invention or a method, you should keep an inventor's notebook or similar documentation. For independent inventors or small companies, this method should work fine.

Larger companies, however, should take additional precautions. The most reliable means of demonstrating independent development is the use of a clean room technique. Various forms of clean rooms exist, but all involve isolating certain engineers or designers and filtering information to them. These engineers or designers are usually given an objective (such as to create a software program which connects a telephone to a computer) and are then presented with publicly available materials, tools, and documents.

The progress of the development team is carefully monitored and documented, and any requests for further information by the team are reviewed by a technical expert or legal monitor.

CAUTION

The effect of a patent application on trade secrecy. Filing a patent application does not end trade secrecy protection, because the application isn't immediately published. Trade secrecy protection will be lost when the USPTO publishes the application 18 months after the filing date. If the application isn't published and the patent issues, trade secrecy protection will be lost because the patent will be published. If your patent application is rejected and has not been published, you can still claim the protection of trade secret laws. Publication, not filing, of the patent is what ends the trade secret protection.

Keeping Trade Secrecy for a Patented Invention

Although the issuance of a patent usually ends trade secret protection for an invention, there may be features of the invention that are not described in the application and could therefore still be trade secrets. Say Sam developed a peanut butter dispenser. The dispenser uses a unique combination of a tube and pump technology. The tube and pump technology is patentable. Sam also devised a method of speeding the peanut butter flow by using a combination of vegetable oils in the peanut butter. This method is a trade secret. Sam can license both the patent and the trade secret.

Public Disclosure Program

Generally, the USPTO publishes pending applications, for public view, 18 months after the patent's earliest effective filing date (or earlier if requested by the applicant). The application will not be published, however, if, at the time of filing, the applicant files a Nonpublication Request stating that the application will not be filed outside the United States.

If the applicant later files the application abroad, the applicant must notify the USPTO within 45 days. A failure of the applicant to provide such notice within the prescribed period will result in the application being regarded as abandoned.

There is one advantage to early publication. An applicant whose application is published may seek royalties from an infringer from the date of publication, provided (a) a patent later issues and (b) the infringer had actual notice of the published application. If an applicant is concerned that a patent will not issue and wishes to preserve trade secrecy rights in the invention, the applicant must withdraw the application in order to prevent publication within 18 months of the filing.

Managing Your Trade Secrets

As a rule, you cannot be passive as a trade secret owner. You must actively protect your secrets by taking reasonable steps to maintain secrecy.

Smaller Businesses/ Independent Inventors

Smaller businesses or independent inventors need not be concerned with issues such as building security (see below) and should focus primarily on maintaining information in a secure location, stamping it with appropriate legends ("Confidential" or "Secret"), and using disclosure agreements, as described in Chapter 7. A disclosure agreement preserves the secrecy of the information during disclosure.

Larger Businesses

The following precautions should be considered by larger businesses:

- **Control access to the building.** The entrance to the building should be secure, and visitors or after-hours employees should sign in. The building should have a fence, an alarm, or a guard system. Employees' access should be restricted in areas where confidential material is located. Employees should be instructed and reminded on how to handle trade secrets. File cabinets and desks with confidential information must be locked, and the business should implement a document control policy.
- **Secure computers, copying devices, and other devices.** These devices should be in secure areas, and the company should require users of machines to log their usage. A machine (such as

a paper shredder) should be used to destroy confidential material.

- **Use security systems for computer and telephone networks.** Passwords should be required for access and be changed frequently.
- **Use stamps and signs.** The company should use stamps, such as "Confidential Material" or "Restricted," on relevant documents, and post signs at restricted access areas.
- **Secure documents.** All notebooks or other materials used in the development or maintenance of trade secrets should be properly documented, labeled, and filed in the restricted access area and treated with confidentiality and secrecy.

Trademarks

Trademark law protects your right to exclusively use a name, logo, or any device that identifies and distinguishes your invention. In addition to names and logos, trademark law can be used to protect "trade dress" and product configuration. Trade dress is the product's packaging— all the elements that give your invention's appearance an identifiable quality, such as the combination of color, geometric shapes, imagery, and lettering on a pain reliever bottle. Product configuration refers to the shape or design of your invention (for example, a distinctive oval-shaped stapler). To acquire protection for trade dress or product configurations, you must demonstrate that your product design is nonfunctional and distinctive. Functional designs are not protected under trademark laws.

You Must Have "Trade" to Have a Trademark

Trademark law differs from copyrights, patents, and trade secrets, because trademark protection is not based upon creating something. It's based on selling something that features your trademark. In other words, trademark rights don't occur until the public has been exposed to your invention and its trademark. If you never sell or advertise your invention, you will not have any trademark rights. The first day that you use your trademark in commerce is referred to as the "date of first use," and you acquire superior rights over later users.

Length of Protection

Generally, trademark protection begins once you use the mark in commerce (that is, when you begin selling or advertising your invention). You don't have to register your trademark to acquire this trademark protection (although registration has many advantages, as explained below). Trademark protection lasts for as long as you continually use the mark in

commerce. Many trademarks have survived for over a century (Coca-Cola and Kellogg's, for example). If you register your trademark, you must periodically renew the registration.

Federal Registration

If you use your mark in federally regulated commerce (for example, across state lines or foreign exports), you can register your mark with the federal government. Owners of registered marks can use the federal registration symbol—®—and the use of the symbol serves as notice of your claim to rights. Federal registration can also serve as the basis for filing a trademark application in certain foreign countries, and it creates a presumption that you have a right to national ownership of the mark.

However, federal registration will not always give you superior rights. In some cases, a person who hasn't registered a mark could have superior rights in a geographic area over a person who later uses a similar mark and registers it. This is because trademark rights in the United States are based on first use, not on registration. The first to use the mark in commerce has superior rights. For example, say you sell an antitheft device called The Perpetrator through a national home shopping cable channel and a large national company later registers and sells a similar device with the same name. Based on your first use of the trademark on the shopping channel, you could petition the government to cancel the larger company's registration or litigate in court to stop the larger company from selling the device under The Perpetrator trademark.

Intent-to-Use Registrations

To protect your trademark before using it in commerce, you can reserve a mark, provided that you have a good-faith intent to use the mark in interstate commerce (or other types of commerce regulated by the federal government) within six months. You can extend that period to three years by filing extensions. In order to reserve your mark, you must file an intent-to-use trademark application with the assistant commissioner of trademarks at the USPTO. If the mark is not used within the required time period, then the intent-to-use application has no value.

The Application Process

You can file a federal application for a trademark at the USPTO website (www.uspto.gov). It's possible to file without the aid of an attorney. Nolo, the publisher of this book, also offers assistance for electronic filing of trademark applications. Before filing, review the free material on trademarks at the Nolo website (www.nolo.com), or check out *Trademark: Legal Care for Your Business & Product Name*, by Steve Elias and Richard Stim (Nolo).

If you only use your trademark within your state, you can register it with your state government. The forms and filing information can be obtained from your secretary of state. Keep in mind, though, if you plan to use your trademark on a website, your use will necessarily be considered national because your site is accessible worldwide. Thus, federal registration would be your best option.

Design Patents

Design patents protect the ornamental features of inventions. A design patent doesn't protect the manner in which an invention functions (that's protected by utility patents and trade secret laws), nor does it protect two-dimensional surface ornamentation, such as photographs or drawings (they're protected by copyright law, covered below). Design patents protect the aesthetic appearance of an invention, such as the shape of a lamp or a telephone.

As the owner of a design patent, you have the right to exclude others from making, selling, or using the design for the term of the design patent. Your patent protection is limited to the category of invention in which you have designed. For example, if you obtained a design patent for a trumpet-shaped hanging lamp, that patent would not enable you to stop someone from making a trumpet-shaped clock.

Standard for Obtaining a Design Patent

The requirements for a design patent are that it be new, original, and ornamental. The requirement of ornamentality means that the design is not utilitarian or functional. For example, the unique shape of a tennis racquet might not be protectable because the shape may affect how the racquet functions—that is, how well it works in the game of tennis. On the other hand, a telephone shaped like a shark (for use in law offices) would be protectable by a design patent because the shape doesn't affect the function of the device (its ability to be used as a telephone).

Deadlines and Length of Protection

You must file your design patent prior to public disclosure. The design patent lasts 15 years from issuance, if it was filed on or after May 13, 2015. For filings before that date, the design patent lasts 14 years from issuance.

Dear Rich:
Emailing Stuff to Yourself Won't Provide Protection

Dear Rich: I'm planning to set up a blog where I'll post multiple sketches, poems, and short stories, but I don't want to go broke paying for copyright registrations. What is your view on just sending myself an email with each work in it as time-stamped evidence that I created it, and then registering the works in big groups once or twice a year?

We don't think it's a worthwhile form of protection. Date-stamped emails and letters won't offer much in the way of copyright protection because at best—and this would still require expert validation—they prove only that you sent something to yourself on or around a certain date. (They don't prove that you actually created the work.) In any case, copyright disputes are rarely about who created something first. You may be confusing them with patent disputes where being first matters. (Note: The "poor-man's patent"—accomplished by mailing a copy of your invention specs to yourself—also won't protect your invention.) Copyright disputes are about whether someone had access to your work and copied it. Since you're posting this material in a blog, you should be able to demonstrate that the work is yours and there should be ample ways to prove when you first published it using cached or archived Internet pages.

Registration

Compared to a utility patent application, the design patent application is relatively simple. For more information on pursuing a design patent, check the USPTO website (www.uspto.com).

Copyright Law

Copyright law protects writing, music, artwork, computer programs, photographs, and other forms of artistic expression. The creator of an original work (known as the author) is automatically granted exclusive rights under copyright law. Registration—though it has its benefits—is not required to receive the exclusive rights to make copies and prevent others from copying the work or creating a derivative work (a work that is derived from or based on the artist's protected work).

There may be nonfunctional features of your invention that are protectable under copyright, such as its packaging, the accompanying literature, software programs used in it, artwork included on the invention, or advertisements for the invention.

What Copyright Won't Protect

Copyright protection doesn't extend to ideas, only the manner in which an idea is expressed. To separate an unprotectable idea from a copyrightable expression, examine the amount of detail in the work. A soft doll with a big puffy face, for example, is an idea. There are very few unique details. However, the Cabbage Patch dolls with their unique faces, names, and "adoption papers" contain many specific details and are a copyrightable expression.

Copyright law will not protect the functional features of your invention, and will not generally protect names, titles, short phrases, blank forms, facts, and any works within the public domain.

Unlike patent law, it doesn't matter who is the first to create a work of art. All that matters under copyright law is that the work is original to an author.

Length of Protection

For most copyrighted works, protection generally extends for the life of the author plus 70 years. So, if you have a copyrighted work, protection continues for 70 years after your death, allowing your family (or other beneficiaries of your will) to reap financial rewards from the work. For works created by companies, the term may be 95 years from date of first publication or 120 years from creation, whichever is longer. (The length of copyright protection also depends upon when the work was first published. Different rules apply for works distributed before 1978.) For more information, review the copyright resources in Chapter 18, "Help Beyond This Book."

Sorting Out Nonfunctional Features: Design Patents, Product Configurations, and Copyright

It might seem like a great deal of overlap exists when it comes to the protection of product designs and shapes. Copyright, trademark, and design patent protection all seem to offer the same forms of protection for nonfunctional designs. How do you determine which form of protection can be used to enforce your nonfunctional features? Below is an explanation of some of the differences.

Not All Designs Qualify for All Forms of Protection

Copyright, trademark, and design patents do not protect functional works; rather, they protect only the ornamentation or design of an object. But, not all designs qualify for copyright, trademark, and design patent protection.

> **EXAMPLE:** Consider the external appearance of a computer monitor. Imagine that designers at Apple Computer created a monitor that was housed within an apple-shaped case. The concept of an apple-shaped monitor might be protectable under a design patent if it is a novel, nonobvious, and an ornamental industrial design. The design shape of the apple might also be protectable under a product configuration trademark, provided it is unusual and memorable, conceptually separable from the monitor, and likely to inform people that it's a product of the Apple Computer company. But, it would be difficult to protect the apple monitor design under copyright law, because copyright protection generally does not extend to common shapes, colors, or items found in nature. Unless the monitor had some unusual or trivial creative feature, it would probably not be protectable under copyright law.

Not All Forms of Design Protection Cost the Same

You might also want to consider the cost and ease of acquiring protection when determining your method of protecting a product design. Consider the differences:

- Design patent protection requires filing fees of approximately $240–$960 and an "issue fee" of $175–$$700. Registration can take one or two years to acquire, and protection doesn't begin until the patent is issued. Protection lasts 15 years from issuance.

What About Computer Chip Protection?

If your invention includes a semiconductor chip, you might need to review special rules regarding semiconductor chip protection. Semiconductor chips are tiny plastic and ceramic devices which transmit information inside computers and other machines. On each chip is encoded an integrated circuit pattern. These patterns are known as "mask works" and are governed by the Semiconductor Chip Act.

Mask works may be protected for a limited time (ten years) provided that the mask work is registered within two years after it is commercially exploited. The mask work is commercially exploited when the work is distributed to the public or when a written offer is made to sell it and the chip is fixed. (A work is considered fixed when it is stored on some medium in which it can be perceived, reproduced, or otherwise communicated.)

Mask works are registered by using the Copyright Office's Form MW. Contact the Copyright Office for more information. See Chapter 18, "Help Beyond This Book," for contact information.

- Federal trademark registration filing fees are under $400. Trademark protection begins once the item is sold to the public and achieves distinction (either by being very unique or through extensive sales and advertising). Protection is perpetual as long as the shape is continuously used in commerce.
- If you choose to register a copyright, electronic filing costs $35–$55. Copyright protection exists once you create a design. There is no registration requirement (unless you want to pursue infringers).

The protection for copyright lasts the life of the author plus 70 years (or 95 to 120 years for a work made for hire).

Stopping Infringers: Trademarks, Copyrights, and Design Patents

The different forms of protection for your product design (trademarks, copyrights, and design patents) require different burdens of proof to stop infringers:

- In order to stop an infringer under design patent law, you need only prove that you have a valid design patent and that the two works are equivalent. You wouldn't have to prove that the competitor saw your work and copied it.

- Under trademark law, you must be able to demonstrate that your product design is distinctive and nonfunctional and that the competing company's mark is so similar to yours that it is likely to confuse consumers.

- In order to stop someone from infringing a copyright, you must prove they had access to, and copied, your work. In other words, there's no copyright infringement if they independently developed the work without first seeing your work.

 INTELLECTUAL PROPERTY MYTH

You Have to Be an Intellectual to Understand Intellectual Property Law

Don't be fooled by the term "intellectual property." Although some aspects of copyrights, trademarks, trade secrets, and patents are complex, you don't need to be a lawyer or techie to understand the basic principles. Common sense and a rudimentary knowledge of the law, as explained in this chapter, will help you grasp the major concepts and determine whether you possess or should pursue or register patent rights, copyrights, trademark rights, trade secrets, or a mix of the above.

Ownership Issues for Inventor Employees

What Type of Intellectual Property Is Involved?..70

Employer/Employee: Patent and Trade Secret Ownership................................71

    Written Employment Agreements and Preinvention Assignments 71

    Employed to Invent 75

    Shop Rights 78

Inventions Covered by Copyright 79

Special Employment Situations..79

    Government Employees and Contractors..79

    University Employees 81

Working Out Ownership Issues With Your Employer 84

n order to license your invention, you must actually own the legal rights to the invention. Sometimes, however, it's not entirely clear who owns the rights to an invention, especially in an employee-employer context. In this chapter, we review how ownership of your invention is affected by employment relationships. You should review this chapter if either of the following is true:

- You created an invention while working for someone.
- Your current employer is interested in licensing an invention from you.

What Type of Intellectual Property Is Involved?

Each form of intellectual property—patent, trade secret, copyright, and trademark—has different rules regarding ownership. Before addressing the question of whether your employer has any legal rights to your invention, you need to have a clear idea of what area of intellectual property is associated with it. (See Chapter 2 for more information.)

In very broad strokes, here are some general rules regarding employment and invention ownership:

- If you created a patentable invention or a trade secret at work, your employer owns the invention or trade secret if you:

  - signed an employment agreement assigning invention rights, or
  - were specifically hired (even without a written agreement) for your inventing skills or to create the invention.

  Note: Even if an employer doesn't acquire ownership under one of the above two methods, the employer may still acquire a limited right to use your patent or trade secret—called a "shop right." (Shop rights are discussed later in this chapter.)

- If you created something copy-rightable at work, your employer will own the copyright if the work was within the scope of your employment duties. (The rules regarding independent contractors are more complex.)

- If you created a name or distinctive appearance for your employer's products, your employer is probably entitled to the trademark rights because these rights are owned by whoever first uses the mark in conjunction with the sale of goods (although there are exceptions to this rule, as discussed in Chapter 2). Trademark rights are usually not an issue in employer–employee disputes.

At the end of the chapter, we'll look at special rules for employees of the government or universities and ways to handle disputes between you and your employer.

Employer/Employee: Patent and Trade Secret Ownership

The rules regarding employer–employee ownership of trade secrets and patents are essentially the same. As a general rule, your employer can acquire the rights to your invention if you were originally hired to create an invention or through a written agreement (such as an employment contract). Employers can also obtain more limited shop rights to employees' inventions in certain circumstances.

Written Employment Agreements and Preinvention Assignments

Some employment agreements require an employee to assign any inventions to the employer. Because such an employment agreement is signed before an employee creates an invention, it's sometimes referred to as a preinvention assignment. You should examine your employment agreement (or other agreements you have with your employer) to determine if it contains any preinvention assignment

---

Dear Rich:
Who Owns Software Created After Hours?

Dear Rich: Who owns the rights to software that is developed voluntarily and during one's own free time (after work hours) but who offers use of the software to his or her employer?

As a general rule, if the software isn't something you would create in the course of your employment and you created it on your own time, using your own equipment, then you own it. If you let your employer use it, then you probably have granted a nonexclusive implied license. To get a more comprehensive answer, the *Dear Rich* staff would need to know:

- Did you create the software at work (or using work equipment)?

- Does the software use code or trade secrets owned by or developed for your employer?
- Did you sign an employment agreement that discusses ownership of employee creations?
- Does your employee handbook at work have rules regarding employee-created innovations?

If the answers are all "No," then you own the rights. If you answered "Yes" to some or all of the questions, you may still own the rights but you will need to sort out some murkier issues. Keep in mind that even if your employer owns the rights, you might still be able to earn revenue from the software.

provisions. These provisions might also be located in your employee manual or in other employee guidelines—which are often considered as legally binding terms of your employment agreement. A preinvention assignment often includes three parts:

- an assignment provision which guarantees the employer ownership of an invention—the most important (and the only necessary) requirement for the employer's total ownership of the patent
- a power of attorney provision which guarantees the employer can register and administer the ownership rights (whether or not the employee is willing and able to assist), and
- a disclosure provision which requires an employee to report any discoveries to the employer. (Advice regarding disclosures is provided below.)

If your employment agreement contains provisions such as these, you will not own inventions created for your employer. If you disregard the agreement and attempt to license your invention, the employer can sue you for breach of the employment agreement. If your employment agreement is found valid and your employer wins the lawsuit, you may have to pay monetary damages.

Sample provisions from a pre-employment agreement appear below.

As with any provision or restriction, the language can vary from agreement to agreement and might even be set out under a separate title or heading. Generally, you should look for key phrases such as: "shall be the sole and exclusive property" or "assignment of all rights of employee."

Disclosure of Inventions to Employers

Disclosure provisions require that you report to your employer all inventions made by you during your period of employment that:

- relate to the company's business
- result from tasks assigned to you by the company, or
- are created using the company's resources.

The purpose of the disclosure provision is to allow the employer to evaluate your inventions and determine if the company has any rights (either by assignment or under shop right rules).

If you create an invention with your own resources and outside the scope of the employer's business, you won't need to disclose the invention under the terms of the sample provision below.

However, each disclosure provision can be different. For example, some employers might ask for a list of all inventions you create outside the scope of your employment. Others might ask for a list of inventions created before your employment. If you have any doubts about making a disclosure to your employer, you should consult with a patent attorney before making the disclosure. Generally, however, it is a good idea to furnish the employer with a list of inventions you created before your employment. This list can help to avoid any claims of employer ownership for these inventions.

Preinvention Agreement: When an Inventor Patents Immediately After Quitting a Job

A chemist employed by an optics company signed a preinvention agreement without a holdover clause (a clause requiring employees to assign ownership of their inventions for a certain amount of time after their employment ends). The chemist prepared a patent disclosure four days after leaving his job. The disclosure described his discovery of four chemical compounds useful to manufacture contact lenses. A federal court determined that it was unlikely the chemist could have conceived the work-related compounds so soon after quitting, and ruled that the chemist had to assign patent ownership to the company. (*Syntex Ophthalmics, Inc. v. Tsuetaki*, 701 F.2d 677 (7th Cir. 1983).)

Limitations on Preinvention Assignments

To protect employees, several states (including California) impose restrictions on the permissible scope of assignments of employee-created inventions to employers. These restrictions apply only to "inventions" an employee creates—that is, items for which a patent is sought. The California restrictions are typical. Under California law, an employee cannot be required to assign any of his or her rights in an invention he or she develops "entirely on his or her own time without using the employer's equipment, supplies, facilities, or trade secret information" unless either of the following is true:

- When the invention was conceived or "reduced to practice" (actually created or a patent application filed), it related to the employer's business or actual or "demonstrably anticipated" research or development.
- The invention resulted from any work performed by the employee for the employer. (Cal. Lab. Code § 2870.)

As you can see, even these limitations on employee invention assignments are not very generous to employees. The only inventions an employee isn't required to assign to the employer are true independent inventions—those that are developed completely without company resources and that don't relate to the employee's work or the employer's current business or anticipated future business.

The following states impose restrictions similar to California's:

- Delaware (Del. Code Ann. tit. 19, § 805)
- Illinois (765 Ill. Comp. Stat. § 1060/2)
- Kansas (Kan. Stat. Ann. § 44-130)
- Minnesota (Minn. Stat. Ann. § 181.78)
- North Carolina (N.C. Gen. Stat. §§ 66-57.1, 66-57.2)

Sample Employer Ownership Provisions of an Employment Agreement

Assignment of Innovations. Employee agrees that any invention, process, system, or patentable creation (Innovations) conceived, originated, discovered, or developed in whole or in part by Employee: (1) as a result of any work performed by Employee with Company's equipment, supplies, facilities, trade secret information, or other Company resources; or (2) on Company's time, shall be the sole and exclusive property of Company, provided that the Innovation relates either to Company's business or anticipated research. Employee agrees to sign and deliver to Company (either during or subsequent to term of employment) such documents as Company considers desirable to evidence: (1) the assignment to Company of all rights of Employee, if any, in any such Innovation, and (2) Company's ownership of such Innovations.

Power of Attorney. In the event Company is unable to secure Employee's signature on any document necessary to apply for, prosecute, obtain, or enforce any legal right or protection relating to any Innovation or copyrightable work referred to above, Employee irrevocably designates and appoints Company (and each of its duly authorized officers and agents) as agent and attorney-in-fact, to act for and in Employee's behalf and to execute and file any such document and to do all other lawfully permitted acts to further the prosecution, issuance, and enforcement of patents, copyrights, or other rights.

Disclosure. Employee agrees to promptly disclose in writing to Company all discoveries, developments, designs, programs, code, ideas, innovations, improvements, inventions, formulas, processes, techniques, know-how, and data (whether or not patentable or registrable under copyright or similar statutes) made, written, conceived, reduced to practice, or learned by Employee (either alone or jointly with others) during the period of Employee's employment, that are related to or useful in Company's business, or that result from tasks assigned to Employee by Company, or from the use of facilities owned, leased, or otherwise acquired by Company.

- Utah (Utah Code Ann. §§ 34-39-2, 34-39-3), and
- Washington (Wash. Rev. Code Ann. §§ 49.44.140, 49.44.150).

Under several states' laws (including California, Illinois, Kansas, Minnesota, and Washington), an employer must provide you with written notice of your state's restrictions on an employer's right to obtain an assignment of employee inventions. If this is not done, the assignment could be unenforceable.

What if you live in one of the states that does not have laws restricting invention assignments? Even in most of these states, preinvention assignments can't be grossly unfair to employees.

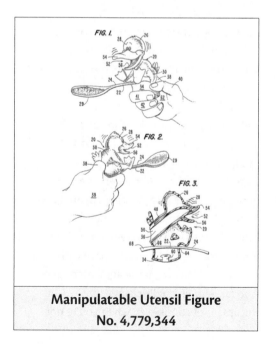

**Manipulatable Utensil Figure
No. 4,779,344**

Invention Assignment Restrictions Inapplicable to Contractors

None of the state law limitations on invention assignments discussed above apply to independent contractors; they only apply to employees. So, even if you live in a state like California that has such a law, companies that hire you as an independent contractor have more latitude in how they word their assignment agreements. Even so, a court might hold an unconscionable or fraudulently obtained assignment invalid, just as if you were an employee.

Employed to Invent

It's possible that, even without a written employment agreement, an employer may own rights to your patent or trade secret under what's called the "employed-to-invent" doctrine.

As the name suggests, if an employer hires you for your inventing or designing skills or to create an invention, the employer owns all rights to your subsequent invention that you were employed to invent. This doctrine is derived from a Supreme Court ruling that stated, "One employed to make an invention, who succeeds, during his term of service, in accomplishing that task, is bound to assign to his employer any patent obtained." (*United States v. Dubilier Condenser Corp.*, 289 U.S. 178 (1933).)

Dear Rich:
Who Owns Lighting Invention?

Dear Rich: I am an engineer employed by a large corporation that owns multiple businesses and often buys new businesses and sells them off depending on market conditions, etc. Over the past couple of years, I had been designing and experimenting with electrical circuits related to commercial lighting. Until recently my employer was not in this business but then recently purchased a lighting company. I was working on this stuff before my employer purchased the lighting company, and also, I do not work on lighting designs for my employer—the lighting business is in another state. I also have no contact with the lighting business whatsoever because I design electronics for a different industry. When they hired me, I was asked to sign a bunch of documents, basically signing off all my patent and copyrights. One of the documents went as far as to say that I was not allowed to consult on my free time. A few years ago I asked our HR department for a copy of the documents I signed. The only thing they came up with was a statement saying that if I used my employer's equipment to design something, they would claim the IP. They then asked me to re-sign a similar document. I never did this and they never pressed the issue.

As a very general rule, if you developed the innovation (1) on your own time, (2) using your own tools, and (3) at the time of innovation, your employer wasn't engaged in the industry of the innovation (or likely to be), you will probably retain rights, in the absence of agreements to the contrary. Employee ownership of inventions is governed by state laws, most of which are influenced in varying degrees by whether:

- you signed any documents agreeing to transfer ownership of inventions (known as preinvention assignments)
- you used employer information, time, or tools in developing your innovation
- you were hired to invent, and
- the invention is related to the employer's business or actual or "demonstrably anticipated" research or development.

Things to consider ... The fact that the HR department can't furnish you with agreements doesn't mean they don't exist. It's possible, for example, that general counsel or outside counsel retained copies. If there is a legal dispute, chances are good that if the documents exist, they'll be "found." Your written agreement trumps any other arrangement you may have with your employer. However, if the agreement goes too far—for example, claims rights to all future innovations even when you're not

Dear Rich:
Who Owns Lighting Invention? (continued)

working for the employer—you may be able to challenge it (unfortunately, you'll have to do that in court). At the same time, you may complicate your situation if your innovation has some application within the employer's (nonlighting) industry, even if it's not a direct application. If there is any evidence that employer tools were involved in your innovation—even in the absence of a written agreement—the employer might obtain an implied license known as a shop right. By the way, some states—California, Delaware, Illinois, Kansas, Minnesota, North Carolina, Utah, and Washington—require that the employer furnish a copy of the law on preinvention assignments to new employees.

The real world ... Your biggest concern may be if a company wants to license your innovation. That company will not want to enter into a license agreement if they believe there is a dispute as to your ownership, or alternatively, if they believe you may have used employer trade secrets in your innovation. You will most likely be asked to include an indemnity provision.

What's an inventor to do? We regret to tell you this ... but if you're interested in patenting, commercializing, or licensing your innovations you will need the advice of an attorney. Unfortunately, there are too many unknowns and wild cards to predict the outcome of any potential disputes.

Generally, most companies prefer to use a written agreement, which is more reliable and easier to enforce than an implied agreement based on the employed-to-invent doctrine. However, the issue of employed to invent still arises.

EXAMPLE: An engineer had no written employment agreement with his employer. He was assigned as the chief engineer on a project to devise a method of welding a "leading edge" for turbine engines. The engineer spent at least 70% of his time on the project.

He developed a hot forming process (HFP) for welding a leading edge and built the invention on his employer's time and using his employer's employees, tools, and materials.

The engineer claimed that he was the sole owner of patent rights. A court held that the company owned the patent rights because the engineer was hired for the express purpose of creating the HFP process. That fact, combined with the use of the employer's supplies, payment for the work, and the payment by the employer for the patent registration, demonstrated that there was an implied contract to assign the patent rights to the employer. Therefore, even without a written employment agreement, the employer acquired ownership.

Shop Rights

Written employment agreements and hiring employees to invent are the two most common ways that employers obtain full rights to employee-created patents and trade secrets. Employers can also obtain limited rights to employees' inventions in certain circumstances based on "shop rights." Under a shop right, you retain ownership of the patent or trade secret, but the employer has a right to use the invention without paying you.

A shop right can only occur if you use the employer's resources (materials, supplies, time) to create an invention. Other circumstances might be relevant, but use of employer resources is the most important criterion. Shop right principles are derived from state laws and precedents in court cases. Generally, the shop right claim arises when an inventor sues a former employer for patent infringement. The employer defends itself by claiming a shop right.

EXAMPLE: An inventor was a consultant (independent contractor) for a power company and conceived of a device for detecting the levels of fly ash (fine particles of ash sent up by the combustion of a fuel) at steam-electric stations. The inventor applied for and received a patent on his device. The power company contracted to have the fly ash invention installed (without the inventor's authorization) at several of its stations. The inventor sued for patent infringement, claiming the power company had no right to use or install his invention without his permission. The power company defended itself by claiming it had a shop right. The federal court agreed with the power company, since the inventor had developed the invention while working at the power company.

If you don't have a written employment agreement assigning patents and were not hired to create the invention, you might be able to prevent the creation of a shop right by making a statement to the employer

Car Radio
No. 1,944,139

at the time you create the invention that you do not consent to a shop right or any royalty-free use of the invention. This method was effective in one federal court case. However, it's also possible that an employer will balk at your claim and initiate a dispute over the invention.

You should only be concerned about shop rights if the invention was created on the employer's time or using the employer's resources (materials, supplies, or trade secrets). If it wasn't, the shop right rule is irrelevant.

Inventions Covered by Copyright

The rules for employer ownership are different if the invention (or some part of it) is subject to protection under copyright law. Under copyright law, an employer always owns copyrights created by an employee which are within the scope of the employment, even without a written agreement. When a copyrightable work is created while the inventor is employed, the work is said to be a "work made for hire" or "work for hire," and the employer, rather than the inventor, owns it. For example, if you work for a toy company and create a copyrightable design for a new toy rocket, your employer will own all copyright in the design. If the copyrightable design is not within the

scope of your employment (for example, you are employed as a bike messenger but create a copyrightable computer program), then you retain ownership.

For independent contractors, however, the rules on copyright ownership are much different. The hiring party will own the copyrights created by an independent contractor only if there is a written agreement that specifies the work is made for hire and the work fits within one of the categories listed in the copyright act. (See "Copyright and Independent Contractors" below.)

These categories apply only to independent contractors. Any work created by an employee within the course of employment will be owned by the employer regardless of the category.

Special Employment Situations

Special rules for ownership of inventions apply to anyone who works for a government agency or university.

Government Employees and Contractors

Are you a government employee or contractor (or an employee of a government contractor)? When it comes to patent ownership, the rules differ depending on your worker status.

Government Employees

Federal law provides that all rights to inventions created by federal employees (whether civilian or military) belong to the government if the invention was:

- made during working hours
- made with the government's resources, including money, facilities, equipment, materials, information, or the help of other government employees on official duty, or
- directly related to the inventor's official duties or made because of those duties. (37 C.F.R. § 501.6.)

In short, if you're a federal employee, you can forget about owning any invention that falls within these rules.

But there is one exception: If the government doesn't plan to file a patent application for the invention or promote its commercialization, the government agency for whom the employee works must leave title and ownership of rights to the employee-inventor. If you are able to keep ownership (either because the three criteria listed above don't apply or the government lacks interest in the invention), you could license it to others and make money or sue others for patent infringement. But even so,

---

Copyright and Independent Contractors

If you are an independent contractor, the person hiring you will own the work only if your work belongs in one of the following categories listed in Section 101 of the Copyright Act of 1976 as:

- a contribution to a collective work;
- a part of a motion picture or other audiovisual work;
- a translation;
- a supplementary work (for example, a work prepared for publication as a supplement to a work by another author for the purpose of introducing, concluding, illustrating, explaining, revising, commenting upon, or assisting in the use of the other work,

such as forewords, afterwords, pictorial illustrations, maps, charts, tables, editorial notes, musical arrangements, answer material for tests, bibliographies, appendixes, and indexes);

- a compilation;
- an instructional text (an instructional text is a literary, pictorial, or graphic work prepared for use in day-to-day instructional activities—for example, a textbook would be an instructional text, but a novel used in a literature class would not be an instructional text);
- a test or as answer material for a test; or
- an atlas.

the government is entitled to a nonexclusive, irrevocable, royalty-free license in the invention with power to grant licenses for all governmental purposes.

If the government obtains ownership of your invention, you have some solace. Federal law provides that, if the government licenses the invention and earns money from it, it must give 15% of the money to the inventor. This is more generous than most private companies are with their employee-inventors. (Note: None of these rules apply to the Department of Energy, Tennessee Valley Authority, or U.S. Postal Service.)

Many states have laws similar to the federal government's. For example, Connecticut law provides that the state obtains ownership of any state employee's invention that (a) was conceived during the employee's job duties; (b) emerged from any state research or development or other program; or (c) was conceived or developed wholly or partly at state expense or with its equipment, facilities, or personnel. If you're a state employee, you need to examine your state's law to determine its patent ownership policies.

Government Contractors

If you are an independent contractor who contracts with the federal government, your ownership situation is brighter than that of government employees. According to a federal policy implemented in 1983,

federal agencies may waive or omit patent rights when awarding government contracts (although there are some exceptions for space research, nuclear energy, or defense). If you're contracting directly with the federal government (that is, you are not working for the federal government through a private company), you should ask about patent ownership at the time of contracting.

You might be able to retain patent rights to a government-sponsored invention. If you are working for an employer who has contracted with the federal government and you want to assert patent rights, (1) your employer would have to retain patent rights from the federal government; and (2) you must have some basis to assert your claim to patent rights, as discussed in Chapter 2.

University Employees

As a result of their constant research and development, many universities earn substantial royalties from patented inventions. To keep those royalties flowing, most universities seek to obtain ownership of inventions created by their employees. Moreover, if the research leading to the invention was federally funded, universities are required by law to obtain ownership. (See "University Licensing: The Bayh-Dole Act," below.)

A university usually requires that faculty and others who might create inventions

University Licensing: The Bayh-Dole Act

The Bayh-Dole Act, enacted in 1980, permits universities to claim patent rights in inventions created with federal funding. The university may then license these discoveries to private industry—a practice some critics have likened to corporate welfare.

As a result of Bayh-Dole, university patent acquisition and licensing has expanded dramatically. Before 1980, the total of all U.S. university patents was less than 150 per year. In 2018, the USPTO issued over 5,000 patents to U.S. universities, generating billions in patent licensing revenue as well as revenue from patent infringement lawsuits. For example, in 2016, Carnegie-Mellon University won $750 million in a patent infringement lawsuit against Marvell Technology Group. And in 2017, the University of Wisconsin won $506 million in a patent lawsuit against Apple.

Regulations for the Bayh-Dole law (35 U.S.C. §§ 200-212) can be found at 37 C.F.R. Part 401. The key regulations are:

- The university must have written agreements with its faculty and technical staff requiring disclosure and assignment of inventions.
- The university has an obligation to disclose each new invention to the federal funding agency within two months after the inventor discloses it in writing to the university.
- The decision whether or not to retain title to the invention must be made within two years after disclosing the invention to the agency.
- The university must file a patent application within one year, or prior to the end of any statutory period in which valid patent protection can be obtained in the United States.
- Any company holding an exclusive license to a patent that involves sales of a product in the United States must substantially manufacture the product in the United States.
- In their marketing of an invention, universities must give preference to small business firms (fewer than 500 employees), provided such firms have the resources and capability for bringing the invention to practical application.
- However, if a large company has also provided research support that led to the invention, that company may be awarded the license.
- Universities may not assign their ownership of inventions to third parties, except to patent management organizations.
- Universities must share with the inventor(s) a portion of any revenue received from licensing the invention. Any remaining revenue, after expenses, must be used to support scientific research or education.
- Under certain circumstances, the government can require the university to grant a license to a third party, or the government may take title and grant licenses itself (these are called "march-in rights").

sign separate formal preinvention assignment agreements granting the university rights to all discoveries made by them. If you have such an agreement, read it carefully. It must comply with the same rules as any other preinvention assignment. If it does, you must live with its provisions. If it doesn't, it could be invalid and could be challenged. Some universities don't use formal assignments, and instead, rely on invention ownership policies set forth in bylaws, manuals, employment letters, or similar documents. An assignment contained in such a document might not be legally enforceable. This is something to discuss with an intellectual property attorney.

If you never assigned your rights to the university or the purported assignment is found invalid, the university would still own the invention if you were directed to (a) invent the specific item or (b) perform inventive work in a particular field and the invention came from that work.

Normally, when an invention or discovery is successful and results in a

licensing deal, the university pays some portion of the revenues to the inventor. Some universities are quite generous. At one major university, for example, inventors get 50% of the first $100,000 of net revenue; 40% of the second $100,000; and 30% of any sums after that.

The Battle for Gatorade

In the mid-1960s, a football coach at the University of Florida asked a team of school physiologists to create a high-energy drink that would provide fluid replacement for perspiring athletes. The physiologists created a drink which eventually came to be known as Gatorade. At the time, the University of Florida and the physiologists had no written arrangement regarding the ownership of employee-created inventions. On their own, the physiologists licensed Gatorade to a food company and started reaping huge revenues. The university felt it should own the rights to the drink and sued. After a long lawsuit, the university was awarded 20% of the money paid to the physiologists, far less than the school would have gotten under current employment agreements. But even at 20%, the university is still believed to earn over $4 million a year from licensing Gatorade (now owned by PepsiCo), which generates over $2 billion in annual sales.

Shoe Protector
No. 4,780,970

Working Out Ownership Issues With Your Employer

What do you do if you and your employer dispute ownership? Your employment agreement, if there is one, might control how the dispute is resolved. For example, the agreement may call for mediation or arbitration in case of a dispute over the agreement's provisions. If not, you can always invite the employer to submit to arbitration or mediation in an effort to avoid a costly courtroom battle. And if all else fails, you could end up in court.

In any ownership dispute, you should seek the advice of an intellectual property attorney before proceeding. (See Chapter 18, "Help Beyond This Book.") The attorney can assess your position in relation to the state law and explain your options. If your attorney believes you have rights to the invention, the attorney will work with you to clear ownership so you can license the invention freely. If the employer claims a shop right, your attorney may be able to reach an agreement as to the extent of this right.

If, for some reason, your employer owns rights to your invention and is willing to transfer those rights to you, you should confirm the arrangement in writing. It's rare that an employer is willing to transfer rights to an employee. However, it could occur in some situations—for example, the company is in financial difficulty, the company is attempting to settle a dispute with the employee, or the company doesn't believe the invention has any commercial potential.

The letter agreement shown below enables an employee to retain control over a specific invention. If the invention already has been patented by the company, you will also need the company to assign the patent to you, and the assignment should be recorded with the USPTO. See Chapter 2 for more information on patent procedures and Chapter 4 for more information on patent assignments.

DOWNLOAD FORMS
You can download this form (and all other forms in this book) from this book's companion page on Nolo.com; see the appendix for the link.

Letter Confirming Employee's Ownership of Intellectual Property Rights

Dear [*insert name of company's representative*]:

This confirms the agreement between [*name of company*] and myself that I shall own exclusive rights to the invention known as [*name of invention*], which is more specifically described below.

Although I created [*name of invention*] during employment, [*name of company*] agrees that I shall be the owner of all rights under patent, trademark, trade secret, and copyright law to [*name of invention*], as well as to any derivative versions under copyright law or improvements under patent law. You represent and warrant that you have the power to grant these rights on behalf of [*name of company*] and that, if required, a representative of [*name of company*] will furnish any other necessary documents that are required to demonstrate my ownership.

Description of Invention:

[*Name of invention*] comprises [*Describe invention in detail. If there is a patent application, use the claims section to describe it. If a patent has already been issued to the company, you will need a patent assignment and the assignment will have to be recorded with the USPTO.*]

If this letter accurately reflects our agreement, please sign and return one copy to me.

Yours truly,

_____

Inventor

_____

Date

Acknowledged and Agreed to:

_____

Representative, [*Name of Company*]

_____

Date

For the Employer: Employee or Independent Contractor?

Although this chapter was written from the point of view of inventor employees, keep in mind that inventors can be employers as well. In other words, all of the ownership rules discussed here apply to your workers, whether you hire them as employees or independent contractors (ICs).

How do you categorize a worker? When you are the employer, the distinction between employees and independent contractors has legal significance. For example, in the absence of a written agreement, you are more likely to own intellectual property rights (copyright, trade secrets, patents) that are created by an employee versus an IC. On the other hand, the administrative burdens of tax reporting, tax withholding, and workers' compensation are more burdensome if you hire employees, not ICs.

Initially, it's up to you to determine whether a person you hire is an employee or an IC, and often the distinction is fairly clear. All ICs have one thing in common—they are in business for themselves. Anyone with an independent business qualifies. In contrast, employees are not in business for themselves. They work for other peoples' ventures.

People who have their own businesses—and who would be considered independent contractors—usually have certain working characteristics in common. They typically:

- offer their services to the general public, not just one person or company
- have their own business offices

- invest in tools, equipment and facilities
- take care of their own taxes, and
- make a profit if the business succeeds, but risk going broke if it fails.

Good examples of ICs are professionals with their own practices, such as industrial designers, patent lawyers, agents, and accountants. An IC can also be a programmer, a prototype builder, or a consultant you hire to advise your business.

In deciding employee/IC status, courts typically assess the degree of control the hiring party has over the worker. An independent contractor maintains personal control over the way he or she does the work contracted for, including the details of when, where and how the work is done. The hiring party's control is limited to accepting or rejecting the final result of the independent contractor's work. An independent contractor is just that—independent.

If the distinction between employee and IC is not so clear, you can consider the IRS guidelines on the issue. The agency is more likely to classify a worker as an independent contractor if he or she:

- can make a profit or suffer a financial loss as a result of the work
- furnishes all tools and materials necessary to do the work
- gets paid per job, rather than per time period
- works for more than one company at a time

For the Employer: Employee or Independent Contractor? (continued)

- invests in/pays for his or her own equipment, facilities, and traveling expenses.
- hires and pays assistants, and
- determines his or her own working hours.

On the other hand, the IRS is more likely to classify a worker as an employee if he or she:

- can be fired at any time by the hiring company
- gets paid by the hour
- receives instructions and/or training from the hiring company
- works exclusively for the hiring company
- receives employee benefits
- has the right to quit without incurring liability, and
- provides services that are an integral part of the hiring firm's day-to-day operations.

If you decide that a worker is an employee, you should have the worker sign a preinvention employment agreement, and you must comply with federal and state tax requirements.

If you decide the worker is an IC, you should have him or her sign an independent contractor agreement that includes an intellectual property assignment, and comply with the income reporting and tax identification number requirements for ICs.

Making matters more confusing, in 2019, California adopted a state law that requires companies to classify workers as employees, unless the company can demonstrate all of the following conditions:

- The worker is free from the company's control.
- The worker performs duties that are outside the company's usual course of business.
- The worker is customarily engaged in an independently established trade, occupation, or business in the same industry.

This controversial law applies only to workers in California. (Make sure to check the law for exceptions and legal challenges.) (Cal. Lab. Code § 2750.3.)

Invention Financing and Joint Ownership

How Much Money Do You Need to License Your Idea?...91

    Define Your Invention in Writing and Drawings...91

    Assess Marketability...91

    Determine If Your Invention Is Patentable...93

    Make a Prototype...93

    Patent It (If Possible)...94

    Test Market...94

    Other Licensing Expenses...94

Sources of Funding...94

    What's the Difference? Loans Versus Investments...95

    Borrowing With Credit Cards...96

    Signature Loans...96

    Bank Loans...97

    Online Funding: Crowdsourcing and Beyond...97

    SBA Loans...98

    Borrowing From Family and Friends...98

    Angel Investing...100

    Venture Capital...102

Joint Ownership...103

How Income, Loans, or Investments Can Create Joint Ownership...106

    Gifts...106

    Loans...106

    Investments...108

    Advance Payments...108

The Joint Ownership Agreement 108

    Introduction 109

    Ownership Percentage Interests 109

    Decision Making 109

    Rights to Manufacture and Sell 109

    Improvements, Revisions 110

    Disputes 110

    Miscellaneous 110

    Signature 110

D o you need money to assess the marketability of your invention, file a patent, or make a prototype? If you're like the vast majority of inventors, you won't get that money from your local bank or from investors. Fewer than 20% of business start-ups are able to fund themselves from these sources.

Instead, you should expect—at least initially—your money will come from credit cards, signature loans (small loans from large financial institutions), or family and friends. Later, after a few years of successful licensing, you might be able to tap into sources such as angel investors, bank loans, or even venture capitalists.

In this chapter, we'll give you the lowdown on how to fund your licensing effort and discuss the relationship of funding and joint ownership of your invention.

How Much Money Do You Need to License Your Idea?

The good news is that an inventor seeking to license an invention needs far less money than an inventor seeking to manufacture and sell an invention. While the latter often needs hundreds of thousands of dollars, a licensing inventor rarely needs more than $10,000 to $20,000.

So, how do you determine how much you need to translate your idea into a licensed product? The amount depends on several factors, including the complexity of your idea, the market for your invention, and the degree of protection necessary to guarantee that your idea is proprietary.

To figure out your budget, consider the following six tasks required to define, develop, protect, and perfect your invention.

Define Your Invention in Writing and Drawings

Having a simple but adequate written and visual explanation is the bottom line for beginning the licensing process. We're not referring to all of the details required in a patent application here—just a basic explanation of how to make and use your unique idea. Without this, you cannot protect or communicate your idea. Expect to pay $200 to $1,000 if you need an artist to help you visualize your idea.

Assess Marketability

Licensees know that a brilliant invention without an equally brilliant demand can be a dud. Before embarking you must ask yourself: "Are there some customers who will perceive the invention as more valuable than an existing product that currently serves their needs?" This is a different question from, "Is this a brilliant invention?"

In *Patent It Yourself*, by David Pressman and David E. Blau (Nolo), you'll find a list of more than 60 positive and negative factors that can help you determine whether your invention has commercial potential—in other words, will someone be interested in licensing your invention. Among the factors to consider are:

- **Cost:** How much will the parts cost? How much will assembling the parts cost? How much will the packaging cost?
- **Competition:** Are opposing products firmly entrenched in the market? Is there a niche in the market just waiting to be filled by your invention?
- **Ease of use:** How simple is it to obtain results from your invention?
- **Demand:** How many people are really going to want your creation? As to this factor, you may wish to do your own research on the reactions of family and friends.

Additional factors were developed by the University of Oregon's Innovation Center, including:

- Will there be legal problems commercializing your invention?
- Are there safety issues (for example, a potential for consumer injuries) that may scare away investors or licensees?
- Will your invention have a positive or negative effect on the environment—

and how will this affect the commercial potential?

- Will your invention have a positive or negative effect on society—and how will this affect the commercial potential?
- Who will buy your invention?
- Will your invention's usefulness diminish over time?
- How long does it take to learn how to use your invention?
- Will your product be distinctive? Will it stand out in the marketplace?
- Will your product provide a valuable service?
- How sturdy is your invention? Will it require frequent maintenance?
- What is the likelihood of new competitors appearing once your invention is commercialized?
- How practical is it to produce your invention for sale?
- Will the demand for your invention die off?
- Will consumers find that your invention is compatible with their needs or lifestyles?
- What does marketing research tell you about the demand for your product?
- How can your invention reach consumers? What methods of distribution are available, and what will they cost?
- What do you perceive as your invention's primary function? Will consumers have the same perception?

- What competition exists for your product now?
- Do you have any way of estimating the potential sales?
- In what stage of development is your invention?
- What type of start-up expenses do you anticipate in order to manufacture the device?
- What do consumer trends indicate about the demand for your invention?
- Is there a potential to expand your invention into a line of products?
- Is there a need for your invention?
- What type of promotion will be needed to sell your invention?
- Does your invention's appearance add to its commercial appeal?
- Is your invention affordable to the relevant market?
- What forms of legal protection are available for your invention?
- How long will it take to receive a payback on your invention?
- What is the margin between the cost and sales price?
- Is your invention dependent on or related to another device or product?
- Is further research and development necessary before you sell the invention?

It may be difficult for you to answer these questions, particularly at the beginning of the invention process. And the significance of each factor will vary, depending on your field and the purpose of your invention. However, if you look at all of these factors together and it becomes obvious that the brilliance of your invention may pale under commercial scrutiny, it's time to reconsider your options. For example, an invention that has fluctuating demand, an unfeasible production system, and a slow payback period will be difficult to successfully commercialize.

Determine If Your Invention Is Patentable

If your invention isn't novel or doesn't otherwise meet the standards of patent protection, you will have a difficult time obtaining a license. Expect to pay between $1,000 and $2,000 for a novelty search to determine patentability for a simple invention.

Make a Prototype

The capability to demonstrate your invention may be the key to funding success. It's not essential to create a prototype, but many invention experts recommend it. A prototype or working model of your invention might enable your patent agent or attorney to get a stronger patent, because a prototype can reveal refinements or even essential features that your written definition lacks. Not only is a prototype useful when filing for a patent, it can also aid in your quest for financing. However, don't spend money on a prototype unless your patentability opinion is favorable. Expect to pay between $300 and $5,000 for a prototype, depending on the complexity of your invention.

Patent It (If Possible)

Acquiring a patent (or filing an application) is often crucial when seeking a licensee. Expect to pay $5,000 to $10,000. See Chapter 2 for information on the patent application process.

Test Market

Though not essential in licensing arrangements, it sometimes helps to have potential customers test a real version of your invention in order to provide information that is essential to licensing decisions. Expect to pay several hundred to several thousand dollars for test marketing.

Other Licensing Expenses

In addition to the expenses for the six tasks discussed above, don't forget these other expenses incurred in the licensing process, such as those for travel, presentation, office and administrative tasks, and negotiating a license agreement. Although varied and hard to estimate, these expenses rarely exceed $2,000 and can often be as low as several hundred dollars.

In order to estimate your licensing expenses, you can create a simple spreadsheet. A sample is provided below. If possible, try to spread the expenses over the expected time period—that is, all of these expenses won't occur at the same time.

Sources of Funding

Now that you have a rough idea of your expected costs, you're prepared to analyze which sources of financing are best suited for your expenses. Keep in mind that the best route is often self-financing of your licensing venture—meaning you'll likely have to use money from personal sources, such as savings, credit cards, or signature loans.

Using your own money, if possible, can be a good option for two reasons. If your effort is self-financed, you will avoid having to share an interest in your invention. Second, as a general rule, most investors are hesitant to invest or lend money unless the inventor has committed some money to the venture as well.

But how much of your own money can you afford to invest? Will your spouse or partner object to this use? This is a matter you must discuss with your family and perhaps your financial adviser. Below, we discuss the various types of funding for a licensing venture.

Sample Licensing Spreadsheet

Task	Mar	Apr	May	Jun	Jul	Aug	Sep	Oct	Nov	Dec	Total
Marketability study	300										300
Patent search			1,000								1,000
Prototype					3,000						3,000
Patent filing							7,500				7,500
Test market										1,500	1,500
Total for Year											$13,300

What's the Difference? Loans Versus Investments

There are two ways to fund your business: loans (debt financing) or investments (equity financing).

Loans. When someone lends you money under the terms of a loan agreement (sometimes referred to as the "note"), you are obligated to repay the amount borrowed (the principal) along with interest.

Investments. Someone who invests in your enterprise, on the other hand, acquires partial ownership, usually in the form of a joint ownership interest in the invention or shares of stock in your corporation, or both. In order to explore investments, you must have a business entity that can accommodate investment—generally a limited liability company or corporation.

The advantage of a loan is that it is *not* an investment. In other words, you are not giving up any ownership in your proprietary idea, and the lender has no management say or direct entitlement to profits in your business. Your only obligation to the lender is to repay the loan on time, and you can deduct the interest payments at tax time.

The disadvantage of a loan is the debt— the looming monthly payments and the potential for personal liability (if you guaranteed the loan), loss of property (if you secured the loan), or a lawsuit (if you default on the loan payments). In a worst-case scenario—one in which you secured the loan or guaranteed it—defaulting could result in the loss of your business, attachment of your wages, or a judgment that could be used against your property.

The advantage of investments is that you will not have to repay investors if your business goes under, and your personal property is unlikely to be at risk. You might also get advice and guidance from those who have a vested interest in your business's success.

The disadvantage of investments is that you get a smaller piece of the pie because you are giving up a share of the business. And if an investor seeks to control your business, it may be more of a nuisance than a help.

The trick with either type of financing is convincing someone that your licensing venture is stable enough to merit a loan or an investment. We discuss that issue in more detail below.

Borrowing With Credit Cards

Credit card companies charge high interest rates and extraordinary penalties. And if you miss a payment on one card, all of your cards can raise their interest rates. When you take a cash advance, there are more unbearable fees and usually no grace period, which means you pay interest from the day you take the advance, even if you pay off your balance within a month. Is there any way to alleviate the negatives of credit cards? Here are a few suggestions.

When shopping for a card, be wary of teaser rates (low introductory rates that jump after a few months) and check the grace period (the number of days before you're charged interest on purchases). Many companies have been shortening their grace period for purchases from 30 to 20 days. Shop around for perks: airline miles, travel discounts, or other purchasing credits. Always compare the periodic rate that will be used to calculate the finance charge. You can find rates at websites comparing current credit offers (type "credit card compare" into a search engine).

CAUTION
Don't charge inventing expenses if your credit card balances are greater than 80% of your credit limits; you've already got a credit card problem. One other thought: Bankruptcy laws make it harder to get rid of credit card debts even if you file for bankruptcy—particularly if your income is greater than the median income for your state.

Signature Loans

Signature loans—loans for $5,000 or less—are often available from your bank, a credit card company, or a large financial company, based on your credit rating and your history with the lender. (The name "signature loan" refers to the fact that you may get a loan offer in the mail or from a bank; all that is required is your signature to make it binding.) These loans are not much different from taking a cash advance with a credit card. You pay high interest rates on monthly payments along with an assortment of fees.

Usually, if you have a good credit history or own a home, you can borrow a few thousand dollars using a signature loan without pledging collateral.

Tread Carefully When Securing or Personally Guaranteeing a Loan

If you *personally guarantee* a debt, you will have to pay if the loan goes bad. In other words, the buck doesn't stop at your business; it can stop at your home or personal bank account. If you personally guarantee a loan, having an LLC or a corporation won't protect your personal assets from creditors.

A *secured loan* is one in which you pledge property as part of the loan agreement—for example, you take out a second mortgage on your house. If you fail to honor the loan agreement—for example, you miss several payments—the lender can take the secured property (collateral) and sell it to recover the amount you owe.

Bank Loans

The old saying about bank loans—that you can qualify for a bank loan only when you don't need it—unfortunately rings true. Inventors, for the most part, are engaged in a remarkably tentative business. And the more imagination required to envision your venture's success, the less likely you will get a loan—unless you have assets beyond the amount of the loan. Conversely, the more evidence you have pointing to your eventual success, the more likely you'll obtain the loan. As a general rule, an inventor seeking to launch a licensing effort will have a hard time getting a bank loan without a personal guaranty. See "What Motivates a Lender to Lend Money?" below, for some criteria used by banks when making loans.

Online Funding: Crowdsourcing and Beyond

All three of the crowdsourcing methods discussed next—crowdinvesting, crowd-lending, and crowdfunding—have successfully funded inventions. But these funding mechanisms are primarily geared toward the manufacturing of an invention, not licensing it. If you're only interested in licensing, crowdlending might be the most reasonable method of raising development revenue.

One concern about crowdsourcing is disclosure. If you have a potentially patentable invention and you disclose the patentable features to obtain crowdsourcing funds but haven't yet filed for a patent, you might find it impossible to later obtain a patent. With a few exceptions, public disclosure prior to filing under the patent law will kill patent chances. Even if you are not patenting your innovation, you are making it publicly known, which may encourage imitators—something you may not be ready for just yet.

Crowdinvesting. Crowdinvesting (or equity crowdfunding), was pioneered by companies such as EquityNet (www.equitynet.com). Crowdinvesting enables investors to fund a startup company in return for an equity share in the company. Because investment funding can easily run afoul of securities laws, legal and accounting advice is essential before using this type of solicitation.

Crowdlending. If you want to borrow money but don't want to deal with a bank, consider sites such as Funding Circle (www.fundingcircle.com) in which individuals offer loans to small businesses. Be aware that these are personal loans and interest rates may vary.

Crowdfunding. With crowdfunding, those who invest receive something in return—for example, a copy of the new product once it has been manufactured. Some crowdfunding sites appeal specifically to inventors hawking their ideas, such as Fund an Idea (www.fundanidea.com), while others like Indiegogo (www.indiegogo.com) cater to a wide range of ventures. But the king of crowdfunding is Kickstarter (www.kickstarter.com).

But there are drawbacks to crowdfunding—the most notable of which are that more than half of projects don't fund (Kickstarter is an all-or-nothing enterprise, meaning that if you don't achieve your funding goal, you don't get any money), and about three-quarters of Kickstarter projects don't deliver on time (making

for many unhappy patrons). In addition, a successful Kickstarter campaign does not mean you have created a commercial product. Kickstarter's cofounder Yancey Strickler told Reuters, "Of all the products launched on Kickstarter, very, very few would be a good investment. ... However, if the bar is lower—to simply, do I want this to exist?—suddenly over half the things have a life."

SBA Loans

The Small Business Administration (SBA) doesn't make loans; it guarantees up to 85% of the amount you borrow from someone else in the event of default. Beware, though, despite SBA support, lenders sometimes require collateral or guarantees from the business owner for all (or a portion) of the loan. In other words, getting an SBA-guaranteed loan is often as difficult as getting a regular bank loan. To find out more, check out the SBA website (www.sba.gov).

Borrowing From Family and Friends

In the film *Envy,* an inventor, played by actor Jack Black, offers his friend, played by Ben Stiller, a chance to invest in his novel process of removing dog excrement. Stiller's character passes on the investment opportunity, and (as often happens in the movies), the invention goes on to earn

What Motivates a Lender to Lend Money?

Lenders will typically check out you, your invention, and your business before handing you money. The decision is traditionally based on the five "Cs" of credit, described below. Practically, you're much more likely to qualify if you can personally guarantee the loan or you can secure the loan with property equal to the value of the loan. You're less likely to qualify if your cash flow is erratic or the forecast for your industry is poor.

Capacity. Capacity, usually the most important factor, refers to how you intend to repay the loan. The lender looks at your business's cash flow and your payment history on existing credit relationships—personal and commercial.

Collateral. The lender ideally wants collateral or "guarantees" that equal the value of the loan. Business assets (equipment, buildings, accounts receivable, and, in some cases, inventory) and personal assets can be sources of collateral. An invention whose success is highly speculative is unlikely to serve as collateral.

Character. The lender will form an opinion as to whether or not you are trustworthy and will run credit checks and background checks—for example, to determine whether you have a criminal record.

Capital. Capital refers to how much you personally have invested in the business. Lenders believe that if you have a significant personal investment in the business, you are less likely to default on the loan.

Conditions. Conditions focus on the economic climate within your industry. Loans are more difficult to obtain when the forecast for your industry is grim.

CRM: The sixth "C." The five Cs of credit are being replaced by a mathematical standard known as credit risk modeling (CRM), which uses software to predict when a firm's assets will fall below liabilities. It looks at financial ratios and historic records of defaulting businesses and predicts—based on your finances—whether your venture will succeed or fail (and when). Though currently in use by only a few lenders, you can expect that this methodology will eventually trickle down to many more loan decisions.

millions. The relationship between the two men sours and Stiller's character becomes bitter. Although the film provides an unrealistic view of invention promotion, it accurately reflects the effect it can have on friends and relatives. Regardless of whether money is invested or the invention succeeds, asking friends and family for money often endangers an otherwise happy personal relationship.

Some inventors recommend against borrowing from family and friends. Instead, they suggest forming a small corporation or limited liability company and selling shares.

In that case, you must inform your investors that they will own part of your company, and that all inventions—even seemingly sure things—have a high degree of risk. In other words, if it fails, everybody loses. Although forming a corporation or an LLC works for many inventors, it's our experience that family and friends are sometimes more comfortable lending money than buying an interest in your company. A loan is a straightforward matter. But ownership (often in the form of shares in your corporation) may seem abstract and risky to Aunt Mary or Uncle John.

If you're going to borrow from family and friends (or from any individual, for that matter), make sure you do it with the appropriate formalities: Sign a promissory note, calculate interest and principal, and set up a payment schedule. If you don't, you may find yourself embroiled in money disputes over Thanksgiving dinner.

You can easily draft your own promissory note (forms are available from Nolo, the publisher of this book, as well as from other providers on the Internet). You can calculate interest and payments using amortization calculators that are easily found online.

Angel Investing

Angel investors don't lend you money—they invest their own money and acquire equity in your business. (The name is derived from the wealthy individuals known as "angels" who fund Broadway shows.) Angel investment—if we can demystify the terminology—merely refers to an investment from an individual, usually a stranger.

There's nothing particularly angelic about the relationship. Basically, it involves finding and convincing a wealthy individual—someone willing to take a risk—to buy a chunk of your business (but not enough to take it away from you). An angel investor usually insists on direct involvement in the business and wants a high rate of return (20% to 50%). Angels are also looking for a great team in much the same way that a gambler looks at the horse, the jockey, the trainer, and the owner.

Why Do Angels Invest?

Unlike venture capital companies that must invest on behalf of their shareholders, angel investors don't have to invest. So why do they take chances on unproven inventors or businesses?

Profit is obviously one motivator. Angels understand that one out of three of their investments will fail. As for the others —the successes—they expect to cash out within seven years (often less) and anticipate a minimum 25% annual return on their investments. Usually angel investors are hoping this will happen in one of two ways: Your company either will be acquired by another or will graduate to an initial public offering (IPO) in which the public is offered shares.

Excitement is the other major motivator. Angels love to participate in high-risk equity investments for the thrill of the game.

What Do Angels Want in Return?

Angels want a piece of your invention business—usually represented by corporate shares. On average, angel investors typically receive about 20% equity in the businesses (or inventions) in which they invest. The actual amount an angel pays to your company for an ownership interest depends on the value of your business. If your invention business is valued at $100,000, an angel would, as a very general rule, expect to pay $25,000 for a 25% ownership interest.

If you're seeking an angel investment, review the material at Angel Capital Association (www.angelcapitalassociation.org), an umbrella alliance of many angel groups, and click on "Find Angels."

Watch Out for Fraudulent Angel Brokers

The popularity of angel financing has spawned a business for angel brokers, finders, or intermediaries—companies that, for a fee, find angel financing. Unfortunately, many of these brokers are scams. Watch out for brokers who charge large up-front fees. When a finder starts talking more than a few hundred dollars, you're probably wasting your money.

You should also beware of brokers who make repackaging pitches. These finders or brokers may want to charge you a large fee to create a business plan and other marketing materials. That's a waste of your time.

What People With Money Want to Know About Your Invention

Just as you wouldn't buy a house without an inspection, investors and lenders will not open their checkbooks without performing "due diligence"—an investigation of the risks and potential value of your invention business. This includes:

- **Verifying facts in your business plan.** Lenders and investors will want to see all supporting information and may conduct their own investigations and prepare their own financials.
- **Digging up background information about you.** A lot of personal information—including criminal records, judgments in civil lawsuits, and bad debts—is available to anyone willing to pay $50 to $100 for an Internet background check. There's little sense trying to hide any of that from potential lenders or investors.
- **Studying the competition.** Investors and lenders will study your actual and prospective competitors and examine the channel in which you plan to compete—for example, to determine whether there may be problems with distribution.

State Lending Assistance

Your state may provide small business lending assistance in several ways, including the following.

Business Development Centers. Approximately 20 states offer SBA-style loan assistance to their residents. Check your state government website to find out whether your state offers Business Development Centers.

Local development funds. Many communities offer small loans or grants to businesses in order to encourage development. Check with your city or county government.

State loans. Some states lend money directly to small businesses to encourage certain industries within the state. For example, Hawaii intends to encourage technology companies by offering loans through the Hawaii Strategic Development Corporation. Check your state's website for more information.

Another sign of a scam is if a finder or broker pressures you to act quickly, then they're probably just after their fee. And, as always, beware of dealing with anyone who cannot furnish references.

Venture Capital

It's unlikely you'll be dealing with venture capitalists (VCs)—which is basically an institutionalized version of angel investors but with a lot more cash. Unlike angel investors, who invest their own money, VCs invest money acquired from financial institutions and wealthy individuals. Angels don't have to invest (they can bank their money if they wish); VCs do—their business is to earn profits for their investors. VCs are exceptionally discerning, choosing to invest in fewer than 2% of the proposals that come their way. When they do invest, it's usually because they've determined there's a very experienced management team, an untapped niche, and a chance for remarkable returns. They generally expect a minimum return of 40% annually on their investment and won't hesitate to withdraw funding if they change their minds about the prospect of success.

 CAUTION

Don't conceal, lie, or exaggerate about invention opportunities. Always give potential investors everything that is available for them to make knowledgeable decisions. When in doubt, disclose, disclose, disclose (with a nondisclosure agreement).

There are two reasons for this: It's unethical and illegal to dupe someone into investing in your business, and falsifying investment claims violates federal and state securities laws.

Visit the U.S. Securities and Exchange Commission (SEC) website (www.sec.gov) for more information about securities laws and exemptions. A quick way to research your state's exemption rules is to go to the home page of your state's securities agency, which typically posts the state's exemptions rules and procedures. To find your state securities agency, go to your secretary of state's website. If in doubt, speak with an attorney.

Joint Ownership

So far, we have discussed ways to fund your licensing venture. In this section, we look at a concept that's often related to invention financing: joint ownership of your invention.

Joint ownership (sometimes called co-ownership) occurs when two or more people share in the ownership rights of an invention. Below are some examples of how joint ownership occurs.

EXAMPLE 1: Joint Ownership Created by Joint Invention. Dr. Wilcox was stumped and unable to finish his modem invention until Fran, his daughter, showed him how to triple the telephone transfer rate. A patent was granted for the invention to Dr. Wilcox and Fran, as joint inventors. As joint inventors, they are also joint owners.

Deduct Your Inventing Expenses

You might be able to deduct your inventing expenses from your ordinary income. To qualify for a deduction, you must satisfy three basic requirements:

- **You must be in the "inventing" business.** Inventing qualifies as a business for tax purposes only if (a) you work at it regularly, and (b) your primary motive for doing it is to earn a profit.
- **You must keep records of your expenses.** You need to keep records of your expenses to (a) know, for sure, how much you actually spent, and (b) prove to the IRS you really incurred the expenses listed on your tax return in the event you're audited.

- **You must have a legal basis for the deduction.** Inventors are fortunate in that the tax law gives them more ways to deduct their expenses than most businesspeople. If you're audited by the IRS, you'll have to provide a legal basis for all your deductions. If the IRS concludes you lack such a basis, it will deny the deduction and you'll have to pay back taxes and penalties. If, like most independent inventors, you're a sole proprietor, your deductions will be listed on IRS Schedule C, *Profit or Loss From Business.*

EXAMPLE 2: Joint Ownership Created by Assignment for Money. Tom invents a metal detector that works underwater. He needs money to build a prototype and to promote the invention. Jerry agrees to give Tom $100,000 in return for an assignment of 50% ownership interest in the invention. Tom and Jerry become joint owners.

EXAMPLE 3: Joint Ownership Created by Will. Sam patents a process for scrambling and cooking eggs within their shells. He dies, and in his will, he leaves half ownership interest in the invention to his daughter, Carol, and the other half to Dartmouth College. Carol and Dartmouth become joint owners.

EXAMPLE 4: Joint Ownership Created by Assignment to a Partnership. Jill invents a new style of camping stove. Ian wants to invest money to perfect the invention. Jim, a lawyer, wants to contribute his legal and licensing experience to help license the invention. Jill, Ian, and Jim form a partnership, and Jill assigns the invention to the partnership. Each partner is a joint owner in the invention.

When there are joint owners, all of the owners must consent to an assignment of all rights to the invention. That is, none of the owners can give up all rights to the invention without obtaining agreement from the other owners (although a joint owner can assign his or her partial rights).

Generally, the joint owners decide among themselves how to split the revenue from sales and licensing (for example, a 65%–35% split). If the joint owners cannot decide and a dispute results, a court will make the final determination.

The Married Inventor

Many inventors acknowledge that without the support of a faithful spouse, their inventions would never have reached fruition. Alexander Graham Bell's wife, for example, testified on his behalf in a patent case and helped preserve his rights to the telephone. But, being married while you create an invention has legal implications. Under state laws, when one spouse creates intellectual property (patents, trade secrets, copyrights) during the marriage, the other spouse is entitled to a share of the revenue. (How much of an interest depends upon state laws and the facts in your case.) Because a spouse is entitled to the revenue, some attorneys require that a spouse sign any assignments in order to avoid a dispute in the event of divorce (for example, the spouse claims that the assignment was an improper transfer of her rights). A sample spouse signature provision is provided in Chapter 1.

Dear Rich:
Can a Joint Owner Assign All Patent Rights?

Dear Rich: Please tell me where I can get background information about this statement from your book, "When there are joint owners, all of the owners must consent to an assignment of all rights to the invention. That is, none of the owners can give up all rights to the invention without obtaining agreement from the other owners." I have not been able to find this in Title 35 of the United States Code.

Joint owners of patents can do some strange stuff—they can license the patent without the consent of the other joint owners, and without paying them either. But an assignment, unlike a license, is a permanent transfer of ownership. It's an outright sale of the patent, and for that reason, a joint owner can only assign his or her interest. As stated in 37 C.F.R. § 3.1 (Definitions: Assignment):

Each individual inventor may only assign the interest he or she holds; thus, assignment by one joint inventor renders the assignee a partial assignee. A partial assignee likewise may only assign the interest it holds; thus, assignment by a partial assignee renders a subsequent assignee a partial assignee. All parties having any portion of the ownership in the patent property must act together as a composite entity in patent matters before the Office.

If it were any other way, any joint owner could easily "steal" the rights of his or her co-owners, depriving them of any possibility of revenue. There's also case law prohibiting joint owners from granting exclusive licenses (rights that exclude other inventors from licensing) without the consent of all owners. Joint owners can contradict these rules by a written agreement, but absent a written owners' agreement, assignment of all patent rights is prohibited.

However, in the case of joint owners of a patented invention, special rules exist regarding joint ownership and division of income. Patent law provides that:

In the absence of any agreement to the contrary, each of the joint owners of a patent may make, use, offer to sell, or sell the patented invention within the United States, or import the patented invention into the United States, without the consent of and without accounting to the other owners. (Title 35 of the United States Code, § 262.)

In other words, any joint owner of a patented invention can make, sell, or use the invention without the consent of the other owners and without compensating the other owners. For example, one owner can enter into a nonexclusive license and keep all the revenue. Seem unfair? If you are a joint owner of a patented invention, know that your interest in the patent can only be protected by entering into a joint ownership agreement, as provided below.

How Income, Loans, or Investments Can Create Joint Ownership

Our concern in this section is to determine if your acceptance of money affects your ownership rights. Review your income to determine if you have received money from anyone in relation to your invention, particularly for services, supplies, equipment, or rent. Then determine if the money can be assigned to one of the categories below:

- salary or other payment for services
- loans
- investments, or
- advance payments.

If the money was paid as salary, you should review Chapter 3 on employer–employee ownership issues. If there's a written document referencing your receipt of the money and what it was for—such as a loan agreement, an employment agreement, or an investment agreement—that document should explain your rights in relation to the invention. If not, you will need to review the materials below to guarantee that you own the rights to your invention.

Gifts

When you receive a gift, you have no legal obligations to the giver and the gift will not affect your ownership rights to your invention—even if the gift is money, supplies, or services. For example, if your Uncle Joe saw your invention, loved it, and said, "I am so proud of you for inventing something; here is $2,000 to continue your work," the money he gave you would be a gift. However, if Uncle Joe puts some condition upon the money such as, "Here's $2,000 if you name it after me," or "Here's $2,000 and you can pay me back when you're successful," then the money is not a gift. If you accept it, a contractual obligation may be created and Uncle Joe might own a right to income from your invention.

Other examples of gifts include: a friend giving you spare parts, or a neighbor allowing you to use her garage or workspace without demanding anything in return. As long as money given to you is truly given as a gift, you will have no obligation to the gift giver, and you will not have lost any legal rights to your invention.

Loans

Did someone lend you money, services, or supplies with the expectation of a return? A loan is a contract that is usually in writing. In some states, a loan of money must be documented by some form of writing, but this writing doesn't necessarily mean a signed contract. It can simply be a notation above a check endorsement, such as "By cashing this check you acknowledge that you owe me $1,000."

Dear Rich:
Provisional Patent Application for Someone Else's Idea

Dear Rich: A former coworker developed a new business idea. I signed a nondisclosure agreement (NDA) and we both worked on commercializing the idea and planned to form a start-up. He lost interest. An attorney reviewed the now-expired NDA and said I was fine to pursue the idea on my own, that I was under no obligation by the NDA. Can I file a provisional patent on the business idea? I would like to protect the idea by fixing a date in case I decide to file a formal patent application within the year. Any thoughts?

First, there is no such thing as a "provisional patent" (a common misconception). There is only a provisional patent application (or PPA)—a document that establishes an official U.S. patent application filing date. Second, you mentioned that you've already hired an attorney; why not ask your attorney whether to file? Your attorney knows more details about your case and could provide specific, client-centric advice. As for filing your PPA with the USPTO, the PPA must be filed in the name of the inventor (or a coinventor). A coinventor is someone who contributes at least one novel and nonobvious concept that makes the invention patentable. If you didn't add anything patentable to the concept—no Eureka! moments—the PPA must be filed in the name of your coworker. As for preserving the date of invention, you don't need a PPA to do so. Many inventors preserve their dates via inventors' notebooks. The important thing to keep in mind is that if you publicize or commercialize the idea, a patent application would have to be filed within one year in order to preserve patent rights. One way to avoid potential hassles is to work out a joint ownership agreement with your former coworker that will provide you with the right to exploit the idea while compensating him.

Some loans are unsecured, and some are secured. A loan is secured when the borrower guarantees to hand over some item of property (sometimes referred to as collateral) in case of a loan default. As a general rule, a secured loan can only be created by a written agreement signed by the borrower, usually called a security agreement.

If you use the rights to your invention as collateral for your secured loan, you will most likely limit your ability to license the invention. Even if you make timely payments, while a loan balance exists and your invention is the collateral, you won't be able to license your invention. Secured loans usually forbid the license (or other transfer) of the invention until the loan is paid off.

EXAMPLE: Jerry borrows $10,000 from a bank and secures the loan with his patent. His loan agreement prohibits him from licensing or otherwise transferring his patent rights. He's unable to license his invention to other companies, because his patent rights are being used as collateral for his loan. He later defaults on the loan and the bank acquires the security—Jerry's patent rights.

Investments

A common form of investment occurs when you create a corporation to exploit your invention and someone buys shares in your corporation. Even a loan may be a form of investment, if repayment of the loan is secured by profits from an invention. Usually a written document memorializes an investment. It's important to review that document with an attorney in order to determine the respective rights of the parties.

Advance Payments

Has someone given you money as an advance payment for the right to make, sell, or distribute your invention? Such an advance payment arrangement (with or without a written agreement) could be a major obstacle in licensing your invention to someone else. As explained

in Chapter 9, advance payments can be refundable (so that the inventor must pay it back if sales are not sufficient) or recoupable (the inventor doesn't have to pay it back, but it will be deducted against future royalties). Read Chapter 9 for more information on advances.

The Joint Ownership Agreement

We recommend that joint owners enter into a joint ownership agreement in order to avoid disputes over revenue and rights. An explanation of common agreement terms and a sample agreement follows. If the sample agreement below doesn't meet your requirements, consult with an intellectual property attorney.

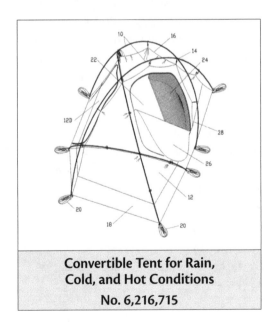

Convertible Tent for Rain, Cold, and Hot Conditions

No. 6,216,715

Introduction

Insert the names of the joint owners. If any of the owners are corporations or partnerships, indicate the correct business form (for example, The Techno Consortium, a New Jersey general partnership). You should insert a description of your invention at the end of the introductory paragraph. Choose the correct option: patent, patent application, or no patent. If you have two patents or a patent and a patent application, we recommend that you execute separate agreements for each invention.

Ownership Percentage Interests

Provide a statement setting forth the percentage interest and proportionate share of revenues each owner is to receive and, likewise, the share of expenses and liabilities to be shared. The owners must agree on what percentage each of them will receive (for example, each partner receives one-half of the revenue). The total of all of the owner percentages must equal 100%.

Decision Making

Decide which issues require unanimous approval (all parties must agree) or majority approval (or ⅔ approval if you wish). However, as mentioned above, entering into an assignment of all rights to the invention must be with the consent of all parties. In the sample agreement, all other decisions require a majority vote. These decisions include the following:

- entering into agreements with other parties to make, license, use, distribute, or sell the invention
- permitting any party to make, use, distribute, or sell the invention
- filing foreign patent applications
- filing a lawsuit to stop infringement of the invention, and
- hiring someone to help prepare and file the patent application or help file an infringement lawsuit.

If you want any decisions to be made by unanimous vote (for example, entering into an exclusive license), you may list them as requiring a unanimous vote in this section.

The owners can establish any decision-making process that suits them and, if necessary, they also may establish a method of breaking a tie. In the sample, we suggest the use of mediation and arbitration.

Rights to Manufacture and Sell

Specify who is authorized to negotiate deals, and which owners can also make, use, or sell the invention. The provision in the sample agreement, for example, permits any joint owner to sell the invention (provided the owner sells it on the same terms as a nonowner licensee).

Improvements, Revisions

The provision in the sample agreement permits all co-owners to share in improvements of the invention, provided that the owners have made themselves available to assist in such improvements. For example, if the relationship between the owners becomes hostile and they can no longer work together to improve the invention, the revenues from improvements will be divided according to the contributors. This can be a touchy subject. For example, what if the improvement is minor? Should the owners who made this improvement be entitled to all of the revenue from it? Some co-owners use a sliding system, such as splitting only one quarter of the first improvement among those who contributed to it and dividing the rest according to the original agreement. The percentages can change as more improvements are made.

Disputes

In the event of disputes, the sample agreement below provides for discussion, mediation, and then arbitration. Some people, however, do not like arbitration (see Chapter 14), and you may need to delete any sentences dealing with arbitration from the agreement.

Miscellaneous

The provisions in the "Miscellaneous" section are explained in Chapter 14. In the blank space, we recommend that you insert the name of your state of residence or the state agreed upon by the joint owners.

Signature

Most joint owners are individuals acting as sole proprietors and can simply sign the agreement. However, if any joint owner is signing as a general partner representing a partnership or on behalf of a corporation, that person must have the authority to sign the agreement. If you have any doubt about any joint owner's authority to sign the agreement, review the material on "Signatures" in Chapter 11.

DOWNLOAD FORMS
You can download this form (and all other forms in this book) from this book's companion page on Nolo.com; see the appendix for the link.

Joint Ownership Agreement

Introduction

This Agreement is made between [*insert name, address, and business form of owner #1*] and [*insert name, address, and business form of owner #2*] (the "Parties") as of [*insert date agreement is to be effective*]. The Parties wish to set forth their respective rights to and obligations for the invention tentatively named [*insert the name of invention*] (the "Invention") and more accurately described below. The ownership rights to the Invention include all patent rights, copyrights, trade secrets, and trademark rights comprising, associated with, or derived from the Invention

The Invention [*select one*]

☐ **Patent Issued**

The Invention as described in the U.S. Patent No. _____ , dated _____ .

☐ **Patent Application Pending**

The Invention as described in the application for U.S. patent (U.S. Patent Office Application Serial No. _____).

☐ **No Patent**

Description of Invention: _____

_____

_____

Therefore, the Parties agree as follows:

Ownership Percentage Interests

The Parties to this Agreement are the owners of all legal rights in the Invention described above. The percentage ownership interests of the Parties are as set forth below. Unless otherwise agreed: (a) All income derived from exploiting the Invention shall be apportioned according to the percentage interests set forth below; and (b) any costs, expenses, or liabilities relating to the Invention and agreed to by the Parties under this Agreement shall also be apportioned by the same percentage interests. In the event any Party is unable to contribute a proportionate share for any cost or expense, the other Parties may contribute the noncontributing Party's share and shall be reimbursed from subsequent revenues related to the cost or expense. Reimbursement shall include interest at 1.5% per month or the maximum rate permitted by law, whichever is less.

Name _____ Percentage Interest _____

_____ _____

_____ _____

_____ _____

_____ _____

Decision Making

Each Party shall have the right to participate in the decisions regarding the Invention, including decisions regarding exploitation, protection, and enforcement of legal rights associated with the Invention. All decisions require a majority vote except for an assignment of all rights to the Invention. In the event there are equal votes in a case where a majority decision is required, the issue shall be resolved through the procedures set forth in the Disputes section below.

Decision-Making Process/Time Limits

All decisions shall be made promptly and with the cooperation of all Parties, acting fairly and in good faith. If a decision requires some time to contemplate (for example, an offer to license, a decision by one Party to manufacture), the Parties may agree to postpone a decision for a period of up to 30 days.

Rights to Manufacture and Sell

Any Party may make, sell, or use any product embodying the Invention (or any portion of the Invention) providing that the Parties have approved such action by a vote required under this Agreement. In the event that any Party desires and is approved to license, manufacture, sell, or distribute the Invention, the terms of such arrangement shall be the same as those available to third parties in similar transactions. That is, a Party to this Agreement will have to pay a competitive royalty to the joint owners after deduction of reasonable manufacturing and overhead expenses.

Improvements, Revisions

Each Party to this Agreement shall share, according to the proportions set forth in this Agreement, in any revenue derived from improvements to or revisions of this Invention provided that each Party shall have made a good-faith attempt to consult, contribute, or otherwise make themselves available for services on such improvements or revisions of the Invention. In the event that any Party refuses to participate in any work resulting in an improvement to or revision of the Invention, revenues derived from such improvements or revisions shall be distributed on a pro rata basis among the contributing Parties.

Disputes

The Parties agree that every dispute or difference between them arising under this Agreement, including a failure to reach a decision as described in this Agreement, shall be settled first by a meeting of the Parties attempting to confer and resolve the dispute in a good-faith manner. If the Parties cannot resolve their dispute after conferring, any Party may require the other Parties to submit the matter to nonbinding mediation, utilizing the services of an impartial professional mediator approved by all Parties. If the Parties cannot come to an agreement following mediation, the Parties agree to submit the matter to binding arbitration at a location mutually agreeable to the Parties. The arbitration shall be conducted on a confidential basis pursuant to the Commercial Arbitration Rules of the American Arbitration Association. Any decision or award as a result of any such arbitration proceeding shall include the assessment of costs, expenses, and reasonable attorneys' fees and shall include a written record of the proceedings and a written determination of the arbitrators. Absent an agreement to the contrary, any such arbitration shall be conducted by an arbitrator experienced in intellectual property law. The Parties reserve the right to object to any individual who shall be employed by or affiliated with a competing organization or entity. In the event of any such dispute or difference, either Party may give to the other notice requiring that the matter be settled by arbitration. An award of arbitration shall be final and binding on the Parties and may be confirmed in a court of competent jurisdiction.

Miscellaneous

Each Party shall act in good faith and not take any action which hinders the rights of the other parties. The provisions of this Agreement shall be binding upon the heirs, executors, administrators, successors, and assigns of the Parties. If any term, provision, covenant, or condition of this Agreement is held to be illegal or invalid for any reason whatsoever, such illegality or invalidity shall not affect the validity of the remainder of this Agreement. This Agreement constitutes the entire understanding between the Parties and can only be modified by written agreement. This Agreement shall be governed by the laws of the state of [*insert choice of state law*]. In the event of any dispute arising under this agreement, the prevailing Party shall be entitled to its reasonable attorneys' fees.

MY SIGNATURE BELOW INDICATES THAT I HAVE READ AND UNDERSTOOD THIS AGREEMENT.

_____   _____
Signature   Date

_____   _____
Signature   Date

_____   _____
Signature   Date

Licensing Agents and Representatives

Agents.. 116

  The Principal/Agent Relationship... 116

  The Benefits of Using an Agent..117

  Finding a Knowledgeable Agent...117

  Agents in Action 119

Completing the Agent Agreement 119

  Introduction 120

  Obligations of Agent... 120

  Obligations of Inventor... 120

  Payments... 120

  Proprietary Rights; Indemnity.. 121

  Disclaimer 121

  Confidentiality... 121

  Termination 121

  General 126

  Signatures.. 126

Attorneys as Agents... 126

Invention Marketing Scams 128

  How They Operate.. 128

  Invention Promotion Laws 129

  How to Tell an Agent From a Scam Artist 130

  When in Doubt About a Marketing Company... 131

Some inventors use the services of agents to obtain licensing deals. In this chapter, we examine the relationship between inventors and agents and provide you with a sample agreement for agent representation. We also examine scam marketing firms, which are companies that pretend to assist inventors but actually prey on them. You should review this chapter if you answer "yes" to any of the following questions:

- Are you considering using the services of a company or an agent who will help market your invention?
- Are you looking for a sample agreement to use with an agent?
- Are you concerned about falling victim to an invention marketing scam?

Agents

A person or company that represents your invention is known as your agent (sometimes referred to as a product rep). The agent makes the sales pitches and negotiates licenses. In return, the agent is usually paid a commission that is a percentage of royalties. This fee is usually somewhere between 10% and 50% of gross revenues. Gross revenues include all income (including advances) received as a result of the license.

The Principal/Agent Relationship

When you authorize someone to act on your behalf, you create an agency relationship. You are the "principal" and the person who acts on your behalf is the "agent." The principal seeks a result such as a license agreement. The agent is paid to obtain the result.

An agent has a legal obligation to protect your interests and to fully disclose opportunities and dangers. This obligation exists because the law considers an agency relationship to be a fiduciary relationship. A "fiduciary," such as an agent, is a person who owes the highest degree of loyalty and honesty to the principal (you). In other words, an agent is held to a higher standard of care toward the principal than a contractor or an employee would be. For example, it would be a breach of the agent's fiduciary duty if she failed to tell you that she was representing an invention that was in direct competition with yours.

An agency relationship is *not* an employment relationship, because you cannot control how the agent performs the work. You only control the end result: the license agreement that you are willing to sign. An agency relationship is also not a partnership, because you and the agent are not sharing the expenses and losses for your invention and the agent isn't personally liable for your business debts. To ensure a court does not interpret your relationship as either employer–employee or partnership, your agreement with the agent should contain the disclaimer, "Nothing contained in this Agreement shall be deemed to constitute either agent or inventor a partner, joint venturer, or employee of the other party for any purpose."

An agent cannot guarantee a licensing deal, and any attempt by an agent to do so should make you suspicious. Reputable agents don't offer guarantees; rather, they tell you they will assess the likelihood of obtaining a license for your invention and use their best efforts to obtain an acceptable deal.

The Benefits of Using an Agent

Why would you want to give up one-third or more of potential licensing revenues to an agent? The answer depends on two factors:

- your ability to license your invention on your own, and
- the industry within which you are attempting to license your invention.

If you cannot make an effective sales pitch or you're intimidated by the prospect of hawking your invention, you should consider using an agent. An agent understands how to sell a product and make a demonstration and is thick-skinned enough to accept rejection without giving up.

Using an agent may also depend upon the industry within which you are attempting to license. Some industries simply don't want to hear from unknown inventors because these companies either develop their own products or deal with selected agents.

Finding a Knowledgeable Agent

Obtaining an agent can be as difficult as locating a licensee. Most agents are not looking for clients. They rely on word of mouth from friends or other inventors. The agents we spoke with when researching this book requested that their names not be included. Why? Because they already have sufficient client listings and attract business strictly from referrals.

How do you find an agent? There are five common methods:

- referrals from businesses
- referrals from inventors
- trade shows
- trade magazine advertisements, and
- online searching.

Referrals From Businesses

If a company won't speak with you about your invention, ask if they deal with agents and can recommend any in particular. For example, when the author of this book approached a toy company about manufacturing a new toy, the company responded by providing a list of toy company agents with whom it would feel comfortable dealing.

Referrals From Other Inventors

If you know other inventors who use agents, ask if they are satisfied, and if so, find out if they will refer you. A referral from a fellow inventor is the best method of obtaining an agent.

Trade Shows

Each trade show or convention distributes a publication with advertisements and an index of attendees. Agents are often listed in this publication as agents, product reps, or product developers. Occasionally, an agent might have a booth at a convention or trade show. Other times, an agent might be roving the show looking for new products to represent.

Trade Magazine Advertisements

Industry trade publications often contain information about agents. These trade publications usually publish an annual index that includes agents. Some inventors have found agents by placing an "Agent Wanted" ad in trade publications. You can start your search for the appropriate journal or magazine at Wikipedia.com (search "Category: Professional and trade magazines").

Online Searching

You can search online for an agent, but one caveat: Typing the words "invention agent" or "invention representative" into an Internet search engine will likely lead to numerous scam marketing services. For information on sorting out the real agents from the rip-offs, see "Invention Marketing Scams," below.

 RELATED TOPIC

Certain licensing publications also list licensing agents and service organizations that appraise new inventions. For example, *The Licensing Journal* often includes lists of technology agents. See Chapter 18, "Help Beyond This Book."

Face Fly Mask
No. 3,104,508

Agents in Action

Most agents are industrious, type A individuals. Many started by developing their own products and then represented other inventors as additional sources of income. And most agents have a niche, specializing in a certain industry—for example, representing only designers of medical devices.

If an agent is interested in representing your product, you'll have to enter into an agent agreement (a sample is provided below) and furnish a prototype that can be used to demonstrate your invention. You'll need to pay not only the costs of preparing the prototype but also some other expenses, such as shipping of the prototypes or reproduction of presentation materials.

The agent will take a suitable prototype of your invention to company offices, trade shows, or conventions. An agent maintains a database which indicates when presentations were made, with whom, and the date. Once an agent has made a presentation, that company is listed as a "solicited company" on the rep's database.

What happens if an agent's contact list is exhausted and no one is interested? Depending on the terms of the agreement, the agent may retain the invention to try again in six months or a year, or the agent may return the invention to you and terminate the agreement. Some

agreements provide that the agent will get royalties if, within a certain period of time after termination, a previously solicited company decides to license the invention.

For example, assume your agent shows the invention to DesignCo. They decide not to license it. You terminate the agent agreement and five months later show your invention to another DesignCo executive who decides to license it.

Depending on your agreement, you may have to pay royalties to the agent. This type of provision is not uncommon.

 RELATED TOPIC
Executing a nondisclosure agreement with your agent. Before presenting your invention to an agent, you should enter into a nondisclosure agreement with the agent. An explanation of nondisclosure provisions and a sample nondisclosure agreement are provided in Chapter 7.

Completing the Agent Agreement

The sample agent agreement set out below is created in a letter format. Although a letter agreement appears less formal than a contract, the agreement is just as enforceable. If you don't want to use the letter format, simply remove the date, salutation, and final paragraph.

Below is an explanation of the provisions in the agent agreement.

Introduction

Insert your name, business form (if
any), and address (for example, "George
Earth, a sole proprietor, with his address
at 14 East 40th Street, New York, NY
10017"). If you are unsure of your
business form, review Chapter 4. Insert
the same information for your agent.
You should attach a separate piece of
paper to the agreement containing a
detailed description of the invention. This
description may only be a few paragraphs,
but it will provide the basis for the agent
to license your invention. If drafted
properly, this description will probably
also be used in any license agreement
that is subsequently negotiated. If your
invention is patented, you can attach a
copy of the patent or make a reference to
the patent (for example, "the invention
and claims embodied in Patent No.
_____"). If the invention is the
subject of a patent or copyright application,
refer to that application. Finally, insert the
name of the industry in which the agent
will represent your invention, for example,
"the toy, hobby, and game" industry.

Obligations of Agent

This section establishes the agent's duties:
evaluating, representing, and negotiating.
It also establishes that the agent is the
exclusive representative for the properties
within the specified industry. This means
that while the agreement is in force, only
the agent (not you or another agent) can
represent the properties within those
industries. ("The properties" refers to your
invention and associated legal rights.) If
the agency relationship is nonexclusive,
then others (including yourself) could
solicit potential licenses within the
specified industry.

Obligations of Inventor

It's possible that the agent will need
assistance from the inventor, for example,
if the product presentation requires
technical assistance or the prototype must
be modified. These duties, once agreed
upon, can be inserted in the final agent
agreement.

Payments

Insert the proper percentage payment for
the agent. Under most agent agreements,
the agent receives 25% to 40% of all
"Properties Income" (as defined), and the
properties income is paid directly to the
agent. After deducting the appropriate
percentage, the agent pays the remaining

sum to the inventor. Some agents might seek to deduct reasonable expenses before splitting the revenues. If the agent wants to deduct expenses, be sure these expenses (postage, telephone, or travel) are spelled out. You can also request approval of any expenses over a certain amount (for example, over $500).

If you are uncomfortable with the agent receiving the licensing money directly, you can suggest providing for an escrow account to hold properties income. For example, you could insert the statement below at the end of the payment section:

Separate Agent Escrow Account—Optional

Agent agrees to maintain a separate interest-bearing escrow account for all Properties Income. Inventor's rights to the account shall be established in a separate escrow agreement and Inventor's access shall be triggered by Agent's death, incapacity, bankruptcy, or insolvency.

Many banks can assist you in the creation of an escrow account and will usually provide the escrow agreement. Maintaining an escrow account will incur additional fees.

Proprietary Rights; Indemnity

The agent (like a potential licensee) will not want any surprises. For this reason, the agent will want your indemnification—a guarantee that you own the invention and that you have the right to license it. You should review the section on indemnity in Chapter 12. Also, review the material on ownership of inventions in Chapters 2 and 3.

Disclaimer

An agent almost always requests a disclaimer provision, which reinforces what you already know—that the agent cannot guarantee a license deal.

Confidentiality

The confidentiality provision contains a standard nondisclosure agreement. For more information on such provisions, see Chapter 7.

Termination

What happens if you terminate (end) the agent agreement and enter into a licensing agreement with a company that the rep had previously solicited on your behalf? Generally, a termination provision stipulates that, if you enter into a licensing agreement within a certain number of months after termination of the agency agreement, you must pay the agent a fee. The time period often ranges from six to 18 months. The amount of the rep's fee can also be altered. For example, you can establish that the agent will only get one-half of the fees if any agreement is entered into after three months but before six months.

Agent Letter Agreement

Date: _____

Dear: [*insert name of agent*]

Introduction

This letter sets forth the terms and conditions of this agreement (the "Agreement") between [*insert your name, business form, and address*] ("Inventor") and [*insert Agent's name, business form, and address*] ("Agent"). Inventor is the owner of licensing rights to various processes and technologies, referred to in this Agreement as the "Properties" and described more fully in Attachment A [*attach a description of the invention to the Assignment and label it "Attachment A"*] to this Agreement. Inventor agrees to have Agent serve as an exclusive representative and agent for the Properties within the [*indicate the industry(ies) in which the agent will represent your invention*] industry (the "Industry").

Obligations of Agent

Agent shall perform the following services:

Evaluation and consultation. Agent will identify potential licensees for the Properties within the Industry.

Sales representation. Agent shall serve as Inventor's exclusive agent for the exploitation of the Properties within the Industry. As Inventor's agent, Agent shall contact and solicit potential licensees or purchasers and present and communicate potential license information between the parties.

Negotiation of agreements. Agent shall work in association with Inventor in the negotiation of sales, licensing, option, or other agreements transferring licensing rights to the Properties.

Obligations of Inventor

Inventor shall perform the following services:

Technical assistance and support. Inventor will consult with licensees of the Properties and provide technical assistance and support for the Properties.

Payments

Inventor agrees that all income paid as a result of any agreement solicited or negotiated by Agent for the Properties (the "Properties Income") shall be paid directly to Agent and that Agent shall issue payments to Inventor within ten (10) days of Agent's receipt of any Properties Income along with any client accountings as provided by the licensee. As compensation for the services provided above, Agent shall receive [*indicate percentage of income paid to Agent*]% of any Properties Income, including, but not limited to, any advances, guarantees, or license fees. The provisions of this Payments Section shall survive any termination of this Agreement.

Proprietary Rights; Indemnity

Inventor represents and warrants that it has the power and authority to enter into this Agreement and that it is the owner of all proprietary rights, whether they are patent, copyright, or otherwise, and that the Properties are not in any way based upon any confidential or proprietary information derived from any source other than Inventor. Because Agent is relying on these representations, Inventor agrees to indemnify Agent and its assignees and hold them harmless from any losses or damages resulting from third-party claims arising from a breach of these representations. Inventor's indemnification of Agent shall survive any termination of this Agreement.

Disclaimer

Nothing in this Agreement shall be interpreted by Inventor as a promise or guarantee as to the outcome of any solicitation or negotiation by Agent on behalf of Inventor or the Properties.

Confidentiality

The parties acknowledge that each may be furnished or may otherwise receive or have access to information that relates to each other's business and the affairs of the respective clients (the "Information"). The parties agree to preserve and protect the confidentiality of the Information and all physical forms. Information relating to the terms, provisions, and substance of this Agreement shall remain within the strictest confidence of both parties, and neither party shall disclose such information to third parties without the prior written consent of the other.

Termination

This Agreement may be terminated at any time at the discretion of either Inventor or Agent, provided that written notice of such termination is furnished to the other party thirty (30) days prior to such termination. If this Agreement is terminated by Inventor, and, within [*number of months*] months of termination, Inventor enters into an agreement to option, license, sell, or otherwise exploit the Properties with any company solicited or contacted by Agent on Inventor's behalf, Inventor agrees to pay the fees established in the Payments Section.

General

Nothing contained in this Agreement shall be deemed to constitute either Agent or Inventor a partner, joint venturer, or employee of the other party for any purpose. Any material contained in an attachment, exhibit, or addendum to this Agreement shall be incorporated in this Agreement. From time to time, the parties may revise the information specified in the attachments or exhibits. Such revisions, if executed by both parties, shall be incorporated in this Agreement and shall be binding on the parties. This Agreement may not be amended except in writing signed by both parties. Each and all of the rights and remedies provided for in this Agreement shall be cumulative. No waiver by either party of any right shall be construed as a waiver of any other right. If a court finds any provision of this Agreement invalid or unenforceable as applied to any circumstance, the remainder of this Agreement shall be interpreted so as best to effect the intent of the parties. This Agreement shall be governed by and interpreted in accordance with the laws of the State of [*insert state law that shall govern the agreement*]. Any controversy or claim arising out of or relating to this Agreement, or the breach of this Agreement, shall be settled by arbitration in accordance with the rules of the American Arbitration Association, and judgment upon the award rendered by the arbitrator(s) may be entered in any court having jurisdiction. The prevailing party shall have the right to collect from the other party its reasonable costs and attorneys' fees incurred in enforcing this agreement. Any such arbitration hearing shall include a written transcript of the proceedings and a written explanation for any final determination. This Agreement expresses the complete understanding of the parties with respect to the subject matter and supersedes all prior proposals, agreements, representations, and understandings.

If these terms and conditions are agreeable, please sign and execute both copies of this Agreement and return one copy to Agent.

INVENTOR: AGENT:

_____   _____
Signature   Signature

_____   _____
Name/Title   Name/Title

_____   _____
Company   Company

_____   _____
Date   Date

In order to be sure that the agent previously solicited the company on your behalf, you should request the agent furnish you a list of companies that were solicited (and the dates of solicitation and the names of the persons contacted). This list can be furnished at the time of termination, or you can request that the agent notify you periodically (every six months) of all solicitations during that period.

General

These general provisions are explained in detail in Chapter 14. Pay special attention to the explanation on arbitration agreements. It's possible that either you or the agent does not want to participate in arbitration in order to settle disputes. Read Chapter 14 for more information on arbitration. In the blank space, we recommend that you insert the name of your state of residence or the state agreed upon by you and the agent.

Signatures

Each party must sign the agreement in relation to the business that is represented (for example, as a general partner representing a partnership), and each party must have the authority to sign the agreement. If you have any doubt about the agent's authority to sign the agreement, review the material on "Signatures" in Chapter 11.

Attorneys as Agents

Sometimes, an attorney might have connections within an industry and be willing to represent you to potential licensees. For example, a patent attorney sees potential in your invention and agrees to represent it and waive attorneys' fees in return for a percentage of the royalties.

EXAMPLE: Phil has invented a drafting system by which an architect, using proprietary ink, can create notes or special instructions that can only be seen under a blue light. A patent attorney, Sam, offers to waive his attorneys' fees and to represent Phil's invention in return for one-third of all revenue. Phil agrees and Sam licenses the invention to a large engineering company, DesignCo.

If an attorney offers to represent your product, you should take the same precautions you would with any agent. Find out if the attorney has represented other clients and ask what the attorney's success rate was. Also, check with your state bar association to determine if the attorney has a record of disciplinary actions. When an attorney performs nonattorney services, such as acting as your agent, the attorney is mixing legal and nonlegal services. In some states, such as California, the law requires that an attorney entering into such a relationship advise the client in writing to seek the advice of another (independent) attorney. The terms of the business arrangement must be in writing and in a manner which "should reasonably have been understood" by the client. In other words, you should understand everything you sign and, if necessary, seek independent legal advice.

You should also obtain a written agreement from the attorney. If the attorney is representing your product or waiving fees, these terms should be stated in the agreement. Also, keep in mind that having an attorney as an agent could result in a conflict of interest. A conflict of interest occurs whenever a lawyer represents adverse interests, for example, if your attorney also represents the licensee. Lawyers are bound by ethical rules to disclose any potential conflicts of interest. When a conflict of interest exists, there's the potential that your attorney may not battle as forcefully for your position. Let's say, in the example above, Phil (the inventor) learns Sam is also the attorney for DesignCo, and Sam earned money by advising DesignCo on the purchase of the license. In this case, a conflict of interest existed and Sam failed to inform Phil about the conflict. By Sam's representing both sides to the agreement, DesignCo might have received more favorable terms than if Sam only represented Phil's interests. (Although it's not common,

attorneys do occasionally represent both inventors and licensors.)

What if an attorney doesn't want to represent your invention but is willing to waive fees for performing legal duties in exchange for a piece of the action? For example, maybe the attorney agrees to draft the patent application or assist in the negotiation of the license in exchange for royalties from the license. Or the attorney is willing to forego a fee for the potential of a percentage of future sales. These types of agreements aren't uncommon, especially in the business of software technology. However, you should proceed carefully. Check the attorney's record. Find out if the attorney has made this type of agreement with other clients, and ask for a list of clients or if it's possible to speak with any clients. Some law firms will furnish lists of clients; others will not. Sometimes, you can find this information through legal directories, such as the Martindale Hubbell guide (available at law libraries and some public libraries or online at www. martindale.com). Becoming intertwined with an attorney in your business dealings can sometimes prove disastrous. It can be difficult to extricate yourself and might be very expensive.

Proceed cautiously. For more information regarding attorneys, review Chapter 18, "Help Beyond This Book."

Invention Marketing Scams

Invention marketing companies (sometimes referred to as "invention promotion" companies) prey on inventors and innovators. Most invention marketing scams combine unrealistic promises of licensing deals and future royalties with high-pressure sales techniques. They offer to evaluate your product, yet they never criticize or reject any products they consider. Inventors pay anywhere from $2,000 to $10,000 for evaluation and marketing advice and (despite the promises of marketing success) are left with no protection and no prospects. When consumers complain or attempt to sue under the contract, they rarely collect damages even if they win their lawsuit. The annual profits for these companies is estimated to be in the millions.

How They Operate

Some common methods employed by these firms include:

- advertising online, and through television, radio, and classified ads in newspapers and magazines
- offering free information to help patent and market inventions
- soliciting contact information so that the company can email or call using high-pressure sales techniques
- making sales calls to ask for information about yourself, your ideas, and a sketch of the invention
- offering to do a free preliminary review of your invention
- suggesting a market evaluation on your idea and charging anywhere from several hundred to several thousand dollars
- supplying a marketing evaluation report that makes vague and general statements that could apply to any invention, not just yours (such as, "You could make $2 to $3 million from your sprocket mirror invention"). And the report provides no hard evidence that a consumer market exists for your invention.
- asking the inventor to pay a fee, plus a percentage of future royalties. By suggesting the possibility of "future royalties," the company is attempting to mislead the inventor into believing the invention has commercial value when no actual research has been done to support this claim.
- seeking more money to promote your invention. The scam marketer informs you that more money is necessary to take your product to the "right" companies. Instead of actually presenting your product, the marketer sends you a list of companies, most (or all) of which will have no relation to your invention.

Periodically the government cracks down on these organizations. The Raymond Lee Organization (RLO) was

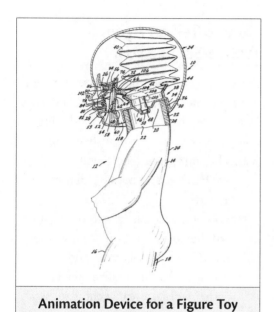

**Animation Device for a Figure Toy
No. 3,855,729**

convicted for falsely alleging that it would obtain patent protection for inventors. A Colorado company, Allied Marketing, was shut down for fraud. The Federal Trade Commission brought an action against one invention marketer and a settlement was reached where the company was ordered to pay $1.2 million into a fund for defrauded inventors (a noble idea, but in reality, one victim reportedly received less than $100 on his $5,000 investment). According to another report, an invention marketing company settled with the government and was required to follow certain guidelines to avoid fraud. The company used this settlement to their advantage, brazenly advertising to be the only invention promotion company "following government guidelines." Sometimes companies close down but reopen under new names.

Invention Promotion Laws

Congress provided some legal controls over scam marketing companies when it enacted the "Invention Developers" law. This amendment to the patent law provides some regulation of unscrupulous invention promotion services that charge substantial fees for marketing efforts that generally are unsuccessful.

There are four parts to the federal law located at 35 U.S.C. § 297. Section 297(a) requires that an invention promoter provide a customer, before entering a contract, a written disclosure that includes:

- the number of inventions evaluated by the invention promoter and stating the number of those evaluated positively and negatively
- the number of customers who have contracted for services with the invention promoter in the past five years
- the number of customers known by the invention promoter to have received a profit as a direct result of the invention promoter's services

- the number of customers known by the invention promoter to have received license agreements for their inventions as a direct result of the invention promoter's services, and
- the names and addresses of all previous invention promotion companies with which the invention promoter has been affiliated in the previous ten years to enable the customer to evaluate the reputations of these companies.

Section 297(b) permits a customer to bring a lawsuit against any invention promoter who caused injury to a customer as a result of a false statement or an omission or through failure of the invention promoter to make all the disclosures. The customer can recover the actual damages or statutory damages up to $5,000, as well as reasonable costs and attorneys' fees. A court can increase damages up to three times the amount awarded if the invention promoter intentionally misrepresented or omitted a material fact.

Section 297(c) defines the terms used in the new law. Section 297(d) requires that the USPTO make publicly available all complaints submitted to the USPTO regarding invention promoters, together with any responses by invention promoters to those complaints.

How to Tell an Agent From a Scam Artist

Scam marketers act like agents. They offer to help protect your invention and license it. However, real agents and marketing companies can be distinguished from scams because legitimate agents:

- are hard to find because they rarely advertise
- do not give a sales pitch to inventors
- will tell an inventor if the invention has flaws or risk factors, and
- provide a list of satisfied clients.

In other words, a real agent is realistic about your invention and is usually willing to take a risk for a percentage of the profits. Some qualified agents might offer to evaluate your product. An evaluation performed by a legitimate rep usually costs several hundred dollars and results in a critique that is particular to your invention and the appropriate industry.

Although scam marketers might seek a percentage of profits, they actually make their money by exorbitant up-front fees that are unrelated to any service that they perform. As a general rule, a person or company that demands more than $1,000 in up-front fees and will not furnish you with a list of clients is probably a scam marketing venture.

When in Doubt About a Marketing Company

If you are in doubt, some of the following methods of checking on a marketing company are recommended:

- Ask for a written estimate of the total cost of services. (If they are running a scam, they will hesitate or be unwilling to provide a firm estimate.)
- Ask what specific standards are used to evaluate your commercial success.
- Ask for a disclosure of the company's success and rejection rates. Under federal law (35 U.S.C. § 297), the company must disclose its track record. Success rates show the number of clients who make more money from their invention than they paid the firm. Rejection rates reflect the percentage of all ideas or inventions that were found unacceptable by the invention promotion company. As a general rule, a reputable marketing firm rejects most of the inventions.
- Ask for a list of satisfied clients.
- Check the National Inventor Fraud Center website (www.inventorfraud. com), which includes a list of helpful links (such as a link to the Federal Trade Commission's site).
- Investigate the company before making any commitments. (See Chapter 18, "Help Beyond This Book.") ●

Soliciting Potential Licensees

Before You Begin Your Search 135

How to Find Potential Licensees 137

    Trade Associations 137

    Newsletters 138

    Trade Magazines 138

    Business Directories... 139

    Sorting Out Your Research 139

How to Overcome a Licensee's Bias Against Submissions............................. 140

    Hurdle #1: Fear of Outside Solicitations 140

    Hurdle #2: Presumptions Regarding Independent Inventors....................... 141

    Hurdle #3: The "We're Doing Okay Without You" Syndrome 142

What's the Best Way to Solicit a Potential Licensee?.................................... 142

    Solicitation Letters... 143

    Phone Calls 143

    Trade Shows.. 144

Product Presentations 146

Should You Solicit Foreign Licensees?.. 147

    What Do You Know About the Market? 149

    What Do You Know About the Licensee?...151

    What About the License Agreement? 152

    Resources 154

"I had a dreadful experience. I went from my house in London up to Glasgow to see this hotshot who I thought might be interested in my radio. I had my first radio (which ran for 14 minutes), and I had my patent in my pocket and my tie was straight and my nails were clean. I went to his office and I was kept waiting for 20 minutes without even a cup of tea, and then this woman went into this office and I heard her say, 'There's a silly little man with a silly clockwork thing who's come to see you. Have you got time to see him?' And he said, 'Not now, give him an excuse.' And then I came all the way back from Glasgow thinking, 'I'm a silly little man.' It's so degrading. So hurtful. But what can you do? You've got to swallow all that stuff."

—Trevor Bayliss (inventor of the Freeplay Radio),
interview on "Todd Mundt Radio Show," February 8, 2001

This chapter explains how to seek out and approach potential licensees, a process we refer to as solicitation. As the experience of inventor Trevor Bayliss indicates above, many inventors find the solicitation process to be far more difficult and frustrating than the invention process.

Solicitation occurs in three steps. First, you find likely candidates. Then, once you've gathered the names of prospective licensees, you contact them in the hopes of getting an appointment to pitch your invention. Third, if you manage to get an appointment, you make your pitch or presentation.

You should read this chapter if you answer "yes" to any of the following questions:

- Are you trying to locate potential licensees but are unsure what companies might be suitable?
- Are you looking for information about a particular industry?
- Are you undecided on how to approach a potential licensee?
- Are you unsure of how to present your invention?

If you're not interested in soliciting licensees directly and plan on having someone else, such as an agent or product representative, do this for you, be sure to review the previous chapter on dealing with agents and reps.

To Prototype or Not to Prototype

A prototype is a working model of your invention and can be quite helpful in making a presentation since it allows a licensee to actually see the invention, not simply listen to your idea. If it's possible to create a prototype for several hundred dollars, it might be worth the expense. However, if the prototype will cost thousands of dollars, you might want to consider an alternative. One method of demonstrating an invention without using a prototype is by furnishing a copy of the Provisional Patent Application (see Chapter 2). Another method is to create a computer simulation.

For example, a musician/inventor conceived of a new type of carrying case for musical instruments but couldn't afford to build a prototype. Instead, at a much cheaper cost, he used graphics and animation facilities and created a three-minute computer presentation that included an accurate rendering of the device. He took this computer rendering to a musical instrument manufacturer to demonstrate the product and to solicit an opinion as to its commercial potential. The musical instrument manufacturer liked the product, but not enough to manufacture the device.

Although this may not seem like a happy ending, it would have been more tragic if the inventor had spent thousands of dollars creating a prototype, only to learn that it could not be licensed. If you decide you want a prototype created, you should look into a company that specializes in building them. These companies often advertise online or in the back of scientific and inventor magazines. For more information, see the section on "Licensing and Intellectual Property Resources" in Chapter 18, "Help Beyond This Book."

Before You Begin Your Search

Before beginning your search for a licensee, consider the following suggestions:

- **Learn about the industry.** One of the worst mistakes you can make as an inventor is to solicit a company blindly, without knowledge of that company or the overall industry. According to one successful inventor/ agent, inventors commonly make the mistake of being unfamiliar with a company's product line and end up pitching a product that is similar to something already being marketed. Before pursuing any leads, you should research the product lines, understand the industry, learn the major players, and, in particular, learn about the chains of distribution. You will soon learn that distributors and retailers exert incredible influence over the potential success of a new invention. For example, it is unlikely that a toy company will release a new product unless it's confident that retailers will carry it. It's essential to know this type of background information, if you want to establish credibility when soliciting a company.

- **Be realistic.** In the business world, it's not enough to be a creative genius. If you intend to profit from your creations, you must be able to deal with business realities. Your invention might be your baby, but to someone at a large company, it's just another unsolicited product. Remember that most businesspeople are oriented toward the bottom line—that's how they keep their jobs. For this reason, we suggest you seriously review the costs and commercial potential of your invention using one of the methods suggested in Chapter 1.

- **If you can't pitch your invention, find someone who can.** If you're not an aggressive or persuasive sales-person, consider affiliating with a businessperson or an agent. Don't be afraid of working with an agent who is ethical and with whom you feel comfortable in the working relationship. In Chapter 5, we provide agreements that can help you work with an agent.

- **No license is better than a bad license.** Some inventors assume that any license is better than no license at all. This is not true. Entering into a licensing agreement is like a marriage. A license agreement—no matter how well drafted—cannot shield you from the aggravation and expense of dealing with the wrong company. The goal is not simply to get licensed, but to find the right partner for the license. Generally, this proves to be a much harder proposition than inventing or patenting your invention.

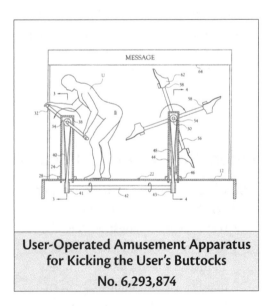

User-Operated Amusement Apparatus for Kicking the User's Buttocks No. 6,293,874

How to Find Potential Licensees

In order to solicit prospective licensees, you need to gather a list of the most likely choices. Below are some methods for gathering this information.

Working Within the Industry

Some of the best information and resources for selling your invention come from working within an industry. If you have created an invention that is applicable to the trade in which you work, you have an advantage because you probably already have contacts, understand the economics of the industry, know the trade magazines and trade shows, and are aware of the major players. You are also familiar with the technology available in the trade and may be able to find new uses for old inventions.

However, there is a drawback to inventing in the industry within which you work. As discussed in Chapter 3, depending upon state law and your employment contract, you might have to relinquish title of your invention to your employer. See Chapter 3 for more on ownership issues between employers and employees.

Trade Associations

A trade association (also referred to as a trade group or business association) is a group comprising the various companies within an industry. For example, the American Pet Products Association (APPA) (www.americanpetproducts. org) is a trade group composed of over 1,000 pet product manufacturers. The APPA holds numerous networking events, gathers market research, and provides industry links, trends, and product guidelines. Almost every industry has a trade association. Once you locate such an organization, you can obtain literature from it, as well as information about conventions, meetings, and directories.

One of the best sources of industry trade groups is Wikipedia (www.wikipedia. org). In addition to generalized lists of links (such as "List of industry trade groups in the United States"), Wikipedia provides specialized lists—for example, "List of food industry trade associations." You can also use Wikipedia's search feature to locate individual trade organizations. Typing in "toy association" will locate the Toy Association, which represents 85% of toy manufacturers.

A complete listing of all trade associations can also be found in the *Encyclopedia of Associations* (Gale Research, Inc.), which is available at many libraries and online for a subscription fee at www.gale.com. For example, say you invented an automotive diagnostic tool for determining spark plug life. Using the *Encyclopedia of Associations*, you could search automotive service associations and find the address for the Equipment and Tool Institute (ETI), which is the trade association for manufacturers of automotive service equipment and tools. The ETI publishes an annual directory of all manufacturers. (By the way, you could also locate the ETI through Wikipedia's search engine.)

Newsletters

Newsletters—often distributed monthly, biweekly, or weekly—offer inside information about an industry. Some newsletters are free, some cost hundreds per year, and some can be obtained only through membership in a trade association (see above). However, most newsletters will furnish a sample upon request. Newsletters can be helpful because they provide backgrounds on major companies (and their executives) within an industry and information about industry trends.

You might find newsletters and relevant blogs on the Internet. Use your search engine and type in keywords for the industry. Many trade newsletters are available through private online subscription services, such as LexisNexis or Dow Jones.

Trade Magazines

Trade magazines are similar to newsletters. They include information about major companies, sales charts, advertisements for products, and general news about particular industries. For example, the trade magazine *FoodService Director* offers insight into the fast food industry. *Automotive Industries* provides inside information on the car industry.

Trade magazines are subsidized by trade advertising, and for this reason are often inexpensive. You might find the trade advertising helpful in learning about the product lines of various companies. One advantage of a subscription is that it often places you on a mailing list for industry-related publications, books, lectures, and other materials.

 RESOURCE

Internet license exchanges. Several Web-based businesses seek to bring patent owners and potential licensees together. Sites such as Yet2.com offer—for a fee—the ability to post information about patented inventions for would-be licensees. To explore patent exchanges, type "patent exchange" or "patent license exchange" into your Internet search engine.

Business Directories

Two types of business directories exist: general business directories, which list all businesses throughout the country, and trade directories, which list specific companies within an industry. You can often obtain the latter through an industry trade group website—for example, the Solar Energy Industries Association posts its membership directory at its website (www. seia.org).

General Business Directories

As for general business directories, one of the best-known is ThomasNet (www. thomasnet.com), which allows you to search online using various criteria, and provides manufacturer profiles and phone numbers. You can also find a number of general business directories online—for example, SuperPages.com (www.superpages.com) lets you search by business category, name, street address, state, or zip code.

Trade Directories

A trade directory is usually more helpful than general business directories because it lists only the companies in one specific industry. If a trade directory is available for the industry related to your invention, we recommend that you obtain it. Most trade directories are published by trade magazines (see above) or as part of a trade show (see below).

Sorting Out Your Research

After you've finished researching your industry, you'll probably have a list of companies suitable as licensees. In some industries, you might be surprised to find only a small number of prospects exist. This is often the result of corporate takeovers—one or two companies have cornered the market by acquiring the smaller players.

If, however, you are faced with many prospects, you can do more research in order to sort your list and perhaps eliminate some listings. To help in this sorting process, you should search for economic news and reports for the companies on your list.

SIC Codes

Most corporate directories utilize a system known as the Standard Industrial Classification (SIC) Code. The SIC is a four-digit number created by the Department of Commerce and is used to classify a business by the type of work it does. For example, if you invented a product to be worn while handling explosives, you might review companies classified as 1795, which is the code for the Wrecking and Demolition Industry. If you invented a timer for video cameras, you would check companies classified as 3651 for Video Equipment and Household Audio. The SIC is helpful when searching, since most corporate directories, whether in print, digital, or online form, include an index of SIC codes.

You can obtain financial statements and news articles about many companies on the Internet. For example, check out these online sites: D&B Hoovers (www.hoovers.com) or Dow Jones (www.dowjones.com). If you are fortunate enough to have access to the expensive Lexis/Nexis database, you can obtain a wide range of corporate information, including whether a company has been in a lawsuit, a company's assets, and any financial claims against a company, as well as news articles, bankruptcy reports, financial statements, and other information. This background information will be helpful before you make your pitch.

How to Overcome a Licensee's Bias Against Submissions

Once you locate prospective licensee companies, how do you convince them to review your product? This is the toughest hurdle you will face in the licensing process, and you will need tenacity and patience. As a general rule, most companies are not actively seeking outside ideas or inventions. In fact, many companies are biased against ideas that come from the outside world. This bias stems from three major factors:

- fear of outside solicitations
- misunderstanding of independent inventors, or
- the notion that the company is doing well enough with its own internally created products.

Hurdle #1: Fear of Outside Solicitations

Just as you might be paranoid about showing your idea to a company (you're afraid they will steal it), a company might be fearful of you and your idea.

One reason could be that the company is concerned it could get sued if it rejects your idea but later comes out with something similar. Or, if it accepted your idea, the company could later find out the idea was taken from someone else (a former employer or another inventor) who might then sue the company.

For these reasons, the only way some companies will respond to your solicitation phone call or letter is by sending you a legal document to sign before even looking at your invention. These agreements might have different titles, such as disclosure agreement, nondisclosure agreement, waiver agreement, evaluation agreement, or confidentiality agreement. Chapter 7, on confidentiality, provides explanations, samples, and advice regarding these types of agreements.

Some companies might not send you one of the preliminary agreements (listed above) because the company has a simple policy of refusing to see outside solicitations. This is not uncommon, especially among larger companies. Unfortunately, unless you play golf with the company's CEO, there's generally no way around this policy.

Hurdle #2: Presumptions Regarding Independent Inventors

Like it or not, independent inventors are perceived as eccentric, kooky loners who have little knowledge of the business world. This cliché is commonly portrayed in Hollywood films: *The Absent-Minded Professor, The Nutty Professor*, and so on. For this reason, one of the first things you must do when pitching your invention is establish your credibility and create a climate in which

**Tongue-Snatching Creature Toy
No. 6,107,262**

the company may be more receptive to your ideas. Demonstrating any of the following experiences or skills should help strengthen your credibility:

- **Academic training, if appropriate.** For example, "I've studied hydroponic gardening at Purdue University, where I first began experimenting with the idea of a hydroponics starter kit for children."
- **Previous business success or experience, even if in another industry.** For example, "For 25 years, I've managed a company that sells auto parts, and that's given me a good perspective on the needs of automotive consumers."
- **A link between yourself and the company's products, even as a consumer.** For example, "I've been using your frying pans for 20 years, and I think I've come up with an improvement on the design."
- **Past inventing experience.** For example, "I've been doing research and development at LapCo for ten years, where I was part of the team that invented the LapLander all-terrain vehicle."
- **Patent protection.** For example, "I recently received a patent for a device that I think would fit in well with your current line of rototilling machines." If your patent is pending but hasn't yet been issued, mention the patent status either from a regular application filing or a provisional patent application filing.

Hurdle #3: The "We're Doing Okay Without You" Syndrome

Another common reason a licensee might not want to consider your submission is the company feels that it's doing well enough without you and your invention. For example, "We have plenty of products. We have a lot of in-house developers. Why do we need you?" This theory pervades many large businesses and is difficult to overcome because it's entwined with the company's internal vision of itself.

Only one method really exists to crack this type of company, and that is to use someone with insider contacts, either a business rep/manager or a contact of yours within the company. Short of that, you may be better off seeking out a smaller or midsized company that is still competitive and not yet stifled with inertia.

 RELATED TOPIC

What about selling it yourself?
Because many companies are hostile to outside ideas, some innovators prefer trying to get the attention of these companies by making their inventions successful under their own ventures. In Chapter 1, we discuss selling your invention.

What's the Best Way to Solicit a Potential Licensee?

There is no surefire guaranteed way to successfully solicit a licensee. Each industry is different. Generally, you will have the best chance of reaching an executive at a trade show, but you might also have good luck writing a letter or calling by phone. Probably some combination of these various approaches will be needed.

The goal of your solicitation is to obtain an appointment for you to make your formal presentation. If possible, avoid disclosing more than necessary about your invention during your initial contacts.

How Do the Big Shots Do It?

Some companies that own and manage large collections of patents or trade secrets (known as portfolios) solicit licensees by means of a licensing memorandum. This is a letter that introduces the property, describes the scope of legal protection (patents, trade secrets, trademarks, and so on), and includes the general business terms for a proposed agreement. The memorandum often also includes a nondisclosure agreement (see Chapter 7) and a sample license agreement. Basically, the memorandum is a licensing kit, and if the prospective licensee is interested, the owner can move rapidly toward a licensing deal.

We do not recommend this course for you, because it's unlikely you will have the contacts or the clout to receive a response to a licensing memorandum. Instead, we recommend that you make a contact by letter or phone, present your invention, and then work out the business terms.

Solicitation Letters

Based on our limited experience and that of other inventors, letters might work as a form of solicitation, but don't expect a deluge of responses. Below is a sample solicitation letter. Remember to do your best to include one or more of the credibility factors listed above in the previous section.

Does Letter Writing Work?

As an experiment to determine if letters were an effective method of soliciting companies with product ideas, we sent out solicitation letters to approximately 25 companies in a variety of fields such as health, hosiery, luggage, electronic musical equipment, bottling, biscuits, toys, and paints. Each letter indicated that we had an invention suitable in the relative fields and included a self-addressed and stamped envelope. We received two letters back and one phone call, each asking for more information.

Phone Calls

Soliciting a company by phone requires a sales mentality. You need to reach the right person and, in a very short time, convince that person you have something worth presenting to the company. Remember, as a general rule you need to befriend every person you speak with at

January 10, 2020
Mr. Robert Rysher
Chief Operations Officer
Cookies, Inc.
1234 Main Street
Lakewood, NJ 08701

Re: Improved Biscuit Package

Dear Mr. Rysher:

I am an inventor with considerable experience in the field of packaging and design. I'm a graduate of the Rhode Island School of Design. I am also a consumer of your biscuit and cookie products. Several years ago, I began researching a better method of mass-market packaging of baked goods. Last year, I invented a novel method of packaging that I believe could be less expensive than your present method and can better protect your baked goods. I am presently applying for patent protection for this process. I would very much like to discuss this innovation with you as I believe Cookies, Inc., would find it to be a valuable method of preserving your product and reducing costs. I look forward to speaking with you.

Sincerely,

Frances Kimberly

Frances Kimberly, Inventor

the company. Therefore, it is foolish ever to speak curtly or act rudely.

How do you reach the right person? If it is a large company, the receptionist may be helpful. Ask if there is someone at the company who considers new product ideas. If the person with whom you wish to speak is not expecting your call, chances are very good that you will be put through to voicemail. In this case, you have about one minute to make a brief pitch.

To get the most out of your message, we suggest you have your major credibility points written down and handy during your call. For example, you (1) are an inventor with two patents and a graduate of Pratt Institute, (2) are knowledgeable about the company's products, such as Products X and Y, and (3) have a patent pending on a device that is more cost-efficient than the company's present device. Having a list of points to cover will help prevent you from forgetting them if you're nervous or flustered.

If you do reach a real person (and not voicemail), you should follow the same approach. Also, you should:

- Get the name of the person; always keep a record of every person you speak with.
- Keep the conversation short; don't get sidetracked. You should be friendly, but remember, the person on the phone is at work and your call is the equivalent of a sales pitch.
- Get a direct mailing address; you want to follow up the call with a letter.
- Stick to the facts and stick to the truth; don't deceive the caller in the hopes of making a sale. Any pitch based upon deceptions will eventually fall apart.
- Thank the person at the end of the call and indicate how you intend to follow up.

Trade Shows

In today's security-conscious atmosphere, many executives are wary of being approached personally. However, one place where this rule doesn't apply is a trade show. Trade shows are conventions in which companies gather to show new products and exchange information. For in-person solicitations, trade shows and other industry gatherings are logical choices, because executives attend prepared to do business and network. Almost everyone wears a name tag, so you know whom you're talking to. You can locate information about industry trade shows through trade associations, magazines, or newsletters or by researching sites such as www.allconferences.com.

On the downside, trade shows are often expensive to visit (airfare, hotel fare) and to attend as a participant (booth costs, employees, and so on). Admission fees for some conventions can run into the thousands of dollars.

If your goal is to make contacts and begin the licensing process at a trade show, you should find one that focuses on your area of invention, write to the show organizers for information on the show, and attempt to determine who will be exhibiting. If an exhibitor directory is not available, find out if you can obtain a directory from the last convention.

When you register for the show, you will be given a name tag that identifies you (for example, "Joan Smith, Inventor"). The show organizers may be able to direct you to appropriate booths. You can make contacts at a trade show three different ways, and all three methods require an assertive personality and self-confidence:

- **Read the name cards.** This is, by far, the most challenging method. You walk through the convention, introduce yourself at booths, and ask to speak with representatives of companies that are exhibiting.
- **Attend with someone who is knowledgeable.** A better strategy might be to attend the convention with someone who has been there before. This person can walk you through, introduce you, and help you make contacts. It may be possible to find such a guide beforehand by corresponding with the organizers of the event or the trade organization. If necessary, offer to pay for someone's services on an hourly basis as a consultant. For example, talk to someone exhibiting at a booth and ask if, during their off-time, you can pay them to walk you through the convention. It will probably be worth the expense.
- **Set up your own booth.** Exhibiting might enhance your ability to license, because agents and licensors walk the floor examining the booths. Ideally, your invention will attract attention. But exhibiting can also be costly. The average booth is 200 square feet and ranges from $10 to $100 per square foot. You may also be charged set-up and dismantling fees and premiums for location on the floor and for electricity and furniture. Plus, you might need extra people to work the booth who need to be paid. Because of these costs, most trade show veterans advise that you attend a show once before you exhibit. That way, you can determine if exhibiting is worthwhile and see the layout of the booths and the quality and appearance of the exhibitors.

Your goal during a trade show solicitation is to make contacts that you can follow up with a letter, phone call, or presentation. As a general rule, don't expect large or midsized companies to set up presentations with you during the trade show, as most of these executives are already booked up with appointments.

Even so, according to one successful agent, in case an executive asks to see a presentation on the spot you should always carry a nondisclosure agreement with you. (Nondisclosure agreements are covered in Chapter 7.) On-the-spot presentations sometimes happen with executives from smaller companies, who are more likely to have time to meet with you during trade shows.

 TIP

Personal appearance counts. Unlike letters and phone calls, an in-person solicitation may be affected by your appearance. Your grooming, clothes, and personal hygiene should demonstrate that you are a credible businessperson. You should have business cards available and ask for a business card from any individual that you speak with. And, as with phone conversations, keep the discussion short and stick to the facts.

Product Presentations

If you manage to secure an appointment for a product presentation—Congratulations! You've already gotten farther than most inventors. Your next step is to prepare yourself for the presentation (or what is often referred to as "the dog and pony show").

Some suggestions for presentations include:

- **Be clear, fast, and concise.** Your presentation is a sales pitch, not a dissertation. Hit the high points (cost, effectiveness, product superiority, and so on) quickly.

- **Practice your presentation but don't memorize or read it.** Your talk should have a conversational quality, which is most likely to engage your listeners.

- **Know your costs.** A potential licensee's number one concern will probably be costs. What will it cost to manufacture and sell your invention? How much can be earned?

- **Stick to the facts; stick to business.** It's fine to be friendly, but focus on the purpose of your visit, which is to convince people at the meeting to license your invention.

- **Be prepared.** Give your presentation a trial run. If you will need electrical power or additional facilities, even just a desk or bulletin board, make sure you will have them. Every marketer has disaster stories about prototypes that failed or facilities that were unsuitable for presentation. Have a contingency plan. For example, "I'm afraid my power supply has died. In any event, I have a video that shows how this device functions and I'd be happy to leave it with you so you can see a demonstration."

- **Be flexible.** Be open to ideas and suggested modifications that are offered. Always "take them under advisement," although you probably shouldn't make changes until you can determine the seriousness of the licensee's commitment.

- **Be positive, without being foolishly upbeat.** Nobody wants to hear from a sad sack. Walk a line between enthusiasm for your invention and a calm business demeanor.

- **Have written materials to supplement your demonstration.** Use simple written materials, such as numbered lists of your product's strengths, to make your point. Determine the right moment to hand out paperwork—before, during, or after a presentation. Charts, graphs, and tables have a powerful effect in presentations and can make your point better than a spreadsheet.

- **Get feedback.** Ask for opinions. Even if the current audience is not interested, they might have suggestions that can benefit you in your next presentation.

- **Don't take it personally.** Don't appear offended by rejection. You should never have to accept a solicitee's bad manners, but don't confuse rudeness with simple rejection. If you want to stay in the invention business, you might have to deal with the same people over and over. Curb your anger and resentment, as they will be interpreted as a lack of professionalism and could affect your ability to license in the future.

Inventors' Associations

Over the past decade, groups of inventors have banded together to help each other and get their new ideas to the marketplace. Once fragmented, these groups are now becoming more effective thanks to national networks like InventNet (www.inventnet.com) and the National Congress of Inventor Organizations (NCIO) (www.inventionconvention.com). These inventors' associations and groups can be quite helpful. For example, an Illinois man devised a lap board for quadriplegics but was unsure of how to manufacture his invention. He spoke with a volunteer from the Chicago-based Inventor's Council of Mid-Michigan. The Council helped connect the Illinois inventor to a group of Amish woodworkers who eventually manufactured the device. For more information on inventor organizations, see Chapter 18, "Help Beyond This Book."

Should You Solicit Foreign Licensees?

The United States is said to make up one-quarter to one-third of the world's marketplace. Europe comprises a marketplace equally large and potentially as profitable as the United States. The nations of Asia are said to have a similarly large segment of marketplace share. How do you approach, analyze, and reconcile these markets and your licensing opportunities?

Infant Blanket With Teeth Pacifier
No. 6,292,962

First, you might not have to wrestle with this issue if you are licensing to an international licensee that intends to exploit your invention internationally. In that case, someone else will handle the heavy lifting for international exploitation.

Second, a licensee might be interested in foreign rights only if you also obtain patent rights in other countries (since your U.S. patent can only stop infringers within U.S. borders). In that case, you must consider whether it's worth pursuing these rights.

Third, your invention might not lend itself to foreign licensing. For example, you might have created an adjunct product for an item that is distributed only within the United States.

But in many cases you may have licensed only U.S. rights and you are unsure as to whether it's worth your time and expense to seek licensing opportunities outside the United States. Below, we discuss some of the issues that arise when making such decisions.

Foreign Patent Rights: Bang for Your Buck?

One factor in deciding whether to pursue foreign licensing is often the cost of obtaining foreign patent rights. In the United States, an inventor pays between $2,500 and $15,000 to acquire a patent (depending on whether a patent attorney drafts the application and on the complexity of the patent). This covers the patent search, preparation of an application, and shepherding the application through the USPTO. In return, the inventor acquires rights in the world's single largest national market.

In contrast, the cost of patent protection in eight European nations (with approximately the same population as the United States), including ten-year renewals, is approximately U.S. $27,500 to $35,000.

What Do You Know About the Market?

The first step in analyzing foreign licensing is making a marketability-per-nation analysis. You need to ask yourself the questions listed below. Although these questions require some degree of speculation, it's possible to acquire sufficient economic data about the trade potential, business climate, and demographics abroad to make an educated guess about seeking a license agreement (and filing for a patent, as well) in a foreign country. Ask yourself about:

Dear Rich:
Stopping Patented Invention From Being Imported

Dear Rich: I am preparing to license a U.S. "patent pending" invention to a U.S.-based company. Even though the market for the product is clearly worldwide, it is sparse enough that it does not justify expensive foreign patent filing. The company's supplier and its competitors are located in China and Korea. If any of these other companies sell to U.S. customers via the Internet (typical), I believe the sale legally occurs in a foreign country, therefore sidestepping my patent. If so, I question if the company I will deal with has any reason to enter a license agreement with me. Is there any way I can be protected in cost-permissible way?

The short answer to your question is that once you acquire patent protection, you can stop Internet sales to U.S.-based customers. U.S. patent holders can stop anyone from importing infringing products or offering infringing products for sale (advertising or marketing) within the U.S.

There are also federal court decisions indicating that a foreign supplier cannot "induce" infringement in the United States. So, whether copies of your product are sold online, slip out of the factory's back door, or result from competitor's copying, you can stop these from coming into the U.S. The bigger concern is who will bankroll the policing and enforcement needed to stop this activity. One of the reasons inventors license (rather than manufacture themselves) is so that the licensee (the company to whom you're licensing) will watch your back. You may be able to enhance that protection by authorizing (via the licensing agreement) the licensee to go after infringers and to split the resulting court awards after deducting legal expenses. You should discuss this matter with an IP attorney before agreeing on important licensing agreement terms, such as territory, indemnity, and grant of rights.

- **Current sales potential.** Does your invention have sales potential currently in the targeted nation? Without sales potential, there might be no reason to seek patent protection.

- **Future market.** Does a possible future market exist for the invention within the next ten to 15 years? Even if the current market is weak, a nation may be worth pursuing if a future market is expected.

- **Competition.** What is the status of competitors in this nation? The presence of competitors can be interpreted in different ways. It's possible that many competitors indicates a healthy, substantial market with room for more competition. On the other hand, a lack of competitors— particularly in an emerging technology —might prove to be a positive sign, given that a major competitor (especially one that has dominated the market for five to ten years) could prove difficult to challenge.

- **Production costs.** Can the invention be cost-efficiently produced in this nation? Although inventions can always be imported, it may be more cost-efficient (or even necessary, in some cases) to produce an invention within the nation.

- **Day-to-day operations.** Do you have the means to observe and administer the licensee and licensed products in this country? You do not need to control day-to-day operations, but you should have a means of reviewing activity from a distance. Otherwise, you could have a difficult time making a success of the market.

- **Ability to sue infringers.** How difficult will it be to chase infringers in the foreign country? As you're aware, your U.S. patent will not provide you with any rights abroad. You will need to acquire rights in the country in which you are licensing—often an expensive process. (See "Foreign Patent Rights: Bang for Your Buck?" above.) In any event, having a patent doesn't automatically stop an infringer; you must pursue the infringer in the nation where the patent was granted. For example, even if you acquire a patent through the European Patent Office, no European-wide method of stopping patent infringement exists. You must sue in each country where an infringement has occurred.

- **Obstacles to sales.** Do any impediments exist to selling in this market? You might need to determine if a nation's regulations (for example, safety standards for medical devices) or trade or union rules will affect your ability to sell there.

EXAMPLE: Franklin developed an Internet software process that is the subject of a U.S. patent application. Franklin decides to research the commercial potential for his software in European nations. Using Internet resources, he learns that the German software market is booming with two-digit growth and anticipated growth rates in the 13% range. Franklin also learns that Internet-related software products are expected to be the best sales prospects and that more than 60% of sales is achieved by medium- to small-sized vendors. Most importantly, Franklin learns that approximately 80% of software sold in Germany originates from United States developers. Armed with a list of potential German licensees acquired from his Internet research, Franklin decides to solicit licensees in Germany.

It's usually wise to begin your analysis by examining the general economic health of each nation that you are considering. The most common indicator is the annual gross national product (GNP, sometimes referred to GDP for gross domestic product). The GNP is a measurement of the nation's financial output of goods and services calculated by a combination of personal consumption, government expenditures, private investment, inventory growth, and trade balance.

For example, the GNP for the combined European Union (EU) nations is similar to that for the United States—approximately ten trillion dollars. In other words, the EU, as a whole, comprises a market as large and as potentially profitable as the United States. But France, Germany, and Spain account for a large chunk of that GNP, so it may be worth your while to seek patents and licensing opportunities only in these EU nations (plus the United Kingdom, which left the EU in 2020).

While information such as GNPs provides a "big picture," this general market knowledge is insufficient for predicting the marketing success of specific inventions. To help you determine the specific market for your particular invention, we provide some suggestions for Internet research below.

What Do You Know About the Licensee?

The most important issue that arises when entering into a foreign license has to do with people, not paper. After all, you can draft a bulletproof foreign license agreement, but if the other party is a scoundrel, a cheat, or simply inept, it doesn't matter what's printed on the agreement. To enforce your contractual rights, you will have to chase the licensee into court in a foreign country and—assuming you are lucky enough to win—you'll still have to collect your judgment before the licensee goes bankrupt or "folds the corporate tent."

So, when dealing with a foreign licensee, start by asking two questions:

- **Has this company or person ever licensed from a U.S. company before?** Remember the business maxim that "a pioneer is the person with the arrow in his back." In other words, don't be the first U.S. inventor-artist to deal with a foreign licensee. If a company has no experience with American licensors, then you'll need a strong reason to proceed with them (for example, even though the foreign company is new, the principals are all experienced in international licensing).
- **If the company has licensed from U.S. inventors, who are they and how can you contact them?** Get the names and contact info for all—not just those recommended by the company—of the inventors who license with the foreign company. Find out whether they are satisfied with the company's quality, accounting, and general responsiveness.

What About the License Agreement?

Assuming you're satisfied that the company is reliable, either you'll be given a standard licensing agreement or you'll furnish one.

Below is a summary of some important foreign licensing issues to keep in mind:

- **Jurisdiction.** Jurisdiction (sometimes referred to as forum selection, as explained in Chapter 14) is the power of a court to bind the parties by its decision. The only way to get a foreign licensee into a U.S. court—unless the company does substantial business in the States— is to include a provision in the license that requires the licensee to consent to U.S. jurisdiction. This could prove difficult to negotiate, as foreign licensees are often hesitant about submitting to the U.S. judicial system.
- **Choice of law.** Every country has laws as to how contracts are interpreted. The licensee will want the disputes to be resolved under the laws of its country. Unless you're interested in learning about the laws of Sierra Leone or Singapore, try to have disputes resolved under U.S. law (for patent purposes) and the laws of your state (when it comes to contract issues).
- **Right to terminate as to territory not exploited.** Even if you license for a worldwide territory, your agreement should include a provision that provides if foreign markets are not exploited within a fixed time period, those foreign rights revert to you.

A sample optional provision is included in the model agreement in Chapter 11.

- **Arbitration.** Arbitration, as explained in Chapter 14, is similar to litigation but with less formality and expense. You'll often benefit by agreeing to have disputes arbitrated. Hopefully, the licensee will agree to arbitrate the matter in the United States. If not, there are three popular (though expensive) spots for international arbitration: London (the London Court of International Arbitration), Paris (the International Court of Arbitration of the International Chamber of Commerce), and Stockholm (the Arbitration Institute of the Stockholm Chamber of Commerce). Also, if possible, your agreement should award attorneys' fees to the victor in the arbitration.

- **Approval of licensed goods.** When major U.S. manufacturers license products abroad, they often arrange periodic inspections of the manufacturing facilities to ensure the quality of the goods (and also to monitor whether the licensee is siphoning off products or engaging in illegal labor practices). It's unlikely you'll be able to afford such onsite inspections, but you can demand that copies of your licensed work be sent to you on a regular basis for approval. This offers you some assurance of consistency and quality

for your work. An approval provision is included in the model license provided in Chapter 11.

- **Foreign patent registrations.** As noted above, you should determine whether it's worth your while to obtain foreign patent registration in the countries where your work is being manufactured or distributed. Often, licensors require that the licensee handle these administrative tasks as part of the license. The provision "Intellectual Property Protection" in the model license agreement in Chapter 11 can be adopted to include filing and prosecution of foreign as well as U.S. patents.

- **Royalties and accounting.** Payment of royalties from a foreign licensee can get tricky, especially when you consider issues like currency conversion rates (probably best to always insist on payment in U.S. currency), how the money will be paid (best to use wire transfers), and what taxes may be applied against your sales or royalties (before signing the license, inquire into national or local tariffs or taxes that might apply). Also, although it's unlikely you can afford to hire an accountant in India or Malaysia, it's still wise to include the audit provision discussed in Chapter 9 (which allows you to inspect the foreign licensee's books).

Okay, once you've absorbed all of these suggestions, here are two final suggestions:

- **Learn the lingo.** Become familiar with international trade terminology and rules so you can speak knowledge-ably about things like "F.O.B." and "letters of credit." You can get a crash course by reviewing the resources listed below.
- **If in doubt, don't do the deal.** Don't let your desire to earn royalties over-come your common sense. Always keep in mind that no foreign license might be better than a bad foreign license.

Resources

Below, you'll find resources to assist you in making your decision of whether to solicit a foreign licensee:

- **The U.S. Department of Commerce** (DOC) (www.commerce.gov) and the **U.S. Small Business Administration** (SBA) (www.sba.gov) are interested in helping the sales of U.S. goods overseas. If an inventor has a track record and the possibility of actually placing a product in the market (or already has a product and is seeking to market it overseas), the DOC and SBA offer assistance. Also, check out two additional DOC-managed sites: the International Trade Association (ITA) (www.trade.gov) and Export.gov.
- **The Federation of International Trade Associations** (FITA) website (www.fita.org) offers many links, leads, and statistics that can be helpful for international businesses.
- **The European Patent Office** (www.epo.org) provides links to patent licensing exchanges, mailing lists, patent information providers, registered European patent agents, law offices, and patent offices for member states.
- **EUBusiness** (www.eubusiness.com) is a reliable source of information for facts and statistics on the economy and specific industries within the European Union.

CAUTION
If you are interested in acquiring foreign patent rights, you must act within limited time periods triggered by your U.S. patent filing. For more information on acquiring foreign patent rights, review *Patent It Yourself,* by David Pressman and David E. Blau (Nolo).

Protecting Confidential Information

Confidential Information and Nondisclosure Agreements............................ 156

    Nondisclosure Agreements.. 157

    One-Way Nondisclosure Agreement 160

Proceeding Without an Agreement.. 168

    The Limits of Trade Secret Laws 169

    Disclosing "Around" the Secret 170

    Confidential Relationships Without Written Agreements............................ 170

Waiver Agreements... 170

    Identifying a Waiver Agreement.. 171

    Waivers and Patentable Inventions... 171

When You Have Sufficient Bargaining Power 172

    Indemnification 172

    Injunctions... 172

    Jurisdiction and Choice of Law.. 173

Disclosing to Employees and Contractors 174

Disclosing to an Attorney.. 175

The best way to protect yourself when describing or showing an invention to a prospective licensee is by having a nondisclosure agreement signed before you disclose any secrets. A nondisclosure agreement is a contract in which the parties promise to protect the confidentiality of secret information that is disclosed. For example, if you have a nondisclosure agreement with a company and it uses your secret without authorization, you can sue for damages and can request a court to stop the company from making any further disclosures. Sometimes, however, a prospective licensee is unwilling to sign a nondisclosure agreement and the inventor is placed in a predicament: whether to risk confiding secret information or lose a prospective business opportunity. In this chapter, we discuss the inventor's three choices when making a disclosure:

- provide a written nondisclosure agreement
- provide no agreement, or
- provide a waiver agreement.

Using a nondisclosure agreement, you can prohibit someone from disclosing your secret invention design or from disclosing the trade secrets in your copyrighted software program. In this chapter, we explain the nuances of the various provisions in a standard nondisclosure agreement, and we help you evaluate another company's nondisclosure agreement. We also review situations when a company refuses to sign a confidentiality agreement or asks you to relinquish (waive) any claims of secrecy.

CAUTION

Nondisclosure agreements are often known by other names, such as disclosure agreements and confidentiality agreements. However, the name of the agreement is not as important as the content. Some agreements are titled Disclosure or Confidentiality Agreements yet their terms have the opposite effect. Instead of agreeing to secrecy, the inventor effectively waives any claim of trade secret confidentiality. By signing one of these waiver agreements, you can lose rights that may affect your invention. For example, you might risk disclosing secret information about a pending patent. An explanation of waiver agreements is provided later in this chapter.

Confidential Information and Nondisclosure Agreements

In Chapter 2, we explained that confidential business information that is not known by your competitors can be protected under an area of intellectual property law known as trade secrets. In a sense, trade secrets relate to all forms of intellectual property. In the early stages of development, trademarks, copyrighted designs, and patentable inventions can be confidential business information. Once a patent is published, a trademark is printed, or a copyright is distributed, its secret status will end. But until the information is made public, it has a value because it is your secret.

The best strategy to protect your secret information is by signing a written nondisclosure agreement—a contract in which both parties agree to maintain certain information in confidence. If the agreement is breached (the information is disclosed without your authorization), you can sue for monetary damages.

Brewing Beer and Ale
No. 135,245

Nondisclosure Agreements

The sample agreement provided below includes many provisions that are considered standard. This agreement is designed for a one-way disclosure. You (the disclosing party) are disclosing secrets and the person or company who receives the secrets (the receiving party) is obligated to maintain secrecy. If the company wants to give you confidential information, such as sales information, then you use a mutual (two-way) non-disclosure agreement. It's also possible a prospective licensee might furnish you with its own version of a confidentiality agreement. We discuss how to review a nondisclosure agreement below in "Reviewing Their Nondisclosure Agreement."

 CAUTION
You must protect your confidential information. Although a nondisclosure agreement will ensure your right to sue, it will not guarantee your success in court. You can never rely solely on an agreement as a basis for protection of confidential information. As explained in Chapter 2, you must also be able to prove that you took reasonable steps to protect your secret and the secret has not become known to the public.

Dear Rich:
What If They Won't Sign an NDA?

Dear Rich: I started a product design company and have a design that a company might be interested in licensing. To date, I have not told them specifics about the design, only that it fits into their product line. We're meeting soon and I want to be sure to protect the idea for future patentability (by not making it public as defined by patent law), as well as prevent the company from disclosing the idea to others. I've read that having representatives from the company write a quick entry in my invention notebook to the effect that we're meeting to discuss the idea is legally sufficient to protect patentability and disclosure. I've also been told not to bother with an NDA as most companies will not sign them.

You are correct to be concerned about public disclosures because, as a general rule, a public disclosure can, if made prior to filing a patent application, prevent you from obtaining a patent.*

Disclosing in confidence. To prevent this result, the company must agree your disclosure was made in confidence (and treat it accordingly). It's true that many companies will not sign NDAs, particularly with individuals that they do not know. However, that's usually not the case when the company knows the other party or has

solicited the idea. So, we recommend starting with an NDA.

Signing your book. Signing an entry in your invention notebook may preserve confidentiality provided it includes a statement to the effect that the disclosure is being made in confidence and the company will take necessary steps to preserve the confidentiality of the disclosure. Still, it's not as ideal as an NDA, which may contain provisions for dispute resolution, attorneys' fees, jurisdiction, or injunctive relief.

Authority to bind. Finally, make sure the person signing the NDA or book has the authority to bind the company (include the person's title; be wary of "agents"), and if in doubt, verify the person's authority.

If they won't sign anything. Be wary of companies that won't sign anything. Sometimes companies have a legitimate reason—they don't want to be limited in case they're developing something similar independently—and sometimes they're just using their bargaining power to see what you have without any restrictions. Keep in mind that almost any "publication" that shows how to make and use the invention, or any offer for sale—licenses are not typically considered an offer for sale—will prevent you from seeking a patent. Disclose sparingly in the absence of a confidentiality agreement.

Reviewing Their Nondisclosure Agreement

*If the inventor makes the public disclosure. One exception to the public disclosure rule described above is: If the inventor made the public disclosure, the inventor has up to one year from the date of public disclosure to file a U.S. patent application.

A company may want you to sign their written nondisclosure agreement or modify yours. Generally, it doesn't matter who furnishes the nondisclosure agreement. If a company is willing to enter into a nondisclosure agreement, you're already ahead of the game. If the nondisclosure agreement contains the basic elements to limit disclosure (described below) and your research indicates a sense of trust about the other party, sign the agreement rather than arguing about details. Save your serious negotiations for the licensing contract.

EXAMPLE: In the early 1980s, IBM was considering two different operating system programs for its first personal computer. Bill Gates owned one operating system, and the other was owned by a rival of Mr. Gates. IBM first went to Gates's rival. What followed was a lengthy negotiation about the terms of the nondisclosure agreement involving lawyers for both sides. When the negotiations bogged down, IBM offered the same nondisclosure agreement to Gates, who read it once and signed it. IBM reviewed Gates's program and quickly licensed the DOS program. Out of this relationship, Microsoft was created.

This is not to imply you should blindly sign any nondisclosure agreement. *You shouldn't!* But you *should* avoid lengthy negotiations over disclosure issues, particularly if the agreement contains the minimum elements of protection.

The nondisclosure agreement you will be furnished can vary in format. You should make a copy so that you can mark it up and then identify and label each of the basic elements. Generally, there are five important elements to a nondisclosure agreement:

- a definition of confidential information
- exclusions from confidential information
- obligations of receiving party
- time periods, and
- miscellaneous provisions.

One-Way Nondisclosure Agreement

The sample nondisclosure agreement below provides the minimum level of protection necessary for an inventor. It's possible to draft an agreement that provides stronger protection. You can insert provisions that will provide for legal remedies, such as injunctions (the right to obtain a court order) or personal jurisdiction (the right to force someone to bring or defend against a lawsuit in your geographic area). However, these provisions often raise flags with prospective licensees, who routinely seek to have them removed. If you would like to use these provisions, they are provided below in "When You Have Sufficient Bargaining Power."

Parties and Summary

The introductory "Parties" paragraph defines the parties and indicates which party will disclose information and which will receive it. Some companies will want to give you confidential information, not just receive it. For example, a company might want to disclose marketing or sales information in order to prepare a course of action with your invention. Or, perhaps, a company is unsure whether it intends to disclose confidential information with you but wants to have the option available. In this case, a mutual nondisclosure agreement will be needed. In order to modify the sample agreement to be a mutual agreement, substitute the following title and introductory paragraphs.

Creating a Mutual Nondisclosure Agreement—Optional

> **Parties.** This nondisclosure agreement (the "Agreement") is entered into by and between [*insert your name, business form, and address*] and [*insert name, business form, and address of other person or company with whom you are exchanging information*] (collectively referred to as the "parties") for the purpose of preventing the unauthorized disclosure of Confidential Information (as defined below).
>
> **Summary.** The parties may disclose confidential and proprietary trade secret information to each other for the purpose of exploring a possible business relationship. The parties mutually agree to enter into a confidential relationship with respect to the disclosure by one or each (the "disclosing party") to the other (the "receiving party") of certain proprietary and confidential information (the "Confidential Information").

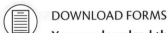

DOWNLOAD FORMS
You can download this form (and all other forms in this book) from this book's companion page on Nolo.com; see the appendix for the link.

Definition of Confidential Information

Every nondisclosure agreement provides a definition of confidential information or trade secrets. The purpose is to establish the boundaries or subject matter of the disclosure. You might be furnished a nondisclosure agreement that defines confidential information by listing the types of confidential information, such as: "Confidential Information includes programming code, financial information, materials or innovative processes, and so on." You can safely sign this type of agreement, provided you can find something on the list that fits your type of disclosure.

Many nondisclosure agreements include an obligation to certify the confidentiality of the disclosure (for example, by stamping it "confidential"). In some nondisclosure agreements, an oral disclosure will only be protected when confirmed with a follow-up letter such as the one shown below.

Notice that the actual trade secret is not disclosed in the letter. The inventor has described the disclosure without revealing anything proprietary. In some cases, the nondisclosure agreement may not permit oral disclosures.

Dear Sam:

Today at lunch, I disclosed information to you about my kaleidoscopic projection system (specifically, the manner in which I have configured and wired the bulbs in the device). That information is confidential (as described in our nondisclosure agreement) and this letter is intended to confirm the disclosure.

William Smith

William Smith

CAUTION

Whatever you disclose (or is disclosed to you) should be noted in your business file, along with the dates of disclosure and to whom the disclosure was made.

Human-Powered Device With Removable Flywheel Power Unit

No. 6.983,948

One-Way Nondisclosure Agreement

Parties

This nondisclosure agreement (the "Agreement") is entered into by and between [*insert your name, business form, and address*] ("disclosing party") and [*insert name, business form, and address of person or company to whom you will disclose information*] ("receiving party") for the purpose of preventing the unauthorized disclosure of Confidential Information (as defined below).

Summary

Disclosing party may disclose confidential and proprietary trade secret information to receiving party. The parties mutually agree to enter into a confidential relationship with respect to the disclosure of certain proprietary and confidential information (the "Confidential Information").

Definition of Confidential Information (Written or Oral)

For purposes of this Agreement, "Confidential Information" shall include all information or material that has or could have commercial value or other utility in the business in which disclosing party is engaged. In the event that Confidential Information is in written form, the disclosing party shall label or stamp the materials with the word "Confidential" or some similar warning. In the event that Confidential Material is transmitted orally, the disclosing party shall promptly provide a writing indicating that such oral communication constituted Confidential Information.

Exclusions From Confidential Information

Receiving party's obligations under this Agreement shall not extend to information that is: (a) publicly known at the time of disclosure under this Agreement or subsequently becomes publicly known through no fault of the receiving party; (b) discovered or created by the receiving party prior to the time of disclosure by disclosing party; or (c) otherwise learned by the receiving party through legitimate means other than from the disclosing party or anyone connected with the disclosing party.

Obligations of Receiving Party

The receiving party shall hold and maintain the Confidential Information of the other party in strictest confidence for the sole and exclusive benefit of the disclosing party. The receiving party shall carefully restrict access to any such Confidential Information to persons bound by this Agreement, only on a need-to-know basis. The receiving party shall not, without prior written approval of the disclosing party, use for the receiving party's own benefit, publish, copy, or otherwise disclose to others, or permit the use by others for their benefit or to the detriment of the disclosing party any of the Confidential Information. The receiving party shall return to disclosing party any and all records, notes, and other written, printed, or tangible materials in its possession pertaining to the Confidential Information immediately on the written request of disclosing party.

Time Periods

The nondisclosure and confidentiality provisions of this Agreement shall survive the termination of any relationship between the disclosing party and the receiving party.

Miscellaneous

Nothing contained in this Agreement shall be deemed to constitute either party a partner, joint venturer, or employee of the other party for any purpose. This Agreement may not be amended except in a writing signed by both parties. If a court finds any provision of this Agreement invalid or unenforceable as applied to any circumstance, the remainder of this Agreement shall be interpreted so as best to effect the intent of the parties. This Agreement shall be governed by and interpreted in accordance with the laws of the State of [*insert your state of residence*]. Any controversy or claim arising out of or relating to this Agreement, or the breach of this Agreement, shall be settled by arbitration in accordance with the rules of the American Arbitration Association, and judgment upon the award rendered by the arbitrator(s) may be entered in any court having jurisdiction. The prevailing party shall have the right to collect from the other party its reasonable costs and attorneys' fees incurred in enforcing this agreement. Any such arbitration hearing shall include a written transcript of the proceedings and a written explanation for any final determination. This Agreement expresses the complete understanding of the parties with respect to the subject matter and supersedes all prior proposals, agreements, representations, and understandings. This Agreement and each party's obligations shall be binding on the representatives, assigns, and successors of such party. Each party has signed this Agreement through its authorized representative.

DISCLOSING PARTY:

[*Business name*]

_____   _____
Signature   Date

_____
Disclosing Party's Name

RECEIVING PARTY:

[*Business name*]

_____   _____
Signature   Date

_____
Receiving Party's Name/Title

Exclusions From Confidential Information

Every nondisclosure agreement excludes some information from protection. That is, the receiving party has no obligation to protect certain information. These exceptions are based upon established principles of law—the most important one being that information is not protected if it was created or discovered by the licensee prior to (or independent of) any involvement with you. For instance, say a prospective licensee develops an invention with similar trade secret information before learning about your secrets. Under the law, the company is free to use its independently created invention. While this seems fair, some companies go further when excluding information. They might request the right to exclude information that is independently developed after the disclosure. In this situation, a company doesn't want to be prohibited from independently developing similar trade secrets after learning your secrets.

If you can avoid this provision, great. But it's not quite as frightening as it might seem. The fact is, under most state laws, the prospective licensee has the right to independently develop a similar product after exposure to your trade secret. The prospective licensee only violates the law if it improperly uses your secret to develop its product. It's possible, for instance, that one division of a large company could invent something without any contact with the division that has been exposed to your secret. However, if a company comes out with a competing product soon after you disclosed your trade secret to them, it might be difficult for you to believe that the company's creation was independent.

Common sense (or a natural suspicion of business practices) would lead you to believe that the company stole your secret. How do you prove it?

That's the real issue with excluding information developed after the disclosure: proof of independent development. How do you prove your secret was (or was not) used improperly in a company's product? How does the company prove that the product was developed independently? The best you can do is to document your exchange of information and have proof that you used reasonable standards to protect the information. The rest is in the hands of your attorney, who will apply legal standards of proof.

Nondisclosure agreements commonly exclude information that is in the public domain. This public domain exclusion is based on the principle that no party should have a monopoly over publicly known information, but this type of provision has a downside. A company could sign a nondisclosure agreement, use a submitted idea without permission, and when sued, conduct an extensive prior art patent search to locate a patent that is similar to the idea. Even though the company did not rely on the prior art patent, the published patents qualify as public domain information. A defense such as this was successfully used by a toy company accused of violating a non-disclosure agreement. (*Kublan v. Hasbro Toy Division*, 50 U.S.P.Q.2d 1539 (S.D. N.Y. 1999).) The only means of avoiding such a defense is for the inventor to conduct a prior art search, list any patents relating to the disclosure, and modify the exclusion statement in the section regarding public domain material as shown below (the added material is in bold type).

Exclusions From Confidential Information
Receiving party's obligations under this Agreement shall not extend to information that is: (a) publicly known at the time of disclosure under this Agreement or subsequently becomes publicly known through no fault of the receiving party, **excluding information contained in pending or issued patents other than those patents listed in Exhibit A: [*list of prior art patents would then be attached to the agreement in an Exhibit A*]**; (b) ...

Obligations of the Receiving Party

The receiving party generally must hold and maintain the information in confidence and limit its use. Under most state laws, the receiving party cannot breach the confidential relationship, induce others to breach it, or induce others to acquire the secret by improper means. Most companies will accept these contract obligations without discussion. If you enter into a mutual nondisclosure agreement, you should also feel comfortable with these requirements.

Time Periods

The sample agreement does not contain a time limit for how long the secret must be kept confidential. Some agreements require that the receiving party maintain the secret information for a limited number of years. For example, the receiving party must not use or disclose the secret for a period of five years from the date the agreement was executed. The time period is often an issue of negotiation. Disclosing parties want an open period with no limits; receiving parties want a short period. Five years tends to be a common length in American nondisclosure agreements (although many companies insist on two or three years). In European nondisclosure agreements, it's not unusual for the period to be as long as ten years. Ultimately, the length you decide to use will depend on the relative bargaining power of the parties.

One factor you might consider when determining the length of a nondisclosure agreement is the shelf life of your idea. Ask the following questions:

- How long will it be before others stumble upon the same innovation?
- If the product were licensed in the next year or two, how long would it be before the secret was reverse engineered? (See Chapter 2 for an explanation of reverse engineering.)

If the answer to these questions is a few years, you are unlikely to be damaged by a shorter (two- to three-year) period.

Miscellaneous

Miscellaneous provisions (sometimes known as "boilerplate") are included at the end of every agreement. The miscellaneous provisions provided at the end of our sample agreement are standard and often used without question in most licensing agreements. Even though they are standard, each element is important. Before striking or adding language to the Miscellaneous section, you should review the discussion on boilerplate provisions in Chapter 14.

Signing the Agreement

Each party must sign the agreement in relation to the business that is represented (for example, as a general partner representing the partnership), and each party must have the authority to sign

the agreement. To further reinforce this, you will note the language in the sample agreement: "Each party has signed this Agreement through its authorized representative." Use the following rules when determining the proper signature line.

Sole proprietorship. If you or the other party are a sole proprietorship, simply sign your own name. If you have a fictitious business name (sometimes known as a dba), then list the name of the business above the signature line. For example, Tom Stein is a sole proprietor calling his business Eine Stein Inventions. He would sign as follows.

Eine Stein Inventions

By: _____
      Tom Stein

Partnership. If you or the other party are a general or limited partnership, the only person authorized to sign the agreement is a general partner or someone who has written authority from a general partner (usually in the form a partnership resolution). The name of the partnership must be mentioned above the signature line, or the partnership will not be bound (only the person signing the agreement will). Cindy Barrett is a general partner in Reality Manufacturing Partnership. She would sign as follows.

Reality Manufacturing Partnership

By: _____
      Cindy Barrett, a general partner

Corporation or LLC. If you or the other party are a corporation or limited liability company (LLC), only a person authorized by the corporation or LLC can sign the agreement. The president or chief executive officer (CEO) usually has such power, but not every officer of a corporation has the authority to bind the corporation. When in doubt, ask for written proof of the authority. This proof is usually in the form of a corporate resolution. The name of the corporation should be mentioned above the signature line, or the corporation may not be bound (only the person signing the agreement will). For example, Marya DeRosa is CEO of Sincere Marketing. She would sign as follows.

Sincere Marketing, Inc., a New York corporation

By: _____
      Marya DeRosa, CEO

Note: If you have reason to question the credibility of the company representative, investigate the company. (See Chapter 6.)

If you have doubts about the person's authority, don't proceed until you are satisfied that the person has full authority to represent the company.

Proceeding Without an Agreement

We advise you to get a prospective licensee to sign a nondisclosure agreement, but we are also aware of business realities. Many prospective licensees refuse to sign an unknown inventor's nondisclosure agreement. If you disclose without the agreement, you risk losing the secret, which could have a devastating effect. If you don't disclose the information, you risk losing a business opportunity.

Probably the most important factor to consider when deciding whether to proceed without an agreement is the reputation of the prospective licensee. If the company has a poor reputation, the dangers of losing your secrets outweigh the business opportunity. You can research the company using techniques discussed in Chapter 6.

Although a nondisclosure agreement provides the best form of protection, there are methods of guarding your rights in the absence of an agreement. We discuss some of these methods below.

The Limits of Trade Secret Laws

The Defend Trade Secrets Act (DTSA), signed into law on May 11, 2016, "federalizes" trade secret law by providing a procedure for trade secret owners to file civil lawsuits in federal court. The DTSA applies if the trade secret is "related to a product or service used in, or intended for use in, interstate or foreign commerce." Prior to the DTSA, trade secret owners could only bring civil lawsuits in state courts, under state laws based on the Uniform Trade Secrets Act (UTSA). (Except for New York, every state has adopted some version of the UTSA.) In many important ways the DTSA and state laws based on the UTSA are similar. However, you should not rely solely on federal and state laws to protect you for product disclosures. Without an NDA in place, the potential licensee has no obligation to maintain secrecy. These state laws only protect against the misappropriation of a trade secret. Misappropriation is:

- the acquisition of a trade secret by a person who has reason to know that the trade secret was obtained by improper means
- the unauthorized disclosure or use of a trade secret by a person who had a duty to maintain secrecy, or

- the disclosure or use of a trade secret by a person who used improper means to acquire it.

"Improper means" refers to unethical methods, such as deliberate theft, burglary, industrial espionage, or knowingly obtaining the secret from someone who has a duty not to disclose the information. If you voluntarily disclose your secrets to a prospective licensee, that would not be an improper means of acquiring the information, and state laws will not be helpful.

Most Companies Will Not Steal Your Secret

One study of trade secret cases determined that trade secret owners prevailed in 75% of the cases—poor odds for parties planning to steal. Most companies don't want to risk a lawsuit when the trade secrets can be acquired through a license. Since royalties and advances amount to a small portion of the overall costs, it is less expensive to license the work legitimately than risk litigation. In addition, the company may want more golden eggs from the inventor. For these reasons, companies generally play fairly. Still, you must investigate a company's reputation before making a disclosure without an agreement.

Disclosing "Around" the Secret

A licensee is primarily concerned with two questions about your invention: (a) What does it do? and (b) Is it profitable? Try to determine if you can present your invention and provide an estimate of its costs in a way that doesn't disclose any trade secrets. (As discussed in Chapter 1, this cost analysis is often more crucial to your licensing ability than the invention itself.) If you can provide the licensee with this limited information, the licensee might agree to enter into a nondisclosure agreement to learn more about the invention.

Confidential Relationships Without Written Agreements

A confidential relationship can, in some cases, be established without a signed agreement. An implied confidential relationship occurs when the conduct of the parties indicates they intended to create a confidential relationship. In an implied confidential relationship, you have legal rights similar to those created by a written agreement. A confidential relationship can be implied if certain factors are present:

- The prospective licensee solicited the idea from you—that is, you did not send the information without prompting.
- You indicated that the invention was a business proposition—you hoped for payment.

- At the time of disclosure, you requested that the information be kept secret.
- The information is a trade secret—it has commercial value and is not known by competitors.

Although a confidential relationship can be implied, it's difficult to prove. In one case, an inventor developed a ratchet by combining parts of two existing tools and brought it to the attention of an independent dealer for the Snap-On Tools company. Later, the inventor submitted a tool suggestion form to Snap-On's corporate headquarters. The inventor never requested confidentiality and never indicated that he expected compensation for his idea. Snap-On manufactured and sold the ratchet without paying the inventor. The inventor sued, but the court ruled against him because he disclosed the information without stating that it was a business proposition in which he hoped for payment.

Waiver Agreements

Some companies are wary of reviewing an unknown inventor's information. In addition to lawsuits, a company might be developing a similar product and is concerned a confidential relationship could preclude the company from proceeding with its own research and development. Not only won't the company sign a nondisclosure agreement, but it might require the inventor to waive (give up) all claims of confidentiality before it will even look at the invention. This waiver is accomplished by having the inventor sign a written waiver agreement.

Waiver agreements, needless to say, can be dangerous. Since trade secret protection is based upon confidentiality, your waiver could result in the loss of trade secret rights, and you will have no legal recourse. This section offers advice on how to identify and deal with waiver agreements.

Identifying a Waiver Agreement

A waiver agreement usually contains the following language:

- "This agreement does not create a confidential relationship."
- "No confidential relationship is established or implied by the exchange (or disclosure) of information (or submission)."
- "The exchange (or disclosure) of information (or submission) is not made in confidence."
- "No obligation of any kind is created (or assumed or implied or imputed) by the receipt (or exchange or disclosure) of information (or submission)."

Waivers and Patentable Inventions

If the only secrets you had were in a pending patent application and you were certain the patent would issue, signing a waiver would not be as risky. Why? Because once the patent issues, your secrets would be public and protected under patent law. The fact that you waive confidentiality would not matter. However, there are still considerable risks to this approach:

- Even if a patent is issued, additional aspects of your patented device or process might be protected only by trade secrets.
- You might devise improvements which, until patented, would only be protected by trade secret law. In such cases, only a confidential relationship will protect your trade secrets.
- If the patent is pending (remember the patent application process can take 18 months to two years), you could face a trade secrecy problem if you sign a waiver and ultimately don't get the patent.
- Trademarks (names for your products) will have no effective protection until they are distributed to the public. Therefore, if you disclose a clever trademark name or logo, it would not be protected.

The decision whether to sign a waiver agreement should be made using the risk analysis described above. You'll need to weigh the risk of losing the business opportunity against the risk of losing trade secret rights.

When You Have Sufficient Bargaining Power

Normally, an inventor has little bargaining power and cannot control whether a prospective licensee signs a nondisclosure agreement. The three scenarios described above (written agreement, no agreement, and waiver agreement) reflect this lack of bargaining power. However, in some cases, you might have sufficient bargaining power to control the content of an agreement. In that case, you can consider strengthening your confidentiality agreement with the following additional provisions.

Indemnification

Some inventors seek to add an obligation —that the receiving party will pay for all damages (lost profits, attorneys' fees, or other expenses) incurred as a result of the receiving party's breach of the nondisclosure agreement. This obligation is known as indemnification and is discussed in Chapter 12. Leaving out the indemnity provision does not prevent you from collecting damages for a breach (contract law holds the

receiving party responsible for a breach); however, the clause makes it easier to claim damages. To include indemnity in your nondisclosure agreement, add the following language at the end of the Obligations section.

> The receiving party shall take all necessary action to protect the confidentiality of the Confidential Information and agrees to indemnify the disclosing party against any and all losses, damages, claims, or expenses incurred or suffered by the disclosing party as a result of the receiving party's breach of this Agreement.

Injunctions

An injunction is a court order directing a person to do (or stop doing) something. In the case of trade secrets, it would be a court order directing the company to stop using your secrets. Normally, as the inventor seeking the injunction, you must be able to demonstrate that you have suffered or will suffer an irreparable harm as a result of a company's using your secrets.

Proving these issues in court is expensive and time-consuming. In order to cut through some of that legal work, some nondisclosure agreements include a provision similar to the one below. This provision is an admission by the receiving party that the harm caused by a breach is irreparable. With this provision, you will have less to prove if and when you seek a court order. This provision only enhances your ability to obtain an injunction; by itself, it will not compel a judge to order an injunction.

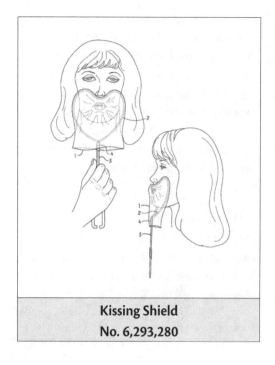

**Kissing Shield
No. 6,293,280**

Injunctive Relief. The receiving party understands and acknowledges that any disclosure or misappropriation of any of the Confidential Information in violation of this Agreement may cause the disclosing party irreparable harm, the amount of which may be difficult to ascertain. Therefore, the receiving party agrees that the disclosing party shall have the right to apply to a court of competent jurisdiction for an order restraining and enjoining any such further disclosure or misappropriation and for such other relief as the disclosing party shall deem appropriate. Such right of the disclosing party is to be in addition to the remedies otherwise available to disclosing party at law or in equity.

Jurisdiction and Choice of Law

In Chapter 14, we provide background on jurisdiction and choice of law. As we explain in that chapter, choice of law refers to what law will be applied if the matter is litigated or arbitrated. For example, if the agreement states, "This Agreement shall be governed in accordance with the laws of the State of California," then California law will apply even if a lawsuit is filed in Virginia. Generally, we recommend that the choice of law be the law of your state of residence.

Jurisdiction is different from the choice of law. Jurisdiction—also called forum or venue—refers to the place where you must go to argue the dispute. We advise against being dragged to a distant location to litigate or arbitrate disputes. Distance increases the cost of litigating and defending a lawsuit, and the cost might be enough prevent you from bringing a lawsuit or greatly harm your ability to defend one. If your bargaining power permits it, you should seek to have choice of jurisdiction in your state and county of residence. Below is a sample provision.

Jurisdiction. The parties consent to the exclusive jurisdiction of the state courts and federal courts located in [*insert your county of residence*] County, [*insert your state of residence*], in any action arising out of or relating to this Agreement, and waive any other venue to which they might be entitled by domicile or otherwise.

If the nondisclosure agreement doesn't mention jurisdiction, it will be determined by state laws. In such a case, the first person to file a lawsuit generally determines jurisdiction.

Disclosing to Employees and Contractors

If you're paying an employee or an independent contractor for services, you should be concerned about confidentiality and require them to sign nondisclosure agreements. Fortunately, you still have substantial protection under state trade secret laws, if you fail to obtain a nondisclosure agreement with an employee.

Because state trade secret laws were drafted primarily to protect employers, they don't protect you as well when

New Provision for Employee/Contractor NDAs

Under the Defend Trade Secrets Act (DTSA), employers are now advised to include a notice of immunity (intended to protect whistleblowers) "in any contract or agreement with an employee that governs the use of a trade secret or other confidential information." (The notice should also be included in agreements for independent contractors as well.) The failure to include the provision does not prevent filing in federal court under the DTSA. But an employer who fails to include the provision is prohibited from recovering exemplary (double) damages and attorneys' fees from the employee or IC. A sample provision would include the following language:

Notice of Immunity from Liability. An individual shall not be held criminally or civilly liable under any federal or state trade secret law for the disclosure of a trade secret that is made (i) in confidence to a federal, state, or local government official, either directly or indirectly, or to an attorney; and (ii) solely for the purpose of reporting or investigating a suspected violation of law; or is made in a complaint or other document filed in a lawsuit or other proceeding, if such filing is made under seal. An individual who files a lawsuit for retaliation by an employer for reporting a suspected violation of law may disclose the trade secret to the attorney of the individual and use the trade secret information in the court proceeding, if the individual (i) files any document containing the trade secret under seal; and (ii) does not disclose the trade secret, except pursuant to court order.

working with independent contractors (for example, consultants, agents, vendors, or manufacturers). So, be sure to sign a nondisclosure agreement if you will disclose secrets to an independent contractor. For more information about service agreements, see Chapter 15.

Disclosing to an Attorney

When you retain the services of an attorney, a privileged relationship is created. The attorney cannot divulge information given in confidence. The attorney can only disclose information you've shared with your consent or under special circumstances, such as a court order. This confidential relationship (attorney/client privilege) also applies to employees and agents of an attorney. You should observe the following guidelines regarding attorney/client relationships:

- Disclosures to an attorney are only protected when made in confidence. For example, public disclosures (in a diner or a ballpark) that could be overheard might not be protected.
- The attorney/client privilege only applies to *your* attorney—the attorney you have retained. A casual discussion with another attorney (sometimes known as "street corner advice") will usually not set the privilege in motion.

The Key Elements of Your Agreement

From Handshake to License 178

Identifying the Parties 179

    Statement of Parties 180

    How to Include Agents in Your Agreement 180

Describing Your Invention and the Licensed Products 180

    Defining the Invention 181

    Defining Licensed Products 184

Specifying Which Rights Are Granted 185

    Grant of (Intellectual Property) Rights 186

    Reservation of Rights 188

    Sublicenses 191

Defining the Territory 192

Setting the Length (Term) of the Agreement 194

    Commencement of Term 195

    Right to Terminate a License 196

    Licensing Terms for Patents 196

    Fixed Terms and Renewals 197

Once you find a company interested in licensing your invention, you and the prospective licensee must agree on a number of essential business issues. This chapter (and the next) will walk you through the basic foundations of the contract. You should read this chapter if you answer "yes" to any of the following questions:

- Do you need to better understand the difference between your invention and the licensed product?
- Do you need help determining the sort of license that best suits your invention?
- Do you need an explanation of the difference between an exclusive or a nonexclusive license?
- Do you need help in deciding the territory or length of your license agreement?

From Handshake to License

License agreements usually develop in two stages. First, the parties—the licensor and the licensee—negotiate the essential elements of the agreement (sometimes referred to as the "business terms"; see "The Term, Business Terms, and Term Sheets," below). These basic elements provide the foundation of a license and they include:

- identification of the parties
- a description of the invention

- a description of the licensee's products containing the invention
- the rights granted by the license
- how long the license will last
- whether or not it will be exclusive
- what territory it will cover
- how much and at what intervals you will get paid, and
- provisions for dispute resolution.

After agreeing on these basic elements, the parties incorporate this information into a more detailed written agreement. A licensee may refer to this second stage as "turning it over to the lawyers," because the licensee's lawyer becomes involved in revising or drafting the agreement. During this second stage, the parties may negotiate over a wide range of contract provisions, such as posttermination rights, warranties, or indemnity (discussed in Chapters 12 and 13).

The Term, Business Terms, and Term Sheets

Although we have tried to avoid confusion, you should be aware that the word "term" can have different meanings in a license agreement. The basic contract elements are often referred to as the "business terms," and the sheet that contains these business elements is sometimes referred to as a "term sheet." The length of the agreement is also referred to as the "term."

If We Don't Get It Right, Can We Change the Agreement Later?

We urge you to work toward creating a final licensing agreement. It's true that if both parties agree to do so, you can amend contract terms and definitions after the contract is signed. However, it's not always easy to agree on alterations once the product is licensed and sales have begun. In addition, amendments and modifications are time-consuming. Concentrate on getting the agreement right before you sign it, and use amendments only if necessary.

Both stages of contract negotiation are important. Don't assume the deal is done just because you've agreed upon the essential business terms.

In order to assist you in your negotiation, we've prepared a worksheet that includes each of the essential elements of your license agreement. It is located at the end of this chapter. This worksheet can be converted into an exhibit (a separate document attached to the agreement). For example, see the exhibit for a sample license agreement discussed in Chapter 11.

Identifying the Parties

Perhaps the most basic element of your licensing agreement is identifying the people or businesses that are entering into the agreement, otherwise known as the parties. The parties are the people signing the agreement—you (the licensor), the licensee, and an agent (if there is one)—who must abide by its terms. The parties should always be identified at the beginning of the agreement by name, the business form, and the business address. If you are not sure of your business form (sole proprietorship, partnership, or corporation), you should review Chapter 4.

Check out the business cards you received from the licensee. They should provide you with information about the entity that is licensing the invention. If you are licensing to a company that is owned by another, ask which party will sign the agreement. Sometimes the parent company—the company that owns the other—signs the licensing agreement. If the licensee is incorporated, find out in which state it incorporated.

It's fairly simple to determine the parties, so this essential element does not require much discussion. Because the license agreement refers to the parties many times, they are sometimes referred to as Licensee and Licensor or given abbreviated names. For example, you can refer to a licensee named Medco Affiliated Industries, Inc., as MEDCO. Like most defined elements of the license, these names are capitalized throughout the agreement for easy reference.

Statement of Parties

You'll usually find information about the parties in the first paragraph of the agreement. A sample is provided below.

> This License Agreement (the "Agreement") is made between Joe Smith, a sole proprietor, of 34 Westwood Ave., Rolling Brook, New Mexico (referred to as "Licensor") and Flameco International Products, Inc., a California corporation with its principal address at 4356 Industrial Drive, Collingswood, California (referred to as "Licensee"). Licensor and Licensee shall be collectively referred to as "the parties."

> This License Agreement (the "Agreement") is made among Joe Smith, a sole proprietor, of 34 Westwood Ave., Rolling Brook, New Mexico (referred to as "Licensor"); Licensor's agent, Frances Representatives, a New Jersey corporation with its principal place of business at 27 Lodisco Drive, Burlinghead, Nevada (referred to as "Licensor's Agent"); and Flameco International Products, Inc., a California corporation with its principal address at 4356 Industrial Drive, Collingswood, California (referred to as "Licensee"). Licensor, Licensee, and Agent shall be collectively referred to as "the parties."

How to Include Agents in Your Agreement

If there is an agent, the agent may or may not be a party to the agreement. (A "party" is named in the first paragraph, signs the agreement, and is bound by the provisions.) Many agents want to be a party in order to obtain their payments directly from the licensee. Generally, we recommend that the agent become a party, because the agent should be bound by the contract, particularly the dispute resolution procedures. In addition, if the agent signs as a party, then both you and the agent can sue for recovery of royalty payments. A sample provision to include an agent is provided below.

Describing Your Invention and the Licensed Products

Although it might seem obvious, two essential elements of your agreement are: (1) specifying exactly what invention you are licensing and (2) defining the products or processes in which the licensee will use your invention. In other words, don't assume that there's anything self-evident about what the invention is or how the licensee will use it.

It's important that you understand the difference between your invention and the licensed products. As you discuss the product or process that will form the basis for the licensing agreement, you and the licensor will refer to two versions of your invention. One is the invention as you created or patented it. The other is the invention as the licensee will sell it, which is usually referred to as the licensed product. In other words, your invention goes in one door and a licensed product (or products) comes out the other. The licensed product is your invention as packaged or modified by the licensee. Both versions of the invention—as you created it and as it is sold—require separate names (for example, "Property" and "Licensed Products"), because your payments are based upon sales of the licensed product.

> **CAUTION**
>
> **Do not underestimate the importance of these definitions.** Both definitions will have an impact on the license agreement. The definition of your invention explains what the licensee is getting from you. The definition of licensed products describes what the licensee is doing with your invention and affects how you are paid.

Defining the Invention

As part of your agreement, you and the licensee will need to agree upon a definition of your invention. It may seem obvious—it's your invention. But you will need to write a succinct statement of what you are licensing and agree on that definition, because it will be incorporated into the definition of the licensed product. Definitions of inventions are usually labeled or abbreviated with a term such as the "Invention," "Property," "Licensed Patents," "Process," "Technical Information," or "Intellectual Property."

Below are some suggestions for creating a definition of your invention. Use the suggestions that apply to your situation.

You Have a Patent or Pending Patent Application

If you have a patent or have applied for one, you should define your invention based upon your patent claims and include a copy of the patent (or the claims listed in your application) with the final agreement. For example, you could use one of the following clauses.

Interactive Toy
No. 6,253,058

Patent Issued

The "Property" refers to the invention(s) described in U.S. Patent No(s). [*insert patent number(s)*].

Patent Not Yet Issued

The "Property" refers to the invention(s) described in U.S. Patent Application No(s). [*insert patent application number(s)*], a copy of which is/are attached to this Agreement.

If the licensee wants to acquire more rights to your invention, such as improvements on your patent or foreign patent rights, you'll likely need a more detailed definition, as shown in this example.

Patents and Improvements

The "Property" is defined as the invention(s) described in U.S. Patent No(s). [*insert patent number(s)*] and any improvements, reissues, or extensions, as well as any continuations, divisions, or substitute U.S. patent applications that shall be based on U.S. Patent No(s). [*insert patent number(s) (same number(s) as above)*]; and any patent applications corresponding to the above-described patents and patent applications that are issued, filed, or to be filed in any and all foreign countries.

The term "improvements" might need its own definition, because some inventors may not want to permit a licensee to use every improvement that results from a patent. For example, if you only wanted the licensee to obtain rights to improvements that reduced the production cost, you could state that an improvement is defined as "any modification or method that reduces the production cost of the Licensed Product." By limiting the definition of improvements, the licensee only obtains rights to the improvements that fall within the definition. However, before you make a decision about improvements, read the section "Improvements by the Licensee: Grant Backs," in Chapter 15. Remember, the definitions often define the scope of your license.

**Vehicle Direction Signal
No. 4,556,862**

You Don't Have a Patent

In the case of a nonpatented invention, the definition of the invention should describe it and indicate the proprietary rights that you have acquired. For an explanation of proprietary rights, review Chapter 2. The description of the invention should specify what it looks like, what it is, and what it does, as shown in this example.

Copyrights, Trade Secrets, and Trademarks: No Patents

The "Property" refers to all proprietary rights, including, but not limited to, copyrights, trade secrets, formulas, research data, know-how, and specifications related to the invention commonly known as the [*name of invention*], as well as any trademark rights and associated goodwill. A more complete description is provided in the attached [*Exhibit A, for example*].

You Have a Copyright Registration for Your Invention

If you have a copyright registration for some aspect of your invention, you should make reference to that registration by number and date. Chapter 2 provides information about copyrights. You can use the same provision as for nonpatent proprietary rights with the following modification to the first sentence.

Copyright Issues

The "Property" refers to all proprietary rights, including, but not limited to, copyrights as embodied in Copyright Registration No. _____ dated _____ ; trade secrets; formulas; research data ....

Trademark Rights

If you've acquired trademark rights, the licensee would want the right to use the mark. For a registered trademark, you should make reference to the registration by number and date. To incorporate these provisions, just modify the first portion of the nonpatents proprietary rights as shown below.

Trademark Rights Registered

The "Property" refers to all proprietary rights, including, but not limited to, copyrights, trade secrets, formulas, research data, know-how, and specifications related to the invention commonly known as the [*name of invention*], as well as all trademark rights and goodwill associated with the Federal Trademark Registration Number _____ dated _____ . A more complete description is provided in the attached [*Exhibit*   ].

See Chapter 2 for more information about trademark rights

Your Invention Has Patented and Nonpatented (but Protectable) Features

If you have a patent on some features of your invention and other features are protected by trade secret or copyright law, the definition of your invention would be a combination of the two definitions above.

Ball-Throwing Apparatus No. 6,076,829

Patents, Copyrights, Trade Secrets, and Trademarks

The "Property" refers to all inventions described in U.S. Patent No. [*insert patent number*], and to all other proprietary rights, including, but not limited to, copyrights, trade secrets, formulas, research data, know-how, and specifications related to the invention commonly known as [*name of invention*], as well as any trademark rights and associated goodwill. A more complete description is provided in the attached [*Exhibit ___*].

Defining Licensed Products

The licensed products are the products sold by the licensee that incorporate your invention. For example, say you patented a device that can clean the submerged portion of a ship's hull. You license the invention to a swimming pool supply company. They sell your invention incorporated in a product called Aqua Buddy that can clean the bottom of swimming pools. Aqua Buddy would be the licensed product.

As we explained above, the definition of licensed products could affect how much money you make. Royalties are usually tied to the sales of licensed products. That is, you only receive payment for the sales of licensed products. For example, consider an agreement in which licensed products are defined as "any products in which the Property is the primary component." Your invention, a new type of hair comb, is incorporated into a three-way product that includes a brush, comb, and curling iron. You might not receive a royalty for sales of this three-way product, because your invention is not the primary component.

How do you decide on a definition for licensed products? The simplest method is to state that a licensed product is "any product that incorporates the Property." If the licensee incorporates several inventions into one product, you can suggest creating a category of "Combination Products" with a separate royalty rate. In Chapter 9, we discuss how royalty rates can be set for different types of products.

When you define licensed products, you should refer to the invention as previously defined, as shown in the following examples.

Specific Listing of Licensed Products

> Licensed Products are defined as those Licensee products incorporating the Property and more specifically described in [*Exhibit A (the "Licensed Products")*].

No Limitations on Licensed Products

> Licensed Products are defined as any products sold by the licensee that incorporate the Property.

If you are licensing a process and not a product, you will need to determine which uses of your invention (rather than products) will be counted as licensed processes. As with products, you should refer to the invented process (normally called "Process") when defining the licensed processes. For example, say you are licensing a method of filtering gasoline. You can define Licensed Process as follows.

No Limitations on Licensed Process

> A Licensed Process is any commercial application of the Process by Licensee. [*Change all references in the agreement to Licensed Process, rather than Licensed Products.*]

Royalties can be tied to use of the process rather than the sale of products. See Chapter 9 for more information on use royalties.

Specifying Which Rights Are Granted

The heart of the license agreement—known as the grant—sets out the rights that you, as the licensor, are transferring to the licensee. This essential term of your licensing agreement conveys and sets limits on the licensee's right to make and sell your invention. A grant deals with the following:

- **Grant of (intellectual property) rights.** The grant describes the intellectual property rights transferred to the licensee in the license, for example, the right to manufacture the patented invention. The grant also establishes whether the license is exclusive or nonexclusive. If it is exclusive, then only the licensee can have the rights conveyed in the grant provision.
- **Reservation of rights.** The grant may also describe the intellectual property rights you are not giving; for example, you reserve all rights to license the invention to medical supply companies.
- **Sublicense.** A grant to sublicense allows a licensee to license its rights to other companies.

Each aspect of the grant is discussed below.

Grant of (Intellectual Property) Rights

As we explained in Chapters 1 and 2, you don't license the invention itself, you license the intellectual property rights associated with your invention. These rights are conveyed or transferred in the grant section. If your invention is patented, for example, you convey the right to make, sell, or use the invention (the rights that come with a patent) as

used and incorporated within the licensed products. If you have a copyright, you can convey the right to copy and sell your copyrighted material. You must also determine whether the license is exclusive or nonexclusive.

Exclusive or Nonexclusive?

Among the most important issues that a prospective licensor faces is whether to grant exclusive or nonexclusive rights.

Exclusive means that only the licensee can have the rights granted in the agreement. A licensee often wants exclusive rights because that prevents a competitor from intruding on the licensee's market. More often than not, the licensor's decision on this issue will be based on:

- the willingness of a prospective licensee to take a nonexclusive license (many won't), and
- the amount that the licensee is willing to pay for an exclusive as opposed to a nonexclusive right.

As a general rule, when you grant exclusive rights, you are giving up your opportunity to license your invention to another company. Whenever you see (or use) the term exclusive, review the language carefully.

To make a license exclusive or non-exclusive, the magic words exclusive or nonexclusive are simply inserted within the grant. See the following example.

> Licensor grants to Licensee an [*exclusive or nonexclusive*] license to make, use, or sell the Property.

In the following sections, we will explain how you can limit exclusive licensing rights. Meaning, you can grant an exclusive right to license while still placing some restrictions on the exclusivity. These limitations fall into four areas:

- time (length of the exclusive arrangement)
- scope (the right to make, use, or sell)
- geographic area (the territory of exclusivity), or
- industry (exclusive only as to a particular industry).

For example, say you want to enter into an exclusive license of your brush product for one year with a company in the "dental care products and supply industry." And you want to limit this exclusive license to sales (not manufacturing) in North America. If you defined your grant accordingly, you would be free to (1) license all rights to anyone after one year, (2) license the right to sell to any non-North American dental supply companies immediately, (3) license rights to any companies for nondental supply uses immediately, and (4) license manufacturing rights (not sales) to any companies immediately.

What Rights Are Granted?

Usually the licensee wants every right you possess. For that reason, the licensee (or licensee's attorney) might propose a long list of rights to be conveyed in the grant, such as the right to sell, distribute, manufacture, modify, and so on. You should primarily be concerned if this list of rights also conveys ownership. At that point, you might be moving away from a license (which allows you to retain ownership) and toward an assignment (which is an outright sale of all your rights). For example, giving a licensee the right to improve or revise the licensed products does not necessarily mean that the licensee will own the rights to the improvement.

Ownership rights of improvements to your invention, particularly if the licensee makes the improvements, can be a tricky issue. Information about improvement ownership is provided in Chapter 15. Below is a sample grant provision that does not assign ownership rights.

> **Grant of Rights.** Licensor grants to Licensee a/an [*exclusive or nonexclusive*] license to make, use, or sell the Property solely in association with the manufacture, sale, use, promotion, or distribution of the Licensed Products.

Including, But Not Limited to ...

You might see the phrase, "including, but not limited to ..." used throughout a license agreement. This contract language is used to present an example without restricting rights to that example. For instance, a licensee may want to describe the term "licensed products" as "any hair care products that incorporate the Property, including, but not limited to, hair care products for pets." This way, licensed products includes hair care products for animals as well as humans. Because this phrase is often used to expand the licensee's rights, review carefully any use of "including, but not limited to ...." If you think this phrase grants rights beyond what you feel comfortable with, negotiate to have it excluded from the contract.

Below is an example of a grant that is too broad because it includes ambiguous or repetitive terms (recast, transform, revise, condense).

> **Grant of Rights.** Pursuant to the terms and conditions herein, Licensor conveys, grants, and transfers to Licensee an exclusive license to manufacture, sell, copy, create derivatives, make improvements, transform, condense, lease, distribute, advertise, promote, market, edit, recast, or revise the Property as incorporated and embodied in the Licensed Products.

Reservation of Rights

Under the law, it's presumed that if you haven't expressly transferred a right, you have retained (or reserved) it. For example, if you do not convey the right to sell the licensed products in Thailand, then you've reserved that right for yourself—or for anyone to whom you wish to license it. So, technically, you don't have to make an express statement that you reserve a certain right.

But, unfortunately, disputes can arise about this issue, so we recommend that you specifically reserve whatever rights you don't wish to transfer. The easiest method of reserving rights is to add the following sentence in the grant.

> Licensor expressly reserves all rights other than those being conveyed or granted in this Agreement.

If you wish to be even more specific, you can do so. For example, preserve your right to license your invention for the computer game market, you could use the following wording.

Reservation of Rights Expressly Excluding a Particular Industry

Licensor expressly reserves all rights other than those being conveyed or granted in this Agreement, including, but not limited to, the right to license the Properties in [*list a particular market which you want to expressly exclude, for example, "the computer and video game market"*].

If you have already licensed or plan to license to two parties (for example, Company A and Company B), it's wise to specifically reserve those rights you granted to Company A when licensing rights to Company B. For example, you invented a new type of brush bristle and first licensed it to a dental company. Now you are licensing the bristle to a vacuum cleaner company. Your grant

Assignments

If a licensee sublicenses its rights to manufacture or distribute your invention, the licensee is still responsible for overseeing production and sales and for paying you. However, if the licensee assigns its rights, it has permanently removed itself from its obligations and the new company (the assignee) has stepped into the licensee's shoes. This new company will market the invention and pay you royalties.

Most licenses are specifically made nonassignable because the licensor does not want to have another company replace the licensee. However, there are two occasions when an assignment may be necessary:

- The licensee might be purchased by another company and wants to reserve the freedom to transfer its rights to that company.
- The licensee might create a subsidiary company and wants to be able to assign the agreement to its subsidiary.

A separate section in the agreement, entitled "Assignment," will detail the conditions under which an assignment can be made. This provision may set the same standards ("cannot withhold consent unreasonably") as the right to sublicense, discussed below. We provide samples of this Assignment section in Chapter 14. Sometimes, to make sure that the licensee can't escape its obligations to you, the words "nonassignable" and "nontransferable" are inserted in the grant. For example, "Licensor grants an exclusive, nonassignable license ...."

Keep in mind that an antiassignment provision can only prevent "voluntary" assignments; it cannot prevent assignments that are ordered by a court or that are mandatory under law. For example, if you licensed to a sole proprietor who dies, the sole proprietor's company would be assigned to the estate, then to the heirs. These involuntary assignments cannot be prevented by the antiassignment provisions in the agreement. Similarly, an assignment by a bankruptcy trustee cannot be prevented under the agreement.

That's What FRANDS Are For...

Competing companies benefit when they cooperate to create industry standards. For example, computer manufacturers like Apple and Microsoft benefit when they agree on the size, shape, and functionality of USB ports and cables. The alternative would be marketplace chaos. To generate these industry standards, companies meet to establish standard-setting organizations (SSOs). These SSOs devise a rulebook that ensures, for example, that gas pump nozzles fit all cars.

To implement these standards, companies might need to share patents. These patents, which are essential for companies to meet the industry standard, are referred to as "standard-essential patents" (SEPs), or "necessary claims" or "essential claims." For example, media streaming companies, such as Hulu, Netflix, and Amazon Prime Video, might need shared licensing of streaming and compression patents to transmit their content.

All this sharing seems great. But let's say a company that owned an SEP were to charge outrageous licensing fees to all its competitors. Or, what if the patent owner decided to license the patent rights for a new streaming application to Hulu at a low rate, but charged Netflix ten times the amount? Is there any way to prevent or stop these abuses from occurring?

To avoid these unfair business practices, industries have adopted FRANDs (Fair, Reasonable, and Non-Discriminatory terms) for SSO members (and often, nonmembers).

Laws do not create FRANDS; contracts do. FRANDS are incorporated in licensing agreements between SSO members or established in SSO governing documents. FRANDs can include rules for use and royalty rates for SEPs.

A SEP owner typically has three choices when faced with a FRAND: (1) License the SEP without charge (or alternatively, agree not to sue any SSO members who used the SEP), (2) reserve the right to charge a "reasonable" royalty, or (3) refuse to license the SEP.

Options One and Three are clear and straightforward to execute. But what constitutes a "reasonable royalty"? Surprisingly, after several years of FRANDS, there is no consensus or template for resolving their application. Courts approach FRAND disputes on a case-by-case basis. In one case, a court examined Qualcomm's royalty rates for modem chips used in mobile phones. The court imposed a formula referred to as the smallest-saleable patent practicing unit ("SSPPU") royalty theory. (*FTC v. Qualcomm*, No. 17-CV-00220-LHK (N.D. Cal. May 21, 2019).) In another case, a court rejected a rote formula for fixing a FRAND royalty and based its determination on industry practice and market evidence. (*HTC v. Ericsson*, No. 18-CV-00243 (E.D. Tex. May 23, 2019).)

to the vacuum cleaner company should specifically reserve "all rights to exploit the Properties within the dental care products and supply industry."

Sublicenses

A sublicense is like a sublease. A person acquires property rights and transfers the rights to someone else. Under a sublicense, the licensee can transfer its rights to a company that can make or sell your invention.

Multi-Station Bird Feeder With Squirrel Guard

No. 6,269,771

Licensees like to have the freedom to sublicense. For example, perhaps the licensee doesn't have a strong sales force in France, so it sublicenses the French rights to a strong French company (assuming the French rights were included in the original license). The French company then pays money to the licensee, who then pays you a portion of the sublicensing revenue, often 50%.

You might not like the idea of sublicensing, because a different company —perhaps a company whose philosophy or sales practices you don't agree with— can sublicense and sell your invention. You can attempt to prohibit sublicensing altogether, but a better solution would be require the licensee to seek out your prior approval before granting a sublicense. The grant section can accomplish this limitation by using the following language.

Licensee may sublicense the rights granted pursuant to this Agreement provided Licensee obtains Licensor's prior written consent to such sublicense, and Licensor receives such revenue or royalty payment as provided in the Payment section below. Any sublicense granted in violation of this provision shall be void.

Under this provision, you can withhold your consent to a sublicense for any reason —no matter how arbitrary. Sometimes, this requirement to seek permission is not suitable for a licensee who wants more predictability. You can satisfy the licensee's needs by adding the following language.

Consent to Sublicense Not Unreasonably Withheld

Licensee may sublicense the rights granted pursuant to this Agreement provided Licensee obtains Licensor's prior written consent to such sublicense and Licensor receives such revenue or royalty payment as provided in the Payment section below. Licensee's consent to any sublicense shall not be unreasonably withheld. Any sublicense granted in violation of this provision shall be void.

Under this provision, you must have a good or "reasonable" motivation for rejecting the sublicense. That is, your decision must be based upon sound business reasons, such as proof that the licensee cannot adequately market the invention. Of course, such a provision has occasionally led to litigation as the parties attempted to determine the standards for what was a "good or reasonable motivation."

Defining the Territory

Where can the licensee sell the licensed products? The territory sets the geographical limits for sales. Generally when licensing a patent, the choice of territory is limited to the country or countries where patent protection has been obtained. However, if you and the licensee agree to seek patent protection in foreign countries, then the territory can go beyond the boundaries of the initial patent protection. To create a worldwide license, simply insert the word "worldwide" in the grant.

Licensor grants to Licensee an exclusive, worldwide license …

If the territory is limited to a country or region, insert that information in the territory section of the agreement, as follows.

Territory. The rights granted to Licensee are limited to the United States and Canada (the "Territory").

Limiting Cross-Territory Sales

Consider that you may want to enter three separate licenses: for North America, Europe, and Asia. These are known as split territorial licenses. The licensees are relying on your assurance that they will have exclusive rights to their respective territories. But what's to prevent someone from buying a lot of products in Asia at a low price and then shipping them to Europe to compete with your European licensee?

One suggestion for limiting this type of cross-territory activity is to add a provision such as the following.

Limiting Cross-Territory Sales

The rights granted to Licensee are limited to [*insert the territory*] (the "Territory"). Licensee shall not make, use, or sell the Licensed Products, or any products which are confusingly or substantially similar to the Licensed Products, in any country outside the Territory and will not knowingly sell the Licensed Products to persons who intend to resell them in a country outside the Territory.

Needless to say, this type of provision isn't bulletproof. It's quite easy for companies to sell licensed products to distributors who then ship the licensed products to a country outside its territory (a procedure known as "gray marketing" products). For example, PhotoCo licenses its camera technology in Europe and Russia and uses a provision such as the one above in its license agreement. The European distributor sells the licensed products to a Central American company which then sells it to stores in the United States. Even with contractual language limiting cross-territory sales, the potential for abuse remains and can lead to litigation. For the same reasons, be aware that split territorial licenses might not work for products that will be sold and distributed over the Internet.

In other words, for a license to be worldwide, you don't need a separate Territory section. But if you want the territory limited to a certain area, you need to indicate the area in a separate Territory section.

What's the best approach for you as a prospective licensor? If the licensee has a history of worldwide sales and good sales connections throughout the world, then grant a worldwide license. But for a licensee familiar only with the U.S. market, it doesn't make sense to license rights to other geographic areas. Doing so would restrict your ability to grant a license to another party for a foreign market.

You and the licensee might have a difference of opinion over the territorial scope of the license. In that event, one solution would be to initially grant worldwide rights but also provide that if the licensee has not exploited or sublicensed rights in an area after a certain period of time—say, two years— then that area would be excluded from the territory. For example, if after three years the licensee has sold the licensed products everywhere but in France, the licensee would lose rights for France. Usually, this type of provision is included in another portion of the license agreement, titled "Right to Terminate a Portion of the Agreement" (discussed in Chapter 13). The language would read as shown below.

Licensor's Right to Terminate as to Territory Not Exploited

Licensor shall have the right to terminate the grant of license under this Agreement with respect to any country or region included in the Territory in which Licensee fails to offer the Licensed Products for sale or distribution or to secure a sublicensing agreement for the marketing, distribution, and sale of the product within two years of the Effective Date.

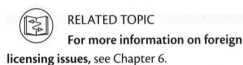 RELATED TOPIC
For more information on foreign licensing issues, see Chapter 6.

Setting the Length (Term) of the Agreement

The "term" refers to the length of time that the license lasts. For how long should you license your invention? Reasons exist for both long and short terms:

- A short term (two to five years) can be beneficial if the licensee is not doing a good job or if the product is a success, because you can terminate or renegotiate for a better license.
- A long term can be beneficial if you are happy with the licensee and want to make sure that you are locked in for a long period.

A licensee will usually want as long a term as possible because a long term guarantees a maximum period for exploitation of the invention. Sometimes, however, a product has a limited lifespan and a licensee may want to limit the agreement to only as long as the licensee sells the product. Sometimes, the parties compromise on term issues by establishing renewal periods. For example, if certain conditions are met—sales or royalty payments at a certain level, for instance—the licensee will have the right to renew the agreement for a period of time, say, one or two years.

In practical terms, you should be aware that if the invention is not profitable, the term makes little difference. It's difficult to force the licensee to keep selling the product if it is losing money. The licensee will either seek to amend the agreement to permit termination or sue to terminate the agreement.

With these considerations in mind, you have three basic choices for determining the length of the term:

- The term can be for a fixed length (say, ten years).
- The term can be for as long as the licensee manufactures and sells the licensed products.
- The agreement could permit either party to terminate. For example, one party (or either party) could announce they want to end the agreement. The agreement would then terminate within a set period of 30 or 60 days.

CAUTION
Patents and license length. Note that in the case of a patent license, the term cannot be for longer than the length of the patent (see "Licensing Terms for Patents," below).

Commencement of Term

The date that a contract commences is usually referred to as the "date of execution" or the "effective date." It's the date when obligations begin—for example, the date when the licensee must pay an advance or when a licensor must deliver documentation.

The effective date is usually the date when you (the licensor) sign the license agreement. Sometimes, the effective date occurs when the licensee signs, when both of you have signed, or the later of the two. If the contract has a fixed date of termination, say, ten years, the contract would end ten years from the effective date.

CAUTION
Record the effective date. It's always wise to record the effective date and any subsequent termination or renewal dates in your calendar.

Right to Terminate a License

Even if your license has a fixed term, the agreement might be cut short for various reasons, including a failure to pay royalties or a failure to offer the licensed products for sale. These reasons are often listed in a contract section entitled "Termination Rights" or "Termination." Termination provisions work in conjunction with the term section. For example, the licensor may have the right to terminate the agreement if the licensee fails to include the licensed products in its annual catalog.

Because the term and termination rights provisions are in different portions of the license agreement, the term section usually includes a statement that the agreement can "be terminated pursuant to any provision of this Agreement."

We discuss the bases for termination in Chapter 13.

Licensing Terms for Patents

You cannot license a patent for longer than the length of the patent—20 years from the filing date for most patents. A longer patent license violates federal antitrust laws (as explained in Chapter 17). If other aspects of your invention are protected—by copyright or trademark, for instance—these elements can be licensed for longer periods. When drafting the term section, a licensee typically will seek language similar to the following.

Term for the Length of Patent Only

> This Agreement shall commence upon the Effective Date and shall expire simultaneously with the expiration of the longest-living patent (or patents) or last remaining patent application as listed in the definition of the Property, whichever occurs last, unless sooner terminated pursuant to a provision of this Agreement.

**Sleeping and Meditation Bag
No. 4,330,989**

According to this provision, the patent license lasts as long as some form of patent protection exists or until termination of the agreement for some other reason. Remember, this provision (and the one below) are based solely upon patent rights.

From the licensor's perspective, we recommend, if possible, licensing for a shorter period with renewal rights based upon sales or other criteria as shown below.

Short Term With Renewal Rights Based Upon Sales

This Agreement shall commence upon the Effective Date and shall extend for a period of two years (the "Initial Term") and thereafter may be renewed by Licensee under the same terms and conditions for consecutive two-year periods (the "Renewal Terms"), provided that:

(a) Licensee provides written notice of its intention to renew this agreement at least thirty days before the expiration of the current term,

(b) Licensee has met the sales requirements as established in Exhibit A, and

(c) in no event shall the Agreement extend longer than the date of expiration of the longest-living patent (or patents) or last-remaining patent application as listed in the definition of the Property.

What happens if you apply for a patent and the patent does not issue? In that case, the licensee may want the right to terminate the agreement. This right to terminate is discussed in Chapter 13.

If you do not have a patent but have a valuable trademark or trade secret, the license for trade secret and trademark rights can extend indefinitely. In this case, you may use language like the following.

No Patents; Indefinite Term

This Agreement shall commence upon the Effective Date and shall continue until terminated pursuant to a provision of this Agreement.

Fixed Terms and Renewals

You or the licensee might want to limit the license to a fixed period with no renewal rights. How long? That depends upon how long you and the licensee believe is necessary to exploit the invention. Usually, there is little danger in agreeing to a fixed term because both parties will be motivated to negotiate a new agreement if it's still working out for both of them. If it isn't working out for one of them, then the agreement probably isn't much good, anyway.

Fixed Ten-Year Term

This Agreement shall commence upon the Effective Date and shall continue for ten years unless sooner terminated pursuant to a provision of this Agreement.

A right of renewal could be included as shown below.

Initial Term With Renewals

This Agreement shall commence upon the latest signature date (the "Effective Date") and shall extend for a period of [*insert number of years for initial term, for example, "two years"*] (the "Initial Term"). Following the Initial Term, this Agreement may be renewed by Licensee under the same terms and conditions for [*insert number of renewal terms*] consecutive [*insert length of each renewal term, for example, "two-year"*] periods (the "Renewal Terms"), provided that Licensee provides written notice of its intention to renew this Agreement within thirty days before the expiration of the current term. In no event, shall the Agreement extend longer than the date of expiration of the patent listed in the definition of the Property.

As we explained, the renewal can be tied to some event, such as sales. For example, you could state that you must receive $100,000 in royalties in the preceding term in order for the Licensee to exercise a renewal right.

Short Term With Renewal Rights Based Upon Sales

This Agreement shall commence upon the Effective Date and shall extend for a period of [*insert number of years*] years (the "Initial Term") and thereafter may be renewed by Licensee under the same terms and conditions for consecutive [*insert number of years*]-year periods (the "Renewal Terms"), provided that:

(a) Licensee provides written notice of its intention to renew this agreement at least thirty days before the expiration of the current term,

(b) Licensee has met the sales requirements as established in [*Exhibit____*], and

(c) in no event shall the Agreement extend longer than the date of expiration of the longest-living patent (or patents) or last-remaining patent application as listed in the definition of the Property.

Finally, if you want to permit the term to extend for as long as the licensee sells the invention, you could draft a term provision as shown below.

This Agreement shall commence upon the Effective Date as specified in [_Exhibit_   ] and shall continue for as long as Licensee continues to offer the Licensed Products in commercially reasonable quantities or unless sooner terminated pursuant to a provision of this Agreement.

The worksheet below is intended to help you keep track of the essential business facts. (Information on royalties, audits, and net sales is provided in the next chapter.)

DOWNLOAD FORMS

You can download this form (and all other forms in this book) from this book's companion page on Nolo.com; see the appendix for the link.

Contract Worksheet

Licensee

Name of licensee business _____

Licensee address _____

Licensee business form _____

    ☐ sole proprietorship   ☐ general partnership   ☐ limited partnership

    ☐ corporation   ☐ limited liability company

State of incorporation _____

Name, position, and phone number of person signing for licensee: _____

_____

_____

Property Definition

Patent No. _____

Patent Application Serial No. _____

Copyrightable features _____

_____

Copyright Registration No(s). _____

Trade secrets _____

_____

Trademarks _____

_____

Trademark Registration No(s). _____

Licensed Products Definition

Industry (Have you limited the license to a particular industry?)

_____

Product (Have you limited the license to a particular product or products?)

_____

Territory

☐ Worldwide   ☐ Countries _____

☐ States _____

Rights Granted (check those rights granted to licensee)

☐ sell   ☐ make or manufacture   ☐ distribute

☐ use   ☐ revise   ☐ import

☐ lease   ☐ right to improvements   ☐ derivatives (copyright)

☐ copy (copyright) ☐ advertise   ☐ promote

☐ other rights _____

☐ other rights _____

☐ other rights _____

Rights Reserved

☐ all rights reserved (except those granted in license)

☐ no rights reserved

☐ specific rights reserved

Have you signed any other licenses? If so, do you need to reserve specific rights?

_____

_____

Term

Have you agreed upon:

☐ a fixed term (How long? _____)   ☐ a term limited by patent length

☐ unlimited term until one party terminates   ☐ an initial term with renewals
(see below)

☐ other _____

Renewals

If you have agreed upon an initial term with renewals:

How many renewal periods? _____   How long is each renewal period? _____

What triggers renewal?

☐ Licensee must notify of intent to renew.

☐ Licensor must notify of intent to renew.

☐ Agreement renews automatically unless Licensee indicates it does not want to renew.

Net Sales Deductions

What is the licensee permitted to deduct when calculating net sales?

☐ quantity discounts   ☐ debts and uncollectibles   ☐ sales commissions

☐ credits and returns   ☐ fees   ☐ freight and shipping

☐ promotion and marketing costs   ☐ other _____

Is there a cap on the total amount of the deductions?   ☐ Yes   ☐ No

If so, how much? _____

Royalty Rates

Licensed products   _____%   Combination products   _____%

Accessory products   _____%

Per-use royalty   _____%   or   Usage standard _____

Other products _____%   Other products _____%

Do you have any sliding royalty rates? _____

Advances and Lump Sum Payments

Advance $ _____   Date due _____

Lump sum payment(s) $ _____   Date due _____

Guaranteed Minimum Annual Royalty (GMAR)

GMAR $ _____   Date due _____

Does the GMAR carry forward credits?   ☐ Yes   ☐ No

Does the GMAR carry forward deficiencies?   ☐ Yes   ☐ No

Audit Rights

No. of audits permitted per year _____   No. of days' notice _____

Money: It Matters

Some Basic Royalty Definitions 207

Ways to Get Paid 209

    Royalties Based on Net Sales 209

    Per-Unit Royalties 210

    Per-Use Royalties 210

    Lump Sum Payments 211

    Fluctuating Royalty Rates 211

    Hybrid License Royalties 212

    Minimum Annual Royalty 212

The Mysteries of Net Sales and Deductions 214

    Quantity Discount Deduction 215

    Debts and Uncollectible Account Deductions 215

    Sales Commission Deductions 215

    Promotion/Marketing/Advertising Deduction 215

    Fee Deduction 215

    Freight/Shipping Deduction 216

    Credits and Returns Deduction 216

    Tax Deductions 216

    Putting a Cap on Net Sales Deductions 216

How Much Do You Get? 216

    Basing Royalty Rates Upon Industry Standards 217

    Basing Royalty Rates Upon Financial Analysis 218

    Basing Royalty Rates Upon Both Industry Standards and
        Financial Analysis 219

    If They're So Rich, Why Won't They Give Me More Money? 219

Royalty Provisions...220

Royalties...220

Net Sales...221

Advance Against Royalties...221

Royalty Rate..222

Hybrid Royalty Payments..222

Guaranteed Minimum Annual Royalty Payments............222

Royalties on Spin-Offs...223

Adjustment of Royalties for Third-Party Licenses...........223

F.O.B. Royalties...225

Sublicensing Revenues..225

Payments and Statements to Licensor.............................225

What's an Audit?..226

How Do You Deal With Late Payments?............................229

n this chapter, we'll discuss the various ways that a licensor is paid, such as royalties, advances, guaranteed minimum payments, lump sum payments, and "per-use" royalties. We will explore the difference between gross and net sales and review the types of deductions that are often claimed by licensees. We will also examine a few sample royalty and audit provisions. Finally, we'll review how to anticipate payment predicaments, such as late payments or a failure to pay. You should read this chapter if you answer "yes" to any of the following questions:

- Would you like an explanation of basic royalty accounting principles?
- Would you like definitions for terms such as advances and net sales?
- Do you need an explanation of the methods you can use to audit a licensee's books?
- Do you need information about how your royalty income will be taxed?

CAUTION

Remember that the decisions you reach with a licensee may be binding and enforceable even without a written agreement. Therefore, keep notes of your conversations and close your discussions by reminding the licensee that any deal is subject to approval of the final contract. This reminder should be included on written correspondence as well.

Spreadsheets to the Rescue

When you work with royalties, you will want to be able to compute your potential earnings accurately and quickly. For this reason, you should consider using a spreadsheet program, such as Microsoft *Excel*. Spreadsheets will prove invaluable when negotiating royalty payments.

Some Basic Royalty Definitions

Below are some simple royalty definitions. Don't worry if you don't fully grasp these concepts right away. A more complete explanation is offered in subsequent sections.

Gross sales. This is the total money received from the licensee's sale of the invention.

Net sales. This includes the gross sales (mentioned above) minus deductions such as shipping costs or returns (products returned by retailers).

EXAMPLE: A licensee receives $1,200,000 from gross sales and has shipping deductions and returns of $200,000. Net sales equal $1,000,000.

Royalty. A royalty is a payment for licensing your invention—usually calculated as a percentage of the sales and paid periodically. You might receive royalty checks once, twice, or even four times a year. (A system of continuous royalty payments is sometimes referred to as a "running royalty.")

Net sales royalty. This is the most common form of royalty payment—a percentage of net sales. How do you compute your net sales royalty payment? Multiply the royalty rate against net sales.

> **EXAMPLE:** A royalty rate of 5% times net sales of $1,000,000 equals a net sales royalty of $50,000. (Note: In some cases, royalties can be a percentage of unit sales or production. See below for an explanation.)

Per-unit royalty. A per-unit royalty is tied to the number of units sold, not the money earned by sales.

> **EXAMPLE:** Under a per-unit royalty, a licensor could receive $1 per product sold.

Per-use royalty. A per-use royalty is based upon the number of times that the invention is used. This royalty is tied to production, not sales. A per-use royalty is commonly chosen when the invention is a process, not a product, such as a method of sealing canned goods. The inventor receives a royalty based upon the amount of production (for example, the number of sealed cans produced).

> **EXAMPLE:** Under a per-use royalty, a licensor could receive ten cents for every 100 cans produced using his patented system.

Advances. This is an up-front payment to the licensor, usually made at the time the license is signed. An advance is almost always credited or "recouped" against future royalties unless the agreement provides otherwise. It's as if the licensee is saying, "I expect you will earn $10,000 in royalties, so I am going to advance you that sum at the time we sign the agreement." When you do earn royalties, the first $10,000 will be kept by the licensee to repay the advance. If you don't earn the $10,000, the licensee usually takes a loss and you do not have to return the advance. To ensure that you don't have to return the advance, you'd want your agreement to state the advance is "nonrefundable." (See "Nonrefundable and Nonrecoupable," below.)

Lump sum payments. Instead of receiving royalties, a licensor might prefer a onetime or lump sum payment for transfer of licensing rights.

EXAMPLE: The licensor receives a lump sum payment of $100,000. In return, the licensee has the exclusive right to sell the invention for five years. The licensor gets no other payments or royalties regardless of whether the invention sells hundreds or millions of units.

Minimum annual royalty payments. A minimum annual royalty payment—sometimes referred to as guaranteed minimum annual royalty or GMAR—is a guarantee that you will receive a certain royalty payment each year. Think of a minimum annual payment as an advance that is paid every year of the agreement.

Nonrefundable and Nonrecoupable

The terms "nonrefundable" and "nonrecoupable" are sometimes used in license agreements. Nonrecoupable means that the payment cannot be credited against royalties. It's as if the licensee is saying, "Take this $10,000 payment and I won't deduct it from your future royalties." The term nonrefundable is often used to ensure that a licensor will not have to personally pay back an advance or minimum annual royalty payment. For example, say you receive a $10,000 advance but the sales are dismal and the royalties never equal the advance. Although a licensor rarely has to return an advance, the term "nonrefundable" is often added to the agreement as reinforcement to guarantee that you don't have to write a check to the licensee.

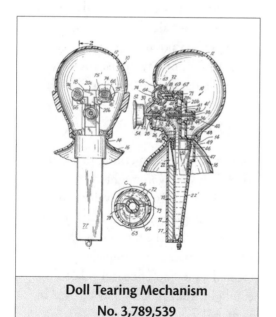

Doll Tearing Mechanism
No. 3,789,539

Ways to Get Paid

Assuming you have a choice, how do you choose between the various payment methods? We explain your options below.

Royalties Based on Net Sales

The payment of royalties based on net sales is the most common method of licensing payment. In business terminology, these royalties are a direct cost that can be charged against the cost of goods. In other words, they are a predictable expense that is figured as part of the cost of selling the product. If the invention is not successful, there will be no royalties. Licensors prefer this system because if the invention is successful, the licensor will be richly rewarded over the life of the invention. We generally recommend choosing a royalty payment over a lump sum payment for invention licensing.

Per-Unit Royalties

In some instances, an inventor might not want to use a royalty system based upon net sales. For example, computer hardware prices often drop radically. Even if units continue to sell at the same rate, the net sales revenue decreases because the price has dropped. If the wholesale price for your product drops, you might be better suited with royalties tied to unit sales. A payment of two dollars per unit could be more profitable than 5% of net sales. Unfortunately, licensees generally don't want to risk committing to unit royalties when the wholesale price can drop dramatically. But if you have the bargaining power, look into a per-unit royalty system.

If you use the per-unit system, you should check that box under the payment section of the agreement and then tweak the agreement as follows:

- If you use a guaranteed minimum annual royalty, tie that section ("Guaranteed Minimum Annual Royalty Payment") to annual per-unit sales, not annual net sales—so, change all references made to "Net Sales" to "Unit Sales" in that section.
- In the "Payments and Statements to Licensor" section, change the term "Net Sales of Licensed Products" to "Per-Unit Sales of Licensed Products."
- If you use the "Royalties on Spin-Offs" section, replace the words "Net Sales" with "Per-Unit Sales" (if you and the Licensee agree to pay on that basis).
- Under "Licensor's Right to Terminate," replace the words "Net Sales" with "Per-Unit Sales."
- If you are not using the term net sales for any payments, you may strike the section entitled "Net Sales."

Per-Use Royalties

If you've invented something that is used, rather than sold, you might choose a per-use royalty. This is a royalty applied to the number of units produced or the number of times the method is used in manufacture. For example, if you patented a method of coating glass for neon light, your process may be used in the manufacturing operation. That is, you are licensing a procedure that is used as part of a production process. Because the process could be used in a variety of ways, a royalty system based on net sales is difficult to justify and hard to audit, making the per-use royalty a better option.

> **EXAMPLE:** Fred has devised a method of compacting and sealing aluminum cans to produce building blocks. He licenses the method to RecyCo and receives a per-use royalty of 15 cents for every cubic foot.

Lump Sum Payments

Lump sum payments are a gamble. When should you take one large payment over a royalty? If your invention is wildly successful, you may always regret the lump sum choice.

But if the invention is not successful, you won't see any royalties and the lump sum would be to your benefit. You can attempt, if possible, to estimate potential sales over the period of the license. However, that is a speculative approach and the fact is, no proven method exists for successfully picking the form of payment.

There are two reasons that some licensors prefer a lump sum payment. First, the licensor doesn't have to be concerned with accounting or auditing records.

Second, some licensors prefer lump sum payments for foreign licenses because of currency conversion rates. These rates— which measure the foreign currency against

U.S. currency—may change dramatically, making your foreign royalty payments less valuable. If you are in doubt whether to choose a lump sum or royalty, you may wish to consult a patent attorney to evaluate your invention's commercial potential.

Note: A lump sum payment for a license is different from a lump sum payment for an assignment. A license may be limited in time, for example for two or three years. Under an assignment, however, you lose ownership of your invention. (See Chapter 1.)

Fluctuating Royalty Rates

A fluctuating royalty rate (sometimes referred to as a sliding royalty) is a rate that changes during the licensing period. The rate may change each year or it may change because of other circumstances, such as sales or inflation. For example, the royalty rate may go up if sales exceed a million units in one year. Similarly, a licensee may seek a decreasing royalty in the event that sales fall below a certain mark.

> **EXAMPLE:** Page has licensed a device to patch bicycle tubes. His royalty rate is 5% for net sales up to and including $100,000 and 6% for net sales above $100,000 in any one year. If net sales are $150,000 in one year, Page receives $8,000 [($100,000 x 5%) + ($50,000 x 6%)].

Hybrid License Royalties

If you are licensing a pending or issued patent and a trade secret, your arrangement is referred to as a "hybrid license." A hybrid license requires special attention because of antitrust laws. (See Chapter 17.) When you license a patent and some other intellectual property rights for an invention (such as a trademark or trade secret), courts presume that the patent is inherently more valuable than the other form of intellectual property. Therefore, if your pending patent does not issue or if your patent expires, it is unfair to require the licensee to pay the same royalty as if the patent existed.

Therefore, we suggest a modification to your license agreement if you meet both of the following criteria:

- You are licensing a patent or pending patent and some other form of intellectual property (such as a trademark or trade secret).
- Your license agreement is expected to continue longer than the life of the patents.

If your license is longer than the life of the patents, you can continue to collect royalties provided that the royalty percentage decreases to reflect the value of the expired patents. We suggest allocating the royalty between the patent and the nonpatented property. For example, 85% of the royalty can be attributable to the patent and 15% for a trademark. After the patent expires, the royalty rate would diminish by 85%.

You do not need a hybrid royalty provision if the term (that is, the length) of your agreement does not exceed the length of your patent protection. For example, if you licensed a patented invention and trade secrets and your license provided for termination "with the expiration of the patent," then you would not need to include the hybrid language.

Minimum Annual Royalty

The minimum annual royalty or guaranteed minimum annual royalty (we'll refer to it as a GMAR) is an annual payment that the licensor is guaranteed to receive, regardless of how well the product sells in any year. How does a GMAR work? Each year, you receive your GMAR payment. At the end of each year, the earned royalties are totaled. (The earned royalties are the actual royalties that accumulated from net sales that year.) What happens next depends upon the agreement.

Credits—When Royalties Exceed the GMAR

The GMAR is a minimum payment to compensate you for royalties that are expected that year. But what happens if the royalties exceed the GMAR payment? In that situation, the licensee has paid you less royalties than you actually earned. Depending upon how your agreement is negotiated, either (1) you may receive a credit payment at the end of the year, or (2) the licensee may hold onto this money as a carryforward credit, and then deduct it against your account in the following years if you have a loss.

We recommend against the carryforward credit, because it prevents you from receiving earned royalties for another year. However, licensees prefer it because new product sales may be unpredictable. The first year may be booming, but sales could slow down the second year.

Deficiencies—When the GMAR Exceeds the Earned Royalties

What happens if the GMAR payment is more than the royalties you actually earned in a year? For example, say you were paid a $10,000 GMAR but the royalties only totaled $9,000 that year. The licensee paid more royalties to you than you earned.

Depending on how you negotiated the agreement, (1) the licensee may have to absorb the deficiency; (2) the licensee may carry forward or cumulate royalty deficiencies, diminishing next year's GMAR payment accordingly; or (3) if there is a carryforward credit provision (see above), the licensee may apply the deficiency against a previous year's credit.

EXAMPLE: Your license agreement provides for a GMAR of $10,000 to be paid on January 1 of each year.

The first year's total royalty was only $6,000, which results in a deficiency of $4,000. The second year's total royalty was $14,000—$4,000 more than the GMAR. So, for the second year, there is a credit of $4,000.

If you had a carryforward provision, you would have received a total of $20,000 for the two years because the first-year deficiency of $4,000 would have canceled out the second-year credit of $4,000. If you had no carryforward provision, you would have received a total of $24,000. You would have received $14,000 the second year ($10,000 GMAR payment plus the $4,000 credit), plus the $10,000 GMAR payment from the first year (the $4,000 first-year deficiency having no effect on your payment).

To sum up, if you are fortunate enough to negotiate a GMAR, your preference should be for a GMAR without a carryforward (sometimes referred to as noncumulating) requirement. You should also be aware that GMARs can be suspended (that is, no payment is required) if certain things occur. Sometimes a contract will provide that no GMAR has to be paid if, through no fault of the licensee, it's impossible to manufacture the product or to obtain the raw materials for the product.

GMARs, Royalties, and Diminished Profits

The licensee doesn't necessarily lose money just because there is a deficiency (that is, your royalties were less than the GMAR). It's possible that the licensee profited, because the GMAR and royalties represent a fraction of the cost of the invention. All that can be definitely concluded in this case is that the profit margin for the invention has been diminished. That is, the licensee did not make as much money as it hoped.

The Mysteries of Net Sales and Deductions

Net sales are the most common measurement for royalty payments. In a net sales license, the royalty rate is multiplied against the net sales. There's no standard definition of net sales, and it can change in every license agreement.

During negotiations, a licensee will attempt to define net sales in a very narrow way with many deductions. This way, the licensee can make a lower royalty payment. The licensor, on the other hand, wants a broad definition. The licensor would prefer if net sales were the same as gross sales.

The big issue when negotiating net sales is what deductions should be included in the definition of net sales. A net sales definition that favors a licensor would read as follows.

"Net Sales" are defined as Licensee's gross sales minus returns that are actually credited. Gross sales are the total amount on invoices billed to customers.

Using this definition, a licensor would receive royalty payments based solely upon sales that had occurred. The only deduction is for products that are actually returned and credited, which are either defective or unsold merchandise.

**Tennis Racket
No. 3,999,756**

License agreements often include many more deductions. To help you to sort through these deductions, the common ones are explained below.

Quantity Discount Deduction

Sometimes a licensee may seek to increase sales by offering a discount on large quantity orders. The licensee then deducts this discount (also referred to as a volume discount) from net sales. A volume discount can be favorable to the licensor because it increases sales. If you choose to include it, you should qualify the discount by describing a quantity discount as "a discount made at the time of shipment" or a "discount actually shown on the invoice," since it's possible that an unscrupulous licensee may attempt to offer a discount after items are shipped, splitting the discount with the purchaser and diminishing your royalty payment.

Debts and Uncollectible Account Deductions

Sometimes a licensee will seek to deduct bad debts and uncollectible accounts. For example, say a third party orders products and then fails to pay. The licensee feels no royalty should be paid since no money was earned for these sales. On the other hand, you are not a collection agency and

should not have to lose money because of the licensee's bad business dealings. Even though insolvency and uncollected debts are not especially common, it would be better for you to avoid this deduction.

Sales Commission Deductions

Sometimes a licensee pays a salesperson a commission for each sale of the licensed product. The licensee may seek to deduct these commissions under the net sales definition. We would discourage the deduction of commissions, because they are a cost of the licensee's business.

Promotion/Marketing/ Advertising Deduction

As we have stated, net sales are supposed to be total sales, not a collection of business deductions. For that reason we discourage the use of promotional, marketing, or advertising deductions in the definition of net sales. Marketing should be a cost of doing business, not a licensor expense.

Fee Deduction

This vague term—fee deduction—includes a wide range of costs and business expenses. If the term "fees" can be made more specific, you may be more comfortable with the deduction. Otherwise, we discourage the deduction of fees from net sales.

Freight/Shipping Deduction

Freight and shipping costs of the product, although a cost of doing business, are traditionally treated as a deduction against net sales. We recommend that you accept this as a deduction from net sales.

Credits and Returns Deduction

It's acceptable for a licensee to deduct credits and returns from the total net sales, since returns reflect merchandise which was not purchased or was defective. Some licensors prefer to qualify the definition to state "bona fide returns" or "returns actually made or allowed as supported by credit memoranda" in order to weed out returns which are part of some unscrupulous arrangement between distributors and retailers.

Tax Deductions

If a product is taxed locally, it's common to include the local taxes as a deduction against net sales.

Summing up, it's generally acceptable for net sales to include deductions for shipping, freight, taxes, credits, returns, and discounts made at time of sale. It's less desirable to include—and we recommend against—deductions for sales commissions, debts, uncollectible accounts, promotions, marketing, and advertising.

Putting a Cap on Net Sales Deductions

You can limit net sales deductions by placing a limit on the amount to be deducted. For example, in your license agreement, you could include a statement that reads as follows:

> In no event may the total amount deducted from net sales (for discounts, credits, or returns) during any royalty period exceed ten percent of the gross sales of the products during that royalty period.

A provision such as this guarantees that the deductions will never be more than 10% of gross sales. Some license agreements forgo a listing of the deductions and simply state that net sales are "gross sales minus 10% for shipping, freight, taxes, returns, and other deductions." This provision might not accurately reflect the actual deductions, but it does remove any accounting issues. That is, you no longer have to wonder whether net sales deductions are accurate.

How Much Do You Get?

In an ideal world, there would be a chart describing the correct value and appropriate royalty payments for new inventions. You'd need only consult this chart and you would know how much

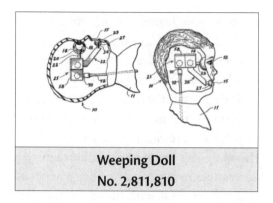

**Weeping Doll
No. 2,811,810**

your invention was worth. There would be no need for negotiation or discussion. Unfortunately, the decisions about advances and royalties are often arbitrary. Sometimes, they're based upon industry standards, and sometimes, the licensee bases them on projections of savings or earnings.

Usually, a licensee makes an offer of an advance and a royalty. This offer is usually determined by one of three methods:

- The licensee offers royalty payments based upon the industry standard.
- The licensee offers royalty payments based upon financial analysis.
- The licensee offers royalty payments based upon a combination of industry standards and financial analysis.

Basing Royalty Rates Upon Industry Standards

A licensee might offer you a $10,000 advance and a 5% royalty, telling you that these numbers are "the industry standard." This means that the royalty rate is customary and every company within the industry uses these same numbers. Licensees can be stubborn about industry standards. As the licensee will explain, the company's projected sales are based upon these numbers and these rates have worked within the industry for other inventors and generated profits.

If an industry standard exists, you will probably be stuck with it. But your first objective should be to verify the rates. If you are working with a product rep or agent, it's easy. They should have information about industry rates. Otherwise, it's tricky. Although invention licensing rates fluctuate between 3% and 10% of net sales, some dip to 1% or 2% and some rise higher than 10%.

If you're not working with a rep or don't have experience in the industry, it can be very difficult to obtain information about standard rates. You will need help from fellow inventors or others familiar with the industry. A fellow inventor who has already licensed or a friendly executive within the trade will prove to be an invaluable colleague when determining industry standards. If such personal contacts are not available, you will have to dig into trade publications as discussed in Chapter 6 and attempt to discern the current rates. Even if you are not using a rep, you might be able to pay an hourly consulting fee to reps, agents, or other industry consultants to obtain basic rate information.

Basing Royalty Rates Upon Financial Analysis

Sometimes a licensee calculates royalty payments and advances based upon the value of your invention. This calculation is established by facts, guesses, and a little bit of financial voodoo. Often, the licensee predicts the cost of manufacturing and raw materials and then attempts to predict sales based upon history, politics, or marketing trends. Sometimes, the rates are also affected by whether the invention is a "pioneer," that is, a breakthrough invention, such as the first instant camera or facsimile machine.

Earnings and Savings

Two common indicators are used to make financial determinations: an earnings analysis and a savings analysis. An earnings analysis determines how much the licensee will earn. If you have a new product, an earnings analysis measures the costs of materials, production, and advertising, and subtracts this total from the potential sales. The result is the potential earnings or profit.

A savings analysis determines how much the licensee will save. If you have a method or an invention that will save money, the licensee will determine the amount of the potential savings. For example, you devised a more efficient method of manufacturing paper bags. The method will save a licensee several hundred thousand dollars each year.

If there's money to be made or saved by your invention, the licensee will attempt to project those earnings or savings. Once the analysis is made, the licensee then determines royalty and advance payments that will coincide with the predictions. If predictions are high, for example, the advance payment may be high. If it is expected that the item will sell more in the second or third year, the royalty rate may increase over time.

The 25/75 Split

If an invention is expected to sell well for a period of years, a common starting point for calculating a royalty rate is the 25/75 split. Under this split, the licensor receives 25% of the profit. That is, for every four dollars of profit, the licensor receives one dollar. Note that this is not the same as a 25% royalty—royalties are a percentage of sales, not profits. But some licensees begin the royalty calculation process by estimating future profits, deducting 25% for the licensor and then recalculating this sum in the product pie (described below) to arrive at the licensor's royalty.

The Product Pie

The licensee may make further financial calculations based upon a product pie. Each company sets aside a certain amount of money for a new product based upon forecasts of sales and expenses. For example, a company may allocate $200,000 for a new product: $5,000 for administrative costs and insurance, $70,000 for manufacturing, $100,000 for marketing. That leaves $25,000 which is earmarked to you as an advance. If you seek more money, the company has to either increase the total amount of the new product pie or subtract money from another portion. Most companies don't like to increase the total allocation, because that means a greater risk—more products will have to be sold. Cutting another portion, such as marketing, may impact potential sales.

The company may cook up a second product pie which details the costs and revenues once the product has been introduced. This pie is usually based upon revenue. For example, if the company sells the product for $20, then the pie would be divided as $5 for materials, $5 for manufacturing, $1 for royalties, $4 for advertising, and $5 profit. Your slice of royalties and advances is sometimes based upon the size of the product pie.

Basing Royalty Rates Upon Both Industry Standards and Financial Analysis

This might be the most common method of figuring how much you get for licensing your invention. A licensee will offer you the industry standard royalty rate but give you an advance or a series of minimum annual payments based upon a financial analysis. For example, say that based upon market research, it looks like your invention will be very successful. The company may offer you the industry standard royalty rate— say 5%—but also offer you a guaranteed minimum royalty payment of $50,000 a year. In other words, the royalty rate may not fluctuate, but the company is flexible about advances or minimum annual payments.

If They're So Rich, Why Won't They Give Me More Money?

You believe your invention will be very successful. However, the licensee is offering you what seems to be the minimum royalty rate and a relatively small advance. Having worked for years to perfect your invention, you feel that the proposed royalty and advance are too small. After all, the licensee is a successful company, so it should be able to pay more money.

First, you need to ask yourself whether you really should be seeking more money. Remember, the number one reason license negotiations fall apart is because the inventor wants more money than the licensee is willing to pay. Are you being unrealistic about how much the company can or will pay? Have you made any financial analysis of projected earnings or savings? Have you asked to see the licensee's projections?

There are usually two reasons why a licensee won't offer more money:

- Offering more money means taking a bigger risk on the product and the company can't afford to take risks.
- The company knows you have no other choices and has a "take it or leave it" attitude.

The first reason is valid. Your success is tied to the company's success, so you don't want them taking unnecessary risks. The second reason is more difficult to navigate. You may have to weigh the alternatives before rejecting an offer.

One possible solution might be to accept an offer but make the time period for the agreement as short as possible. That way, if the product is successful, you can renegotiate for a better arrangement. (For more information about limiting the time period of the agreement, see Chapters 8 and 13.) As another possible solution, you could suggest a fluctuating or sliding royalty that increases as sales increase.

Royalty Provisions

You have reviewed a great deal of information about royalties. How do you incorporate it into your agreement? Below, you'll find sample provisions for royalties with some additional commentary.

Royalties

The first part of the royalty provision, below, states that the royalties accrue on a certain date. This means the date for recording sales—either the sale date, shipping date, or payment date, whichever comes first. This guarantees that net sales are recorded on the earliest possible date. In other words, you don't have to wait for the following quarter before the transaction is considered a sale.

The final sentence of the provision states that: "Royalties shall also be paid by the Licensee to Licensor on all items, even if not billed (including, but not limited to, introductory offers, samples, promotions, or distributions) to individuals or companies which are affiliated with, associated with, or subsidiaries of the Licensee." What does this mean? Sometimes a company will give promotional items (claiming they're not subject to royalties) to an affiliate or subsidiary who then sells them. The company makes money through its affiliate or subsidiary, but the transaction does not register as a net sale. Although this practice is not common, this contract provision establishes that all such transactions are subject to royalty.

> All royalties ("Royalties") provided for under this Agreement shall accrue when the respective items are sold, shipped, distributed, billed, or paid for, whichever occurs first. Royalties shall also be paid by the Licensee to Licensor on all items, even if not billed (including, but not limited to, introductory offers, samples, promotions, or distributions) to individuals or companies which are affiliated with, associated with, or subsidiaries of the Licensee.

Net Sales

Net sales refers to the total revenue from the licensed product that is subject to royalty payments. In other words, if a transaction doesn't register as a net sale, you will not get paid a royalty. For that reason, licensors will want to have as broad a definition of "net sales" as possible (and as few deductions as possible).

A licensed product is usually defined in the license agreement as a product that is sold by the licensee that includes your licensed technology. It may be the invention as you created it or it may be your invention with some additions, such as packaging or other design features. (See Chapter 8 for more information on the difference between your invention and licensed products.)

> "Net Sales" are defined as Licensee's gross sales (that is, the gross invoice amount billed customers) less quantity discounts and returns actually credited. A quantity discount is a discount made at the time of shipment. No deductions shall be made for cash or other discounts, for commissions, for uncollectible accounts, or for fees or expenses of any kind which may be incurred by the Licensee in connection with the Royalty payments.

Advance Against Royalties

This provision establishes the amount of the advance payment. Execution refers to the date when you sign the agreement.

> As a nonrefundable advance against royalties (the "Advance"), Licensee agrees to pay to Licensor upon execution of this Agreement the sum of [*insert the amount of the advance, if any*].

Royalty Rate

The provision below establishes the royalty rate.

Royalty for All Rights

> Licensee agrees to pay a Royalty of [*insert appropriate royalty percentage*]% of all Net Sales revenue of the Licensed Products ("Licensed Product Royalty").

Hybrid Royalty Payments

If you have a hybrid license that lasts longer than the length of your patents, we suggest allocating a value between the various forms of intellectual property. You can add the following language after the last sentence of the sample royalty provision. Remember, when making these allocations, the courts presume that a patent has inherently more value than other forms of intellectual property. For example, the patents might account for 80% or more of the value of the license.

Hybrid Royalty; Patent and Nonpatented Rights

> Licensee agrees to pay a Royalty of [*insert appropriate royalty percentage*]% of all Net Sales revenue of the Licensed Products ("Licensed Product Royalty"). The "Licensed Product Royalty" shall be allocated according to the percentage as provided in this Agreement. In the event that a patent does not issue or an issued patent expires or is otherwise terminated, the allocated percentage for such patent or pending patent shall be subtracted from the Licensed Product Royalty. The Licensed Product Royalty shall be adjusted accordingly.
>
> _____% of the royalty for the license of the Patent No.
>
> _____ .
>
> _____% of the royalty for the license of Pending Patent No. _____ .
>
> _____% of the royalty for the license of [*trade secrets, trademarks, copyrights, or other intellectual property*].

Guaranteed Minimum Annual Royalty Payments

The last sentence of this sample provision prohibits cumulating or carrying forward royalty deficiencies or credits, which we recommend.

In addition to any other advances or fees, Licensee shall pay an annual guaranteed royalty (the "GMAR") as follows: [*insert the terms of your GMAR: for example, $10,000 per year*]. The GMAR shall be paid to Licensor annually on [*insert the date when the GMAR should be paid each year*]. The GMAR is an advance against royalties for the 12-month period commencing upon payment. Royalty payments based on Net Sales made during any year of this Agreement shall be credited against the GMAR due for the year in which such Net Sales were made. In the event that annual royalties exceed the GMAR, Licensee shall pay the difference to Licensor. Any annual royalty payments in excess of the GMAR shall not be carried forward from previous years or applied against the GMAR.

Royalties on Spin-Offs

Sometimes, an invention can lead to sales of related products or accessories. For example, say you invented a toy car. In addition to selling the car, the licensee might also sell T-shirts featuring pictures of your cars. This provision entitles you to be paid for these spin-offs. Normally, a spin-off royalty is smaller than a licensed product royalty.

Licensee agrees to pay a Royalty ("Spin-Off Product Royalty") of [*insert appropriate royalty percentage*]% for all Net Sales of "Spin-Off Products." A "Spin-Off Product" is any product derived from, based on, or adapted from the Licensed Product.

Adjustment of Royalties for Third-Party Licenses

Sometimes, a licensee wishes to enhance sales of your product by including another company's trademark, such as Mickey Mouse. Mickey's owner, the Disney Company, will charge the licensee a royalty. The licensee is now faced with two royalties: yours and Disney's. Because Mickey will be increasing your sales, the licensee will ask you to take a reduced royalty known as a third-party license royalty. For example, if your regular royalty rate is 5%, the third-party license rate might be 3%.

Car Radio
No. 1,944,139

Spin-Offs and Antitrust Law

When the licensor charges a royalty for devices that don't infringe the patent but are "derived" from the invention, there is always a potential for antitrust abuse. (See Chapter 17.) In many cases, a licensee will only agree to pay for spin-offs if the derivative invention falls under the claims of the licensed patent. Should you use this provision in your agreement? Here are some things to consider.

A spin-off is a product that is introduced to capitalize on the success of an existing product. If, for example, you license an invention to the Apple Computer Company, they can accept or reject the spin-off provision. If they accept it, they are acknowledging that the invention will generate sufficient revenue *and* create a potential spin-off market. As the owner of rights in the invention, Apple can capitalize on their trademark and the shelf space they acquired selling the product to cash in on the accessories market (as Apple has done with many of its products). This way, they create a new market and get a head start on all competitive spin-offs. Many companies, like Apple, welcome this market because it enhances the invention and often makes it more popular, even if they're paying more of a royalty for it than competitors—for example, the spin-off market has been a strong revenue generator for the Apple iPod and iMac.

The spin-off provision also recognizes the possibility that other rights come with the license—such as trade secrets, copyrights, or trademarks that may be used in the spin-off, even if the patented technology is not.

Keep in mind, this is an *optional* provision and in some cases it may not work—for example, the licensee may reject it outright.

Occasionally, an inventor with a great deal of clout may bully a licensee into accepting a spin-off provision that amounts to an abuse of patent rights—for example, a spin-off requirement that lasts longer than the patent term. If you have doubts as to the enforceability of a spin-off provision, consult with an attorney knowledgeable in licensing law before proceeding.

In the event that any Licensed Product (or other items for which Licensee pays Royalties to Licensor) incorporates third-party character licenses, endorsements, or other proprietary licenses, Licensor agrees to adjust the Royalty rate to [*insert appropriate royalty percentage*]% for such third-party licenses. Licensee shall notify Licensor of any such third-party licenses prior to manufacture. Third-party licenses shall not include licenses accruing to an affiliate, associate, or subsidiary of Licensee.

F.O.B. Royalties

Sometimes, the licensee's products are manufactured outside the United States (also referred to as offshore) and then sold to U.S. retailers through a "letter of credit" or F.O.B. system (the initials stand for "free on board"). F.O.B. sales are made at a much lower rate, sometimes one-third less than similar sales within the United States. If a licensee uses F.O.B. sales, we recommend that you include an F.O.B. royalty rate (usually two to four points higher than the net sales rate). For example, if your net sales royalty is 5%, your F.O.B. royalty rate might be 7% or 8%.

Licensee agrees to pay the Royalty ("F.O.B. Royalty") of [*insert appropriate royalty percentage*]% for all F.O.B. sales of Licensed Products.

Sublicensing Revenues

Before agreeing to a sublicensing provision (example below), you should review the section on sublicensing in Chapter 8. Fifty percent is the common rate for sublicensing payments. Note that this is not a royalty. You will receive 50% of all revenues from licensing. There is no need for a net sales formula or deductions. Why? Because there are no production, freight, or other costs incurred by the licensee. All of this is being done by the sublicensee.

In the event of any sublicense of the rights granted pursuant to this Agreement, Licensee shall pay to Licensor [*insert the amount of the sublicensing percentage*]% of all sublicensing revenues.

Payments and Statements to Licensor

The sample payment provision below provides when payment shall be made ("within 30 days after the calendar quarter"). Sometimes licensees want to pay 90 days after the end of the quarter. This is common, though undesirable—especially because, in reality, most agreements provide for a 30-day "cure" provision. This means that if anything goes wrong during the agreement, the licensee has 30 days after the payment date to cure or fix the problem. So it could take 120 days from the end of the quarter before you get your payment. It's to your advantage to keep this period as short as possible.

The payment provision below also provides that: "The acceptance by Licensor of any of the statements furnished or royalties paid shall not preclude Licensor from questioning the correctness at any time of any payments or statements."

This protects you by establishing that your acceptance of a payment does not prevent you from later claiming the payment was inaccurate. Finally, this provision provides that you get paid in U.S. currency—guaranteeing that you will not have to deal with fluctuating currency conversion rates.

Within thirty days after the end of each calendar quarter (the "Royalty Period"), an accurate statement of Net Sales of Licensed Products along with any royalty payments or sublicensing revenues due to Licensor shall be provided to Licensor, regardless of whether any Licensed Products were sold during the Royalty Period. All payments shall be paid in United States currency drawn on a United States bank. The acceptance by Licensor of any of the statements furnished or royalties paid shall not preclude Licensor questioning the correctness at any time of any payments or statements.

What's an Audit?

So you've negotiated a good royalty, but how do you know the payments you receive are accurate? Because sales figures and deductions are within the control of the licensee, you will want the right to audit, or review, licensee records. This right can be provided in the license agreement and is traditionally referred to as an audit provision.

The "Audit" provision generally provides:

- that the licensor (or the licensor's representative) shall have access to the licensee's books and records
- that the audit information will remain confidential, and
- a method for resolving any disputes over discrepancies.

Opening Up the Books

An audit provision provides who can audit the books and how often. Normally, a licensee will want to limit the frequency of audits. It's common for a licensee to limit the number of audits to once or twice a year. Also, the licensee will want several days' notice before the audit is to occur—typically around five days.

The licensee may also seek to limit who can audit the books. For example, a licensee might request that you hire a Certified Public Accountant (CPA) to perform the audit. It will be more expensive for you to hire a CPA, and, therefore, we would recommend that you avoid this requirement. It would be less expensive if any accountant can serve as your representative for an audit. It also would be helpful to obtain the licensee's cooperation by designating an individual at the licensee's company to be available to assist you or your representatives. Because you might not discover or suspect a discrepancy right away, you should negotiate an audit provision that requires the licensee to keep all books and records available for at least two years after the termination of the license agreement.

Contingency Auditors

Sometimes, a licensee will attempt to prohibit a licensor from using an accounting firm that works on a contingency basis. Working on a contingency basis means that the company will not get paid unless it finds a discrepancy. Licensees are not comfortable with these firms, because they believe that contingency accountants "manufacture" discrepancies in order to receive bigger commissions. As a general rule, we would recommend that you retain the right to use whomever you want as your representative for an audit.

Keeping the Audit Confidential

Because the licensee's books may contain confidential information about sales and prices, your representative may be required to sign a confidentiality agreement. You might also be requested to keep the information confidential. Such confidentiality agreements are reasonable but should not apply in the event of litigation about payments.

Interest Rates

You cannot arbitrarily choose an interest rate. State laws, known as usury laws, prohibit excessive interest rates. Some agreements provide for interest "at a rate of 1% or 1.5% per month, or the maximum rate permitted by law, whichever is less." This language prevents the interest rate from exceeding the limits of state usury laws. The interest rate provided in the sample agreement is tied to the prime rate, a fluctuating national rate that is commonly used in business.

Settling Audit Disputes

In the case of an underpayment (you receive less money than you should), the license agreement should provide for a method of settling the dispute. Usually, there are three parts to this dispute resolution.

First, the licensee must promptly pay you the money you should have received.

Second, you should seek an interest payment. If you had received the proper payment in the first place, you could have deposited it in a bank and earned interest on it.

Third, you may seek to have the licensee pay for the costs of your audit. A licensee will not want to pay for the audit for just any discrepancy, only substantial ones. What counts as substantial? Some agreements set a dollar amount, for example, $1,000. Other agreements set a percentage (for example, if any underpayment was more than 2% of the amount paid).

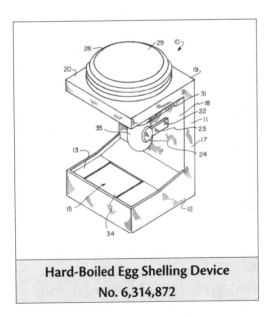

Hard-Boiled Egg Shelling Device
No. 6,314,872

Audit. Licensee shall keep accurate books of accounts and records covering all transactions relating to the license granted in this Agreement. Licensor or its duly authorized representatives shall have the right upon five days' prior written notice, and during normal business hours, to inspect and audit Licensee's records relating to the Property licensed under this Agreement. Licensor shall bear the cost of such inspection and audit, unless the results indicate an underpayment greater than [*insert either amount of underpayment, for example, "$1,000," or percentage, such as "2% of the amount paid"*] for any six-month period. In that case, Licensee shall promptly reimburse Licensor for all costs of the audit along with the amount due with interest on such sums. Interest shall accrue from the date the payment was originally due and the interest rate shall be 1.5% per month, or the maximum rate permitted by law, whichever is less. All books of account and records shall be made available in the United States and kept available for at least two years after the termination of this Agreement.

EXAMPLE: A licensor had received a $10,000 royalty payment. An audit determined that the licensee should have received $10,300. The underpayment was $300, or 3% of the amount actually paid. In the licensing agreement, the licensee had agreed to pay for the audit if any underpayment was more than 2% of the amount paid. The Licensee must pay the $300 plus interest, plus the costs of the audit.

How Do You Deal With Late Payments?

Late payments are similar to underpayments: You are losing money because you could have invested the payment earlier and earned interest. Therefore, a license agreement can require that the licensee pay interest from the date that the payment should have been made. The interest rate can be the prime rate (see the audit provision above) or any legal rate. Monthly rates of 1% or 1.5% are common in audit and late payment provisions.

The sample agreement also includes the language "time is of the essence," which is basically legal double-talk meaning that you and the licensee agree that it's a material aspect of the agreement for you to get paid on time.

> **Late Payment.** Time is of the essence with respect to all payments to be made by Licensee under this Agreement. If Licensee is late in any payment provided for in this Agreement, Licensee shall pay interest on the payment from the date due until paid at a rate of 1.5% per month, or the maximum rate permitted by law, whichever is less.

 RELATED TOPIC
For information on taxation of licensing income, see Chapter 17. ●

Negotiating Your Agreement

What, Me Negotiate?..232

    Negotiate in Person Whenever Possible..232

    Ask Questions..232

    Things to Avoid..232

    Take It or Leave It..234

    Negotiating Resources...235

Documenting the Important Contract Elements......................................235

    License Summary..236

    What Do You Do With the Fact Sheet?...236

Letter of Intent..238

    What If the Letter of Intent Is Binding?..244

Option Agreements..244

    Attaching the License Agreement to the Option Agreement....................245

    Option Payments...246

    Sample Option Agreement..246

**What If the Licensee Wants to Proceed Without a Written
License Agreement?**..252

n this chapter, we provide negotiating tips and suggest some ways to incorporate the important contract elements into a formal document, such as a license agreement, an option agreement, or a letter of intent. You should read this chapter if you answer "yes" to any of these questions:

- Do you want suggestions about negotiating?
- Would you like to prepare a summary of the important contract elements?
- Would you like information about option agreements?
- Would you like to learn about letters of intent?

What, Me Negotiate?

Negotiation is like navigating a trip. You need to know where you're going and then decide the best route. We can't teach you how to negotiate, but we can provide you with some tips.

Negotiate in Person Whenever Possible

Email, faxes, and phone work fine, but a personal meeting creates an atmosphere where solutions and compromises are more likely to result. Don't get upset if you are outnumbered at a business meeting.

During the meeting, you'll be able to see who the real decision maker is among the group and address your comments to him or her. Face each person you speak with, speak directly, and make eye contact. Pay attention to responses and demonstrate your attention by nodding your head or stating your opinion. Avoid talking while another person is speaking or making gestures of disgust or disrespect, such as rolling your eyes, snorting, or sighing. And try not to crowd anyone—that is, don't sit or stand too close.

Ask Questions

Avoid confrontations by asking questions. For example, say the licensee is offering you less than the industry standard. Don't create a confrontation and demand a higher rate. Start by asking why. A question rather than a demand is more likely to result in a change because questions articulate the underlying issues without creating a conflict.

Things to Avoid

Negotiations can be stressful. It might be easier to remember what not to do so you can avoid potentially costly mistakes. Below is a list of "don'ts" to help you in your negotiations:

Dear Rich:
When Do You Have a Deal?

Dear Rich: How do you know when you have an enforceable contract? I thought I had a handshake deal for a license and then when I got the full written agreement it had all of the things we agreed upon but it also had this other stuff that we hadn't agreed upon. Can I make the other side abide by the handshake deal?

Maybe. Maybe not. You must start with the idea that license negotiations often have two distinct stages: negotiation of the basic business terms followed by negotiation of the legal terms. Unless you have agreement on all of the material elements of your contract, then there is no enforceable deal. Here's an example:

EXAMPLE: Sam agrees to license Camille's water bottle invention. Camille negotiates for a three-year license with a 6% royalty on net revenue with no deductions. She will make the deal exclusive and worldwide. Sam and Camille shake hands and Sam promises to send along his "standard" license agreement.

A week later Camille obtains the written license. It includes all of the basic terms she and Sam negotiated, but it also includes several objectionable provisions, including a requirement that she obtain insurance, a material element to her. Until the parties reach an agreement as to this material element, they have no license. Eventually Sam agrees to remove the insurance requirement and Camille signs the agreement.

In cases like this—where the parties have agreed to the business terms of the deal—the parties can use an escrow account or condition the release of funds on the execution of a written agreement. This avoids the problem of having to chase after money laid out if the deal never materializes. If the negotiations fall apart, the funds are returned and everyone moves on.

- **Don't have unrealistic expectations.** The major reason licensing negotiations fall apart is unrealistic expectations. Know what you want. A good negotiator knows this and has a range of "worst to best" alternatives. Create flexible expectations based upon the realities of the business.
- **Don't bluff.** The false display of confidence might work in a poker game, but it's not recommended in business negotiations. It could cause a licensee to walk out or to call your bluff. If your bluff is called, you will lose credibility when you accept less.
- **Don't keep negotiating after you've agreed on terms.** According to one consultant, inventors often talk themselves into a sale and then out of it again because they won't stop talking.
- **Don't ask for an exorbitant amount of money when you're willing to settle for a fraction of it.** In his book *Smart Negotiating: How to Make Good Deals in the Real World* (Simon & Schuster, 1992), author James C. Freund suggests that your starting point for payments be no more than 15% to 25% away from your realistic expectation.
- **Don't reject an offer today if you can put it off till tomorrow.** Even if you're sure you won't accept an offer, it's usually better to delay so you can reflect on your decision.

Take It or Leave It

Sometimes a licensee presents you with a finalized agreement and asks you to sign it, explaining that you can take it or leave it. For example, say the president of a licensee company tells you, "You get a $10,000 advance and a 5% royalty and we get exclusive worldwide rights for the life of the patent. Take it or leave it." This type of offer really says, "We dictate the terms and we don't negotiate." If you have no other prospects and are afraid of losing an opportunity, then you must decide on their terms. Don't mistakenly assume the company is bluffing. They're probably not.

Review the elements of your deal according to the principles provided in this chapter and the subsequent contract chapters. Research the licensee company to determine whether it is stable or financially precarious, and find out what you can about the company's reputation within the industry. A good general rule is if the company is stable and respected and the terms are standard (or close to standard), you should accept the offer. However, if the arrangement is inherently unfair and the licensee company's reputation is not good, you're better off rejecting the offer.

Be Careful How You Characterize Other Inventors

If the licensee has a business relationship with a competing inventor, be careful how you characterize the competition. If you make false statements about another inventor or invention, or about your own invention, in order to induce the licensee to break a business relationship, you could be setting yourself up for several lawsuits including defamation, a claim known as "interference with a business (or contractual) relationship," or "interference with prospective economic advantage." Every state has laws prohibiting such behavior.

Negotiating Resources

If you'd like more background on negotiating, the negotiating bible is *Getting to Yes: Negotiating Agreement Without Giving In*, by Roger Fisher, William Ury, and Bruce Patton (Penguin Books, 1991). Other good sources are James Freund's *Smart Negotiating: How to Make Good Deals in the Real World* (Simon & Schuster, 1992), *Never Split the Difference: Negotiating as If Your Life Depended on It*, by Chris Voss and Tahl Raz (Harper Business, 2016), and *Negotiator Pro*, a software program that takes you through the steps of a formal negotiation and provides advice from experts in the field. The program is available from Negotiator Pro (www.negotiatorpro.com).

Documenting the Important Contract Elements

Once you have negotiated the essential business terms, we recommend that you prepare a one-page sheet that summarizes the results. This sheet is a simple way of memorializing the contract facts.

This sheet may be attached to your final license agreement or it may be attached to a prelicense document, such as an option agreement or a letter of intent (discussed below). That way, if you change the details later (for example, you extend the length of the agreement), you need only modify the sheet, not the whole agreement. If you include your sheet as an attachment to your agreement, be sure to give it a title such as Exhibit A and make reference to it in the main body of the agreement. (An exhibit is simply a document that is included with the main agreement and that becomes part of the agreement.) For example, in the body of your agreement you could refer to the fact sheet with the following language: "Licensee agrees to pay to Licensor the sum specified in Exhibit A."

! CAUTION
In the event that you fail to nego-tiate a written agreement, the fact sheet may also—although we do not recommend it— become a memorandum of an oral license. For example, you and the licensee sit down for lunch and work out the basic elements of the license. You and the licensee write down these elements on your fact sheet. The licensee is in a hurry and wants to begin manufacturing. He promises to send you a complete license agreement within a month. Six months later, you have not received the license agreement. You sue for royalties and argue that you had an oral agreement, based upon the fact sheet.

License Summary

The sheet below summarizes the basic contract elements between Joan Smith, an inventor (referred to as SMITH), and MEDCO, a medical supply company.

What Do You Do With the Fact Sheet?

What you do with your sheet summarizing the contract depends on the licensee's course of action. Below are the common scenarios:

- **Written license.** The licensee wants a written license agreement. The summary sheet can be used as a reference for filling out the agreement, or it can be used as an exhibit. That is, you would attach it to the license agreement and refer to it as Exhibit A.

For example, "The Royalty shall be as defined in Exhibit A."

- **Letter of intent.** The licensee desires a written license agreement, but because it could take several weeks or months to prepare the agreement, the licensee requests a letter of intent—a nonbinding document that states the intentions of the parties. The summary sheet (or the substance of the sheet) is incorporated into the letter of intent. Review the section on letters of intent, below.

- **Option agreement.** The licensee is not sure about entering into a license agreement and wants more time before executing one—for example, to evaluate or test market the product. In that case, you can incorporate the summary sheet into an option agreement. An option agreement lets a licensee buy time (usually known as the option period) from you, the inventor—a few weeks, months, or years. In return for receiving an option payment, the inventor agrees not to license the invention to anyone else during the option period. Review the section on option agreements, below.

- **Oral license.** The licensee doesn't care about a written license agreement and wants to start selling the product based solely on the basic contract facts. In other words, the licensee wants to operate on your oral

Sample License Summary

Medco-Smith License

1. **The Properties**

    U.S. Patent Pending #09/998,944

    U.S. Patent Application #09/023,484

    PCT Application #US92/15,874

    Copyrighted Packaging Imagery

    All Patent Disclosures including #343,561

    Certain SMITH proprietary information and trade secrets

2. **License**

    Exclusive. No assignment or sublicense without licensor's written consent.

3. **Licensed Products**

    Medical supply products

4. **Term**

    17 years or the life of any patents on the Properties, whichever is longer

5. **Territory**

    World

6. **Advance**

    $25,000

7. **Minimum Annual Royalty**

    None

8. **Licensed Product Royalty Rate**

    Five percent (5%) of Net Sales (all revenues, less credited returns, from the sale, distribution, and transfer of any such products by MEDCO)

    [*Note: When licensing patents, pending patents, and trade secrets (known as a hybrid license), you may choose to allocate the respective percentage values. See Chapter 9 for sample language.*]

9. **Date for Commencement of Sale**

    January 2019

10. **Insurance**

    Licensee obtains standard product liability/$1 million coverage

11. **Dispute Resolution**

    Mediation and arbitration in California

license. We do not recommend that you proceed on the basis of an oral agreement. In the event, however, that you decide to disregard this advice, we suggest adding a dispute resolution provision to the sheet and having the licensee sign it. Review the section on oral licenses below.

Letter of Intent

After agreeing to the essential business terms, a licensee may prepare and sign a letter of intent. The letter of intent sets forth the essential terms and establishes a date when the parties plan to enter into a license agreement.

A letter of intent is usually not a binding contract. That is, even if you sign it, you can still reject the deal for any reasonable basis. For example, you sign a letter of intent but then reject the final contract because you and the licensee disagree about provisions such as warranties or indemnity.

Most letters of intent specifically state they are not binding agreements. Why bother preparing and signing one? Licensees like the letter of intent because it serves as a guide for the final agreement, establishes that both parties are going to work in good faith to consummate the license, and provides some comfort level to the parties as they progress through the contract negotiation.

A letter of intent, like an agreement in principle, usually requires the parties to act in good faith in pursuing their contracting goals. This means that the parties must deal fairly and reasonably with each other—not blow the other party off for arbitrary reasons. Courts in most states will enforce this good-faith requirement even if they do not enforce the actual terms of the letter of intent.

Note also that even though a letter of intent rarely creates a binding agreement regarding its subject matter, it may contain some elements that become binding—for example, a confidentiality provision.

The sample letter of intent below could have included the sheet summarizing the contract facts as an exhibit. Instead, in our sample, the terms were written into the body of the letter. Sometimes, a licensee prefers this format because it starts to flesh out language that may be used in the license agreement.

Letter of Intent. This introductory paragraph guarantees that the letter of intent is not intended to be a contract. Even though it does not impose any legal obligation, some courts have interpreted a letter of intent to require that the parties act in good faith. This means that the parties will deal fairly and reasonably. For example, a licensor would be acting unfairly if the sole purpose of obtaining the letter of intent was to get a better deal from a different company.

Contract Standards: Good-Faith and Best Efforts

Throughout this book, the terms "good-faith" and "best efforts" appear in contract provisions. For example, the mediation provision in Chapter 11 provides that the parties make a good-faith attempt to resolve the dispute. In the letter of intent in this chapter, the parties agree to use best efforts to execute a license agreement. The terms are related but not the same.

Good faith. Even without the magic words "good faith" in the contract, every party to a contract must act in good faith. This requirement, known as the "implied covenant of good faith and fair dealing," is presumed to be a part of every contract. The precise definition of good faith and fair dealing may vary from state to state and from contract to contract, but it refers generally to the duty to act honestly and equitably toward the other parties to the agreement.

When one party does not act in good faith, the contract can be considered breached under the laws of most states. In some states, breaching the covenant of good faith and fair dealing may also constitute a tort—a personal injury that gives rise to a legal claim. The good-faith obligation applies only once a contract is in place; it does not apply to precontractual discussions. It applies to attempts to resolve contract disputes, as well.

When good faith and fair dealing is at issue. In order to breach the implied covenant of good faith, the breaching party must exhibit some fairly egregious behavior. That behavior is measured by an objective, reasonable person's standard. Some examples of acts that courts have found to breach the covenant are:

- An insurance company deliberately and unreasonably denies claim requests.
- A distributor signs an exclusive distribution arrangement with a manufacturer and then "sits" on the product in order to enable a competitor to gain market share.
- The owner of a business sells it and agrees not to compete, and then lends money to a relative to create a competing business.

Remedies. In the event that a party claims a breach of the implied covenant of good faith and fair dealing, the remedies are usually the same as for breach of contract. That is, the wronged party can seek compensation for damages that might reasonably be foreseen by the parties (excluding punitive damages). If breach of the covenant is treated as a tort (personal injury claim) under state law, then compensatory and punitive damages are also available.

Contract Standards: Good-Faith and Best Efforts (continued)

Best efforts. Best efforts is a contractual qualifier by which one party agrees to use diligent efforts to fulfill an obligation. For example, what if a third party has to assist in the performance of a contractual obligation and you can't guarantee that will happen by the deadline set in the contract? One solution is to insert the qualifier that you will use "best efforts" to complete the work. That way, you're not guaranteeing that the third party will come through in a timely manner, only that you'll try your best to make it happen.

> **EXAMPLE:** Gerbik Engineering contracts to complete reconstruction of a boat, which requires a naval inspection and certification by the Coast Guard. Because the inspections are done at the convenience of the Coast Guard, Gerbik can't guarantee that the boat will be ready to go by the contractual deadline, September 1. If the Coast Guard doesn't inspect until September 2, Gerbik would be in breach of the agreement. To avoid this problem but still assure the other party that Gerbik will do its part to meet the deadline, Gerbik's lawyer inserts a statement that "Gerbik Engineering will use best efforts to have the boat reconstructed and inspected by September 1."

By using a best-efforts statement, a party can argue that missing the deadline doesn't constitute a breach of the contract, as long as that party exercised consistently diligent efforts to complete the work on time.

Range of efforts. Lawyers have developed some different ways to describe the various types of efforts that a party can promise to use in a contract. These are listed below, with their usual definitions (as you'll see, despite the number of terms used, they all boil down to either "reasonable" or "best" efforts). However, keep in mind that courts might interpret these terms differently. To the surprise of some practitioners, courts often don't distinguish amongst the types of efforts a party might employ, and instead consider all "efforts" requirements to require only consistent diligence from the person who promises to make them.

> **EXAMPLE:** A film distributor had agreed "to use its best efforts diligently and in good faith to exploit" two motion pictures. In analyzing this "best efforts" standard, the court held that the distributor need act only like the "average, prudent comparable distributor," a standard that sounds closer to the basic definition of "reasonable efforts" as described below.

So why bother to elaborate the differences between best efforts and reasonable efforts? Because some courts do recognize distinctions among these definitions. And, using more precise terms allows each party to understand what the other is promising to do.

Contract Standards: Good-Faith and Best Efforts (continued)

Reasonable efforts. Someone who promises to make reasonable efforts must act like any other reasonable businessperson in a similar position; that is, the person must act diligently and responsibly, but doesn't have to do things that are commercially unfeasible.

Commercially reasonable efforts. This is considered to be the same as "reasonable efforts."

Good-faith efforts. Again, this is interpreted to require "reasonable efforts."

Best efforts. A person who promises to make best efforts must do everything possible to make it happen, even to the point of suffering a commercial loss. As noted, courts often disagree with this interpretation. Many have held that a best-efforts promise does not require the party to act in a commercially unreasonable manner (for example, to risk bankruptcy). In Illinois, for instance, courts will not enforce a best-efforts promise; they consider the terminology too vague.

Reasonable best efforts. Considered to be the same as "best efforts."

What are reasonable efforts? Regardless of whether courts differentiate between best efforts and reasonable efforts, they do require parties who make such promises to make *some* effort that involves diligence, reasonableness, and good faith. Because there are so many vagaries, it's often best for the drafter of such provisions to either specify exactly what the "efforts" will consist of or to specify what will not be required.

The Properties. Insert your name, business form, and address. This introductory statement defines the invention or technology that is being licensed. You should have agreed upon a definition as part of your business negotiation. See Chapter 8 for information on defining the invention. You should strike the patent references if you do not have a patent or pending application for patent.

The Grant. Insert the name, business form (for example, "an Illinois corporation"), and address of the prospective licensing company. This statement establishes the elements of the prospective license. See Chapter 8 for information on defining the license. If an agent is acting on behalf of the licensor, then the agent's name will be inserted into this statement. For example, "JONES is acting as Inventor's agent." You should also insert the territory (for example, "the world"). Insert the length of agreement (the term). See Chapter 8.

Operations. This Operations provision establishes the licensing company's obligations for manufacturing and accounting. This type of provision is not necessary but is often included in a letter of intent. An operations provision is often more detailed and more specific in the license agreement.

Sample Letter of Intent

Dear [*insert name of contact person at company that wants to option invention*]:

This letter reflects our discussions regarding the terms and conditions of the proposed licensing agreement for certain technologies, more specifically described below. Please review this letter of intent, and if it accurately reflects our discussions, return a copy with your signature. We will then proceed to a written draft of the licensing agreement. Thanks for your cooperation.

Letter of Intent. This document is a Letter of Intent only. It is not intended to be, and shall not constitute in any way, a binding or legal agreement, or impose any legal obligation or duty on Inventor and Company.

The Properties. [*Insert your name*] ("Inventor") is the owner of the certain proprietary and intellectual property rights collectively known as "the Properties." The Properties include: U.S. Patent Pending No(s). [*insert patent number(s)*], U.S. Patent Application No. [*insert patent application number*], and certain Inventor proprietary information and trade secrets.

The Grant. [*Insert name of company that wants to option your invention*] ("Company") is a manufacturer and distributor that desires to enter into a Licensing Agreement (the "Agreement") for the purpose of [*choose one: exclusively or nonexclusively*] exploiting the Properties in the form of products (the "Licensed Products") throughout [*insert countries or regions for the license*] (the "Territory") for [*insert the length of the potential license, for example, "five years"*] (the "Term"). The license shall not include the right to assign or sublicense such rights to other parties without the express written consent of Inventor.

Operations. Company will bear all responsibility for manufacturing, advertising, marketing, promotion, and support of the Licensed Products. Company will keep accurate records of accounting, distribution, and costs and will make these records available for inspection on a reasonable basis.

Sample Letter of Intent (continued)

Royalties. Company shall pay to Inventor a royalty rate of [*insert appropriate royalty percentage*]% of all "Net Sales" from the Licensed Products or any Licensed Products that use technology developed or derived from the Properties. "Net Sales" shall be all revenues (less credited returns) from the sale, distribution, and transfer of any such products by Company.

[*Optional clause*] **Advance.** As an advance against future royalties, Company shall pay to Inventor $[*insert amount of advance*] upon execution of the Agreement.

License Agreement. In the event that the parties agree to proceed upon these terms, Inventor and Company agree to use their best efforts to execute a written contract incorporating the terms of this Letter of Intent on or before [*insert date when option must be exercised*].

If this accurately reflects your intention, please sign, date, and return the enclosed copy of this Letter of Intent.

_____   _____
Inventor   Date

_____   _____
Company   Date

Royalties. This provision establishes the basic licensor payments, royalties, and advance and also incorporates the definition for "Net Sales." An explanation of these terms is provided in Chapter 9. The term "execution of the Agreement" refers to the signing of the contract. If royalties are to be paid directly to the agent, then that information would be included in this section.

License Agreement. This provision establishes that the parties will use "best efforts" (see "Contract Standards: Good Faith and Best Efforts," above).

The parties can extend the date for executing a written contract. Even if the date is not extended, both parties can still execute a license agreement at any time. The date is simply a guidepost.

DOWNLOAD FORMS
You can download this form (and all other forms in this book) from this book's companion page on Nolo.com; see the appendix for the link.

What If the Letter of Intent Is Binding?

Most letters of intent are nonbinding and say so with explicit language. A nonbinding letter is often preferred because both parties are free to get out of the agreement if they desire. However, if there is no mention of the word "nonbinding" or if the letter of intent does not disclaim or deny that it is an enforceable agreement (by saying, for example, "this letter is not a contract"), then your signature will bind you to the agreement. Unlike a nonbinding letter of intent, you (and the licensee) will not be able to terminate the arrangement at will. You're both locked in. If you don't meet the terms of the letter—for example, sign a written license on the date set in the agreement—your arrangement with the licensee will terminate unless you agree to extend the time to sign an agreement.

If you are happy with the basic contract elements, entering into a binding letter of intent with a potential licensee might work for you. As an alternative, if a licensee wants a binding commitment to enter into a license agreement by a certain date, you could execute an option agreement. In an option agreement, a licensee pays you for keeping the licensing deal open to it for a certain period of time. We discuss options below.

Option Agreements

An option agreement is essentially a contract to make another contract, if certain conditions are met. A licensee who thinks it may want to enter into a license agreement with you pays you a fee to keep

**Wind-Operated Sprinkler Feature
No. 6,588,679**

Attaching the License Agreement to the Option Agreement

If the licensee exercises the option, you are obligated to sign the license agreement. Shouldn't you see the whole license agreement before signing the option deal? Ideally, yes, you should see the complete license deal that you are expected to sign. It would be great (and we recommend) that the license agreement be attached to the option deal as an exhibit. That way, if the licensee later exercises the option, both of you will have already agreed on the provisions.

Unfortunately, many situations are not as neat and clean as this. The parties—you and the licensee—might be willing to agree on the business terms but not willing to discuss and negotiate all of the contract provisions at the time of the option agreement. Instead, the parties may agree to use "good faith" or "best efforts" to agree upon contract provisions, basically a promise to use reasonable efforts and fair business judgment.

Because a disagreement is always possible, it is wise to use an arbitration or mediation provision in the option agreement. That way, you can bring in a third party to iron out or force a solution for contract provision disputes. For more information about arbitration and mediation, review Chapter 14.

the offer open while it makes its decision. In exchange for the payment, you agree not to enter into a license agreement with anyone else for a period of time—perhaps six months or a year (sometimes referred to as the option period). If the licensee decides to proceed (sometimes referred to as "exercising its option"), you then sign a license agreement. If not, you can keep the option payment and are free to take the invention somewhere else after the option period expires.

Why does a licensee pay for the option? Because the company wants to be sure that you will not take the invention to anyone else during the option period. In other words, the company is paying you to keep the invention away from others for a specified period of time.

Option Payments

Option payments are usually smaller than license payments. Don't expect to get rich off an option. As a general rule, the longer the option period, the more money you should seek for the option. For example, a six-week option payment might cost $1,000 while a three-month option could go for $5,000. Remember, the longer the option, the longer that your invention is out of the marketplace. You might be losing opportunities and money if the option period is longer than a year.

If the option is ultimately exercised, the option payment is usually considered as part of the advance and later deducted against your royalties. But you could try to negotiate a different outcome. If you're in a strong bargaining position, you might be able to negotiate a payment that is not deductible.

If the potential licensee doesn't exercise the option, you keep the money without any obligation. To guarantee this result, you should explicitly state in your option agreement that the option payment is nonrefundable.

Sample Option Agreement

Below we explain provisions found in the sample option agreement.

Introduction. This introductory paragraph establishes the purpose of the agreement and defines the parties. Note that the key terms for the parties are capitalized throughout the agreement for easy reference.

The Properties; Licensed Products. This section provides two definitions—one for the invention and one for the licensed products. The parties are using the term "Properties" to refer to the invention. As we explained in Chapter 8, many names can be used to signify the invention. If you're not familiar with the concepts of defining the invention or the licensed products, review Chapter 8.

Exclusive Option. This provision establishes that the option is exclusive, meaning the inventor cannot option rights to another company. We recommend attaching a copy of the license agreement (or a sample license agreement) to the option agreement. If that's not possible, strike the last sentence and add a sentence that states: "The parties, acting in good faith, shall use best efforts to incorporate the terms set forth in this Option Agreement into the final License Agreement."

Terms and Conditions of Option. This section provides that the option payment is nonrefundable, meaning the inventor does not have to return the money if the option isn't exercised. However, the payment can be deducted against future royalties if the licensee exercises the option. If you have the ability, you should negotiate an option payment that is nonrefundable and nonrecoupable. Nonrecoupable means that the payment cannot be deducted against royalties.

Option Agreement

Introduction

This Option Agreement (the "Agreement") is made between [*insert your name, address, and business form*] (referred to as "Inventor") and [*insert the company's name, address, and business form*] (referred to as "Company"). Inventor and Company shall be collectively referred to as "the parties." Inventor is the owner of certain proprietary rights to an invention tentatively referred to as the "[*insert the name of your invention*]." Company desires to acquire an exclusive option to enter into a License Agreement for these ideas, processes, and technologies. The parties agree as follows:

The Properties; Licensed Products

Inventor is the owner of licensing rights to all inventions embodied in U.S. Patent No. [*insert patent number*], a copy of which is attached as Attachment A, and to all other proprietary rights, including but not limited to copyrights, trade secrets, formulas, research data, know-how, and specifications related to the invention presently known as "[*insert the name of your invention*]" and referred to in this Option Agreement as "the Properties." Inventor has submitted the Properties to Company. Inventor represents that [*insert* he *or* she] has the authority to grant rights to Company for the Properties. Company desires an exclusive option to enter into a License Agreement to sell the Properties as incorporated in Company's products ("the Licensed Products").

Exclusive Option

For the consideration provided below, Inventor grants to Company the exclusive option to enter into a license agreement (the "License Agreement") for the Properties. The License Agreement shall be substantially similar to that attached to this Option Agreement as Attachment _____ and shall incorporate the License Terms as set forth below.

Terms and Conditions of Option

Company shall have six months from the date of execution of this Agreement (the "Option Period") to exercise its option for the Properties. During the Option Period, Inventor shall refrain from offering or granting any third party any rights to the Properties which will interfere with the exercise of the option granted to Company.

In consideration for the option and rights granted in this Option Agreement, Company shall pay to Inventor the nonrefundable sum of $[*insert amount of option payment*]. In the event that Company exercises its option, such payment shall be considered as an advance against future royalties.

License

In the event Company decides to enter into a License Agreement, such agreement shall contain the business terms as set forth below.

License Grant

Exclusive worldwide license of all rights to the Properties, including, but not limited to, any patent, copyright, or similar rights, if applicable. No assignment or sublicensing of rights without written consent of Inventor.

Term

For the life of any patents obtained on the Properties or fifteen years, whichever is longer.

☐ Advances [*optional*]

A nonrefundable advance against royalties of $[*insert amount of advance*] to be paid as follows: [*indicate when advance is to be paid*].

Royalties; Net Sales

[*Insert royalty rate*]% of Net Sales of the Licensed Products. Net Sales are defined as Company's gross sales minus returns that are actually credited. Gross sales are the total amount on invoices billed to customers.

☐ Guaranteed Minimum Annual Royalty [*optional*]

A Guaranteed Minimum Annual Royalty of $[*insert amount of GMAR*] payable (in advance) at the beginning of each calendar year of the Licensing Agreement. Company may carry forward or cumulate royalty deficiencies for any year in which the minimum royalty guarantee did not exceed the actual royalties earned by Inventor.

Confidentiality

The parties acknowledge that each may be furnished or have access to confidential information that relates to each other's business (the "Information"). In the event that Information is in written form, the disclosing party shall label or stamp the materials with the word "Confidential" or some similar warning. In the event that Information is transmitted orally, the disclosing party shall promptly provide a writing indicating that such oral communication constituted Information. The parties agree to preserve and protect the confidentiality of the Information and no party shall disclose such Information to third parties without the prior written consent of the other.

Termination

Company shall have the right to terminate this Option Agreement at any time, upon written notice to Inventor. In the event (a) Company elects to terminate this Option Agreement, or (b) Company has not exercised its option before the end of the Option Period, or (c) Company materially breaches this Agreement, Company agrees to promptly return to Inventor all rights, models, and documentation in and to the Properties and not to use or disclose to any third parties information relating to the Properties. In such an event, Inventor shall be free to license the Properties to others with no further obligation to Company and Company shall have no further obligation to Inventor with the exception of any confidentiality agreements executed by the parties (the terms of which are incorporated in this Option Agreement) and which shall survive the termination of this Option Agreement.

General; Miscellaneous

Any material contained in an attachment, exhibit, or addendum to this Option Agreement shall be incorporated by reference in this Option Agreement. Nothing contained in this Option Agreement shall be deemed to constitute either Inventor or Company a partner, joint venturer, or employee of the other party for any purpose. This Option Agreement may not be amended except in a writing signed by both parties. No waiver by Inventor of any right shall be construed as a waiver of any other right. If a court finds any provision of this Option Agreement invalid or unenforceable as applied to any circumstance, the remainder of this Option Agreement shall be interpreted so as best to effect the intent of the parties. This Option Agreement shall be governed by and interpreted in accordance with the laws of the State of

[*Insert your state of residence*]. Any controversy or claim arising out of or relating to this Option Agreement, or the breach of this Option Agreement, shall be settled by arbitration in accordance with the rules of the American Arbitration Association and judgment upon the award rendered by the arbitrator(s) may be entered in any court having jurisdiction. The prevailing party shall have the right to collect from the other party its reasonable costs and attorneys' fees incurred in enforcing this agreement. Any such arbitration hearing shall include a written transcript of the proceedings and a written explanation for any final determination. This Option Agreement expresses the complete understanding of the parties with respect to the subject matter and supersedes all prior proposals, agreements, representations, and understandings.

If these terms and conditions are agreeable, please sign and execute both copies of this Option Agreement.

_____   _____
Inventor   Date

_____   _____
Company   Date

In this agreement, the inventor (you) expects to license all rights. You are not reserving any rights. If you do not intend to license all rights, you can option rights for specific licensed products or in certain territories.

License. This provision lists all the negotiated business elements (exclusive license, royalties, and so on). Your sheet summarizing the contract facts could have been used instead. In that case, you would state that the "License elements shall be as established in the attached exhibit entitled Exhibit A." For more information on determining these basic elements, review Chapters 8 and 9.

Confidentiality. In the event that the parties have not previously signed a confidentiality agreement, you should include a provision such as this requiring confidentiality. (See Chapter 7.)

Termination. This option agreement terminates if the company does not exercise the option. That is, if the company does not indicate that it wants to proceed, the parties walk away and the inventor keeps the option payment. However, option agreements can include renewals. For example, at the end of six months, the potential licensee can pay a certain sum for another six-month option period. This provision also establishes that the potential licensee must return all materials (prototypes, documentation, and so on) in the event of termination.

General; Miscellaneous. Each state has varying rules regarding contract interpretation, and this section provides which state's law will govern disputes. We recommend that you seek your state of residence, although the potential Company might insist on its home state. Usually, this is not a crucial point. However, be aware that if the potential Company wants you to agree to the jurisdiction of another state, you will have to travel to that state for any dispute arising from the agreement.

Sometimes option agreements omit this miscellaneous section because the parties want a contract that does not appear "too legalistic." However, we recommend that you include these provisions because they are important for resolving disputes. This contract also provides for resolving disputes by a method known as arbitration—a private system for adjudicating disputes and paid for by the participants. These provisions are explained in detail in Chapter 14.

Be forewarned that many companies are reluctant to arbitrate and might ask you to strike that section.

DOWNLOAD FORMS
You can download this form (and all other forms in this book) from this book's companion page on Nolo.com; see the appendix for the link.

What If the Licensee Wants to Proceed Without a Written License Agreement?

Although most licensees prefer a written license—it provides more security and may be required for patent rights—companies sometimes want to proceed without a written agreement. A licensee might want to begin manufacturing your invention based upon your oral agreement of the material terms. Although it's unlikely, it can happen.

If the licensee is adamant about moving ahead without a written agreement and does not want to execute a letter of intent or an option agreement, you have a difficult choice: to proceed without a written agreement or to terminate the arrangement.

We recommend against oral agreements. They are more difficult to prove and enforce and do not provide sufficient protection in the event of infringement or lawsuits. In addition, the law may set limits on oral agreements or interpret the agreements in a manner that does not adequately protect you.

You may be inclined to disregard this advice. In that case, we suggest that you take some precautions. First, ask if the licensee has proceeded with other inventors without written agreements. Ask to speak with the other inventors to determine if the relationship has been successful—for instance, whether they've been paid and are satisfied with the arrangement.

Second, if the licensee insists on moving ahead without a license agreement, use your summary sheet as a skeletal written agreement. Both you and the licensee should sign this document. This will never protect you as well as a complete written license, but it is better than relying solely upon a handshake and an oral agreement.

Finally, because oral agreements are more difficult to interpret and enforce, we recommend that you find some method of dispute resolution if you insist on proceeding without a written agreement. ●

Sample Agreement

License Agreement...255

    Introduction Provision..255

    The Property...256

    Licensed Products...276

    Grant of Rights..277

    Sublicense...277

    Reservation of Rights...277

    Territory..278

    Term...278

    Net Sales...280

    Advance Against Royalties..280

    Licensed Product Royalty...280

    Guaranteed Minimum Annual Royalty (GMAR)..............282

    Sublicensing Revenues...282

    Payment and Statements to Licensor...............................282

    Audit..282

    Warranties and Indemnity..282

    Compliance With Intellectual Property Laws...................283

    Infringement Lawsuits Against Third Parties...................283

    Exploitation..283

    Samples and Quality Control...283

    Insurance..283

    Confidentiality..284

    Termination..284

    Effect of Termination..285

    Survival...285

Attorneys' Fees and Expenses..285

Dispute Resolution...285

Governing Law 286

Jurisdiction 287

Waiver...287

Invalidity 287

Entire Understanding 287

Attachments and Exhibits 287

Notices..287

No Joint Venture 287

Assignability...288

Signatures...288

Exhibit A 290

Optional License Agreement Provisions..290

Force Majeure (Pronounced Fors-Mazhoor´) 290

Escrow...291

Grant Back of Improvements 291

Training 291

Installation..292

Tech Support...292

Deliverables: Schedules and Development Services; Delivery
and Approval 293

Right of First Refusal 296

Most Favored Nations Clause (Sometimes Referred to as a Most
Favored Licensee Provision)...296

Modifying the Sample Agreement for Your Needs 297

Modifications With a Word Processor...297

Modifications by Hand...298

Inserting New Sections 298

n this chapter, we offer a sample agreement. If you're in a hurry, you may have opened to this chapter without reviewing the rest of the book first. You'd like to use the form agreement, fill in the blank sections, and get started. That's okay, but you should be prepared for the fact that this form agreement is not like an income tax form or a lease form. That is, the sample license agreement is not fixed—you may need to modify the content, reorder the sections, or add or remove sections. We'll give you advice on how to do that later in this chapter.

You should take the time to review the other relevant chapters in this book if you run into any of the following problems:

- You don't understand why you need a particular provision.
- You don't know what information should be supplied in one of the blanks.
- You want to remove, alter, or add a provision.

License Agreement

Below, we review the various sections of a standard license agreement.

Introduction Provision

Insert your name, business form (if any), and address (for example, "Phil Patel, a sole proprietor, with his address at

Definitions Up Front

One common variation in a license agreement is to place a list of the contract definitions after the introductory paragraph. That way, you know where to look for a definition, rather than searching through the agreement to find where it was originally introduced and defined. This is mostly a matter of personal preference. If you'd prefer to have your definitions up front, simply pull them out of the body of the agreement and alphabetize them, as in this example.

"Effective Date" is defined as the date when the Agreement commences and is established by the latest signature date.

"Confidential Information" is defined as any confidential information that relates to each party's business.

"Net Sales" is defined as Licensee's gross sales (i.e., the gross invoice amount billed customers) less quantity discounts and returns actually credited.

"Property" is defined as all inventions described in U.S. Patent No. _____.

5678 Hempstead Turnpike, Wantagh, NY 11793"). If you are unsure of your business form, review Chapter 4. Supply the same information for the licensee (for example, "Medco, a California corporation, with its address at Pierpont Plaza, San Francisco, CA 94102"). The licensee will supply you with information about its business form.

You should also supply a name that you are using for your invention. If the item has been sold to the public already, you can use the trademark name. If it is a patented invention, use the title of the patent—for example, "Portable Popcorn-Making Device." Otherwise, just insert whatever nickname you and the licensee have been using to refer to the invention.

The second half of the introductory paragraph starting with "Licensor is the owner of certain proprietary rights ... " replaces the "whereas" provisions that are common in many license agreements. The "whereas" provisions summarize what the parties intend to do. They usually begin with statements such as: "Whereas the parties desire to enter into an agreement ...." There's no need to use the "whereas" format. You can simply summarize the intentions of the parties as shown in the sample agreement. If the sample agreement does not accurately reflect your intentions, it should be modified accordingly. This portion of the agreement is not considered to be enforceable (that is, it's not legally binding), because it occurs before the statement "therefore the parties agree ...." Regardless of its enforceability, this introductory paragraph should accurately summarize the intentions of the parties.

The Property

This provision defines your invention. You can use the term "the Property" (or "Properties") or "the Invention." If you are licensing a method or procedure, you can use the term "the Process." Whatever term is used, it must be consistent throughout the agreement. There are many ways to write a property definition.

If you have applied for a patent but it hasn't yet issued, you should define your invention based upon your patent claims and include a copy of the patent application (or the claims enunciated in your application) with the final agreement. (This will not work if you only have a provisional patent application.) Simply label the application "Exhibit A" at the top and attach it to the end of the agreement. For an explanation of the difference between a provisional patent application and a pending patent application, review Chapter 2. For example, you could use the alternative clause below.

License Agreement

Introduction

This License Agreement (the "Agreement") is made between [*insert Licensor's name, business form, and address*] (referred to as "Licensor"), and [*insert Licensee's name, business form, and address*] (referred to as "Licensee").

Licensor and Licensee shall be collectively referred to as "the parties." Licensor is the owner of certain proprietary rights to an invention referred to as [*insert name of invention*]. Licensee desires to license certain rights in the invention. Therefore the parties agree as follows:

The Property [*select one*]

☐ **Patent Issued**

The "Property" refers to the invention(s) described in U.S. Patent No(s). [*insert patent number(s)*].

☐ **Patent Not Yet Issued**

The "Property" refers to the invention(s) described in U.S. Patent Application No(s). [*insert patent application number(s)*], [a copy of which is *or* copies of which are] attached to this agreement.

☐ **Patents and Improvements**

The Property is defined as the invention(s) described in U.S. Patent No(s). [*insert patent number(s)*] and any improvements, reissues, or extensions, as well as any continuations, divisions, or substitute U.S. patent applications that shall be based on the patent(s); and any patent applications corresponding to the above-described patent(s) and patent applications that are issued, filed, or to be filed in any and all foreign countries.

☐ **Copyright, Trade Secrets, and Trademarks: No Patents**

The Property refers to all proprietary rights, including, but not limited to, copyrights, trade secrets, formulas, research data, know-how, and specifications related to the invention commonly known as the [*insert name of invention*] as well as any trademark rights and associated goodwill. A more complete description is provided in the attached Exhibit A.

☐ **Copyright or Trademark Registration**

The Property refers to all proprietary rights, including, but not limited to, copyrights as embodied in Copyright Registration No. _____ dated _____ (or Trademark Registration No. _____ dated _____ and associated goodwill).

☐ **Patents and Copyright, Trade Secrets, and Trademarks**

The "Property" refers to all inventions described in U.S. Patent No. [*insert patent number*] and to all other proprietary rights, including, but not limited to, copyrights, trade secrets, formulas, research data, know-how, and specifications related to the invention commonly known as [*insert name of invention*] as well as any trademark rights and associated goodwill. A more complete description is provided in the attached Exhibit A.

Licensed Products [*select one*]

☐ **Licensed Products Specifically Defined**

Licensed Products are defined as the Licensee products incorporating the Property and specifically described in Exhibit A (the "Licensed Products").

☐ **No Limitations on Licensed Products Definition**

Licensed Products are defined as any products sold by the Licensee that incorporate the Property.

☐ **No Limitations on Licensed Process Definition**

A Licensed Process is any commercial application of the Process by the Licensee. [*Remember to change all references in the agreement to Licensed Process, rather than Licensed Products.*]

Grant of Rights

Licensor grants to Licensee a/an [exclusive *or* nonexclusive] license to make, use, and sell the Property solely in association with the manufacture, sale, use, promotion, or distribution of the Licensed Products.

Sublicense [*select one*]

☐ **Consent to Sublicense Required**

Licensee may sublicense the rights granted pursuant to this agreement provided Licensee obtains Licensor's prior written consent to such sublicense and Licensor receives such revenue or royalty payment as provided in the Sublicensing Revenues section (the Payment section) below. Any sublicense granted in violation of this provision shall be void.

☐ **Consent to Sublicense Not Unreasonably Withheld**

Licensee may sublicense the rights granted pursuant to this Agreement provided Licensee obtains Licensor's prior written consent to such sublicense (Licensor's consent to any sublicense shall not be unreasonably withheld) and Licensor receives such revenue or royalty payment as provided in the Payment section below. Any sublicense granted in violation of this provision shall be void.

Reservation of Rights [*select one*]

☐ **All Rights Reserved**

Licensor expressly reserves all rights other than those being conveyed or granted in this Agreement.

☐ **Reservation of Rights Expressly Excluding a Particular Industry**

Licensor expressly reserves all rights other than those being conveyed or granted in this Agreement, including, but not limited to, the right to license the Properties in [*list a particular market which you want to expressly exclude, for example, "the computer and video game market"*].

Territory [*select one*]

☐ **Statement of Territory**

The rights granted to Licensee are limited to [*insert the territory*] (the "Territory").

☐ **Limiting Cross-Territory Sales**

The rights granted to Licensee are limited to [*insert the territory*] (the "Territory"). Licensee shall not make, use, or sell the Licensed Products or any products which are confusingly or substantially similar to the Licensed Products in any country outside the Territory and will not knowingly sell the Licensed Products to persons who intend to resell them in a country outside the Territory.

Term [*select one*]

☐ **Specified Term With Renewal Rights**

This Agreement shall commence upon the latest signature date (the "Effective Date") and shall extend for a period of [*insert number of years for initial term, for example, "two years"*] (the "Initial Term").

Following the Initial Term, this Agreement may be renewed by Licensee under the same terms and conditions for [*insert number of renewal terms*] consecutive [*insert length of each renewal term, for example, "two-year"*] periods (the "Renewal Terms"), provided that Licensee provides written notice of its intention to renew this Agreement within 30 days before the expiration of the current term. In no event shall the Agreement extend longer than the date of expiration of the patent listed in the definition of the Property.

☐ **Term for the Length of Patent Only**

This Agreement shall commence upon the latest signature date (the "Effective Date") and shall expire simultaneously with the expiration of the longest-living patent (or patents) or last-remaining patent application as listed in the definition of the Property, whichever occurs last, unless sooner terminated pursuant to a provision of this Agreement.

☐ **Short Term With Renewal Rights Based Upon Sales**

This Agreement shall commence upon the latest signature date (the "Effective Date") and shall extend for a period of [*insert number of years*] years (the "Initial Term") and thereafter may be renewed by Licensee under the same terms and conditions for consecutive [*insert number of years*]-year periods (the "Renewal Terms"), provided that:

(a) Licensee provides written notice of its intention to renew this Agreement within 30 days before the expiration of the current term;

(b) Licensee has met the sales requirements as established in Exhibit A [*if you choose this alternative be sure to include the sales requirements in Exhibit A*]; and

(c) in no event shall the Agreement extend longer than the date of expiration of the longest-living patent (or patents) or last-remaining patent application as listed in the definition of the Property.

☐ **No Patents; Indefinite Term**

This Agreement shall commence upon the latest signature date (the "Effective Date") and shall continue until terminated pursuant to a provision of this Agreement.

☐ **Fixed Yearly Term**

This Agreement shall commence upon the latest signature date (the "Effective Date") and shall continue for [*insert number of years*] unless sooner terminated pursuant to a provision of this Agreement.

☐ **Term for as Long as Licensee Sells Licensed Products**

This Agreement shall commence upon the latest signature date (the "Effective Date") and shall continue for as long as Licensee continues to offer the Licensed Products in commercially reasonable quantities unless sooner terminated pursuant to a provision of this Agreement.

Royalties

All royalties ("Royalties") provided for under this Agreement shall accrue when the respective items are sold, shipped, distributed, billed, or paid for, whichever occurs first. Royalties shall also be paid by the Licensee to Licensor on all items, even if not billed (including, but not limited to, introductory offers, samples, promotions, or distributions) to individuals or companies which are affiliated with, associated with, or subsidiaries of Licensee.

Net Sales

"Net Sales" are defined as Licensee's gross sales (that is, the gross invoice amount billed customers) less quantity discounts and returns actually credited. A quantity discount is a discount made at the time of shipment. No deductions shall be made for cash or other discounts, for commissions, for uncollectible accounts, or for fees or expenses of any kind which may be incurred by the Licensee in connection with the Royalty payments.

☐ **Advance Against Royalties** [*optional*]

As a nonrefundable advance against Royalties (the "Advance"), Licensee agrees to pay to Licensor upon execution of this Agreement the sum of $[*insert the amount of the advance, if any*].

Licensed Product Royalty [*select one*]

☐ **Royalty on Net Sales**

Licensee agrees to pay a Royalty of [*insert amount of royalty*]% of all Net Sales revenue of the Licensed Products ("Licensed Product Royalty").

☐ **Per-Unit Royalties**

Licensee agrees to pay a Royalty of $_____ per Unit. For purposes of computing this Royalty, the term "Per-Unit Sales" shall refer to Licensed Products that have been sold, shipped, distributed, billed, or paid for, whichever occurs first. No deductions shall be made for cash or other discounts, for commissions, for uncollectible accounts, or for fees or expenses of any kind which may be incurred by the Licensee in connection with the Per-Unit Sales payments.

☐ **Hybrid Royalty; Patent and Nonpatented Rights**

Licensee agrees to pay a Royalty of [*insert amount of royalty*]% of all Net Sales revenue of the Licensed Products ("Licensed Product Royalty"). The Licensed Product Royalty shall be allocated according to the percentages as provided in this Agreement. In the event that a patent does not issue or an issued patent expires or is otherwise terminated, the allocated percentage for such patent or pending patent shall be subtracted from the Licensed Product Royalty. The Licensed Product Royalty shall be adjusted accordingly.

_____% of the Royalty for the license of the Patent No. _____ .

_____% of the Royalty for the license of Pending Patent No. _____ .

_____% of the Royalty for the license of trade secrets [*or* trademarks, copyrights, *or other intellectual property*].

☐ **Guaranteed Minimum Annual Royalty Payment** [*optional*]

In addition to any other advances or fees, Licensee shall pay an annual guaranteed Royalty (the "GMAR") as follows: [*insert the terms of your GMAR: for example, $10,000 per year*]. The GMAR shall be paid to Licensor annually on [*insert the date when the GMAR should be paid each year*]. The GMAR is an advance against Royalties for the twelve-month period commencing upon payment. Royalty payments based on Net Sales made during any year of this Agreement shall be credited against the GMAR due for the year in which such Net Sales were made. In the event that annual Royalties exceed the GMAR, Licensee shall pay the difference to Licensor. Any annual Royalty payments in excess of the GMAR shall not be carried forward from previous years or applied against the GMAR.

☐ **License Fee** [*optional*]

As a nonrefundable, nonrecoupable fee for executing this license, Licensee agrees to pay to Licensor upon execution of this Agreement the sum of $_____ .

☐ **Royalties on Spin-Offs** [*optional*]

Licensee agrees to pay a Royalty ("Spin-Off Product Royalty") of [*insert appropriate royalty percentage*]% for all Net Sales of "Spin-Off Products." A Spin-Off Product is any product that is derived from, based on, or adapted from the Licensed Product, provided that if the product uses the Property it shall be considered to be a Licensed Product and not a Spin-Off Product.

☐ **Adjustment of Royalties for Third-Party Licenses** [*optional*]

In the event that any Licensed Product (or other items for which Licensee pays Royalties to Licensor) incorporates third-party character licenses, endorsements, or other proprietary licenses, Licensor agrees to adjust the Royalty rate to [*insert appropriate royalty percentage*]% for such third-party licenses. Licensee shall notify Licensor of any such third-party licenses prior to manufacture. Third-party licenses shall not include licenses accruing to an affiliate, associate, or subsidiary of Licensee.

☐ **F.O.B. Royalties** [*optional*]

Licensee agrees to pay the Royalty ("F.O.B. Royalty") of [*insert appropriate royalty percentage*]% for all F.O.B. sales of Licensed Products.

☐ **Sublicensing Revenues** [*optional*]

In the event of any sublicense of the rights granted pursuant to this Agreement, Licensee shall pay to Licensor [*insert the amount of the sublicensing percentage*]% of all sublicensing revenues.

Payments and Statements to Licensor

Within 30 days after the end of each calendar quarter (the "Royalty Period"), an accurate statement of Net Sales of Licensed Products along with any Royalty payments or sublicensing revenues due to Licensor shall be provided to Licensor, regardless of whether any Licensed Products were sold during the Royalty Period. All payments shall be paid in United States currency drawn on a United States bank. The acceptance by Licensor of any of the statements furnished or Royalties paid shall not preclude Licensor questioning the correctness at any time of any payments or statements.

Audit

Licensee shall keep accurate books of account and records covering all transactions relating to the license granted in this Agreement, and Licensor or its duly authorized representatives shall have the right upon five days' prior written notice, and during normal business hours, to inspect and audit Licensee's records relating to the Property licensed under this Agreement. Licensor shall bear the cost of such inspection and audit, unless the results indicate an underpayment greater than $[*insert amount of underpayment, for example, "$1,000"*] for any six-month period. In that case, Licensee shall promptly reimburse Licensor for all costs of the audit along with the amount due with interest on such sums. Interest shall accrue from the date the payment was originally due and the interest rate shall be 1.5% per month, or the maximum rate permitted by law, whichever is less. All books of accounts and records shall be made available in the United States and kept available for at least two years after the termination of this Agreement.

Late Payment

Time is of the essence with respect to all payments to be made by Licensee under this Agreement. If Licensee is late in any payment provided for in this Agreement, Licensee shall pay interest on the payment from the date due until paid at a rate of 1.5% per month, or the maximum rate permitted by law, whichever is less.

Licensor Warranties

Licensor warrants that it has the power and authority to enter into this Agreement and has no knowledge as to any third-party claims regarding the proprietary rights in the Property which would interfere with the rights granted under this Agreement.

Indemnification by Licensor [*select one*]

☐ **Statement of Licensor Indemnification**

Licensor shall indemnify Licensee and hold Licensee harmless from any damages and liabilities (including reasonable attorneys' fees and costs) arising from any breach of Licensor's warranties as defined in Licensor Warranties, above, provided (a) such claim, if sustained, would prevent Licensee from marketing the Licensed Products or the Property; (b) such claim arises solely out of the Property as disclosed to the Licensee, and not out of any change in the Property made by Licensee or a vendor, or by reason of an off-the-shelf component or by reason of any claim for trademark infringement; (c) Licensee gives Licensor prompt written notice of any such claim; (d) such indemnity shall only be applicable in the event of a final decision by a court of competent jurisdiction from which no right to appeal exists; and (e) the maximum amount due from Licensor to Licensee under this paragraph shall not exceed the amounts due to Licensor under the Payment section from the date that Licensor notifies Licensee of the existence of such a claim.

☐ Licensor Indemnification With Fund

Licensor shall indemnify Licensee and hold Licensee harmless from any damages and liabilities (including reasonable attorneys' fees and costs) arising from any breach of Licensor's warranties as defined in Licensor Warranties, above, provided (a) such claim, if sustained, would prevent Licensee from marketing the Licensed Products or the Property; (b) such claim arises solely out of the Property as disclosed to the Licensee, and not out of any change in the Property made by Licensee or a vendor, or by reason of an off-the-shelf component or by reason of any claim for trademark infringement; (c) Licensee gives Licensor prompt written notice of any such claim; (d) such indemnity shall only be applicable in the event of a final decision by a court of competent jurisdiction from which no right to appeal exists; and (e) the maximum amount due from Licensor to Licensee under this paragraph shall not exceed the amounts due to Licensor under the Payment section from the date that Licensee notifies Licensor of the existence of such a claim. The maximum amount due from Licensor to Licensee under this paragraph shall not exceed [*50 to 100*]% of the amounts due to Licensor under the Payment section [*if you have numbered the sections of your agreement, include the number of the payment section*] from the date that Licensor notifies Licensee of the existence of such a claim. After the commencement of a lawsuit against Licensee that comes within the scope of this paragraph, Licensee may place [*same percentage as listed above*]% of the royalties thereafter due to Licensor under the Payment section in a separate interest-bearing fund which shall be called the "Legal Fund." Licensee may draw against such Legal Fund to satisfy all of the reasonable expenses of defending the suit and of any judgment or settlement made in regard to this suit. In the event the Legal Fund is insufficient to pay the then-current defense obligations, Licensee may advance monies on behalf of the Legal Fund and shall be reimbursed as payments are credited to the Legal Fund. Licensor's liability to Licensee shall not extend beyond the loss of its royalty deposit in the Legal Fund. After the suit has been concluded, any balance remaining in the Legal Fund shall be paid to Licensor and all future royalties due to Licensor shall be paid to Licensor as they would otherwise become due. Licensee shall not permit the time for appeal from an adverse decision on a claim to expire.

Licensee Warranties

Licensee warrants that it will use its best commercial efforts to market the Licensed Products and that their sale and marketing shall be in conformance with all applicable laws and regulations, including but not limited to all intellectual property laws.

Indemnification by Licensee

Licensee shall indemnify Licensor and hold Licensor harmless from any damages and liabilities (including reasonable attorneys' fees and costs) (a) arising from any breach of Licensee's warranties and representation as defined in the Licensee Warranties, above; (b) arising out of any alleged defects or failures to perform of the Licensed Products or any product liability claims or use of the Licensed Products; and (c) any claims arising out of advertising, distribution, or marketing of the Licensed Products.

☐ Limitation of Licensor Liability [*optional*]

Licensor's maximum liability to Licensee under this agreement, regardless on what basis liability is asserted, shall in no event exceed the total amount paid to Licensor under this Agreement. Licensor shall not be liable to Licensee for any incidental, consequential, punitive, or special damages.

Intellectual Property Protection

Licensor may, but is not obligated to, seek in its own name and at its own expense, appropriate patent, trademark, or copyright protection for the Property. Licensor makes no warranty with respect to the validity of any patent, trademark, or copyright which may be granted. Licensor grants to Licensee the right to apply for patents on the Property or Licensed Products provided that such patents shall be applied for in the name of Licensor and licensed to Licensee during the Term and according to the conditions of this Agreement. Licensee shall have the right to deduct its reasonable out-of-pocket expenses for the preparation, filing, and prosecution of any such U.S. patent application (but in no event more than $5,000) from future royalties due to Licensor under this Agreement. Licensee shall obtain Licensor's prior written consent before incurring expenses for any foreign patent application.

Compliance With Intellectual Property Laws

The license granted in this Agreement is conditioned on Licensee's compliance with the provisions of the intellectual property laws of the United States and any foreign country in the Territory. All copies of the Licensed Product as well as all promotional material shall bear appropriate proprietary notices.

Infringement Lawsuits Against Third Parties

In the event that either party learns of imitations or infringements of the Property or Licensed Products, that party shall notify the other in writing of the infringements or imitations. Licensor shall have the right to commence lawsuits against third persons arising from infringement of the Property or Licensed Products. In the event that Licensor does not commence a lawsuit against an alleged infringer within 60 days of notification by Licensee, Licensee may commence a lawsuit against the third party. Before filing suit, Licensee shall obtain the written consent of Licensor to do so, and such consent shall not be unreasonably withheld. Licensor will cooperate fully and in good faith with Licensee for the purpose of securing and preserving Licensee's rights to the Property. Any recovery (including but not limited to a judgment, settlement, or licensing agreement included as resolution of an infringement dispute) shall be divided equally between the parties after deduction and payment of reasonable attorneys' fees to the party bringing the lawsuit.

Exploitation

Licensee agrees to manufacture, distribute, and sell the Licensed Products in commercially reasonable quantities during the term of this Agreement and to commence such manufacture, distribution, and sale within the following time period: [*insert time period, for example, "six months"*]. This is a material provision of this Agreement.

Samples and Quality Control

Licensee shall submit a reasonable number of production samples of the Licensed Product to Licensor to ensure that the Licensed Product meets Licensor's quality standards. In the event that Licensor fails to object in writing within ten business days after the date of receipt, the Licensed Product shall be deemed to be acceptable. At least once during each calendar year, Licensee shall submit two production samples of each Licensed Product for review. The quality standards applied by Licensor shall be no more rigorous than the quality standards applied by Licensee to similar products.

Insurance

Licensee shall, throughout the Term, obtain and maintain, at its own expense, standard product liability insurance coverage, naming Licensor as additional named insured. Such policy shall (a) be maintained with a carrier having a Moody's rating of at least B; and (b) provide protection against any claims, demands, and causes of action arising out of any alleged defects or failure to perform of the Licensed Products or any use of the Licensed Products. The amount of coverage shall be a minimum of $[*insert amount of insurance coverage*] with no deductible amount for each single occurrence for bodily injury or property damage. The policy shall provide for notice to the Agent and Licensor from the insurer by registered or certified mail in the event of any modification or termination of insurance. Licensee shall furnish Licensor and Agent a certificate from its product liability insurance carrier evidencing insurance coverage in favor of Licensor, and in no event shall Licensee distribute the Licensed Products before the receipt by the Licensor of evidence of insurance. The provisions of this section shall survive termination for three years.

Confidentiality

The parties acknowledge that each may be furnished or have access to confidential information that relates to each other's business (the "Confidential Information"). In the event that Confidential Information is in written form, the disclosing party shall label or stamp the materials with the word "Confidential" or some similar warning. In the event that Confidential Information is transmitted orally, the disclosing party shall promptly provide a writing indicating that such oral communication constituted Confidential Information. The parties agree to maintain the Confidential Information in strictest confidence for the sole and exclusive benefit of the other party and to restrict access to such Confidential Information to persons bound by this Agreement, only on a need-to-know basis. Neither party, without prior written approval of the other, shall use or otherwise disclose to others, or permit the use by others of, the Confidential Information.

Termination [*select one*]

☐ **Initial Term With Renewals From the Term Section**

This Agreement terminates at the end of two years (the "Initial Term") unless renewed by Licensee under the terms and conditions as provided in the Term section of this Agreement.

☐ **Fixed Term**

This Agreement shall terminate at the end of [*insert number of years*] years unless terminated sooner under a provision of this Agreement.

☐ **Term Based Upon Length of Patent Protection**

This Agreement shall terminate with the expiration of the longest-living patent (or patents) or last-remaining patent application (as listed in the definition of the Property), whichever occurs last, unless terminated sooner under a provision of this Agreement.

☐ **Initial Term With Renewals**

This Agreement terminates at the end of two years (the "Initial Term") unless renewed by Licensee under the same terms and conditions for consecutive two-year periods (the "Renewal Terms"), provided that Licensee provides written notice of its intention to renew this Agreement at least 30 days prior to expiration of the current term. In no event shall the Agreement extend longer than the date of expiration of the longest-living patent (or patents) or last-remaining patent application as listed in the definition of the Property.

☐ **Termination at Will: Licensee's Option**

Upon 90 days' notice, Licensee may, at its sole discretion, terminate this Agreement by providing notice to the Licensor.

Licensor's Right to Terminate

Licensor shall have the right to terminate this Agreement for the following reasons:

(a) Licensee fails to pay Royalties when due or fails to accurately report Net Sales, as defined in the Payment section of this Agreement, and such failure is not cured within 30 days after written notice from the Licensor;

(b) Licensee fails to introduce the product to market by [*insert date by which Licensee must begin selling Licensed Products*] or to offer the Licensed Products in commercially reasonable quantities during any subsequent year;

(c) Licensee fails to maintain confidentiality regarding Licensor's trade secrets and other Information;

(d) Licensee assigns or sublicenses in violation of the Agreement; or

(e) Licensee fails to maintain or obtain product liability insurance as required by the provisions of this Agreement.

☐ **Terminate as to Territory Not Exploited** [*optional*]

Licensor shall have the right to terminate the grant of license under this Agreement with respect to any country or region included in the Territory in which Licensee fails to offer the Licensed Products for sale or distribution or to secure a sublicensing agreement for the marketing, distribution, and sale of the product within two years of the Effective Date.

Effect of Termination

Upon termination of this Agreement, all Royalty obligations as established in the Payment section shall immediately become due. After the termination of this license, all rights granted to Licensee under this Agreement shall terminate and revert to Licensor, and Licensee will refrain from further manufacturing, copying, marketing, distribution, or use of any Licensed Product or other product which incorporates the Property. Within 30 days after termination, Licensee shall deliver to Licensor a statement indicating the number and description of the Licensed Products which it had on hand or is in the process of manufacturing as of the termination date. Licensee may dispose of the Licensed Products covered by this Agreement for a period of three months after termination or expiration except that Licensee shall have no such right in the event this agreement is terminated according to the Licensor's Right to Terminate, above. At the end of the posttermination sale period, Licensee shall furnish a royalty payment and statement as required under the Payment section. Upon termination, Licensee shall deliver to Licensor all tooling and molds used in the manufacture of the Licensed Products. Licensor shall bear the costs of shipping for the tooling and molds.

Survival

The obligations of Sections [*insert section names or numbers that will survive termination*] shall survive any termination of this Agreement.

Attorneys' Fees and Expenses

The prevailing party shall have the right to collect from the other party its reasonable costs and necessary disbursements and attorneys' fees incurred in enforcing this Agreement.

Dispute Resolution [*select one*]

☐ **Arbitration**

If a dispute arises under or relating to this Agreement, the parties agree to submit such dispute to binding arbitration in the state of [*insert state in which parties agree to arbitrate*] or another location mutually agreeable to the parties. The arbitration shall be conducted on a confidential basis pursuant to the Commercial Arbitration Rules of the American Arbitration Association. Any decision or award as a result of any such arbitration proceeding shall be in writing and shall provide an explanation for all conclusions of law and fact and shall include the assessment of costs, expenses, and reasonable attorneys' fees. Any such arbitration shall be conducted by an arbitrator experienced in [*insert industry experience required for arbitrator*] and in invention licensing law and shall include a written record of the arbitration hearing. The parties reserve the right to object to any individual who shall be employed by or affiliated with a competing organization or entity. An award of arbitration may be confirmed in a court of competent jurisdiction.

☐ **Mediation and Arbitration**

The parties agree that every dispute or difference between them, arising under this Agreement, shall be settled first by a meeting of the parties attempting to confer and resolve the dispute in a good-faith manner. If the parties cannot resolve their dispute after conferring, any party may require the other parties to submit the matter to nonbinding mediation, utilizing the services of an impartial professional mediator approved by all parties. If the parties cannot come to an agreement following mediation, the parties agree to submit the matter to binding arbitration at a location mutually agreeable to the parties. The arbitration shall be conducted on a confidential basis pursuant to the Commercial Arbitration Rules of the American Arbitration Association. Any decision or award as a result of any such arbitration proceeding shall include the assessment of costs, expenses, and reasonable attorneys' fees and shall include a written record of the proceedings and a written determination of the arbitrators. Absent an agreement to the contrary, any such arbitration shall be conducted by an arbitrator experienced in intellectual property law. The parties reserve the right to object to any individual who shall be employed by or affiliated with a competing organization or entity. In the event of any such dispute or difference, either party may give to the other notice requiring that the matter be settled by arbitration. An award of arbitration shall be final and binding on the parties and may be confirmed in a court of competent jurisdiction.

☐ **Alternative Dispute Resolution**

If a dispute arises and cannot be resolved by the parties, either party may make a written demand for formal resolution of the dispute. The written request will specify the scope of the dispute. Within 30 days after such written notice, the parties agree to meet, for one day, with an impartial mediator and consider dispute resolution alternatives other than litigation. If an alternative method of dispute resolution is not agreed upon within 30 days of the one-day mediation, either side may start litigation proceedings.

Governing Law

This Agreement shall be governed in accordance with the laws of the State of [*insert the choice of state law*].

Jurisdiction

Each party (a) consents to the exclusive jurisdiction and venue of the federal and state courts located in [*insert county and state in which parties agree to litigate*] in any action arising out of or relating to this agreement; (b) waives any objection it might have to jurisdiction or venue of such forums or that the forum is inconvenient; and (c) agrees not to bring any such action in any other jurisdiction or venue to which either party might be entitled by domicile or otherwise.

Waiver

The failure to exercise any right provided in this Agreement shall not be a waiver of prior or subsequent rights.

Invalidity

If any provision of this Agreement is invalid under applicable statute or rule of law, it is to be considered omitted and the remaining provisions of this Agreement shall in no way be affected.

Entire Understanding

This Agreement expresses the complete understanding of the parties and supersedes all prior representations, agreements, and understandings, whether written or oral. This Agreement may not be altered except by a written document signed by both parties.

Attachments and Exhibits

The parties agree and acknowledge that all attachments, exhibits, and schedules referred to in this Agreement are incorporated in this Agreement by reference.

Notices

Any notice or communication required or permitted to be given under this Agreement shall be sufficiently given when received by certified mail or sent by facsimile transmission or overnight courier.

No Joint Venture

Nothing contained in this Agreement shall be construed to place the parties in the relationship of agent, employee, franchisee, officer, partners, or joint venturers. Neither party may create or assume any obligation on behalf of the other.

Assignability [*select one*]

☐ **Statement of Assignability**

Licensee may not assign or transfer its rights or obligations pursuant to this Agreement without the prior written consent of Licensor. Any assignment or transfer in violation of this section shall be void.

☐ **Consent Not Unreasonably Withheld**

Licensee may not assign or transfer its rights or obligations pursuant to this Agreement without the prior written consent of Licensor. Such consent shall not be unreasonably withheld. Any assignment or transfer in violation of this section shall be void.

☐ **Consent Not Needed for Licensee Affiliates or New Owners**

Licensee may not assign or transfer its rights or obligations pursuant to this Agreement without the prior written consent of Licensor. However, no consent is required for an assignment or transfer that occurs (a) to an entity in which Licensee owns more than 50% of the assets, or (b) as part of a transfer of all or substantially all of the assets of Licensee to any party. Any assignment or transfer in violation of this section shall be void.

Each party has signed this Agreement through its authorized representative. The parties, having read this Agreement, indicate their consent to the terms and conditions by their signatures below.

LICENSOR: LICENSEE:

_____   _____
Signature   Signature

_____   _____
Name/Title   Name/Title

_____   _____
Company   Company

_____   _____
Date   Date

EXHIBIT A

The Property

[Insert description of the Property.] _____

_____

_____

_____

_____

_____

Licensed Products

[Indicate type of products, for example "medical supply products."] _____

_____

_____

_____

_____

_____

DOWNLOAD FORMS

You can download this form (and all other forms in this book) from this book's companion page on Nolo.com; see the appendix for the link.

Patent Not Yet Issued

> The "Property" refers to the invention(s) described in U.S. Patent Application No(s). [*insert patent application number(s)*], [a copy of which is *or* copies of which are] attached to this agreement.

If the licensee wants to acquire more than the present U.S. patent rights to your invention, such as derivative rights or improvements on your patent or foreign patent rights, then the definition may be more detailed as in the following example.

Patents and Improvements

> The Property is defined as the invention(s) described in U.S. Patent No(s). [*insert patent number(s)*] and any improvements, reissues, or extensions, as well as any continuations, divisions, or substitute U.S. patent applications that shall be based on U.S. Patent No(s). [*insert patent number(s) (same numbers as above)*]; and any patent applications corresponding to the above-described patents and patent applications that are issued, filed, or to be filed in any and all foreign countries.

Note: The term "Improvements" may need its own definition, since some inventors may not want to permit a licensee to use every improvement that results from a patent. By limiting the definition (for example, "improvements related to the sports and recreation industry"), the licensee only obtains rights to the improvements that fall within the definition. Read Chapter 8 for information on defining the Property and read Chapter 15 regarding improvements to your invention.

In the case of a nonpatented invention, the definition of the invention should describe the invention and indicate the proprietary rights that you have acquired. The description of the invention should tell what it looks like, what it is, and what it does.

Copyright, Trade Secrets, and Trademarks: No Patents

> The Property refers to all proprietary rights, including, but not limited to, copyrights, trade secrets, formulas, research data, know-how, and specifications related to the invention commonly known as the [*name of invention*], as well as any trademark rights and associated goodwill. A more complete description is provided in the attached Exhibit A.

If you have a copyright or trademark registration for some feature of your invention that is being licensed, you should reference that registration by number and date.

Copyright or Trademark Registration

The Property refers to all proprietary rights, including, but not limited to, copyrights as embodied in Copyright Registration No. _____ dated _____ (or Trademark Registration No. _____ dated _____ and associated goodwill).

If you are licensing patent rights and other features protected by trademark, trade secret, or copyright law, then your definition of your invention would be a combination of the two definitions above.

Patents and Copyright, Trade Secrets, and Trademarks

The "Property" refers to all inventions described in U.S. Patent No. [*insert patent number*] and to all other proprietary rights, including, but not limited to, copyrights, trade secrets, formulas, research data, know-how, and specifications related to the invention commonly known as [*name of invention*], as well as any trademark rights and associated goodwill. A more complete description is provided in the attached Exhibit A.

Licensed Products

The definition of "Licensed Products" has a crucial impact on your license, because these are the types of products that the licensee can sell. That is, the licensee will package or modify your invention to sell to different markets. If you are unsure of how to define Licensed Products, review Chapter 8. If you are licensing a process or method (not a product), you should review Chapter 8 and modify the grant provision accordingly. If there is no limitation on Licensed Products (that is, you have agreed that the licensee may put your invention in any of its products), you can simply state the following.

No Limitations on Licensed Products Definition

Licensed Products are defined as any products sold by the Licensee that incorporate the Property.

Method of Storing Elongated Implements Between Corner Side Walls No. 6,142,320

If you want to use the same broad definition for a process, state the following.

No Limitations on Licensed Process Definition

A Licensed Process is any commercial application of the Process by the Licensee. [*Change all references in the agreement to Licensed Process, rather than Licensed Products.*]

Grant of Rights

The license is either exclusive or nonexclusive. If it is exclusive, only the licensee can have the rights conveyed in the grant provision. No one else, not even you, can exercise these rights.

Sublicense

Under this provision, the licensee can license its rights to another company, but only with your written consent. Usually, a licensee will sublicense rights to foreign companies. If the licensee finds this too rigid, you can agree not to withhold consent except for a valid business reason.

For more information about sublicensing, see Chapter 8.

Consent to Sublicense Not Unreasonably Withheld

Licensee may sublicense the rights granted pursuant to this Agreement provided Licensee obtains Licensor's prior written consent to such sublicense (Licensor's consent to any sublicense shall not be unreasonably withheld) and Licensor receives such revenue or royalty payment as provided in the Payment section below. Any sublicense granted in violation of this provision shall be void.

Reservation of Rights

This establishes the intellectual property rights that are not being given. Generally, you reserve all rights not granted in the agreement. However, if you already have a license with someone in another industry, you may want to place your new licensee on alert and specifically mention that industry. For example, you could reserve all rights to license the invention to aquatic recreational companies.

Reservation of Rights Expressly Excluding a Particular Industry

Licensor expressly reserves all rights other than those being conveyed or granted in this Agreement, including, but not limited to, the right to license the Properties in [*list a particular market which you want to expressly exclude, for example, "the computer and video game market"*].

For more information, review Chapter 8.

Territory

Generally, if you are licensing a patent, the choice of territory is limited to the country or countries where patent protection has been obtained. However, if you and the licensee agree to seek patent protection in foreign countries, then the Territory can go beyond the boundaries of the initial patent protection. If the license is worldwide, for example, you can simply write "the world," but if the territory is limited to a certain area, then state it here (for example, "the United States and Canada"). We have provided an alternate provision if you are concerned about a licensee selling products in an area where you have another license (referred to as "cross-territory activity"). For a more detailed discussion of territory issues, see Chapter 8.

Limiting Cross-Territory Sales

The rights granted to Licensee are limited to [*insert the territory*] (the "Territory"). Licensee shall not make, use, or sell the Licensed Products or any products which are confusingly or substantially similar to the Licensed Products in any country outside the Territory and will not knowingly sell the Licensed Products to persons who intend to resell them in a country outside the Territory.

Term

As discussed in Chapter 8, there are three common ways to structure the term (or length) of your license agreement: (1) The term can be for a fixed length (say ten years or, alternatively, the length of your patent); (2) the term can be for a fixed length (say, two years) with a series of renewal periods; or (3) the term can be for as long as the licensee manufactures and sells the licensed products or until the agreement is terminated.

If you have negotiated a term for the length of the patents only, the provision should be as below.

Term for the Length of the Patents Only

This Agreement shall commence upon the Effective Date and shall expire simultaneously with the expiration of the longest-living patent (or patents) or last-remaining patent application as listed in the definition of the Property, whichever occurs last, unless sooner terminated pursuant to a provision of this Agreement.

If you want a short term with renewal rights based upon sales or other criteria, consider the sample provision below.

Short Term With Renewal Rights Based Upon Sales

This Agreement shall commence upon the Effective Date and shall extend for a period of two years (the "Initial Term") and thereafter may be renewed by Licensee under the same terms and conditions for consecutive two-year periods (the "Renewal Terms"), provided that:

(a) Licensee provides written notice of its intention to renew this Agreement within 30 days before the expiration of the current term;

(b) Licensee has met the sales requirements as established in Exhibit A; and

(c) in no event shall the Agreement extend longer than the date of expiration of the longest-living patent (or patents) or last-remaining patent application as listed in the definition of the Property.

If you are using this provision, you will need to prepare an exhibit—an additional document added to the end of the agreement—that details the conditions when renewal occurs.

Here's an example:

EXHIBIT A: Sales Requirement

In the event that Licensee achieves sales revenue [*or units, depending on how you're structuring the deal*] of [*insert sales requirement*] during the Initial Term, this License shall renew for a period of [*insert number of years*] years (First Renewal Term).

In the event that Licensee achieves sales revenue of [*insert sales requirement*] during the First Renewal Term, this License shall renew for a period of [*insert number of years*] years (Second Renewal Term).

If Licensee fails to achieve the sales requirements set forth above, this Agreement shall terminate and rights shall revert to Licensor.

If you want an agreement that will continue indefinitely until terminated, use the provision below.

No Patents: Indefinite Term

This Agreement shall commence upon the Effective Date and shall continue until terminated pursuant to a provision of this Agreement.

If you want a fixed term with no renewal rights, consider the sample provision below.

Fixed Yearly Term

> This Agreement shall commence upon the Effective Date and shall continue for ten years unless sooner terminated pursuant to a provision of this Agreement.

If you want to permit the term to extend for as long as the licensee sells the invention, you could draft a term provision as follows.

Term for as Long as Licensee Sells Licensed Products

> This Agreement shall commence upon the Effective Date and shall continue for as long as Licensee continues to offer the Licensed Products in commercially reasonable quantities unless sooner terminated pursuant to a provision of this Agreement.

Review Chapter 8 for more information on term provisions. Remember to keep track of your exhibits. If you are attaching a copy of your patent application as Exhibit A, then attach the sales requirements as Exhibit B.

Net Sales

The definition of net sales has a substantial impact on how much you will get paid. In Chapter 9, we explain and recommend certain limitations on net sales. Modify the sample accordingly.

Advance Against Royalties

A nonrefundable advance means that you will only have to pay it back by deductions from future royalties. If you are receiving a payment that you do not have to pay back from royalties (that is, no strings attached), substitute the following optional provision:

Advances Against Royalties

> As a nonrefundable, nonrecoupable fee for executing this license, Licensee agrees to pay to Licensor upon execution of this Agreement the sum of $[*insert amount of license fee*].

See Chapter 9 for more information.

Licensed Product Royalty

For an explanation of royalties, review Chapter 9. If you are licensing under a "per-unit" basis or you are licensing a combination of patents and other intellectual property under a hybrid license, you should review Chapter 9.

Hybrid Royalty; Patent and Nonpatented Rights

Licensee agrees to pay a Royalty of [insert appropriate royalty percentage]% of all Net Sales revenue of the Licensed Products ("Licensed Product Royalty"). The Licensed Product Royalty shall be allocated according to the percentages as provided in this Agreement. In the event that a patent does not issue or an issued patent expires or is otherwise terminated, the allocated percentage for such patent or pending patent shall be subtracted from the Licensed Product Royalty. The Licensed Product Royalty shall be adjusted accordingly.

_____% of the Royalty for the license of the Patent No. _____ .

_____% of the Royalty for the license of Pending Patent No. _____ .

_____ % of the Royalty for the license of trade secrets [or trademarks, copyrights, or other intellectual property].

**Telegraphy
No. 174,465**

If you have negotiated a Spin-Off, Third-Party, or F.O.B. royalty, you can use the alternate provisions. An explanation is provided in Chapter 9.

Royalties on Spin-Offs [optional]

Licensee agrees to pay a Royalty ("Spin-Off Product Royalty") of [insert appropriate royalty percentage]% for all Net Sales of "Spin-Off Products." A Spin-Off Product is any product derived from, based on, or adapted from the Licensed Product provided that if the product uses the Property, it shall be considered to be a Licensed Product.

Adjustment of Royalties for Third-Party Licenses [optional]

In the event that any Licensed Product (or other items for which Licensee pays Royalties to Licensor) incorporates third-party character licenses, endorsements, or other proprietary licenses, Licensor agrees to adjust the Royalty rate to [insert appropriate royalty percentage]% for such third-party licenses. Licensee shall notify Licensor of any such third-party licenses prior to manufacture. Third-party licenses shall not include licenses accruing to an affiliate, associate, or subsidiary of Licensee.

F.O.B. Royalties [*optional*]

> Licensee agrees to pay the Royalty ("F.O.B. Royalty") of [*insert appropriate royalty percentage*]% for all F.O.B. sales of Licensed Products.

Guaranteed Minimum Annual Royalty (GMAR)

If you have negotiated a GMAR, you may need to modify the optional provision in the Licensing Agreement sample, according to your conditions. See Chapter 9. Insert the amount of the annual GMAR.

Sublicensing Revenues

For more information on sublicensing revenues, read Chapter 9.

Payment and Statements to Licensor

If you have an agent and your agent wants payments sent directly to him or her, add the following language.

> **Payments and Statements.** All payments and statements made by Licensee pursuant to this Agreement shall be made and remitted to Agent at the following address: [*insert address*].

Audit

This provision establishes your rights to review the licensee's records. See Chapter 9.

Warranties and Indemnity

Warranties are promises upon which the other party can rely. For example, you may warrant that the invention does not infringe other inventions. (In other words, you are not trying to license an invention you don't actually own.) If the warranty is false, you receive financial punishment in the form of indemnity. When you provide indemnity (that is, you indemnify someone), you agree to pay for their damages if they are successfully sued. Such damages might include:

- consumer injuries from the product
- infringement by another company, or
- a challenge to your ownership.

Warranties and indemnity are often the most debated aspects of a license agreement. You should review Chapter 12 for an explanation of the provisions offered here. One alternate provision is the establishment of a royalty fund in the event of indemnity. When a third party makes a claim against the licensee, the licensee stops paying you royalties and instead puts the money into a fund. All or part of the fund is then used for indemnity. If anything is left after the case is resolved, it is returned to you. If you want to establish a fund, you can use the alternate provision.

Compliance With Intellectual Property Laws

This provision deals with the licensee's duty to obey intellectual property laws and to properly mark the licensed products with notices. (For example, if the licensed products are copyrightable, a notice such as "Copyright 2020 Sally Smith" should be included. Review Chapter 2.)

Infringement Lawsuits Against Third Parties

This provision deals with suing people or companies who infringe your patent rights. Who has the right to sue these people, and how do you split any money you recover from infringers? For more information on suing infringers, review Chapters 2 and 17.

Exploitation

It's important to guarantee that your invention is offered for sale by a certain date. You may need to customize this provision to include reference to a specific trade show or a seasonal catalog that you

definitely want to be included in. For more information, read Chapter 12.

Samples and Quality Control

You (the licensor) will want this provision if you wish to review the product before it is offered for sale. If you would like more information about samples and quality control issues, review Chapter 12. If you are licensing a trademark (see Chapter 2), you should insist on these quality controls. Failure of a trademark owner to maintain quality standards over trademark uses can result in the loss of trademark rights (known as "abandonment"). Keep in mind, however, that the important issue for trademark owners is not simply that the agreement provides for quality control, but that the control is actually exercised.

Insurance

The amount of product liability insurance coverage is usually between one to ten million dollars, depending upon the product and the industry. The purpose of this provision is to protect you in the event a consumer is injured because of a defective licensed product. Insurance should be available so that you (and the licensee) can avoid the financial liability. For more information about insurance, review Chapter 12.

Confidentiality

Every license agreement contains some assurance of confidentiality. If you have signed a separate confidentiality agreement, your license agreement may refer to that. For more information about confidentiality, review Chapter 7.

Termination

Have you and the licensee already agreed upon the length of time the license agreement will last? If you have provided for a fixed term in your term provision (see Chapter 8), your agreement has a built-in ending—the conclusion (or expiration) of the term. Some license agreements don't include a term provision. Instead, the parties specify the date the contract will end in the termination provision. If you are using both a term and termination provision, make sure they conform (that is, they both provide for the same basis for termination and the same periods of time).

If you want the license to terminate after a period of years, use the following language.

Fixed Term

This Agreement shall terminate at the end of [*insert number of years*] years, unless terminated sooner under a provision of this Agreement.

If you are licensing a patent, the term should not extend beyond the length of the patent protection.

Term Based Upon Length of Patent Protection

This Agreement shall terminate with the expiration of the longest-living patent (or patents) or last-remaining patent application (as listed in the definition of the Property), whichever occurs last, unless terminated sooner under a provision of this Agreement.

If you have established a fixed term with renewal periods, you may use the following language.

Initial Term With Renewals

This Agreement terminates at the end of two years (the "Initial Term") unless renewed by Licensee under the same terms and conditions for consecutive two-year periods (the "Renewal Terms") provided that Licensee provides written notice of its intention to renew this Agreement within 30 days prior to expiration of the current term. In no event shall the Agreement extend longer than the date of expiration of the longest-living patent (or patents) or last-remaining patent application as listed in the definition of the Property.

Termination at will means that one party can end the agreement simply by notifying the other. In this type of termination, it's not necessary to provide an explanation or reason. The agreement ends simply because one party decides to terminate it. This provision does not have to be mutual. In fact, the licensee usually wants this ability but does not want the licensor to have it. In other words, they can terminate at will but you can't. This is often true if the licensee is required to pay a minimum guaranteed royalty payment. The at-will provision lets the licensee bail out of the agreement (and royalty commitment) if the licensed products are not selling well. An example is below.

Termination at Will: Licensee's Option

Upon 90 days' notice, Licensee may, at its sole discretion, terminate this Agreement by providing notice to the Licensor.

Effect of Termination

What happens when the agreement is over? There's usually still some clean-up work including sales of remaining products and payment of royalties. For more information about posttermination requirements, read Chapter 13.

Survival

When the agreement is terminated, that doesn't mean that all of the obligations in the agreement should end. We recommend that the following provisions survive the agreement:

- payment obligations
- warranties
- licensee indemnity
- confidentiality, and
- product liability insurance.

If you would like more information about survival, review Chapter 13.

Attorneys' Fees and Expenses

In the event of a legal dispute with the licensee, this provides that the prevailing party is entitled to payment for legal fees. If you would like more information about attorneys' fees, review Chapter 14.

Dispute Resolution

This provides a method of resolving disputes without resorting to litigation. Alternatives to litigation, such as arbitration and mediation, are sometimes unpopular with licensees. (See Chapter 14.)

In mediation, a neutral evaluator (the mediator) attempts to help the parties reach a resolution of their dispute. Basically, the parties sit down with the mediator and tell their stories. The mediator advises the parties on ways to resolve the dispute, and the two parties try to agree on a resolution (that hopefully leads to a settlement agreement). The mediator may recommend a course of action but does not make any binding decisions—only the parties can do that. Some licensees prefer mediation because the mediator's recommendations are not binding (only the parties can make a binding settlement), and because mediation is typically less expensive than litigation or arbitration.

Arbitration is like going to court with less formality. Instead of filing a lawsuit, the parties hire and pay for one or more arbitrators to evaluate the dispute and make a determination. The arbitrators are trained to evaluate disputes, and many of them are retired judges.

If the licensee is opposed to arbitration (and many are), you can try a less formal approach to dispute resolution with the following mediation provision. It does not require that the parties commit to arbitration, but it allows for the parties to work out some method of alternative dispute resolution.

Alternative Dispute Resolution

If a dispute arises and cannot be resolved by the parties, either party may make a written demand for formal resolution of the dispute. The written request will specify the scope of the dispute. Within 30 days after such written notice, the parties agree to meet, for one day, with an impartial mediator and consider dispute resolution alternatives other than litigation. If an alternative method of dispute resolution is not agreed upon within 30 days of the one-day mediation, either side may start litigation proceedings.

Governing Law

In the event of a dispute, this clause establishes which state law will govern the arbitration or lawsuit. Generally, we suggest that this state (and the state listed in the next provision) be your state of residence. If you would like more information about governing law (sometimes referred to as choice of law), review Chapter 14.

Jurisdiction

In the event of a dispute, this establishes the state (and county) in which the lawsuit must be filed. In other words, this is the place where you will have to travel to fight the licensee. We recommend that you use your state of residence. If you would like more information about jurisdiction, review Chapter 14.

Waiver

This permits the parties to waive a portion of the agreement without establishing a precedent. For example, imagine that the licensee is several months late making a payment. You agree to accept the delay. The fact that you have "waived" the requirement for prompt payment once does not mean that you will always permit a late payment. If you would like more information about waiver, review Chapter 14.

Invalidity

Also referred to as severability, this permits a court to sever (take out) an invalid provision while keeping the rest of the agreement intact. If you would like more information about invalidity, review Chapter 14.

Entire Understanding

Also referred to as "integration," this provision establishes that the agreement is the final version and that any further modification must be in writing. For more information, review Chapter 14.

Attachments and Exhibits

This guarantees that attachments and exhibits will be included as enforceable parts of the agreement. If you would like more information, review Chapter 14.

Notices

This describes how each party must provide notice of disputes. For more information about the necessity for notice provisions, see Chapter 14.

No Joint Venture

This provision, sometimes referred to as "relationships," prevents either party from claiming a certain relationship with the other, for example, stating that you are a partner or in a joint venture. If you would like more information, review Chapter 14.

Assignability

There may be some instances where you don't want the licensee to transfer rights to your invention to another company—for example, if the licensee is purchased by a third party. The sample provision prohibits any assignment without your consent. If the licensee is afraid that you have too much control, you can soften the effect by withholding consent only if you have a valid business reason. What's a valid reason? Perhaps the company to which your licensee wants to grant an assignment has a reputation for not paying royalties, or maybe it is in poor financial shape. You cannot, however, withhold consent for an arbitrary reason, such as someone from the company having once treated you rudely. For more information about assignments, see Chapter 14.

Consent Not Unreasonably Withheld

Licensee may not assign or transfer its rights or obligations pursuant to this Agreement without the prior written consent of Licensor. Such consent shall not be unreasonably withheld. Any assignment or transfer in violation of this section shall be void.

If you don't have much bargaining power and the licensee wants freedom to transfer to affiliates or new owners (under the same terms as your license agreement), you can use a provision such as the one below.

Consent Not Needed for Licensee Affiliates or New Owners

Licensee may not assign or transfer its rights or obligations pursuant to this Agreement without the prior written consent of Licensor. However, no consent is required for an assignment or transfer that occurs (a) to an entity in which Licensee owns more than 50% of the assets, or (b) as part of a transfer of all or substantially all of the assets of Licensee to any party. Any assignment or transfer in violation of this section shall be void.

Signatures

Each party must sign the agreement in relation to the business that is represented (for example, as a general partner representing the partnership), and each party must have the authority to sign the agreement. To further reinforce this, you will note the language in the sample agreement: "Each party has signed this Agreement through its authorized representative." Use the following rules when determining the proper signature line.

Sole proprietorship. If you or the licensee is a sole proprietor, simply sign your own name. If you have a fictitious business name (sometimes known as a dba), list the name of the business above the signature line. For example, Tom Stein

Can You Fax or Email Your Signature?

A faxed signature is suitable assuming that both parties do not dispute the authenticity of the signature. If there is a dispute about the signature (such as one party claims it's a forgery), you will have difficulty proving the signature is authentic from a fax. If you sign the agreement by fax, follow up the fax by mailing or overnighting signed copies.

According to the Electronic Signatures in Global and International Commerce Act, electronic contracts and electronic signatures are just as legal and enforceable as traditional paper contracts signed in ink. An electronic contract is an agreement created and "signed" in electronic form—in other words, no paper or other hard copies are used. Therefore, an agreement will be valid if emailed and electronically "signed." You're probably familiar with the "Click to Agree" contract, commonly used with software.

However, unless you have a means of confirming the assent of the other party—for example, a digital signature system—you can still run into problems if the other side denies it received or agreed to the electronic agreement. For that reason, it is better to rely on paper rather than "plastic" when executing a nondisclosure agreement.

is a sole proprietor calling his invention business Eine Stein Inventions. He would sign as shown below.

```
Eine Stein Inventions

By: _____
     Tom Stein
```

Partnership. If you or the licensee is a general or limited partnership, the only person authorized to sign the agreement is a general partner or someone who has written authority (usually in the form of a partnership resolution) from a general partner. The name of the partnership must be mentioned above the signature line, otherwise, the partnership will not be bound (only the person signing the agreement will). Cindy Barrett is a general partner in Reality Manufacturing Partnership. She would sign as shown here.

```
Reality Manufacturing Partnership

By: _____
     Cindy Barrett, a general partner
```

Corporation or LLC. If you or the licensee is a corporation or limited liability company (LLC), only a person authorized by the corporation or LLC can sign the agreement. The president or chief executive officer (CEO) usually has such power, but not every officer has the authority to bind the corporation or LLC. If in doubt, ask for written proof of the authority. This proof is usually in the form of a corporate resolution. The name of the corporation should be mentioned above the signature line, or the corporation will not be bound (only the person signing the agreement will). For example, Marya DeRosa is CEO of Sincere Marketing. She would sign as follows:

Sincere Marketing, Inc., a New York corporation

By: _____
     Marya DeRosa, CEO

Note: If you have reason to question the credibility of the licensee's representative, investigate the company. (See Chapter 6.) If you have doubts about the person's authority, don't proceed until you are satisfied that the person has full authority to represent the company.

Exhibit A

As we explain in Chapters 8 through 10, your Exhibit A can include a list of important contract facts. In this sample, we have limited the Exhibit A only to the properties and licensed products. It is quite common to provide a description of several paragraphs of the Property

(or to include a copy of the patent or patent application).

You can also use Exhibit A to reference the territory, the length of the agreement, the royalty and advance payments, dates when the agreement is effective, and when the product must be offered for sale. For example, instead of listing the amount of the royalty in the Payment section, you would state "see Exhibit A." Then you would place the royalty amount in the exhibit. If you were entering into several similar nonexclusive licenses, this would work well because you would only need to modify the exhibit, introductory paragraph, and signature lines each time you entered into a new agreement.

Optional License Agreement Provisions

The sample agreement contains the provisions most commonly used in license agreements. Several others can be included if appropriate. Below is a brief description of additional provisions.

Force Majeure (Pronounced Fors-Mazhoor´)

The force majeure provision (sometimes referred to as "Acts of God") establishes that the agreement will be suspended in the event of unforeseen natural disasters.

For example, if a tornado ruins the licensee's manufacturing plant for three months, the license agreement would be suspended for three months

> In the event of an act of God such as fire, riot, act of public enemy, war, or similar cause not within the control of Licensee, the Licensee shall have the right to suspend the term of this Agreement. Licensee may suspend the term only for the duration of any such contingency. Licensee shall not suspend its obligation to make payments to Licensor if such payments are due and are not otherwise prevented. At the conclusion of the contingency, Licensee shall notify Licensor in writing and the Agreement shall be reinstated.

Escrow

If you execute an escrow agreement, it should be attached to your license agreement and the following provision should be inserted.

> **Escrow Account.** The parties have executed a separate Escrow Agreement (attached to this Agreement and incorporated by reference) for the deposit of escrow materials.

If you cannot execute an escrow agreement at the time of license, you can still express your intention to do so in the license agreement by including the following provision.

> **Establishment of Escrow Account.** The parties shall execute a separate Escrow Agreement to establish an escrow account for the deposit of [*indicate what will be deposited*] ("Escrow Items"). The Escrow Items shall be released to [*name of party, (Licensor or Licensee)*] upon the following conditions: [*list reasons for release from escrow. For example, "The funds will be released to Licensor upon completion of the Services and furnishing of Deliverables."*].

In the event you need an escrow account or want to learn more about the escrow process, review Chapter 14.

Grant Back of Improvements

Who owns the improvements that the licensee makes to your invention? A grant back provision transfers ownership to you. For more information, review Chapter 15.

Training

If you wish to include a training provision in your license agreement, below is a sample provision. As explained in

Chapter 15, if the training is ongoing or more complex, you should use a separate services agreement that will better define your obligations and protect your rights.

> Licensor will provide [*number of days and whether they are consecutive*] days of basic training for [*names or number of Licensee employees to be trained*] Licensee employees at Licensee's facility in [*location of Licensee's facility*]. Training will be performed by [*name of Licensor or person who will provide training*]. Licensee shall bear all costs of travel and accommodations and shall pay Licensor on a direct cost basis computed on the number of hours worked and an hourly rate of [*hourly rate*] for services. Licensee shall indemnify Licensor for any and all claims that may result from such training. All payments for services and other expenses shall be paid by Licensee within 30 days of receipt of Licensor's written invoice.

Installation

If you wish to include an installation services provision in your license agreement, a sample appears below.

> Licensor shall supervise and assist in the installation of equipment as described in Exhibit [*whatever letter you have chosen for the service agreement exhibit, for example, Exhibit B*]. Licensor's installation services will be performed by [*name of Licensor or Licensor employee who will perform services*]. Licensee shall bear all costs of travel and accommodations for Licensor and shall pay Licensor on a direct cost basis computed on the number of hours worked and an hourly rate of [*hourly rate*] for services. Licensee shall indemnify Licensor for any and all claims that may result from such installation services. All payments for services and other expenses shall be paid by Licensee within 30 days of receipt of Licensor's written invoice.

For more on installation services, see Chapter 15.

Tech Support

For a tech support arrangement in which you assist the licensee's support staff, use a provision such as the sample below.

> Licensor will provide reasonable telephone and email assistance to Licensee's designated representatives for Licensee's technical support of licensed products.

If you are providing limited end-user tech support, you will need a more detailed provision. The sample provision below should address most of your concerns.

Licensor shall, for a period of six months after introduction of the licensed products, provide reasonable ongoing [*describe the type of assistance, for example, "telephone"*] assistance to Licensee. Such support shall relate only to troubleshooting and identification of reported problems relating to the use of the Licensed Products. Telephone technical support shall be provided by Licensor [*indicate what days and what times, for example, "Monday through Friday 12:00 p.m. to 4:00 p.m. PST"*] at a rate of [*indicate the hourly, weekly, or monthly rate, for example, "$2,000 per month"*] and not to exceed [*indicate maximum amount of support hours per week, for example, "20 hours per week of Licensor's personnel time"*]. In the event that Licensee needs technical support provided by a third party other than Licensor, such determination shall not affect any other provisions of this agreement.

For more on tech support and other service provisions, see Chapter 15.

Deliverables: Schedules and Development Services; Delivery and Approval

Below is a sample deliverables provision that can be inserted in your license agreement. The two parts of the provision ("Schedules and Development Services" and "Delivery and Approval") attempt to anticipate the problems that result when, for example, the inventor believes the deliverable has been perfected and the licensee thinks the work is insufficient. For more information on deliverables, see Chapter 15.

Disposable Standing Trash Bin
No. 6,315,143

EXHIBIT A

THE PROPERTY

[Insert description of the Property.]

_____

_____

_____

_____

_____

_____

_____

_____

_____

_____

_____

LICENSED PRODUCTS

[Indicate type of products, for example "medical supply products."]

_____

_____

_____

_____

_____

_____

_____

_____

_____

_____

_____

_____

Schedules and Development Services

Licensor shall perform certain development services for Licensee. A description of such services, as well as the delivery schedule and the technology or invention to be delivered ("Deliverables"), is provided in Exhibit A. Payments for such services shall be as provided in Exhibit A. Any Deliverable listed in Exhibit A shall consist of three stages: (1) concept/planning, (2) design/prototype, and (3) development/test.

Licensor shall submit for Licensee's written approval a budget for each Deliverable. Any expenses or charges in excess of those budgeted must be preapproved in writing by Licensee. If requested, Licensor shall, within 72 hours of notification, meet with Licensee and provide a status report on the schedule and budget for any Deliverable. Licensor shall invoice Licensee pursuant to the payment schedule set forth in the appropriate Exhibit A [*or Exhibit B—remember to attach the deliverables and schedule as an exhibit*].

Delivery and Approval

Licensee shall have five working days from receipt of any Deliverable within which to provide Licensor with written notice of its decision to either accept the Deliverable or to reject it because it fails to conform to the specifications in Exhibit A. If Licensee determines that any Deliverable does not substantially conform to the specifications, Licensee shall deliver to Licensor a written report describing each manner that the Deliverables fail to conform. Licensor shall, within five working days of receipt of Licensee's statement, correct such errors or failures and resubmit the Deliverables. After resubmission, Licensee shall have a second evaluation period of five working days to either accept the Deliverables or reject them because they still fail to conform to the original specifications. If Licensee again rejects the Deliverables, Licensee may pay a third party to correct such failures and deduct the cost either from Licensor's next scheduled payment from Licensee or from Licensor's future royalties.

Right of First Refusal

If your license agreement includes a right of first refusal, you must give the licensee the first right to license any improvements. This provision is common in an exclusive license. For more information, see Chapter 15.

> Licensor may identify and develop improvements for the Licensed Property ("Improvements"). Improvements may be patentable or unpatentable and may also be protected under copyright, trade secret, or other legal principles. Licensee shall have the first right to license such Improvements and the parties shall negotiate in good faith to reach agreement as to the terms and conditions for such license. In the event that the parties fail to reach agreement and Licensor receives an offer from a third party for the Improvements, Licensee shall have 30 days to notify Licensor whether Licensee desires to execute a license on similar terms and conditions. In the event that Licensee matches any third-party terms and conditions, Licensor shall enter into a License Agreement with Licensee and terminate negotiations with any third parties.

Most Favored Nations Clause (Sometimes Referred to as a Most Favored Licensee Provision)

This provision is common in a nonexclusive arrangement and guarantees that the licensee won't be charged any more for the invention or improvements than any other licensee. See Chapter 15 for more information.

> Licensor may identify and develop new features or improvements for the Licensed Property ("Improvements"). Improvements may be patentable or unpatentable and may also be protected under copyright, trade secret, or other legal principles. In the event that Licensee enters into a license agreement for these Improvements with a third-party licensee ("Third-Party License"), Licensor agrees to offer Licensee terms and conditions which are as favorable as those for the third-party licensee. Licensor shall promptly notify the Licensee of any Third-Party License as well as any additional obligations or undertakings in the Third-Party License. Licensee shall have 30 days to notify Licensor whether Licensee desires to execute a license on similar terms and conditions.

Modifying the Sample Agreement for Your Needs

You might think, "Since I'm not an expert, I'd better not change anything in the agreement." Surprisingly, lawyers often take a similar view and are equally paranoid about changing the form agreements found in their legal books. They blindly copy unnecessary legal language simply because "that's the way it's always been done."

Because each license agreement is unique, we recommend that you modify the agreement as necessary to suit your needs. Review the appropriate chapter and then make the changes. For example, if you must modify the payment section, first read Chapter 9 and then make your changes. If you use simple, unambiguous language and follow the rules established in each chapter, your agreement will be enforceable and understandable.

If you're unsure of how to write new language or a new section, just use clear language and avoid trying to sound like a lawyer. For instance, avoid using legal language such as "heretofore" and "therein." Review the appropriate chapter in this book to make sure your addition is legal and doesn't conflict with another provision.

Modifications With a Word Processor

You should open (or import) the agreement in your word processing program. For example, if you use Microsoft *Word*, you can download and open the agreement and edit it without any problem. Modify the agreement according to your needs.

EXAMPLE: You and the licensee have a unique element in your agreement: One of the licensed products will only be manufactured in a gold-plated limited edition run of 1,000 units and you will receive a special royalty rate. How do you add this to the form agreement? Simple! Give the product a name ("Gold-Plated Products"), list it in Exhibit A under licensed products, and add a new section under Payment, such as: "Gold-Plated Special Edition Royalties—Licensee shall pay Licensor a royalty of ___ % for Net Sales of Gold-Plated Products," and indicate the royalty rate.

Modifications by Hand

Although we don't recommend modifying your agreement by hand, it can be done for small changes. To strike certain words or phrases or to add words or phrases, you can write them in with a pen on the form agreement. Every time you write something on the printed form agreement, both you and the licensee (and any other parties to the agreement) must initial each modification.

Inserting New Sections

Where do you insert a new section? Wherever it makes sense. There is no legal requirement for the ordering of the paragraphs. You can place them in any order, and as long as they come after the statement "Therefore, the parties agree," they will be legally enforceable. However, certain general principles are followed, such as placing the grant and royalty provisions near the front and the termination and miscellaneous provisions near the end. You may also group provisions together under one heading. For example, you can group all of the miscellaneous provisions under the heading "Miscellaneous."

Warranties, Indemnification, and Proprietary Rights Provisions

Promises, Promises … Warranties, Representations, and Covenants............300

    Licensor Warranties..301

Indemnity: The "Hold Harmless" Provision...303

    What Should You Indemnify?...303

    Indemnity: What to Avoid..305

    Paying for Indemnity..307

Licensee Warranties and Indemnity...310

    Licensee Warranties..310

    Licensee Indemnity... 311

Proprietary Rights..312

    Registering Patent, Trademark, or Copyright Protection

       for the Invention 312

    Marking Products With Appropriate Proprietary Notices.............................313

    Dealing With Infringers 314

Commercialization and Exploitation 316

Samples and Quality Control... 317

Insurance 317

n this chapter we discuss protective aspects of license agreements—legal provisions that protect your interests and the interests of the licensee. These provisions are not directly related to the marketing of your invention, and you might not have discussed them during your business negotiations. However, in the event of lawsuits, infringements, or product injuries, these provisions can have an important impact. You should read this chapter if you answer "yes" to any of the following questions:

- Would you like a definition of warranties, representations, and covenants?
- Are you concerned about making a promise that your invention will not infringe other inventions?
- Would you like indemnity explained?
- Are you concerned about whether the invention will include the proper copyright and patent notices?
- Would you like the right to approve a sample of your invention before it is offered to the public?
- Are you worried about lawsuits caused by a defective product?

In this chapter, we review provisions that protect the interests of the parties or guard against certain problems. For example, warranties provide assurances of the rights granted under the license agreement (for example, the right to license or the right of title to the invention). Indemnity is a method of backing up your contract promises in which you agree to pay for certain damages. (Indemnity is one of the most disputed issues in licensing agreements.) We also discuss provisions that protect your intellectual property rights during the license period (for example, requirements that the licensee use the proper legal notices).

Promises, Promises ... Warranties, Representations, and Covenants

One of the most important and often overlooked sections of a license agreement deals with warranties, representations, and covenants. These three terms are used collectively ("Licensor warrants, represents, and covenants ...") or separately ("Licensor warrants that ...," "Licensor represents that ...," "Licensor covenants that ..."). Although there are subtle distinctions between the terms, all three generally refer to a promise upon which the other party can rely. Here are the differences:

- **Representations.** A representation is a statement of current fact that a party makes with the intent that the other party will rely on it.
- **Warranties.** A warranty is a guarantee or promise that a statement is true. It's similar to an indemnity in that the party making the warranty

must pay damages if the warranty is triggered (that is, if the statement is not true).

- **Covenants.** A covenant is a promise to do something (or in the case of a negative covenant, *not* to do something). Many contracts are composed of big promises, such as "I promise to license your invention and you promise to provide patent rights." Covenants are smaller promises that augment or make possible the big promises, sometimes requiring activity before or after the major action that's the true subject of the agreement. Covenants also provide assurances, such as in a covenant to act in good faith and deal fairly or a covenant to use best efforts.

For purposes of our discussion, we will avoid using the terms "representations" and "covenants," and instead, refer to any such promise as a "warranty." If a warranty proves false, it can be the basis for termination, or, worse, it may cause you to be liable for financial damages.

EXAMPLE: Tommi licenses a film-editing invention to Filmco. In her license agreement, she warrants she owns the rights to the invention. Filmco is later sued by Tommi's former employer, VideoCo. VideoCo claims it owns the rights to the invention. If VideoCo proves that it does, in fact,

own the rights to the invention, Filmco can terminate its license with Tommi and sue her for damages because they relied on Tommi's warranty.

Licensor Warranties

We recommend that you, as the licensor, include the following warranty provision in your agreements. The following sections will explain the provision in more detail.

Licensor Warranties

> Licensor warrants that it has the power and authority to enter into this Agreement and has no knowledge as to any third-party claims regarding the proprietary rights in the Property which would interfere with the rights granted under this Agreement.

Power and Authority— Warranting the Right to License

The first warranty in this provision—the right to license—is what one lawyer refers to as "the Brooklyn Bridge" issue. Many people can claim to sell you the Brooklyn Bridge, but only the person who actually has title can legally sell it to you. As long as you have the "power and authority" to license your invention, you shouldn't have a problem making this warranty. If you are unsure, review ownership issues in Chapters 3 and 4.

Warranting That the Invention Does Not Infringe (With Qualification)

The second licensor warranty—that the invention does not infringe—requires your careful consideration. A licensee will want an assurance that the sale of the invention is not going to trigger infringement lawsuits. On its face, this seems like a reasonable request. After all, the licensee is investing a lot of money in your invention and doesn't want any surprises.

Unfortunately, no matter what precautions you take, the possibility always exists that your invention infringes upon some existing invention or patent. Therefore, we recommend that you qualify your warranty of noninfringement by stating that it is made "to the best of your knowledge." Another way to state it is that you "have no knowledge" of possible infringement. That way, you are qualifying your warranty based upon what you know (see "The 'Best of Your Knowledge,'" below) at the time of execution (signing) of the agreement. If you don't use this qualification, then you will be responsible for any infringement, whether or not you knew about it.

Warranting That the Invention Does Not Infringe (Without Qualification)

What if the licensee demands a warranty of noninfringement without any qualification? In some cases, a licensee may want you to warrant that your invention

does not infringe on another protected invention, period. Being unaware of an infringement would be no excuse. In that case, the licensee wants a provision such as the following:

Warranting Without Qualification

Licensor warrants that it has the power and authority to enter into this Agreement and that the Property does not infringe any valid rights of any third party. The provisions of this section shall survive any termination.

Under this provision, it doesn't matter what you knew or should have known. If any infringement exists, you are responsible. If you are faced with an unqualified warranty like this, you should review your position. Has anyone done a patent search or a similar reliable analysis regarding your invention? If so, review it carefully, because your warranty is based upon this research. If no search has been done or if you are seeking a more thorough opinion, then you should consider obtaining a written opinion from a patent attorney. The cost for this may range from $500 to several thousand dollars.

Sometimes, a licensee may be willing to share the costs of this search. Why? A contract warranty only provides a means of going after the inventor after the agreement has been signed (and the product is for sale). Licensees usually prefer to know ahead of time if they are headed toward a potential infringement problem. Therefore, the search provides information that can benefit both parties. You should propose that the licensee pay for it and deduct half (or all) of the cost from future royalties. Explain that a written opinion is valuable because it might help the licensee head off any potential problem before manufacturing begins.

The "Best of Your Knowledge"

According to some court decisions, a warranty or representation as to your knowledge (that is, "to the best of my knowledge") refers not only to what you know, but also to what a reasonable person in your position *should* have known. For example, if you are an expert on radio-controlled devices, you would not be expected to know every patent in your field, but you would be expected to know about major developments.

Indemnity: The "Hold Harmless" Provision

Warranties and indemnity work together. A licensee relies on your warranty.

Indemnity is your financial punishment if the warranty is false. When you provide indemnity (that is, when you indemnify someone), you agree to pay for their damages for certain situations. For example, if you indemnify a licensee against infringement, then you will have to pay the licensee's damages (and legal fees) if the licensee is sued for infringement.

Indemnity acts like a powerful shield. The licensee can deflect a lawsuit and make you, the inventor, pay for the damages and legal fees. Indemnity provisions are also sometimes referred to as "hold harmless" provisions because the language for an indemnity provision often states that the "Licensor shall hold the Licensee harmless from any losses," and so on.

As you can imagine, providing indemnity to a licensee can have a devastating effect. If there is a challenge to your invention, you might have to pay your own legal fees, as well as the legal fees and damages suffered by the licensee. For that reason, we recommend that you carefully review indemnity provisions and limit your indemnity obligations.

What Should You Indemnify?

There are four types of lawsuits that the licensee might become entangled in:

- lawsuits in which you sue the licensee
- lawsuits in which the licensee sues you

- lawsuits in which the licensee sues a third party (a third party is someone who is not a party to the agreement), or
- lawsuits in which a third party sues the licensee or licensor.

You should only indemnify the licensee against the last category—third-party claims directed at the licensee. And you should only indemnify for claims that relate to your warranties—that is, (a) your right to license the invention and (b) the invention does not infringe upon any other inventions. These warranties—which should be in the "Licensor Warranties" section discussed above—should be referenced in the indemnification section, as shown in the sample provision below.

Besides limiting indemnity to lawsuits in which a third party sues the licensee about ownership or infringement, we also suggest you qualify the indemnification. Even if lawsuits over ownership or infringement are brought against the licensee, you should only have to pay the licensee's damages under the following circumstances:

- The claim prevents the licensee from selling the invention. In other words, it has to be a serious claim that keeps your invention off the market.
- The claim is not about something that the licensee did or added to your invention. That is, the third-party lawsuit has to be about the invention as you furnished it to the licensee.
- The licensee gave you prompt written notice of the third-party claim. The licensee cannot ignore the claim and settle it secretly without your knowledge, and then come after you for payment.
- The indemnity applies only in the event of a final decision by a court. You don't want to have to pay for invalid claims or merely alleged defects that are not proven in court.
- The maximum amount you have to pay for indemnity will not exceed the total sum you were paid under the license agreement. This is usually a controversial issue, and we will provide more information below.

Following is a suggested indemnity provision incorporating the above suggestions.

Indemnification by Licensor

Licensor shall indemnify Licensee and hold Licensee harmless from any damages and liabilities (including reasonable attorneys' fees and costs), arising from any breach of Licensor's warranties as defined in Licensor Warranties, above, provided (a) such claim, if sustained, would prevent Licensee from marketing the Licensed Products or the Property; (b) such claim arises solely out of the Property as disclosed to the Licensee, and not out of any change in the Property made by Licensee or a vendor, or by reason of an off-the-shelf component or by reason of any claim for trademark infringement; (c) Licensee gives Licensor prompt written notice of any such claim; (d) such indemnity shall only be applicable in the event of a final decision by a court of competent jurisdiction from which no right to appeal exists; and (e) that the maximum amount due from Licensor to Licensee under this paragraph shall not exceed the amounts due to Licensor under the Payment section from the date that Licensor notifies Licensee of the existence of such a claim.

Indemnity: What to Avoid

A licensee might want you to indemnify everything in the agreement. Some licensor indemnification provisions are extremely broad and should be avoided. For example, the following is merely the first sentence of one large national licensing company's standard agreement.

Licensor agrees to indemnify, defend, and hold harmless Licensee, its subsidiary, affiliated, and/or controlled companies, and all sublicensees, as well as their respective officers, directors, agents, and employees from and against any and all damage, loss, expense (including reasonable attorneys' fees and costs), award, settlement, or other obligation arising out of any claims, demands, actions, suits, or prosecutions that may be made or instituted against them or any of them by reason of any alleged breach of any representation, warranty, or covenant in this Agreement, or from any injury or death arising from any defect in the Property, or from any other alleged claim or injury.

Avoid Indemnifying for All Warranties

You should avoid a provision that has language such as that shown below.

Not Recommended—Overbroad Indemnification Provision

> Licensor shall indemnify Licensee and hold Licensee harmless from any damages (including reasonable attorneys' fees and costs), arising from any breach of any representation, warranty, or covenant in this Agreement.

This statement is too broad. Many statements within the license agreement can be characterized as either a representation, warranty, or covenant. The indemnity provision should designate which warranties are indemnified. We recommend only two specific warranties (as explained above): (a) that you have the right to license the invention, and (b) that the invention does not infringe any other inventions. These specific warranties should be in a separate section titled "Licensor Warranties" and should be referenced directly in the indemnification section, as shown in the sample provision above.

Avoid Indemnifying for Breaches of the License Agreement

You should avoid a provision like the one that follows.

Not Recommended—Overbroad Indemnification Provision

> Licensor shall indemnify Licensee and hold Licensee harmless from any damages (including reasonable attorneys' fees and costs), arising from any breach of this Agreement.

Indemnifying for a breach of the agreement is the ultimate in licensing masochism. Why? Because you are agreeing to punish yourself if you break the agreement. The license agreement can only be breached by the parties who signed it (or their successors). An indemnification for a breach means that if you do something wrong, you will pay the licensee legal fees when he or she sues you. That hurts! This provision is similar to the one-way attorneys' fees provision discussed in Chapter 14. Indemnification should only be provided for third-party lawsuits. A third-party lawsuit is a suit brought by someone who is not a party to the agreement. An example of a third-party lawsuit would be someone other than the licensee who claims that your invention infringes.

Avoid Indemnifying for Damages or Injuries

You should avoid a provision like the one that follows.

Not Recommended—Overbroad Indemnification Provision

> Licensor shall indemnify Licensee and hold Licensee harmless from any damages (including reasonable attorneys' fees and costs) from any injury or death arising from any defect in the Property.

By agreeing to this provision, you are effectively stepping into the insurance business. You should avoid it and, instead, insist that the licensee maintain adequate product liability insurance (as explained below).

Avoid Indemnifying for Alleged Claims

You should avoid a provision like the following.

Not Recommended—Overbroad Indemnification Provision

> Licensor shall indemnify Licensee and hold Licensee harmless from any damages (including reasonable attorneys' fees and costs) from any alleged claim or injury arising from the Licensed Product.

Watch out for provisions that require you to indemnify for *alleged* breaches of warranties. These provisions require that you open your checkbook to defend against any claims, whether or not they are valid. Your indemnity provision should only require you to be obligated for actual infringement, not alleged infringement. That is why we recommend you include a qualification stating that you only have to pay indemnity if the claim results in a court verdict. Many people bring false lawsuits as a means of "shaking down" a licensee. You should only be responsible for allegations or claims if they result in a final judgment in a court of law.

Paying for Indemnity

All of this talk about indemnity is fine, but how are you going to pay for it? Chances are, the costs will be a massive burden. One successful toy licensor has a rule, "Never give back money." His indemnity provisions permit licensees to take money from royalties that accrue after the date of notification of the claim, but he does not have to pay any money that he has already received.

EXAMPLE: Phil licenses an outdoor lighting invention to OutdoorsCo and indemnifies against infringement. When a rival company sues for infringement,

OutdoorsCo notifies Phil and begins withholding royalty payments to pay for defending the lawsuit. Phil does not pay OutdoorsCo any money that he has already earned from them under the licensing agreement.

Get ready to negotiate, because the issue of how much to pay is a controversial topic. A licensee commonly wants you to pay all of the indemnity costs and doesn't want to limit it to future royalties. This is one area where it may be worthwhile to take a strong stand. Depending on your bargaining power, the following are the three most common choices:

- **Pay only from future royalties.** This is the "we don't give back money" approach which requires the licensee to withhold future royalties after the claim is filed for indemnity costs. You don't have to return advances or previously received royalties. Licensors with strong bargaining positions may even limit this further by requiring that only 50% or 75% of future royalties be deducted.
- **Pay only what you have earned.** The logic behind this is that you shouldn't have to pay the licensee more than what you earned. For example, if your total earnings from royalties is $50,000, then you would

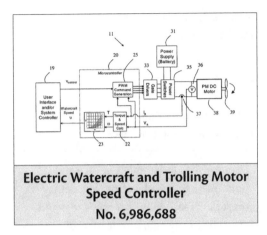

Electric Watercraft and Trolling Motor Speed Controller

No. 6,986,688

have to pay all or a portion of this sum back to the licensee. This is a burden, but at least there is a cap (or limit) on how much is to be paid.
- **Pay whatever it costs.** This is the worst-case scenario where there is no limit and you have to pay all indemnity costs.

Naturally, you should try to avoid paying for everything. If the licensee insists on it (and you lack the bargaining power to avoid it), then at least obtain an opinion from a patent attorney.

Paying From Future Royalties

If you can negotiate to have the indemnity paid from future royalties, then you should consider an indemnity provision such as the following one.

The maximum amount due from Licensor to Licensee under this paragraph shall not exceed the amounts due to Licensor under the Payment section from the date that Licensor notifies Licensee of the existence of such a claim.

Paying From Future Royalties— Establishing a Fund

A more sophisticated approach to the future royalties indemnity provision is to set up a fund. How does the fund work? When a third-party claim is made against the licensee, the licensee stops paying you royalties and instead puts the money into a fund. All or part of the fund is then used for indemnity. If anything is left after the case is resolved, it is returned to you.

This is the ideal method, because you never have to reach into your own bank account and pay for indemnity. You get to keep everything you earned until you were notified of the third-party claim. After notification, royalties are deposited into the fund. A powerful licensor can even negotiate so that only half of the fund is used for indemnity. Some industries do not use indemnity funds, while in others (such as the toy business) it is common.

Sample Fund Provision

The maximum amount due from Licensor to Licensee under this paragraph shall not exceed [*50 to 100*]% of the amounts due to Licensor under the payment section [*if you have numbered the sections of your agreement, include the number of the payment section*] from the date that Licensor notifies Licensee of the existence of such a claim. After the commencement of a lawsuit against Licensee that comes within the scope of this paragraph, Licensee may place [*same percentage as listed above*]% of the royalties due to Licensor under the payment section in a separate interest-bearing fund, which shall be referred to in this Agreement as the "Legal Fund." Licensee may draw against such Legal Fund to satisfy all of the reasonable expenses of defending the suit and of any judgment or settlement made in regard to this suit. In the event the Legal Fund is insufficient to pay the then-current defense obligations, Licensee may advance monies on behalf of the Legal Fund and shall be reimbursed as payments are credited to the Legal Fund. Licensor's liability to Licensee shall not extend beyond the loss of its royalty deposit in the Legal Fund. After the suit has been concluded, any balance remaining in the Legal Fund shall be paid to Licensor, and all future royalties due to Licensor shall be paid to Licensor as they would otherwise become due. Licensee shall not permit the time for appeal from an adverse decision on a claim to expire.

Paying What You Earned

If you can't negotiate a future royalties indemnity provision, then attempt to cap it by limiting indemnity to what you earn under the agreement as follows.

> The maximum amount due from Licensor to Licensee under this paragraph shall not exceed the total sums paid to Licensor under this Agreement.

What If the Licensee's Agreement Doesn't Include Warranty or Indemnity Provisions?

In some instances, a licensee's agreement might not include warranties and indemnity. This could be a result of neglect or because the licensee prefers not to deal with these provisions. Even if warranties and indemnities are not written into the agreement, these legal principles can still be enforced under state court decisions and statutes such as the Uniform Commercial Code. Should you bring up the issue if the licensee leaves out these provisions? Probably not. As a general rule, licensors have a difficult time obtaining favorable indemnification provisions, and you will save negotiating time.

Licensee Warranties and Indemnity

You provide warranties and indemnity for the licensee, and it's logical to expect similar promises and assurances from the licensee. The licensee's warranties and the indemnity will differ, as described below.

Licensee Warranties

We recommend that you seek an assurance that the licensee will sell your invention as promised and obey laws regarding the manufacturing, marketing, sale, or distribution of the final product. You should include a provision such as the following (which will be explained in more detail in the following sections).

Licensee Warranties

> Licensee warrants that it will use its best commercial efforts to market the Licensed Products and that their sale and marketing shall be in conformance with all applicable laws and regulations, including, but not limited to, all intellectual property laws.

Warranting to Sell the Invention

The first warranty—that the licensee will sell the invention—is especially important. Some unscrupulous licensees may license your invention simply to keep it off the market. For example, a tire company might license a method of making indestructible tires and then keep it off the market in order to continue selling its inferior products. It is for this reason that you want the licensee to warrant that it will market the invention.

Exclusive Licensees and the Duty to Market

What if an exclusive licensee refuses to include a warranty that it will market the invention? Even without the provision, you may still have recourse under state laws, which have created a legal obligation for the licensee—known as an implied duty—to market or exploit the invention. For example, under many state laws, the company has a legal obligation (apart from the contract) to sell the product. This implied duty only applies to exclusive licensees. A nonexclusive licensee has *no* obligation by law to sell your invention—unless it has agreed to do so in your license agreement. These laws are usually referenced under your state's commercial or civil code. Review the index for these state codes in your local law library (or on the Internet if your state has posted its state laws).

Warranting to Obey the Laws

It may seem silly to require that the licensee obey all applicable laws. After all, why would the licensee want to risk violating laws? And even if the licensee violates the laws, what difference does it make to you, the inventor? We recommend this warranty because it allows you to hold the licensee responsible in the event there is a violation of these laws, and it may provide a defense for you in case you are named in a lawsuit involving illegal practices.

Licensee Indemnity

We suggest that the licensee indemnify you for its warranties and representations and also in the event of a product liability suit. A product liability suit occurs when someone is injured by a defective product. We discuss product liability later in this chapter in the section regarding insurance.

Indemnification by Licensee

Licensee shall indemnify Licensor and hold Licensor harmless from any damages and liabilities (including reasonable attorneys' fees and costs) (a) arising from any breach of Licensee's warranties and representation as defined in the Licensee Warranties, above; (b) arising out of any alleged defects or failures to perform of the Licensed Products or any product liability claims or use of the Licensed Products; and (c) any claims arising out of advertising, distribution, or marketing of the Licensed Products.

Proprietary Rights

The proprietary rights section of your licensing agreement usually deals with three "what if" issues:

- What if you or the licensee wants to register patent or copyright protection for the invention?
- What if the licensee fails to properly mark the products with the appropriate patent and copyright notices?
- What if someone infringes the invention?

The purpose of this provision is to protect intellectual property rights during the license agreement. This protection deals with registration of the intellectual property, marking the invention with the appropriate legal notices, and suing anyone who infringes the rights licensed under the agreement.

Registering Patent, Trademark, or Copyright Protection for the Invention

You may want to register for patent, trademark, or copyright protection after the license is signed. The provision below grants you that right. Naturally, you can only register those elements that you created. You can't register for trademarks, copyrighted works, or inventions that the licensee has created or added to the licensed product.

If you haven't registered your invention and don't plan to, the licensee might want to register for protection. There's nothing wrong with this, assuming you are named as the author or inventor and obtain the rights that go with the protection. But who pays for this registration? If you have the bargaining power to make the licensee pay, fine. But it's common for the licensee to deduct the costs of registration from future royalties. You will need to make sure that the expenses are reasonable and capped (limited). We recommend the provision below as a means to protect your interests while allowing for registration by the licensee.

Tie With Concealed Pockets
No. 6,266,823

Intellectual Property Protection

Licensor may, but is not obligated to, seek, in its own name and at its own expense, appropriate patent, trademark, or copyright protection for the Property. Licensor makes no warranty with respect to the validity of any patent, trademark, or copyright which may be granted. Licensor grants to Licensee the right to apply for patents on the Property or Licensed Products provided that such patents shall be applied for in the name of Licensor and licensed to Licensee during the Term and according to the conditions of this Agreement. Licensee shall have the right to deduct its reasonable out-of-pocket expenses for the preparation, filing, and prosecution of any such U.S. patent application (but in no event more than $5,000) from future royalties due to Licensor under this Agreement. Licensee shall obtain Licensor's prior written consent before incurring expenses for any foreign patent application.

When the Licensee Acquires Intellectual Property Registration in Its Name

It's sometimes appropriate for the licensee to file a trademark or copyright registration under its own name. For example, if the licensee is the first to sell your invention, then the licensee acquires trademark rights for the licensed product. (See Chapter 1 for an explanation.) If the invention has copyrightable features, the copyright act permits an exclusive licensee to register copyright as the owner (or "claimant"). When the license terminates, the licensee's rights under copyright law will terminate. Patent applications, however, should only be done in the name of the inventor, with one exception. A person to whom the inventor has assigned or is under an obligation to assign the invention may make an application for patent. (See Chapter 1 for an explanation of assignments.)

Portable Sign System
No. 6,972,689

Marking Products With Appropriate Proprietary Notices

Different forms of intellectual property have different notice requirements. The failure to include a proprietary notice (for example, "Java Jacket®"—indicating it is a federally registered trademark) may affect your rights against infringers. The provision below requires that the licensee affix all of the required proprietary notices (copyright, patent, and so on) and obey the intellectual property laws.

Compliance With Intellectual Property Laws

> The license granted in this Agreement is conditioned on Licensee's compliance with the provisions of the intellectual property laws of the United States and any foreign country in the Territory. All copies of the Licensed Product as well as all promotional material shall bear appropriate proprietary notices.

Dealing With Infringers

If your invention is successful, unethical competitors might create imitations. As we explained in Chapter 2, the government rarely gets involved in the prosecution of infringers. If you and the licensee do nothing, there is nothing to stop the infringement.

You might not have the financial resources to fight an infringer by yourself, so it's wise to include a provision that allows both you and the licensee to deal with infringers. The provision below provides for funding of a lawsuit and determining how to divide any money that is recovered from the infringer. This provision establishes a 50/50 division of any award money after payment of attorneys' fees.

EXAMPLE: Bob licenses his self-cleaning urinal invention to SaniCo. SaniCo sues an infringer and recovers $100,000. After deducting their attorneys' fees of $25,000, SaniCo splits the remaining $75,000 on a 50/50 basis with Bob.

Because some risk exists in bringing an infringement lawsuit (there's always the chance that you will lose), it's common for a licensee to seek a provision that provides for the party bringing the lawsuit to get more than 50%. In many license agreements, the party bringing the lawsuit may obtain 75% of the payment or more.

You should also note that sometimes, instead of paying damages, an infringer

Convertible Tent for Rain, Cold, and Hot Conditions
No. 6,216,715

is allowed to continue selling imitation products provided that an ongoing royalty is paid. This royalty would be divided according to the same percentage established for judgments or settlements.

Infringement Lawsuits Against Third Parties

In the event that either party learns of imitations or infringements of the Property or Licensed Products, that party shall notify the other in writing of the infringements or imitations. Licensor shall have the right to commence lawsuits against third persons arising from infringement of the Property or Licensed Products. In the event that Licensor does not commence a lawsuit against an alleged infringer within sixty days of notification by Licensee, Licensee may commence a lawsuit against the third party. Before filing suit, Licensee shall obtain the written consent of Licensor to do so, and such consent shall not be unreasonably withheld. Licensor will cooperate fully and in good faith with Licensee for the purpose of securing and preserving Licensee's rights to the Property. Any recovery (including, but not limited to, a judgment, settlement, or licensing agreement included as resolution of an infringement dispute) shall be divided equally between the parties after deduction and payment of reasonable attorneys' fees to the party bringing the lawsuit.

Can't Afford to Sue? Help Is Available

There are two types of infringement lawsuits:

- lawsuits in which a third party sues you or the licensee (or both) for infringement, or
- lawsuits in which you or the licensee sue a third party for infringement.

There are two types of insurance available to cover these suits.

One type of insurance is defensive and will provide coverage if you are sued for infringement. This insurance is offered by several large insurance companies, which you can find by searching online for patent infringement insurance.

Several companies now offer the second type of insurance—for inventors who want to sue infringers. This insurance is offensive, not defensive, because it permits you to go after imitators. Assuming you can qualify for coverage, these companies will pay a percentage of your legal fees (usually 75%) and take a portion of any settlement. For more information about these policies, contact Lloyd's of London (www.lloyds.com) or Intellectual Property Insurance Services Corporation of Louisville, Kentucky (www.infringeins.com), or search online for patent enforcement insurance.

Dear Rich:
Insurance for Patent Enforcement?

Dear Rich: I am patent pending and am worried about what will happen if my patent is granted and a big company rips me off. I can't afford to sue a big company. Will lawyers take my case for a cut of the profits? What do the little guys do?

There are three common solutions for this issue:

- Align yourself with a strong licensee. As part of your licensing agreement, the licensee will usually chase down (or possibly scare off) thieves and competitors. The right licensee can save you a lot of hassle.
- Consider offensive insurance. There is such a thing as offensive patent insurance, and you can read more about it above.
- Find a "contingency fee" litigator. Some patent attorneys take cases on contingency, meaning they take a percentage of any settlement or court award you receive, and if you don't get paid, the lawyer doesn't get paid. But it's sometimes difficult to find a patent lawyer who will work under this kind of arrangement, and it can be an expensive way to go (you're giving up one third or more of your recovery).

Commercialization and Exploitation

In Chapter 8, we recommended that you discuss the dates for commercialization and include those dates as material terms on your fact sheet. This provision expands on the commercialization requirements. In many industries, companies offer new products at certain times of the year. If a licensee fails to introduce the item at an appropriate trade show or in a seasonal catalog, you might lose a full year of royalties. For this reason, you should define the commercialization provision as a "material" provision. In the event the licensee fails to commercialize the item, you can claim a "material breach," which is a basis for termination of your license agreement. We recommend a commercialization provision such as the one that follows.

Exploitation

Licensee agrees to manufacture, distribute, and sell the Licensed Products in commercially reasonable quantities during the term of this Agreement and to commence such manufacture, distribution, and sale within the following time period: [*insert time period, for example, "six months"*]. This is a material provision of this Agreement.

The term "commercially reasonable quantities" requires that the licensee make a good-faith effort to distribute more than a token number of licensed products. If there's a particular trade show or seasonal catalog you want the product exploited in, you can add a sentence like the following one.

> Licensee agrees to introduce the Licensed Product at the trade show or with the seasonal catalog as specified in Exhibit A.

Newspaper Hanger
No. 6,869,054

Samples and Quality Control

Imagine your disappointment if the licensee begins selling your invention and the product has defects or is inferior to competing products. The provision below permits you to review the quality standards of the licensee.

Samples and Quality Control

> Licensee shall submit a reasonable number of production samples of the Licensed Product to Licensor to assure that the product meets Licensor's quality standards. In the event that Licensor fails to object in writing within ten business days after the date of receipt, the Licensed Product shall be deemed to be acceptable. At least once during each calendar year, Licensee shall submit two production samples of each Licensed Product for review. The quality standards applied by Licensor shall be no more rigorous than the quality standards applied by Licensee to similar products.

Insurance

What happens if a consumer is injured using your product and claims that it's defective? Perhaps the licensee has promised to indemnify you against such a disaster.

Unfortunately, that's not enough. What's really needed is an insurance carrier with a solid rating—a Grade B or higher under the Moody Standard insurance rating system—who will cover both the licensee and you. (If there is a licensing agent, the agent may also want to be named in the policy.) If you are named in the policy, the insurance company will have a duty to defend you, as well as the licensee, in the event of product injuries. This insurance is intended to shield you from claims of product injuries, not infringement lawsuits. That is, it only covers you if consumers are hurt using the product.

It's possible that the licensee already has a policy but the policy isn't as robust as the example below. You may have to be flexible and accept the licensee's policy. However, you should be aware of the difference between two types of policies. They are:

- **Occurrence policies.** If the insurance was in place when the injury occurred, an occurrence policy will cover the suit, no matter when the claim is made or the lawsuit is filed. For example, the policy covers 2019 and the injury occurs in 2019. The injured person files the lawsuit in 2020. There is coverage.

Insurance

Licensee shall, throughout the Term, obtain and maintain, at its own expense, standard product liability insurance coverage, naming Licensor as additional named insured. Such policy shall: (a) be maintained with a carrier having a Moody's rating of at least B; and (b) provide protection against any claims, demands, and causes of action arising out of any alleged defects or failure to perform of the Licensed Products or any use of the Licensed Products. The amount of coverage shall be a minimum of [*insert amount of insurance coverage*] with no deductible amount for each single occurrence for bodily injury or property damage. The policy shall provide for notice to the Agent and Licensor from the insurer by registered or certified mail in the event of any modification or termination of insurance. Licensee shall furnish Licensor and Agent a certificate from its product liability insurance carrier evidencing insurance coverage in favor of Licensor. In no event shall Licensee distribute the Licensed Products before the receipt by the Licensor of evidence of insurance. The provisions of this section shall survive termination for three years.

- **Claims-made policies.** This type of insurance covers claims only if they are made during the policy period. For example, say the policy covers 2019 and the injury occurs in 2019. The injured person files the lawsuit in 2020. There is no coverage.

Because you may not be able to control whether the insurance is claims-made or occurrence, we suggest that you include a statement that this provision shall survive for three years (this time period may be negotiable) after termination. That way, you'll still be protected in the event it is a claims-made policy.

> **TIP**
> **Product liability insurance.** We do not provide you with the suggested amount of coverage, as that may differ from industry to industry. It is not unusual for product liability coverage to range between $1,000,000 and $5,000,000, or more.

Termination and Posttermination

Termination and Posttermination..322

Termination Based Upon a Fixed Term 323

Termination at Will 324

Termination Based on Contract Problems...324

    Don't Rely on a Judge's Discretion 325

    The Cure Period...325

Termination and Bankruptcy...326

Posttermination: What Happens Afterwards?..327

    Posttermination Sales...327

    Return of Molds, Plans, and Related Materials 328

    Posttermination Provision 328

Survival of the Fittest..329

The conclusion of a license—known as termination—can occur for various reasons. Perhaps you agreed to end the license after a period of years or perhaps something has gone wrong, such as the licensee has stopped paying royalties. In this chapter, we discuss the ways by which a license agreement is terminated and what happens after termination. You should read this chapter if you answer "yes" to any of the following questions:

- Would you like to know the reasons a license agreement can be terminated?
- Does either party want the right to terminate without a reason?
- Would you like to know how bankruptcy will affect the license?
- Does the licensee want the ability to sell off inventory after the license is over?
- Would you like designs, plans, materials, or molds returned after termination?

In the following sections, we discuss the various methods of ending a license agreement and provide sample provisions. For example, license agreements may terminate at the expiration of a time period or as a result of a dispute. We also discuss how disputes can be resolved (or "cured"). Bankruptcies can also affect a license agreement, and we explore the difference between licensee and licensor bankruptcies. Finally, we provide you with advice on what to do *after* the license has terminated.

Termination and Posttermination

When negotiating a license agreement, most people focus on the beginning of the relationship and don't think about the end. At some point, however, your license agreement will end, either peacefully or angrily. A well-drafted license agreement should deal with both types of situations. You don't have to include all the termination provisions provided below in your license. They're provided to make you aware of the different possibilities. Some common bases for termination are:

- termination based upon a deadline (sometimes referred to as a "fixed-term" agreement)

  EXAMPLE: The agreement provides for termination after two years.

- termination at will

  EXAMPLE: One party terminates the agreement without providing a reason.

- termination based on a problem arising from the agreement

  EXAMPLE: You terminate because the licensee fails to pay royalties.

Termination Based Upon a Fixed Term

A fixed term means that the license agreement will end at a predetermined time. Some examples of a fixed term could be:

- a license that runs for three years
- a license that runs until the licensee fails to renew, or
- a license that runs until the patent expires.

Have you and the licensee already agreed upon the length of time the license agreement will last? If you have provided for a fixed term in your term provision (see Chapter 8 on establishing the basic elements of your licensing agreement), then your agreement has a built-in ending —the conclusion (or expiration) of the term. Some license agreements don't include a term provision. Instead, the parties express the contract length in the termination provision.

Note: If you are using both a term and a termination provision, make sure they conform (that is, that they both provide for the same fixed period of time).

If you want the license to terminate after a period of years, you might use the following provision.

This Agreement shall terminate at the end of [*insert number of years*] years unless terminated sooner under a provision of this Agreement.

If you have a patent, make sure to limit the term to the length of the patent, as shown here.

This Agreement shall terminate with the expiration of the longest-living patent (or patents) or last-remaining patent application (as listed in the definition of the Property), whichever occurs last, unless terminated sooner under a provision of this Agreement.

If you want to establish a fixed term with renewal periods, use something like the following sample.

This Agreement terminates at the end of two years (the "Initial Term") unless renewed by Licensee under the same terms and conditions for consecutive two-year periods (the "Renewal Terms") provided that Licensee provides written notice of its intention to renew this agreement within 30 days prior to expiration of the current term. In no event, shall the Agreement extend longer than the date of expiration of the longest-living patent (or patents) or last-remaining patent application as listed in the definition of the Property.

If there is no patent, strike the last sentence at the end of the provision.

Termination at Will

Termination at will means that one party can end the agreement simply by notifying the other. In this type of termination, it's not necessary to provide an explanation or reason. The agreement ends simply because one party decides to terminate it. This provision does not have to be mutual. In fact, the licensee usually wants this ability but does not want the licensor to have it. In other words, they can terminate at will but you can't. This is often true if the licensee is required to pay a minimum guaranteed royalty payment. The at-will provision lets the licensee bail out of the agreement (and royalty commitment) if the licensed products are not selling well.

A licensee's right to terminate at will may seem unfair, but it's just a business reality. If a licensee doesn't want to sell your product or is losing money, there's nothing you can do to change that position, no matter how the license is drafted. That's why termination at will is common. If you can avoid termination at will, fine. But if the licensee insists on it, accept it and try to negotiate a long notice period (perhaps 90 days), which will give you more time to find another licensee.

The following is a sample termination at will provision under which only the licensee can terminate:

Termination at Will: Licensee's Option

> Upon 90 days' notice, Licensee may, at its sole discretion, terminate this agreement by providing notice to the Licensor.

Termination Based on Contract Problems

What happens if the licensee fails to honor the agreement? If you sue, a court might award you damages but not terminate the agreement. That is, you could be awarded a payment but the license agreement may continue.

A judge will only terminate an agreement if a material breach occurred. Which breaches are "material"? That depends upon the contract, the events

Weather Vane
No. D436,542

giving rise to the breach, the law governing the contract, and the discretion of the judge. In some cases, for example, judges have determined that a failure to pay royalties is not a material breach.

Don't Rely on a Judge's Discretion

To you, a failure to pay royalties is a material breach. Rather than rely on a judge's discretion or interpretation of the law, you can write a provision stating that the agreement will terminate for specific types of breaches, such as a failure to pay royalties.

We recommend that you specify the particular problems that will be the bases for termination. In particular, we recommend that you consider termination for the reasons provided below:

- a failure to pay royalties (or make other payments as provided in the agreement)
- a failure to sell (or exploit) the invention
- a failure to maintain confidentiality as required under the confidentiality provision
- an assignment or sublicense of your rights in violation of the agreement, and
- a failure to maintain product liability insurance. (If your invention is the type of licensed product that requires product liability insurance, see Chapter 12.)

Not all of these reasons will fit within your agreement. For example, confidentiality, assignment, or product liability might be irrelevant to your invention. Therefore, you should modify the provision shown in the next section accordingly.

All-Purpose Breach Provisions

Some license agreements state that, "In the event of a breach, either party can terminate this agreement." We do *not* recommend this type of provision because it is too broad and it will be left up to a judge to determine whether the activity—for example, failure to pay royalties—is a breach. In other words, this clause is still too discretionary. You will be better served by identifying the particular breaches that qualify for termination.

The Cure Period

Many companies run into temporary problems. For example, payments might be delayed because of computer snafus or cash shortages. For that reason, it's unfair to terminate the agreement until the licensee has had an opportunity to fix or cure the problem. Normally, each side is given 30 or 60 days (the cure period) from the time of notification to cure the defect. For example, if you don't receive your royalty payment, you notify the licensee (see the "Notices" section in Chapter 14), and if you don't get paid within the cure period, then you can terminate the agreement. We recommend a 30-day cure period as a reasonable period to fix the problem.

Not every breach or problem is curable. A failure to obtain product liability insurance, for example, may not be curable, because you're exposed to liability. The right to cure is usually included within the termination provision as shown below.

Licensor's Right to Terminate

Licensor shall have the right to terminate this Agreement for the following reasons:

(a) Licensee fails to pay Royalties when due or fails to accurately report Net Sales, as defined in the Payment section of this Agreement, and such failure is not cured within 30 days after written notice from the Licensor;

(b) Licensee fails to introduce the product to market by [*insert date by which Licensee must begin selling Licensed Products*] or to offer the Licensed Products in commercially reasonable quantities during any subsequent year;

(c) Licensee fails to maintain confidentiality regarding Licensor's trade secrets and other Information;

(d) Licensee assigns or sublicenses in violation of the Agreement; or

(e) Licensee fails to maintain or obtain product liability insurance as required by the provisions of this Agreement.

Terminate as to Territory Not Exploited
[*optional*]

Licensor shall have the right to terminate the grant of license under this Agreement with respect to any country or region included in the Territory in which Licensee fails to offer the Licensed Products for sale or distribution or to secure a sublicensing agreement for the marketing, distribution, and sale of the product within two years of the Effective Date.

Termination and Bankruptcy

What happens if the licensee goes bankrupt? Unfortunately, there is not much you can do to protect yourself against a licensee's bankruptcy. Many license agreements contain a provision stating that the licensor can terminate the agreement in the event of bankruptcy. But such provisions are unenforceable (with the exception of some trademark licenses). That is, you will *not* be able to terminate the license agreement if the licensee goes bankrupt. Once the licensee files for bankruptcy, only a federal bankruptcy court can determine your rights and obligations under a licensing agreement. The bankruptcy court can keep your invention rights tied up for months or years while a bankruptcy trustee attempts to sort out the financial mess. It's even possible that your license may be assigned to another company in order to pay off creditors of the licensee.

Seem unfair? Welcome to bankruptcy law, which, like tax law, relies on arcane rules and regulations that often defy logic. Oddly, if you (the licensor) become bankrupt, the licensee can elect to continue with the license or terminate it. So, if the situation is reversed and you're insolvent, the licensee has the right to terminate or pay royalties to the trustee.

Summing up, you cannot claim bankruptcy or insolvency as a basis for termination. Although these termination provisions (sometimes referred to as ipso facto provisions) are often mistakenly included in license agreements, they're invalid and should not be used.

Posttermination: What Happens Afterwards?

If a license ends bitterly, it will be very difficult to get the licensee to voluntarily return materials. That's why the contract must provide for various contingencies with a clause titled "Posttermination" or "Effect of Termination." These posttermination provisions are like the conditions of a prenuptial agreement for newlyweds describing who gets what and how things should be divided after a split.

After termination, you should be concerned about three things:

- The licensee stops sales as soon as possible.
- The licensee pays you all money that is due.
- The licensee returns all designs, molds, or other furnished materials.

Posttermination Sales

At the time of termination, the licensee may have boxes of licensed products left in the warehouse. If you end the agreement amicably, it seems reasonable to allow the licensee a period of time to sell off the remaining inventory. Naturally, you're entitled to royalties for these products. How long should the sell-off period be? If it's too short, the licensee will be unable to unload its inventory.

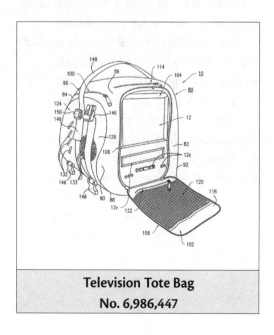

Television Tote Bag
No. 6,986,447

If it's too long, it might conflict with another license. A period between three to six months is probably sufficient. In addition, the licensor should obtain an accounting of the remaining inventory.

Obviously, if the licensee is not paying royalties, it makes no sense to allow a sell-off of inventory. The same is true if no product liability insurance exists or the government recalls the invention. The provision provided below prevents sales unless all of these conditions have been met.

Return of Molds, Plans, and Related Materials

If your invention is a product—an item to be mass-produced—one of the most expensive start-up costs is the preparation of molds or tooling for manufacture.

Since the licensee will have no further use for them, you should request the tooling and molds. It's only fair that you should pay for the shipping of these items.

There are two important reasons to obtain the tooling and molds. First, it removes the materials from the licensee, who no longer has the right to manufacture the invention. And second, in the event you can locate a new licensee, it will give you a head start for manufacturing.

Posttermination Provision

Below is an example of a recommended posttermination provision.

Effect of Termination

Upon termination of this Agreement, all Royalty obligations as established in the Payments section shall immediately become due. After the termination of this license, all rights granted to Licensee under this Agreement shall revert to Licensor, and Licensee will refrain from further manufacturing, copying, marketing, distribution, or use of any Licensed Product or other product which incorporates the Property. Within 30 days after termination, Licensee shall deliver to Licensor a statement indicating the number and description of the Licensed Products which it had on hand or was in the process of manufacturing as of the termination date. Licensee may dispose of the Licensed Products covered by this Agreement for a period of three months after termination except that Licensee shall have no such right in the event this agreement is terminated according to the Licensor's Right to Terminate, above. At the end of the posttermination sale period, Licensee shall furnish a royalty payment and statement as required under the Payment section. Upon termination, Licensee shall deliver to Licensor all tooling and molds used in the manufacture of the Licensed Products. Licensor shall bear the costs of shipping for the tooling and molds.

Survival of the Fittest

Just because the license terminates, it doesn't mean that all of the obligations in the agreement terminate. For example, it's important that the parties maintain confidential information after the agreement ends. It's also important that you receive any other payments that may accrue after termination. Therefore, the parties often designate that some obligations continue or survive the agreement. We recommend that the following sections survive termination:

- confidentiality
- warranties
- licensee indemnity
- product liability insurance, and
- payment obligations.

The licensee may insist that other provisions survive as well.

You indicate which provisions survive by adding a sentence at the end of the provision such as: "This obligation shall survive any termination of this Agreement." Some license agreements have a separate provision that says:

Survival

The obligations of [Sections ____ , ____ , and ____ or the ____ , ____ , and ____ sections] shall survive any termination of this Agreement.

It doesn't matter which method is used, but you should carefully review which sections survive termination.

Boilerplate and Standard Provisions

Paying the Lawyer's Bills.. 333

   Laws That Allow Award of Attorneys' Fees 333

   Attorneys' Fees and Expenses 334

Dispute Resolution 335

   Arbitration... 335

   Mediation 336

Governing Law.. 337

Jurisdiction 338

Waiver... 339

Severability 340

Entire Understanding.. 340

Attachments and Exhibits 341

Notices 341

No Joint Venture 342

Assignments 342

Force Majeure 344

Headings 344

Establishing Escrow Accounts 345

In this chapter, we discuss contract provisions that are sometimes referred to as boilerplate, general, miscellaneous, or standard provisions. These provisions are usually grouped at the end of an agreement and deal with a range of miscellaneous issues, such as resolving disputes and interpreting the agreement. You should read this chapter if you answer "yes" to any of the following questions:

- Would you like an explanation of attorneys' fees provisions?
- Would you like information about the process of arbitration?
- Are you confused about issues such as choice of law or jurisdiction?
- Do you want a definition for "waiver," "integration," "force majeure," "invalidity," or "severability"?
- Would you like to know what is meant when an attachment or exhibit is "incorporated" into an agreement?
- Are you concerned about whether the licensee can assign your invention to another company?

As you read through this chapter, you might wonder why these contract provisions are grouped together. Boilerplate provisions actually have little in common with one another except for the fact that they don't fit anywhere else in the agreement. For that reason, they are usually dumped at the end of the agreement and labeled with titles such as "Miscellaneous," "General," or "Standard."

Don't be misled by the fact that boilerplate is buried in the back of the agreement. These provisions are very important and can affect how disputes are resolved and how the contract is enforced by a court.

Below is a summary of the boilerplate provisions we will discuss in this chapter:

- **Attorneys' fees.** In the event of a legal dispute, this provision determines if the winner receives payment for legal fees.
- **Arbitration.** This provision provides for a method of resolving disputes without resorting to a lawsuit.
- **Choice of law.** In the event of a dispute, this provision determines which state law will govern the lawsuit.
- **Jurisdiction.** In the event of a dispute, this provision establishes in which state (and county) the lawsuit must be filed.
- **Waiver.** This provision permits the parties to waive (forgo or give up claim to) a portion of the agreement without establishing a precedent (without giving up future claims under the same portion).
- **Severability.** This provision permits a court to sever (or take out) an invalid provision and still keep the rest of the agreement intact.
- **Integration.** This provision establishes that the agreement is the final version and that any further modification must be in writing.

- **Attachments.** This provision guarantees that attachments and exhibits will be included as part of the agreement.
- **Notice provisions.** This provision describes how each party must provide notice of disputes.
- **Relationships.** This provision prevents either party from claiming a business relationship with the other, such as that of partner or joint venturer.
- **Assignment.** This provision affects the ability of the parties to sell their rights under the agreement to another party.
- **Force majeure (pronounced forsmazhoor').** This provision establishes that the agreement will be suspended in the event of unforeseen disasters (such as earthquakes, hurricanes, floods, and so on).
- **Headings.** This provision provides that the headings used throughout the agreement have no special significance.
- **Escrow.** This provision allows you and the licensee to place trade secrets, payments, or other information into a special account which will only be opened under certain conditions.

Paying the Lawyer's Bills

Hopefully, your relationship with the licensee will be prosperous and peaceable. But what if the licensee breaches the agreement and you're forced to sue?

The hourly rate for business lawyers is between $200 and $400 an hour. The filing and initial stages of a lawsuit cost between $5,000 and $50,000 and can quickly escalate to more than $100,000, depending on the length of the suit and the subject matter. The amount you pay in attorneys' fees could quickly overshadow the amount you seek in damages.

Unfortunately, in the United States (unlike other countries), the winner of a lawsuit is not automatically awarded his or her attorneys' fees. In other words, each party has to pay its own lawyer, regardless of the outcome of the suit. This is known as the American Rule, and two exceptions exist: (1) A court may award fees if a specific law permits it, and (2) a court must award attorneys' fees if a contract provides for it.

Laws That Allow Award of Attorneys' Fees

Federal statutes provide for the award of attorneys' fees in cases where intellectual property laws (laws involving copyrights, trademarks, trade secrets, or patents, for example) have been violated. Some states' laws also allow an award of attorneys' fees for trade secrets violations. So, if you sue someone for a violation of intellectual property law—say for infringement of a patent—and you win, the judge (under the statute) may award you attorneys' fees.

Did you say the judge *may* award attorneys' fees? That's right. Under these laws, the award of attorneys' fees is not mandatory. It's discretionary (up to the judge). In reality, judges rarely award attorneys' fees unless one party's behavior is especially offensive—for example, a company knew they were infringing and proceeded despite your protests.

In addition, these laws do not cover all licensing lawsuits. Your lawsuit must arise from a violation of the patent, trademark, copyright, or trade secret laws (all of which are geared toward protecting against infringement). Common license agreement problems, such as failure to pay royalties, are not a violation of these laws because such disputes are based on contract law, not intellectual property law.

In summary, don't count on these laws for getting attorneys' fees in a lawsuit against a licensee. Chances are your case will not qualify under the statutes, and even if it does, the discretionary aspect makes the award unpredictable. If you're seeking attorneys' fees, you are far better off using an attorneys' fees provision, as described below.

Attorneys' Fees and Expenses

You and the licensee can create a contract provision that provides for the award of attorneys' fees to the winner (also known as the prevailing party) of any lawsuit arising from the license agreement. However, don't be surprised if the licensee is opposed to the use of an attorneys' fees provision. Why? Because it is the licensee who is usually sued by the licensor, not vice versa, and the licensee believes the provision will encourage the licensor to sue.

If you can get your licensee to agree to it, we recommend the following sample attorneys' fees provision:

> The prevailing party shall have the right to collect from the other party its reasonable costs and necessary disbursements and attorneys' fees incurred in enforcing this Agreement.

 CAUTION

Watch out for one-way attorneys' fees provisions. We encourage the use of mutual attorneys' fees provisions, such as the one above. Under a mutual provision, the party that wins the lawsuit is the party that is awarded attorneys' fees. This is fair and encourages the quick resolution of lawsuits. We discourage a one-way provision that allows only the licensee to receive attorneys' fees. That is, if the licensee wins, you, the licensor, would pay the licensee's attorneys' fees, but if you win, you would get nothing to pay your lawyer. One-way provisions, no matter which side they favor, create an uneven playing field for resolving disputes. Some states, such as California, have recognized this unfairness and automatically convert a one-way attorneys' fees contract provision into a mutual provision. We urge you to strike any one-way attorneys' fees provisions.

Dispute Resolution

Arbitration is like going to court—with less formality and expense. Instead of filing a lawsuit, the parties hire one or more arbitrators to evaluate the dispute and make a determination. Arbitrators are trained to evaluate disputes, and many of them are retired judges. Mediation is similar to arbitration except that instead of making a determination, a neutral evaluator attempts to help the parties settle their dispute. The mediator offers advice so the parties can reach a solution together.

Arbitration

The arbitration process can be relatively simple. Usually it involves some document preparation and a hearing. The arbitrator's determination may be advisory (a suggested resolution), or it may be binding and can be entered in a court. A binding arbitration cannot be overturned unless something especially unfair happened—for example, the arbitrator ruled against you and you later learned that the arbitrator owned stock in your opponent's company.

In order to arbitrate the dispute, both parties must consent. Unfortunately, when you are in the midst of a dispute, it's hard to get the parties to agree to anything. Therefore, the best method of guaranteeing arbitration is to include an arbitration provision in your license agreement.

Despite the advantages of arbitration, many licensees are opposed to the procedure. They might have recently lost an arbitration proceeding and refuse to participate in another one. They could be fearful that the dispute will be placed in the hands of an inappropriate arbitrator, or they might prefer the litigation process in order to intimidate the licensor. In addition, some arbitrations are expensive, require attorneys, and end up being appealed in the court system.

Summing up, below are the pros and cons for arbitration:

- **Pros.** Arbitration is often less expensive and more efficient than litigation. If the subject of the dispute is technical—for example, about a patent—the parties can select an arbitrator who has technical knowledge.

- **Cons.** There's no right to discovery (the process by which the parties must disclose information about their cases). However, you can include a requirement for discovery in your arbitration provision. Unlike a court ruling, a binding arbitration ruling is not appealable. It can only be set aside if it can be demonstrated that the arbitrator was biased or that the ruling violated public policy. Arbitrators must be paid (unlike state and federal judges), and these fees can often run to $10,000 or more. And most participants hire attorneys, so you will still have attorneys' fees (although probably lower than in a lawsuit).

Many associations and companies offer private arbitration, the most well-known of which is the American Arbitration Association (AAA) at www.adr.org. The AAA has special Patent Arbitration Rules and a national panel of patent arbitrators.

We recommend the following sample arbitration provision with your state of residence placed in the blank:

Arbitration

If a dispute arises under or relating to this Agreement, the parties agree to submit such dispute to binding arbitration in the state of [*insert state in which parties agree to arbitrate*] or another location mutually agreeable to the parties. The arbitration shall be conducted on a confidential basis pursuant to the Commercial Arbitration Rules of the American Arbitration Association. Any decision or award as a result of any such arbitration proceeding shall be in writing and shall provide an explanation for all conclusions of law and fact and shall include the assessment of costs, expenses, and reasonable attorneys' fees. Any such arbitration shall be conducted by an arbitrator experienced in [*insert industry experience required for arbitrator*] and in invention licensing law and shall include a written record of the arbitration hearing. The parties reserve the right to object to any individual who shall be employed by or affiliated with a competing organization or entity. An award of arbitration may be confirmed in a court of competent jurisdiction.

Mediation

In mediation, a neutral evaluator (the mediator) attempts to help the parties reach a resolution of their dispute. Basically, the parties sit down with the mediator and tell their stories. The mediator makes recommendations and advises the parties on ways to resolve the dispute, and the two parties try to agree on a solution. Some licensees prefer mediation because the mediator's recommendations are not binding—only the parties can make a binding settlement—and because mediation is less expensive than litigation or arbitration.

The pros and cons of mediation are:

- **Pros.** Mediation is the most "peaceable" method of solving your problem. You can arrive at a settlement rather than being told how to resolve the dispute by an arbitrator or a judge.
- **Cons.** By itself, mediation is often not enough, because it doesn't force the parties to end the dispute. If the parties cannot resolve their dispute with mediation, they must find some binding method of ending the battle: either arbitration or litigation (a lawsuit). In addition, the licensee may elect mediation simply to buy more time. For example, if the licensee owes royalties, mediation will simply prolong the time period before the payment *must* be made.

Mediation and Arbitration

The parties agree that every dispute or difference between them, arising under this Agreement, shall be settled first by a meeting of the parties attempting to confer and resolve the dispute in a good-faith manner. If the parties cannot resolve their dispute after conferring, any party may require the other parties to submit the matter to nonbinding mediation, utilizing the services of an impartial professional mediator approved by all parties. If the parties cannot come to an agreement following mediation, the parties agree to submit the matter to binding arbitration at a location mutually agreeable to the parties. The arbitration shall be conducted on a confidential basis pursuant to the Commercial Arbitration Rules of the American Arbitration Association. Any decision or award as a result of any such arbitration proceeding shall include the assessment of costs, expenses, and reasonable attorneys' fees and shall include a written record of the proceedings and a written determination of the arbitrators.

Absent an agreement to the contrary, any such arbitration shall be conducted by an arbitrator experienced in intellectual property law. The parties reserve the right to object to any individual who shall be employed by or affiliated with a competing organization or entity. In the event of any such dispute or difference, either party may give to the other notice requiring that the matter be settled by arbitration. An award of arbitration shall be final and binding on the parties and may be confirmed in a court of competent jurisdiction.

If you want to use a mediation clause, we suggest a provision like the one above which progresses from informal meeting to mediation and then to arbitration.

If the licensee is opposed to arbitration (and many are), you can try a less formal approach to dispute resolution with the following mediation provision. It doesn't require the parties to commit to arbitration, but it allows for the parties to work out some method of alternative dispute resolution.

Alternative Dispute Resolution

If a dispute arises and cannot be resolved by the parties, either party may make a written demand for formal resolution of the dispute. The written request will specify the scope of the dispute. Within 30 days after such written notice, the parties agree to meet, for one day, with an impartial mediator and consider dispute resolution alternatives other than litigation. If an alternative method of dispute resolution is not agreed upon within 30 days of the one-day mediation, either side may start litigation proceedings.

Governing Law

Every state has laws regarding contract interpretation. The parties can choose any state's laws to govern the agreement, regardless of where they live or where the agreement is signed. The licensee usually favors the state where its headquarters are located, often New York or California.

Does it matter which state is chosen? Some states have a reputation as being favorable for certain kinds of disputes. That's usually because so many similar disputes have been brought in that state that a body of law has developed which makes the resulting decision more predictable. Generally, however, the differences in state law are not great enough to make this a major negotiating issue. Your choice of which state's law will govern your agreement can be stated in a clause such as the following one.

> This Agreement shall be governed in accordance with the laws of the State of
> _____ .

> ⓘ CAUTION
> **Don't confuse jurisdiction and governing law.** The selection of which state is used for governing law is not a crucial negotiating issue. But the selection of the state for jurisdiction, described below, is important. Sometimes these two provisions are grouped in one paragraph, so read them carefully.

Jurisdiction

Jurisdiction (sometimes referred to as personal jurisdiction) is the power of a court to bind you by its decision. If the court doesn't have authority over you, the judgment isn't worth anything. A court can get jurisdiction over you in three

ways: (1) You are a resident of the state in which the court is located; (2) you have sufficient contacts in the state, such as selling a lot of merchandise there; or (3) you consent (or agree) to jurisdiction.

You can specify in your license agreement where any subsequent lawsuits about the agreement will occur. These provisions—sometimes called "forum selection" or "jurisdiction" clauses—require that the parties consent, in advance, to the jurisdiction of a specific court and that the parties waive the right to complain about jurisdiction later or to bring the lawsuit anywhere else.

Forum selection provisions are often overlooked during negotiations—relegated to the "fine print" category—and their full impact is usually not felt until months or years later.

> **EXAMPLE:** A couple opened a Burger King franchise in Michigan. In signing their agreement with Burger King, the Michigan couple consented to a forum selection clause which provided for jurisdiction in Florida. Later, when problems arose, the couple argued that it wasn't fair to require them to travel to Florida, and they shouldn't be bound by the forum selection clause because they weren't aware of its meaning. The courts upheld the jurisdiction clause, and the couple was forced to fight Burger King in Florida. (*Burger King Corp. v. Rudzewicz,* 471 U.S. 462 (1985).)

There are couple of things to keep in mind about forum selection. First, don't confuse forum selection provisions with "governing law" provisions (discussed above). Although the two may be combined in a contract, each establishes a separate requirement. A forum selection provision sets out where a case can be filed (personal jurisdiction). A governing law provision sets out which state's laws will be used to make a decision in the dispute.

Second, several states—including Idaho, Montana, North Carolina, and South Carolina—refuse to honor these provisions. If you attempt to use a jurisdiction provision in these states, it can be invalidated. (Idaho Code § 29-110; Mont. Code Ann. § 28-2-708; N.C. Gen. Stat. § 22B-3; S.C. Code Ann. § 15-7-120.)

The following strategies for forum selection provisions are recommended:

- If you have sufficient bargaining power, obtain jurisdiction in your home county.
- If you cannot obtain jurisdiction in your home county, don't include any reference to jurisdiction. If a contract contains no reference to jurisdiction, the location of the case is usually determined by whoever files the lawsuit.
- If you do include a jurisdiction clause, it may be helpful to have the choice of law (as discussed above) conform to the same state as that of the jurisdiction. Generally, it proves

simpler and more efficient to use the governing law of the state in which you are litigating.

Below is an example of a forum selection (jurisdiction) provision.

Jurisdiction

Each party (a) consents to the exclusive jurisdiction and venue of the federal and state courts located in [*insert county and state in which parties agree to litigate*] in any action arising out of or relating to this agreement; (b) waives any objection it might have to jurisdiction or venue of such forums or that the forum is inconvenient; and (c) agrees not to bring any such action in any other jurisdiction or venue to which either party might be entitled by domicile or otherwise.

Waiver

If you allow the licensee to do something prohibited under the agreement (that is, to breach the agreement), then you may have waived (given up) your right to complain about it later. For example, imagine that the licensee is several months late making a payment. You agree to accept the delay. Let's say that the following year, the licensee is again several months late paying royalties, and you again accept it without a dispute. In the third year, the licensee is again several months late, but you're tired of the late payments and you sue the licensee. The licensee successfully defends himself by claiming that since you allowed the late payments during the past two years, you waived your right to contest the late payment during the third year.

In order to prevent this result, you should include a waiver provision similar to the one below. This clause provides that if you don't contest a breach of the agreement, you are not waiving your right to contest such breaches in the future. The licensee cannot defend itself by claiming it relied on your past behavior of accepting its breaches. (Of course, the provision swings both ways. If you breach the agreement, you cannot rely on the licensee's past acceptance of your behavior.)

> The failure to exercise any right provided in this Agreement shall not be a waiver of prior or subsequent rights.

Severability

The severability clause (sometimes referred to as the invalidity clause) provides that if one part of the agreement is invalid, it can be cut out (severed) and the rest of the agreement will remain valid. In other words, if something is wrong with part of the agreement, that portion can be cut out of the agreement without affecting the rest of the agreement. If you don't include a severability clause and some portion

of your license agreement is deemed invalid, then the whole agreement may be canceled. To avoid this result, your agreement should include the following provision.

> If any provision of this Agreement is invalid under applicable statute or rule of law, it is to be considered omitted and the remaining provisions of this Agreement shall in no way be affected.

Entire Understanding

In the process of negotiation and contract drafting, you and the licensee might make many oral or written statements. Some of these statements will make it into the final agreement. Others won't. The integration provision verifies that the version you are signing is the final version and that neither you nor the licensee can rely on statements made in the past—*this is it!* Without an integration provision, it's possible that either party can claim rights based upon promises made before the deal was signed.

The integration provision (sometimes labeled as "Entire Understanding") also establishes that, if any party makes promises after the agreement is signed, those promises will only be binding if they are done formally (that is, by a signed written amendment to the agreement).

> This Agreement expresses the complete understanding of the parties and supersedes all prior representations, agreements, and understandings, whether written or oral. This Agreement may not be altered except by a written document signed by both parties.

> The parties agree and acknowledge that all attachments, exhibits, and schedules referred to in this Agreement are incorporated in this Agreement by reference.

CAUTION

Watch out for "We'll fix it later" promises. The integration clause closes the door on any oral or written promises. Don't sign an agreement if something is missing, and don't accept an assurance that the licensee will do something later to correct it.

Attachments and Exhibits

Many agreements contain attachments and exhibits—separate documents that are stapled or clipped to the agreement. For example, in Chapter 11, we suggested that you summarize the essential business elements on a sheet that could be attached. These additional pages are attached to the agreement, and special language in the agreement guarantees that attachments and exhibits are considered as part of the agreement—such as, the "exhibit is incorporated by reference." Below is an example of a provision that incorporates all attachments or exhibits. If there are no attachments or exhibits, you don't need it.

Notices

If a dispute arises, each party is entitled to be notified of the problem. The purpose of the notice provision is to establish the method of notification. Sometimes, a licensee makes the procedure more difficult than necessary. For example, the licensee may require notification by certified mail with return receipt and that the licensee's lawyers be notified in the same manner. There's really not much point arguing over notice provisions. However, you should remember that if you don't follow the notice procedures, your claim against the licensee might be delayed until you provide proper notification. The following sample provision establishes a reasonable notice method.

> Any notice or communication required or allowed under this Agreement shall be sufficiently given when received by certified mail or sent by facsimile transmission or overnight courier.

No Joint Venture

Your relationship with the licensee is defined by the agreement. But to an outsider, it may appear that you have a different relationship, such as a partnership or joint venture. It's possible that an unscrupulous licensee will try to capitalize on this appearance and make a third-party deal. That is, a licensee may claim to be your partner and obtain a benefit from a distributor or sublicensee. In order to avoid liability for such a situation, most agreements include a provision (sometimes referred to as "No Joint Venture") disclaiming any relationship other than licensee/licensor. We recommend that you include such a provision.

> Nothing contained in this Agreement shall be construed to place the parties in the relationship of agent, employee, franchisee, officer, partners, or joint venturers. Neither party may create or assume any obligation on behalf of the other.

Assignments

When the licensee assigns an agreement, a new company will sell your product and pay you royalties. This new company steps into the shoes of the original licensee. Assignments occur for a number of reasons: (1) A licensee needs money and is willing to sell its rights to your invention to another company; (2) a licensee creates an affiliate or subsidiary and assigns the licensing business to its affiliate or subsidiary; or (3) a licensee company is acquired by another company.

For example, if you licensed your invention to PCMac, a software company that was acquired by Microsoft, then Microsoft would become your new licensee. Microsoft, even though it didn't negotiate with you, would have to abide by all the provisions of the license agreement and pay you royalties.

There may be some instances where you don't want a company to acquire rights to your invention. For example, perhaps you had a bad experience with a company and now they're in line to become your new licensee. Maybe the new licensee is a competitor of yours. Or perhaps the new licensee plans to sell off your invention as a business maneuver. In today's world of acquisitions and mergers, most companies want some freedom to assign agreements and will oppose a complete prohibition on assignments.

Some suggested strategies:

- If you have the bargaining power, it's best to prohibit any assignment of your contract unless you give written consent.

Statement of Assignability

> Licensee may not assign or transfer its rights or obligations pursuant to this Agreement without the prior written consent of Licensor. Any assignment or transfer in violation of this section shall be void.

- If the licensee is afraid that you have too much control, you can soften the effect by withholding consent only if you have a valid business reason. What's a valid reason? Perhaps the company to which your licensee wants to grant an assignment has a reputation for not paying royalties or is in poor financial shape. You cannot, however, withhold consent for an arbitrary reason, such as someone from the company having once treated you rudely.

Consent Not Unreasonably Withheld

Licensee may not assign or transfer its rights or obligations pursuant to this Agreement without the prior written consent of Licensor. Such consent shall not be unreasonably withheld. Any assignment or transfer in violation of this section shall be void.

Remote Controlled Animated Decoy No. 6,212,816

- If you don't have much bargaining power and the licensee wants freedom to transfer to affiliates or new owners (under the same terms as your license agreement), you can use a provision such as the one below.

Consent Not Needed for Licensee Affiliates or New Owners

Licensee may not assign or transfer its rights or obligations pursuant to this Agreement without the prior written consent of Licensor. However, no consent is required for an assignment or transfer that occurs (a) to an entity in which Licensee owns more than 50% of the assets, or (b) as part of a transfer of all or substantially all of the assets of Licensee to any party. Any assignment or transfer in violation of this section shall be void.

- If you don't have any bargaining power and the licensee wants absolute freedom to assign, then you will have to take out the provision shown above.

CAUTION

When preparing an assignment provision, keep in mind that you can only prevent "voluntary" assignments; you cannot prevent assignments that are ordered by a court or that are mandatory under law.

Force Majeure

The force majeure (sometimes referred to as "Acts of God") provision establishes that the agreement will be suspended in the event of unforeseen natural disasters. For example, if a tornado ruins the licensee's manufacturing plant for three months, the license agreement would be suspended for three months.

How does this delay affect your license? If you had a fixed-term license (say for three years) and the disaster resulted in a six-month delay, the licensee would have a license for three years and six months. Similarly, the payment schedule would be altered and the licensee would have a six-month grace period before the first post-disaster payment is due.

You will notice that we have not included a force majeure provision in the model agreement. That's because a force majeure provision is not essential and you need not include it unless the licensee insists. This provision is intended to deal with unpredictable disasters that are out of the control of the licensee, not business contingencies, such as union disputes. If possible, remove references to things such as "failure of technical facilities," "failure or delay of transportation facilities," "strike," or "shortage of raw materials."

In the event of an act of God such as fire, riot, act of public enemy, war, or similar cause not within the control of Licensee, the Licensee shall have the right to suspend the term of this Agreement. Licensee may suspend the term only for the duration of any such contingency. Licensee shall not suspend its obligation to make payments to Licensor if such payments are due and are not otherwise prevented. At the conclusion of the contingency, Licensee shall notify Licensor in writing and the Agreement shall be reinstated.

Headings

Although it's not really necessary, some licensees like to include a provision stating that the headings used throughout the agreement have no special significance. The headings are the titles of each provision, usually in bold type. It's not necessary, but if requested, it won't hurt to include it.

Headings of the sections of this Agreement are included for reference only and are not intended to affect the interpretation of the Agreement.

Establishing Escrow Accounts

An escrow is like a safety deposit box. You and the licensee place something (for example, trade secrets or money) in an account controlled by an escrow agent, and only under certain conditions will it be released. Escrow accounts are normally used to maintain secret information that has not been licensed but is necessary for maintenance or repair of the invention. For example, you modify your invention to meet the licensee's specifications and the modifications are done using your secret software code. You did not license

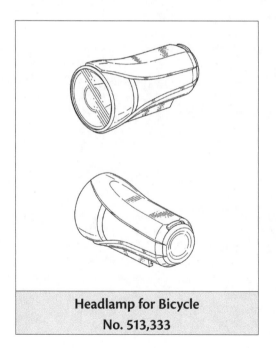

Headlamp for Bicycle
No. 513,333

this code to the licensee but, under certain circumstances, the licensee might need access to it (for example, the invention has to be modified and you are unavailable to make the modification).

Instead of giving the trade secrets to the licensee, you can place them in a special account, monitored by an escrow agent. The contents of the account (the escrow items) will be available to the licensee only under certain conditions, for example, if you, the licensor, are unable to repair the invention.

Escrow arrangements are also used to hold money, stock, or documents transferring ownership of inventions. This arrangement is similar to a traditional escrow account used for selling a house. Like the title to a house, you might place the assignment of your invention in escrow. When the other party makes the proper payment or completes a certain act, the assignment (like the house title) is released.

The rules regarding the release of the escrow items are established in an escrow agreement that is signed by you, the licensee, and the escrow agent. Lawyers or banks often act as escrow agents. If you use an escrow agreement, the following provision should be inserted in your license agreement and you should attach a copy of your escrow agreement to the license agreement.

Established Escrow Account

> The parties have executed a separate Escrow Agreement (attached to this Agreement and incorporated by reference) for the deposit of escrow materials.

If you cannot execute an escrow agreement at the time of license, you can still express your intention to do so in the license agreement by including the following provision.

Future Establishment of Escrow Account

> The parties shall execute a separate Escrow Agreement to establish an escrow account for the deposit of [*indicate what will be deposited*] ("Escrow Items"). The Escrow Items shall be released to [*name of party*—Licensor *or* Licensee] upon the following conditions: [*list reasons for release from escrow. For example, "The funds will be released to Licensor upon completion of the Services and furnishing of Deliverables."*].

As explained, above, the escrow agent often prepares the escrow agreement. Below is a sample escrow agreement for release of trade secrets upon certain conditions.

DOWNLOAD FORMS

You can download this form (and all other forms in this book) from this book's companion page on Nolo.com; see the appendix for the link.

Escrow Agreement

This escrow agreement (the "Escrow Agreement") is made between [*insert your name, address, and business form*] ("Inventor"), and [*insert licensee's name, address, and business form*] ("Company"), and [*insert escrow agent's name and address*] ("Escrow Agent"). Company is a licensee of Inventor's invention (the "Properties") indicated on Exhibit A and pursuant to the Agreement dated [*insert date of license Agreement*] between Inventor and Company (the "License Agreement"). The parties desire to place trade secrets and related materials with the Escrow Agent. Therefore, Inventor, Company, and the Escrow Agent agree as follows:

1. Escrow Items

Inventor will promptly place copies of [*indicate what will be placed into escrow*] (collectively the "Escrow Items") under the control of the Escrow Agent.

2. Release Conditions

Company may submit a request to the Escrow Agent for release of the Escrow Items (the "Company's Release Request") upon the occurrence of one of the following release conditions during the term of the License Agreement:

(a) Inventor's filing of a petition under any chapter of the federal bankruptcy laws; or

(b) the failure by Inventor, within 30 days after Company's request to Inventor, to perform any of Inventor's obligations under the License Agreement.

3. Duties of Escrow Agent

The Escrow Agent's duties are limited to:

(a) safeguarding the Escrow Items against access or disclosure by any person or entity except as expressly provided in this Agreement, and

(b) notifying Inventor and Company that it has received the Escrow Items.

The Escrow Agent is not responsible for verifying the accuracy or completeness of the Escrow Items. The Escrow Agent's performance under this Escrow Agreement is excused when it is prevented by acts of God and other causes beyond its reasonable control.

4. Release of Escrow Items

The Escrow Agent shall, subject to the conditions below, deliver all of the Escrow Items to Company upon receipt of Company's Release Request, signed by an Officer of Company stating that Company has the right to receive all of the Escrow Items.

Company shall deliver its Release Request to the Escrow Agent and, at the same time, deliver a duplicate copy of its Release Request to Inventor. Within 30 days after the receipt of such Release Request, the Inventor shall either (a) submit a written authorization to the Escrow Agent to make the delivery, or (b) submit a written objection to the Escrow Agent and to Company.

If the Inventor authorizes the delivery or does not respond within 30 days, the Escrow Agent shall deliver the Escrow Items. If Inventor objects to the delivery of the Escrow Items in writing, Company and Inventor shall attempt in good faith to agree upon their respective rights to the Escrow Items. If Company and Inventor do so agree, an agreement shall be prepared and signed by both Company and Inventor and delivered to the Escrow Agent. The Escrow Agent shall be entitled to rely on the agreement and shall distribute the Escrow Items. If no such agreement can be reached after good-faith negotiation, either Company or Inventor may demand arbitration of the matter. In such an event, the American Arbitration Association shall be asked to appoint one arbitrator, familiar with the subject matter of the license in the United States, to rule on the matter. Such appointment is to be in accordance with the then-current Commercial Arbitration Rules of the American Arbitration Association. The decision of the arbitrator shall be binding and conclusive upon Company and Inventor, and the Escrow Agent shall be entitled to act in accordance with such decision. Any such arbitration shall be held in [*indicate county and state for arbitration*]. The prevailing party in any such arbitration shall be entitled to receive payments of its attorneys' fees and costs.

The Escrow Agent's duties may be altered, amended, modified, or revoked only by a writing signed by officers of Company and Inventor.

The Escrow Agent shall not be personally liable for any act the Escrow Agent may do or omit to do under this Agreement while acting in good faith and in the exercise of its own good judgment.

The Escrow Agent is authorized to comply with orders, judgments, or decrees of any court and of the arbitrator provided for above. If the Escrow Agent obeys or complies with any such order, judgment, or decree, the Escrow Agent shall not be liable to any of the parties or to any other person, firm, or corporation by reason of such compliance. The Escrow Agent shall not be liable even if such order, judgment, or decree is subsequently reversed, modified, annulled, set aside, vacated, or found to have been entered without jurisdiction.

The Escrow Agent shall be entitled to employ legal counsel and other experts as the Escrow Agent may deem necessary to advise it in connection with its obligations under this Escrow Agreement, and may rely upon the advice of such counsel and pay such counsel reasonable compensation.

The responsibilities of the Escrow Agent shall terminate if the Escrow Agent resigns by written notice to Company and Inventor. In that event, Inventor shall promptly appoint a successor Escrow Agent, subject to the approval of Company. Company's approval will not be unreasonably withheld.

It is understood and agreed that should any dispute arise with respect to the delivery, ownership, or right of possession of any part of the Escrow Items held by the Escrow Agent, the Escrow Agent is directed to retain the Escrow Items in its possession, without liability to anyone, until such dispute is settled either by (1) mutual written agreement, as provided above; or by (2) final order, decree, or judgment of the arbitrator provided for above; or by (3) a court of competent jurisdiction after the time for appeal has expired and no appeal has been perfected. The Escrow Agent shall be under no duty to institute or defend any such proceedings.

5. Miscellaneous

Any notice or communication required or permitted to be given under this Escrow Agreement shall be sufficiently given when received by certified mail or sent by facsimile transmission or overnight courier. If any term, provision, covenant, or condition of this Agreement is held to be illegal or invalid for any reason whatsoever, such illegality or invalidity shall not affect the validity of the remainder of this Agreement. This Escrow Agreement and the License Agreement constitute the entire understanding between the Parties and can only be modified by written agreement. No party may assign or transfer its rights under this Escrow Agreement without the prior written consent of the other parties. This Agreement shall be binding upon the parties and their respective successors and assigns.

LICENSEE:

_____   _____
Signature   Date

LICENSOR:

_____   _____
Signature   Date

ESCROW AGENT:

_____   _____
Signature   Date

Service Provisions

Service Provisions Versus Separate Service Agreements 352

Training the Licensee's Personnel 354

Installation of Equipment 355

Technical Support for the Licensee or for End Users 356

Improving, Modifying, and Delivering the Invention 357

    What Are Deliverables? 357

    Scheduling and Approving Deliverables 358

    Independently Created Improvements 360

    Improvements by the Licensee: Grant Backs 362

n this chapter, we discuss and examine service provisions. These provisions define jobs you agree to perform for the licensee (for example, the licensee wants you to offer technical assistance). You should read this chapter if you answer "yes" to any of the following questions:

- Does the licensee want you to train personnel in the production or use of your invention?
- Does the licensee want your services for the installation of machinery or technology needed to make your invention?
- Has the licensee asked you to provide technical assistance?
- Does the licensee want you to develop improvements to your invention?
- Are you expected to deliver improvements according to an established schedule?
- Are you concerned about who owns rights to improvements?

In some situations, the work that you agree to do for a licensee is so substantial that a separate services agreement is necessary. In those cases, the service provisions discussed in this chapter will not be sufficient. Below, we will briefly explain when a separate service agreement may be necessary and how to include such an agreement with the rest of your licensing agreement. We also provide information (and sample provisions) for service-related activities, such as employee training, installation of equipment, technical support, improvements, and providing and scheduling deliverables. We will also discuss the right of first refusal and a provision known as "most favored nation."

Service Provisions Versus Separate Service Agreements

The service provisions discussed in this chapter are limited in scope. They are geared toward simple, short-term services that you perform for a licensee. These provisions are *not* suitable for larger projects, which could require many employees or contractors. For this reason, we suggest that if services are substantial, you should prepare a separate services agreement, which is beyond the scope of this book. That is, you should execute two agreements: a licensing agreement (as explained in this book) and a services agreement.

How do you know if you will need a separate services agreement? You might need one if you answer "yes" to one or more of the following questions:

- Are the services open-ended with no fixed termination? Will the services last longer than the length of the license agreement?
- Do you need to hire or use employees or contractors?

- Do you need to obtain a separate work space?
- Do you have to create a separate company to perform the services?
- Do the payments for services exceed the amount of money you are receiving for your license?

In the event you need a separate services agreement, we recommend that you read *Working for Yourself*, by Stephen Fishman (Nolo), which contains various sample service agreements. If the services are substantial, you might also need financial advice. For example, there could be tax issues if revenue from services is subject to different taxes than licensing revenue. However, if the services are limited to work that you can perform without employees or contractors and are incidental to your licensing, the provisions below should be suitable.

How Do You Coordinate Two Separate Agreements?

It may seem confusing to have two separate agreements with the same company—one for licensing and one for services. However, much of the confusion can be removed if the two agreements are incorporated. "Incorporating" means that the services agreement, although separately executed, is still a part of the license agreement. For example, many of the license provisions, such as arbitration, attorneys' fees, and indemnity, will apply to both agreements.

To incorporate your services agreement into your licensing agreement, attach it as an exhibit to the license agreement. (Incorporation is discussed in Chapter 14.) The following incorporation provision should be included in the services agreement.

Incorporation

> The provisions of this Exhibit (the Services Agreement) are incorporated within the attached license agreement.

In addition, your license agreement should include an attachments and exhibits provision (see Chapter 14) as shown below.

Attachments and Exhibits

> The parties agree and acknowledge that all attachments, exhibits, and schedules referred to in this Agreement are incorporated in this Agreement by reference.

Training the Licensee's Personnel

If you possess knowledge that can assist in the manufacturing, selling, or pre-production process (sometimes referred to as know-how), the licensee may want you to pass that information to its employees. This is sometimes referred to as training. If you are asked to conduct training, you should consider the following issues:

- How much will you be paid for the services?
- Where will you do the training?
- If you have to travel, how will you be reimbursed for travel, housing, and so on?
- What will the extent of the training be (how long, how many people, and so on)?
- Which person from the licensee's company will you work with?

Human Powered Device With Removable Flywheel Power Unit
No. 6,983,948

- What happens if you are injured or the licensee's personnel are injured during the training period?

Sometimes, as a goodwill gesture, inventors perform training services for free (particularly if no travel is involved). However, training provisions usually provide for compensation. You should be able to determine your own hourly rate. (An hourly rate between $50 to $150 per hour is common.) You'll also want reasonable expenses for travel and lodging. It's likely that you'll have to travel to the licensee's headquarters or plant to train personnel, and the costs of travel can really add up.

You should also define the extent of the training. Try to summarize what type of training you will perform and, if possible, how many people you will train and the length of time you expect the training will take. You may want your fee to increase if any of the training exceeds what was agreed upon. For example, say you agreed to train two employees for 40 hours at $75 per hour. In the event that you had to train for 50 hours, your hourly rate might go up for the time over 40 hours. It's also helpful to list the names or titles of the persons you will train. Defining the training specifications helps both parties prepare for the session.

If you wish to include a training provision in your license agreement, a sample provision would look like the following one.

Training

> Licensor will provide [*number of days and whether they are consecutive*] days of basic training for [*names or number of Licensee employees to be trained*] Licensee employees at Licensee's facility in [*location of Licensee's facility*]. Training will be performed by [*name of Licensor or person who will provide training*]. Licensee shall bear all costs of travel and accommodations and shall pay Licensor on a direct cost basis computed on the number of hours worked and an hourly rate of [*hourly rate*] for services. Licensee shall indemnify Licensor for any and all claims that may result from such training. All payments for services and other expenses shall be paid by Licensee within 30 days of receipt of Licensor's written invoice.

As noted above, if the training is ongoing (such as regular training during the term of the license agreement) or more complex (for example, training employees around the world), you should use a separate services agreement that will better define your obligations and protect your rights.

Installation of Equipment

A licensee may require that you (the licensor) supervise the installation of equipment related to your invention or process. This type of service raises similar issues to the training of personnel (discussed above): Where is the work done? How much is paid for time, travel, lodgings, and so on, and what happens in the event of injuries? What will the installation entail? We recommend that you summarize the work to be done in one or two paragraphs (perhaps in the form of a job summary or an invoice) and attach this information as an exhibit to the agreement. If you wish to include an installation services provision in your license agreement, a sample appears below.

> Licensor shall supervise and assist in the installation of equipment as described in Exhibit [*whatever letter you have chosen for the service agreement exhibit, for example, Exhibit B*]. Licensor's installation services will be performed by [*name of Licensor or Licensor's employee who will perform services*]. Licensee shall bear all costs of travel and accommodations for Licensor and shall pay Licensor on a direct cost basis computed on the number of hours worked and an hourly rate of [*hourly rate*] for services. Licensee shall indemnify Licensor for any and all claims that may result from such installation services. All payments for services and other expenses shall be paid by Licensee within 30 days of receipt of Licensor's written invoice.

Technical Support for the Licensee or for End Users

It's possible that either the licensee or buyers of the products (sometimes referred to as end users) will need technical assistance for your invention. This is particularly common in software licensing where the purchaser of the program needs help using the product. Normally, the licensee will provide this technical assistance to consumers of the licensed products. However, in some cases, the licensee may ask you to provide technical assistance, either to its tech people (similar to personnel training) or to consumers of the product.

If you are willing to provide tech support, the major issues are:

- What are the hours for tech support?
- If it is phone support, who pays for the phone services?
- If it is via email or the Web, who pays for the computer equipment and services?
- How are you compensated for tech service—that is, by the number of phone calls or email responses, length of phone calls, or the total hourly services rendered?

We don't recommend that you get into the tech support business. Tech support is a major commitment of time and usually requires hiring contractors or employees. These types of services usually require a separate services agreement detailing tech support responsibilities. However, if you

have a limited tech support arrangement or you are simply assisting the licensee's tech support people, the following provisions are suitable for insertion in your licensing agreement.

For a tech support arrangement in which you assist the licensee's support staff, use a provision such as the sample below.

Technical Support

Licensor will provide reasonable telephone and email assistance to Licensee's designated representatives for Licensee's technical support of licensed products.

If you are providing limited end-user tech support, you will need a more detailed provision. The sample provision below should address most of your concerns.

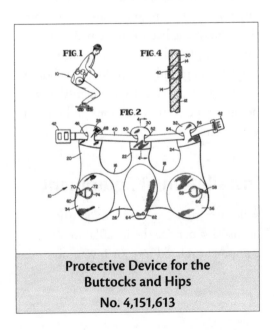

Protective Device for the Buttocks and Hips

No. 4,151,613

Limited End-User Technical Support

Licensor shall, for a period of six months after introduction of the licensed products, provide reasonable ongoing [*describe the type of assistance, for example, "telephone"*] assistance to Licensee. Such support shall relate only to troubleshooting and identification of reported problems relating to the use of the Licensed Products. Telephone technical support shall be provided by Licensor [*indicate what days and what times, for example, "Monday through Friday, 12:00 p.m. to 4:00 p.m. PST"*] at a rate of [*indicate the hourly, weekly, or monthly rate, for example, "$2,000 per month"*] and not to exceed [*indicate maximum amount of support hours per week, for example, "20 hours per week of Licensor personnel time"*]. In the event that Licensee needs technical support provided by a third party other than Licensor, such determination shall not affect any other provisions of this agreement.

Improving, Modifying, and Delivering the Invention

The licensee may want you to modify or develop improvements to your invention. For example, say you've invented a gyroscopic device that, when inserted inside a toy, spins the toy. The licensee wants you to modify your invention to fit into different-sized toys. Or perhaps the licensee wants you to develop a series of gyroscopic toy ideas based around cartoon characters.

These types of services have three major components: defining the services, scheduling delivery of the work, and establishing standards for acceptance of the work.

What Are Deliverables?

The term "deliverables" is commonly used to refer to work that you must deliver to the licensee. That is, if you were obligated to modify your invention or make a specific improvement, that would be a deliverable. These deliverables, which are variations on your invention, must be defined in the license agreement, usually in a separate exhibit to the agreement. For example, your services provision would state that the "Licensor shall provide the Deliverables, as defined in Exhibit A."

Define the deliverables with care and be specific as to what you intend to produce for the licensee. How can you be specific? Here are some tips on what to cover:

- **Functionality.** Describe specifically what the deliverable will do, for example: "It is a flashlight that emits light at both ends."
- **Dimensions.** Describe the size or shape, for example: "It is a mini-flashlight, no longer than 6 inches, no wider than 1 square inch, and weighing no more than 8 ounces."
- **Materials.** Describe the materials used in manufacturing or use, for example: "It is a miniflashlight made of case-hardened steel and using two AA batteries."

Scheduling and Approving Deliverables

A licensee will want to establish deadlines for the deliverables. These deadlines will probably be tied to payments. For example, you must deliver an improvement within 90 days, at which point you will receive a payment.

An acceptance provision defines the standards that the licensee uses for accepting or rejecting your deliverables. The licensee does not have to accept your deliverables. However, the acceptance provision should establish the criteria used in accepting or rejecting your deliverables and should provide a means for you to correct any errors.

Weather Station
No. 6,761,065

Below is a sample deliverables provision that can be inserted in your license agreement. The two parts of the provision ("Schedules and Development Services" and "Delivery and Approval") attempt to anticipate the problems that result when, for example, the inventor believes the deliverable has been perfected and the licensee thinks the work is insufficient.

Schedules and Development Services

Licensor shall perform certain development services for Licensee. A description of such services, as well as the delivery schedule and the technology or invention to be delivered ("Deliverables"), is provided in Exhibit A. Payments for such services shall be as provided in Exhibit A. Any Deliverable listed in Exhibit A will consist of three stages: (1) concept/planning, (2) design/prototype, and (3) development/test.

Licensor will submit for Licensee's written approval a budget for each Deliverable. Any expenses or charges in excess of those budgeted must be preapproved in writing by Licensee. If requested, Licensor will, within 72 hours of notification, meet with Licensee and provide a status report on the schedule and budget for any Deliverable. Licensor will invoice Licensee pursuant to the payment schedule set forth in the appropriate Exhibit A.

Delivery and Approval

Licensee shall have five working days from receipt of any Deliverable within which to provide Licensor with written notice of its decision to either accept the Deliverable or to reject it because it fails to conform to the specifications in Exhibit A. If Licensee determines that any Deliverable does not substantially conform to the specifications, Licensee shall deliver to Licensor a written report describing each manner that the Deliverables fail to conform. Licensor shall, within five working days of receipt of Licensee's statement, correct such errors or failures and resubmit the Deliverables. After resubmission, Licensee shall have a second evaluation period of five working days to either accept the Deliverables or reject them because they still fail to conform to the original specifications. If Licensee again rejects the Deliverables, Licensee may pay a third party to correct such failures and deduct the cost either from Licensor's next scheduled payment from Licensee or from Licensor's future royalties.

CAUTION

Make sure deliverables are included as part of your invention. The reason you are preparing modifications or improvements or developing related inventions is so that they will become licensed products and you will receive royalties. If you are providing deliverables, your grant or definition of the invention should state that it includes "all Deliverables required under this agreement." (The grant provision, discussed in Chapter 8, defines what rights you have transferred. If you are unsure as to what a grant provision or definition of the invention is, refer to Chapter 8.)

In some cases, your modifications or improvements might result in something that goes beyond the rights you granted under the license agreement. For example, say you licensed an invention for controlling stage lighting. The licensee asks you to improve the design of the switch box, and in the process you devise a unique antishock safety feature. This unique safety feature constitutes an improvement but could also be a separately patentable invention—requiring you to determine a new set of licensing rights. Who owns it? That depends on the wording of your license agreement, specifically the definition of the licensed property and the grant provision. Often, the licensee acquires these rights but they revert to the inventor at the end of the license. Sometimes these rights are acquired under a right of first refusal, as explained below. However, absent such provisions, some inventions (particularly if they are independently patentable) might fall outside the license agreement and require a separate licensing agreement.

These issues—determining if the licensee can acquire new invention rights —are often complex and require the advice of an intellectual property attorney. See Chapter 18, "Help Beyond This Book," for information on how to find an attorney.

Independently Created Improvements

You might design new features or improvements to your invention without being required to do so by the licensee. That is, they are not categorized as deliverables under your services arrangement. You may have already agreed to license such features or improvements to the licensee. Any such agreement should be included in the grant or invention definition portion of your license; be sure to review it carefully.

Even if it's not included in the grant provision, the licensee might seek a provision asking for the right to license these improvements at competitive license rates. This request to acquire improvements can be phrased in two ways: a right of first refusal or most favored nations clause.

Right of First Refusal

If your license agreement includes a right of first refusal, you must give the licensee the first right to license any improvements. This provision is common in an exclusive license. For example, say you license a place-kicking invention to SportsCo, including a right of first refusal to any major improvements or new inventions stemming from the place-kicking invention. You later modify the invention for use as a baseball batting tee. You must show the new invention to SportsCo first, who may then license it. If they reject it and you get a better offer from GameCo, SportsCo will also have a limited period of time to match the GameCo offer.

Right of First Refusal

Licensor may identify and develop improvements for the Licensed Property ("Improvements"). Improvements may be patentable or unpatentable and may also be protected under copyright, trade secret, or other legal principles. Licensee shall have the first right to license such Improvements, and the parties shall negotiate in good faith to reach agreement as to the terms and conditions for such license. In the event that the parties fail to reach agreement and Licensor receives an offer from a third party for the Improvements, Licensee shall have 30 days to notify Licensor whether Licensee desires to execute a license on similar terms and conditions. In the event that Licensee matches any third-party terms and conditions, Licensor shall enter into a License Agreement with Licensee and terminate negotiations with any third parties.

CAUTION

New inventions: licensing the unknown. A right of first refusal can also be used for new inventions, not just improvements. For example, the licensee obtains a right of first refusal to license any new inventions you create in the sporting goods field. In that situation, you are tying up rights to an invention that does not yet exist. Whether or not you are willing to make such a commitment as to new inventions depends upon your bargaining power and your level of trust in the licensee. As a general rule, we recommend against committing inventions that you have not yet created.

Most Favored Nations (Most Favored Licensee)

A most favored nations clause (sometimes referred to as a most favored licensee provision) is common in a nonexclusive arrangement and guarantees that a licensee won't be charged any more for the invention or improvements than any other licensee. For example, say you have a nonexclusive license agreement with SportsCo for your place-kicking invention and any improvements. Your SportsCo agreement pays you a 10% royalty rate and includes a most favored nations clause. You subsequently improve your invention and you execute a nonexclusive license with GameCo with a royalty rate of 9% for the improved place kicker. Under the most favored nation provision,

you couldn't enter into this agreement unless you lowered your royalty rate with SportsCo to 9% for the same invention.

Most Favored Nations

Licensor may identify and develop new features or improvements for the Licensed Property ("Improvements"). Improvements may be patentable or unpatentable and may also be protected under copyright, trade secret, or other legal principles. In the event that Licensee enters into a license agreement for these Improvements with a third-party licensee ("Third-Party License"), Licensor agrees to offer Licensee terms and conditions which are as favorable as those offered to the third-party licensee. Licensor shall promptly notify the Licensee of any Third-Party License as well as any additional obligations or undertakings in the Third-Party License. Licensee shall have 30 days to notify Licensor whether Licensee desires to execute a license on similar terms and conditions.

Gun Mount Apparatus
No. 6,986,446

Most Favored Nations and Confidentiality

Try not to sign a confidentiality agreement that prohibits you from discussing a licensing agreement with anyone. Being prohibited from discussing an agreement can prevent you from fulfilling your obligations under a most favored nations clause. For example, you sign a nonexclusive license with GameCo that prohibits you from discussing the terms with anyone. But you had another license agreement with a most favored nations provision with SportsCo. You're supposed to tell SportsCo about the GameCo terms, but you're prohibited by the confidentiality agreement. What do you do? You, as the licensor, have an obligation to get permission from GameCo to discuss the confidential agreement (known as a waiver), or you must draft the agreement so that you can discuss the third-party agreement with any other licensee who has licensed the same invention.

Improvements by the Licensee: Grant Backs

In the process of preparing licensed products, the licensee might improve your invention by adding new features or functions that help sell the product. The licensee owns these improvements because it has paid for and supervised the work. But that doesn't mean the licensee can freely copy your invention when using the improvements. It only means that, in the event your patent expires, the licensee will own the right to use the improvements with the invention—which is now in the public domain.

If you are dealing with trade secrets, trademarks, or copyrightable works, you can control the right to modifications to your work by including a grant back provision in your license agreement. A grant back provision allows you to reclaim rights to any licensee improvements. For example, if you have a trade secret or create a copyrightable computer program and the licensee wants to modify it, you can insist (a) that you will own all such modifications after the license expires, or (b) that the licensee will grant you the nonexclusive right to use the improvements without having to pay royalties.

It's not quite as simple with a patented invention. Although grant back provisions for patentable improvements are usually upheld by the courts, there are cases where they are declared invalid. Generally, a grant back will not be upheld if a court determines that it is anticompetitive. What's anticompetitive? It would be anticompetitive if you are demanding an exclusive grant back as a condition of the license for a patented invention, and as a result the licensee was discouraged from making any innovations (knowing it would later have to give them up). Normally, invalid grant backs occur when large companies stifle competition, for example, in cases where the grant back is linked to illegal price fixing. For more information on these anticompetitive rules (referred to as patent misuse), see Chapter 17.

Handling the Licensee's Agreement

Dealing With Suggested Changes...366

   You Can't Always Get What You Want 366

   Review, Evaluate, and Negotiate Modifications 367

Evaluating an Agreement Presented to You...368

Evaluating the Provisions and Suggesting Changes............................369

   The Modification Chart 378

The Cover Letter..379

What happens if the licensee wants to make substantial changes to your license agreement or, instead, wants to furnish you with its own license agreement? How do you use the information in this book to interpret other agreements? You should read this chapter if you answer "yes" to either of the following questions:

- Has the licensee furnished you with a list of requested changes to your license agreement?
- Has the licensee furnished you with its own license agreement?

In this chapter, we offer advice on how to deal with modifications to a license agreement. We provide tips on dealing with a licensee's suggested changes to your agreement, and we also provide a system that should enable you to identify and modify important provisions in a licensee's agreement.

Dealing With Suggested Changes

It's rare for a licensee to accept a license agreement without requesting at least some modifications. You should expect to receive a list of suggested changes, which might be several pages long. The company could have even revised your entire agreement in a redline/strikeout version (see "What Is Redline/Strikeout?" below) that indicates new additions and material to be stricken.

Some of the requested changes will be stylistic. That is, the licensee might want you to move provisions, use different terminology, or place all of the definitions at the front of the agreement. You should feel comfortable making stylistic changes. The bulk of the changes, however, will be substantive—affecting the rights or obligations of each party. For substantive changes, be prepared to spend several hours reviewing the requests and comparing them to the material in this book.

You Can't Always Get What You Want

As we have explained in other portions of this book, you won't always be able to obtain the ideal provision. Your ability to respond to requested modifications is a reflection of your bargaining power. Very often you, the licensor, have little bargaining power, and you will be forced to accept a modification. There's nothing wrong with giving in on contract issues provided that you understand what you are giving up and that you are not giving up something that will substantially impair your ability to profit from the license.

A Brief Excursion Into Legalese

Throughout this book, we have tried to shield you from unnecessary legalese—the contrived language commonly used in contracts. However, you may encounter such language in license provisions presented to you or in proposed modifications to your agreement. Below are some common examples and translations. For other terms or phrases, consult a legal dictionary or an unabridged English dictionary.

As provided herein ... As provided in this agreement

Hereinafter referred to ... Referred to in this agreement

Heretofore granted ... Previously granted

Notwithstanding ... In spite of

Foregoing ... Previous

Deemed ... Considered.

EXAMPLE: The licensee requests a change to your jurisdiction provision (the provision that states where litigation or arbitration must be filed). The licensee is adamant about using its home state, Michigan. You have offered a compromise—each party can file a respective lawsuit in its home state—and that's been rejected by the licensee.

You weigh the consequences and although it's not your first choice, you decide you are willing to accept the risk of traveling to Michigan for a lawsuit.

Review, Evaluate, and Negotiate Modifications

When you receive requested changes to your agreement, evaluate each request by comparing it to the information in this book. For instance, if there is a requested change to the indemnity section, review indemnity in Chapter 12 and evaluate what is at issue. Then comes the hard part—deciding whether you want to make the change.

Below are two common methods of handling requested changes:

• **The "Yes, No, Maybe" approach.** Make three lists: "Yes" (the changes you will make), "No" (the changes you won't make), and "Maybe" (the changes about which you are undecided or upon which you are willing to negotiate). When negotiating with the licensee, use your Maybe list for bargaining purposes. For example, if the licensee won't agree to one of your Yes or No items, offer to give in on a Maybe.

- **The "Most Important" approach.**
  Make a list of the things that are
  most important to you in a license
  agreement and list them in order of
  importance. For example:
    - size of the advance
    - size of the royalty
    - location for lawsuits, and
    - arbitration as the method for
      resolving disputes.

What Is Redline/Strikeout?

Redline/strikeout refers to a method
commonly used by attorneys to revise
agreements. Before word processors were
commonly used, contracts went through
several drafts and new sections that were
to be added to a contract were underlined
in red ink. A dark line striking out text
signified that this material was to be
removed. Most popular word processing
programs include redline/strikeout
features. In Microsoft *Word*, you can
choose the color and type of marking you
want to use for revisions. If you wish, the
computer will merge these revisions into a
clean (or unmarked) draft.

Review the licensee's suggested changes
and categorize them according to your
list. This helps to sort the modifications
in order of importance to you. Negotiate
accordingly. Fight hardest for those items
that are highest on your list, and be more
flexible on items that are not as important.

Evaluating an Agreement Presented to You

What do you do if the licensee insists that
you use its license agreement? Deciphering
a company's contract is a challenge, even
for experienced attorneys.

If you have turned directly to this
chapter without reviewing any other
material in this book, you may have
some difficulty. In order to evaluate the
agreement, you will need some familiarity
with common licensing provisions. We
suggest you review the sample agreement
in Chapter 11 before you begin.

In order to analyze a new agreement,
we suggest the following strategies:

- *Don't freak out!* Be prepared to spend
  several hours making your analysis.
- If the licensee furnished the
  agreement in paper format, scan it
  into digital format.

- If the other party furnishes you their agreement as a PDF, convert it into word processing files. It is much easier to search for key words and terms using your computer.
- Locate the major provisions (as discussed below) and label them.
- Compare each provision with the language suggested in this book.
- Highlight everything you don't like or don't understand.
- Prepare a chart, listing the number of the provision and your concerns.
- Convert the chart into a response letter detailing your requested changes for the licensee.

Your job, should you choose to accept it, is to untangle the provisions and locate the key ones. Unfortunately, there are no rules for the ordering and placement of provisions in a license agreement. Many agreements seem haphazardly organized (and the order doesn't make any sense).

Below is a list of the provisions you should be looking for, as well as key words that often identify the provisions. The list also includes some tips for evaluating the provisions once you've found them. (To analyze the provisions more fully, review the provisions discussed in Chapters 8, 9, 11, 12, 13, 14, and 15.) Trying to locate phrases within a mass of legal verbiage can be a tedious job, but it will get easier as you go along. The procedure is a little bit like putting together a jigsaw puzzle; once you find a few key parts, the rest fall into place.

Evaluating the Provisions and Suggesting Changes

Once you have identified the key provisions, you must evaluate each section and decide if the language should be modified. This task requires a lot of intellectual labor. In fact, the work may seem incredibly daunting. After all, you're an inventor, not a lawyer. If you're becoming tense, confused, and frustrated, consider hiring an attorney.

If, however, you decide to proceed, you will need to analyze each provision and decide if it adequately protects your interests. If it does not, you'll need to decide what language should be added or stricken in order to bring the agreement in line with your standards.

There's no limit to the number of modifications you can request, but you'll probably have more success if you limit your requests to the most important revisions (that is, those changes that directly affect your rights or finances).

Checklist for Reviewing a License Agreement

Contract Provision & Comments	What to Look For
1. Introductory Statement	Key words: *whereas, introduction* This is usually the first few paragraphs of the agreement and often includes the term "whereas" (as in, "Whereas the parties agree to enter into a license agreement"). This statement should accurately indicate the intentions, names, and addresses of the parties. See Chapter 8 for more information.
2. The Property	Key words: *property, invention, concept, know-how, technology* Locate the word or phrase used to define your invention ("Invention," "Property," or similar names). This term should accurately describe your invention. See Chapter 8 for more information.
3. Licensed Products	Key words: *licensed product, licensed goods, products, licensed property* Locate the word or phrase defining the products the licensee will sell ("Licensed Products" or similar phrase). This term should accurately describe what will be sold. It's possible that a licensee uses the same term for the invention as for the licensed products. See Chapter 8 for more information.
4. The Grant of Rights	Key words: *grant, license, exclusive, nontransferable, nonassignable, perpetual* Find the grant language. It should be somewhere on the first page. You're looking for terms such as "exclusive," "perpetual," or "worldwide." This language should reflect the boundaries of your grant and may include information about the territory. See Chapter 8 for more information.
5. Sublicense	Key word: *sublicense* You might find a reference to sublicensing, but not always. Often sublicensing references are found in the grant section, although sometimes they are located in the payment section or even in the section regarding assignments. If no such provision exists, make a note to include one. See Chapter 8 for more information.

Checklist for Reviewing a License Agreement (continued)

Contract Provision & Comments	What to Look For
6. Reservation of Rights	Key words: *reserve, reservation*
	There may or may not be a reference to "reservation of rights." If there is no reference, make a note to add it. For more information, review Chapter 8.
7. Territory	Key words: *territory, region, area, worldwide*
	It's not unusual for the territorial restrictions to be included in the grant section rather than in a separate territory section. You're looking for any reference to the geographic location of the grant (words such as "worldwide" or "North America"). For more information, review Chapter 8.
8. Term	Key words: *term, length, duration, renew, initial term*
	Term refers to the length of the agreement; it's not unusual for this information to be found in the grant or termination section. You're looking for any reference to the length or renewability of the agreement. For more information, review Chapter 8.
9. Payment	Key words: *payment, royalty, advance, consideration, guaranteed minimum annual royalty, lump sum, nonrecoupable, net sales, per use*
	The payment section is usually in the first half of the agreement. You need to isolate information about advances and royalties. If applicable, look for guaranteed minimum annual royalty payments and sublicensing revenues. If you are selling a product (and not a technology licensed per use), you will need to find the definition of net sales. If you are licensing technology based upon usage, there should be a method for tracking usage. For more information, review Chapter 9.
10. Payment Statements	Key words: *statement, accounting, quarterly, annually*
	You are looking for a provision that details the contents of the payment statement and when it will be mailed. This information is usually incorporated in or near the payment section. For more information, review Chapter 9.

Checklist for Reviewing a License Agreement (continued)

Contract Provision & Comments	What to Look For
11. Late Payments and Audit Rights	Key words: *audit, late payment, accounting, inspect* If it's not in the payment section, then somewhere nearby should be a section explaining what happens when payments are late and what your rights are in the event you need to audit the licensee's records. If you can't find it, the licensee might have deliberately left this information out of the agreement. Make a note to request a modification to include audits and late payments. For more information, review Chapter 9.
12. Warranties and Indemnification	Key words: *warrant, warranty, represent, covenant, indemnify, indemnification* Warranties (or contractual promises) could be in one section or spread throughout the agreement. You are looking for statements that start with "Licensor warrants ..." or "Licensee warrants and represents ..." or some similar variation. If they are spread throughout the agreement, you'll need to index them for your own reference so you will have a list of all the warranties that you are making. Indemnifications, which are your promises to defend lawsuits, are usually grouped together and always use the word "indemnify." For example, "Licensee indemnifies for any and all claims ...." You should list all of your indemnification obligations. You should be searching for language describing who pays for these defensive lawsuits and how the payments are calculated. Compare the provisions to those in Chapter 12.
13. Intellectual Property Protection	Key words: *registration, intellectual property, patent, copyright, trademark, notice, infringement* Somewhere in the license agreement, you should be able to find references to the following: • Registration of patents, copyrights, or trademarks (U.S. or foreign). Who has the right to register, and who pays for the registration? For more information, review Chapter 12.

Checklist for Reviewing a License Agreement (continued)

Contract Provision & Comments	What to Look For
13. Intellectual Property Protection (continued)	• Infringement against third parties. What happens when someone copies your invention? There should be a section discussing who pays for offensive lawsuits against infringers of your invention. (Note: This is different from a defensive lawsuit when someone claims your invention is infringing. That would be covered in indemnification.) For more information, review Chapter 12.
	• Compliance with laws. Look for a provision stating that the licensee will comply with intellectual property laws. If it's missing, make a note to add it. For more information, review Chapter 12.
14. Exploitation	Key words: *exploit, commence, offer for sale, antishelving*
	There should be some reference as to when the licensee must commence sales and that the licensee must continue to sell the invention. If not, make a note to include this provision. For more information, review Chapter 12.
15. Samples and Quality Control	Key words: *samples, examples, prototypes, quality*
	Have you agreed upon a samples or quality control provision? Locate the reference to production samples. If not, make a note to include this provision. For more information, review Chapter 12.
16. Insurance	Key words: *insurance, coverage, claims, product liability*
	The licensee should maintain adequate insurance. This requirement might be in its own section, or it could be located in a provision such as licensee obligations. For more information, review Chapter 12.
17. Confidentiality	Key words: *confidentiality, nondisclosure, trade secrets, information*
	Confidentiality provisions are usually labeled with obvious titles such as "Confidentiality," "Nondisclosure," or "Trade Secrets." For more information, review Chapter 7.

Checklist for Reviewing a License Agreement (continued)

Contract Provision & Comments	What to Look For
18. Termination	Key words: *terminate, termination, breach, default, insolvency*
	Information about termination is usually either in the front of the agreement in the term section or near the back in a separate termination section. You are looking for language describing the conditions for termination. In particular, look for language describing each party's right to terminate. Compare this language with our suggested grounds for termination in Chapter 13.
19. Posttermination	Key words: *sell-off, return, molds, models*
	After the license ends, each party may have additional obligations. The licensor may want a sell-off period (a limited time to sell remaining products), and you may want materials returned. Look for a section that details these and other posttermination rights. For more information, review Chapter 13.
20. Survival	Key words: *survive, survival*
	As you read through the agreement, various provisions could include a survival statement, such as: "The obligations of this section shall survive any termination of this Agreement." Make a list of these surviving provisions. It's also possible there's a separate section entitled "Survival." Compare the list of surviving provisions with our recommendations in Chapter 13.
21. Attorneys' Fees	Key words: *arising, attorney, fees*
	Most likely, the agreement won't have an attorneys' fees provision. Many licensees do not use them in standard agreements. The term "attorneys' fees" could appear in various sections, such as the indemnity or offensive litigation sections. However, you should look for a section that indicates something to the effect of: In the event of a lawsuit arising from the agreement, the prevailing party is entitled to attorneys' fees. For more information, review Chapter 14.
22. Arbitration or Mediation	Key words: *arbitrate, arbitration, arbitrator, mediation*
	It's possible the licensee won't include an arbitration or mediation provision. For more information, review Chapter 14.

Checklist for Reviewing a License Agreement (continued)	
Contract Provision & Comments	**What to Look For**
23. Governing Law	Key words: *govern, state, controlling law*
	This is usually one sentence near the end of the agreement and includes language such as: "This agreement will be governed by the law of the State of _____." For more information, review Chapter 14.
24. Jurisdiction	Key words: *consent, bound, jurisdiction, state forum selection*
	The agreement might not contain a jurisdiction (forum selection) provision. If there is one, it will be near the end of the agreement (usually near the governing law provision) and will include language such as: "The parties consent to the exclusive jurisdiction of the courts located in." This provision indicates where you have to file or defend lawsuits. For more information, review Chapter 14.
25. Assignability	Key words: *assign, assignment*
	Look for any references to the licensee's ability to assign the agreement. This language could be in the back of the agreement near the general contract provisions, or it might be in the grant section (usually near the front). (Note: The word "assign" may appear in other contexts—for example, an assignment of patent rights. However, you are looking for references to assignment of the agreement.) Compare the contract language with our recommendations in Chapters 8 and 14.
26. New Inventions	Key words: *most favored nation, right of first refusal, improvement*
	Sometimes, a licensee wants to claim a right to your next invention or to improvements you make on your invention. An arrangement can be established giving the licensee the first right to review and license these new inventions. This right is sometimes referenced by the use of language such as "favored nation" or "right of first refusal." Look for similar language. For more information, review Chapter 15.

Checklist for Reviewing a License Agreement (continued)	
Contract Provision & Comments	**What to Look For**
27. Grant Back of Improvements	Key words: *grant back, improvement*
	Who owns the improvements that the licensee makes to your invention? A grant back provision transfers ownership to you. It's possible there's no such provision in the agreement. Because there are important legal issues tied to such provisions, you should review Chapter 15.
28. Escrow Provisions	Key words: *escrow, deposit*
	Although it's not a common provision, it's possible that you and the licensee need an escrow provision. An escrow account is a secure location where trade secrets or payments are stored until certain conditions are met for their release. Escrow provisions are easily identifiable by the use of the word "escrow." For more information, review Chapter 14.
29. Miscellaneous Provisions	Key words: *general, miscellaneous (or any of the individual headings provided below)*
	As we explained in Chapter 14, the following are a group of contract provisions that are usually included near the end of every agreement. Sometimes they are grouped in one section titled "General Provisions" or "Miscellaneous Provisions," and sometimes they are listed separately.
a. Waiver	Key words: *waiver, failure*
	This provision protects your contract rights. For more information, review Chapter 14.
b. Invalidity	Key words: *invalid, effect, sever, omit, affect*
	This provision allows you to preserve your agreement even if it contains an unenforceable section. For more information, review Chapter 14.
c. Entire Understanding	Key words: *complete, entire, full, oral*
	This establishes that this agreement is the complete understanding between the parties. For more information, review Chapter 14.
d. Attachments and Exhibits	Key words: *attachment, exhibit, incorporated, reference*
	This guarantees that exhibits and attachments are an enforceable part of the agreement. For more information, review Chapter 14.

Checklist for Reviewing a License Agreement (continued)

Contract Provision & Comments	What to Look For
e. Notices	Key words: *notice, mailed, sufficient* This provides a method for sending and getting notices about the agreement. For more information, review Chapter 14.
f. No Joint Venture	Key words: *joint venture, agent, partner* This confirms that you and the licensee are not partners or joint venturers. For more information, review Chapter 14.
30. Service Provisions	The following provisions are not in every license agreement. Their presence depends upon the nature of the technology or services provided. (Service provisions and service agreements are explained in detail in Chapter 15.) Many of these provisions may be grouped together under one heading, such as "Licensor Services." If you are performing services for the licensee, look for the following, if applicable:
a. Installation	Key words: *install, installation* Look for language describing your obligations and payment for installing equipment. For more information, review Chapter 15.
b. Technical Assistance	Key words: *technical, support, assistance* Look for language defining technical assistance obligations and payments, if any. For more information, review Chapter 15.
c. Training	Key words: *train, teach, instruct* Look for language discussing training obligations and payments. For more information, review Chapter 15.
d. Development	Key words: *develop, improve, modify* Look for language dealing with converting your invention into a form that is sold to consumers. Review Chapter 15.
e. Approval Provisions	Key words: *approve, approval, accept* Look for language that defines what standards the licensee will use for accepting or rejecting your deliveries. For more information, review Chapter 15.

The Modification Chart

We suggest that you prepare a chart like the one below to outline your proposed changes. You'll submit the chart to the licensee with a short cover letter, which is discussed below. On the left side of the chart are the section numbers and titles of the provisions you're concerned with, and on the right side, a space for comments, questions, or modifications. The tone should be civil, not demanding. Refer to yourself as the Licensor, not as "I."

Sample Modification Chart	
Section	**Comment**
Introduction	Please strike the address for the Licensor. It is incorrect. The correct address is 14 Lincoln Road, Salmagundo, California 94366.
2 (Term)	Please modify the Term section to state "This Agreement shall commence as of the effective date and shall continue for the life of any patent (and extensions), if any, issued on the Invention, or until terminated in accordance with the provisions of this Agreement."
6.5 (Patents)	Can this section be modified so that the Licensor approves costs for foreign patents?
8 (Late Payments)	Please modify the second line so that it reads, "If Licensee is late in any payment provided for in this Agreement, Licensee shall be liable to Licensor for the sum of the payment plus interest from due date at a rate of 1.5% per month or the maximum rate permitted by law."
10 (Indemnification)	It seems unfair that the Licensor should have to absorb 100% of the indemnification costs. Could we at least limit indemnification to sums that have been paid under the agreement?
11.2 (Termination)	Please strike Section 11.2. It was my understanding that the Licensor had the right to terminate during any year if (1) Licensee halts sales of the Licensed Products for a period of six continuous months, or (2) annual royalties from sales of the Licensed Products during the preceding year do not exceed $10,000.
11.4 (Termination)	Could you please revise Section 11.4 as follows: "In the event of termination of Agreement, pursuant to this Section 11, no advances shall be repayable to Licensee."
14 (Jurisdiction)	The Licensor should not have to travel to New York for litigation. Either strike the jurisdiction section or provide for jurisdiction in both New York and California.

The Cover Letter

You should submit the chart with a short cover letter. Don't use your cover letter for a long dissertation on contract rights. The letter and chart are basically a guide for a meeting or phone conversation in the future.

October 21, 20xx

Dear Mr. Smith:

I've reviewed the license agreement. Attached is a list of comments and proposed modifications. I think we are close to a final agreement and I look forward to discussing it with you. Please call after you have an opportunity to review this letter.

Sincerely,

Licensor

Licensor

After You Sign the Agreement

Create Your Contract Calendar..383

Dealing With Royalty Statements..385

    Common Royalty Problems..386

    What If the Sales Figures Appear Inaccurate?...386

    Bringing in the Auditors...387

Resolving Licensing Disputes..388

    Creating a Paper Trail..388

    Avoiding Declaratory Actions...389

    When Letters Fail...389

Avoiding Patent Misuse and Illegal Agreements..390

    Tying Arrangements..390

    Illegal License Length and Hybrid Licenses..392

    Preventing Development of Competitive Products...394

The Taxman Cometh...394

    Ordinary Income Versus Capital Gains...394

    Deductions...395

Quality Control...395

Congratulations! You've signed a license agreement and are ready to sit back and collect royalty checks. Not so fast. The signing of the license agreement creates some new responsibilities. How do you review royalty statements? What does it mean to monitor product quality? How do you schedule due dates? What if things begin to break down between you and the licensee? A whole host of business and legal issues will arise once your license agreement takes effect.

You will find that the suggestions and advice in this chapter are a mixture of law and common sense. If you are an experienced businessperson, you are probably familiar with most of this material. However, you should read this chapter if you answer "yes" to any of the following questions:

- Would you like advice on how to schedule contract due dates and intellectual property obligations?
- Will this be the first royalty check you have ever received?
- Would you like advice on how to handle a royalty dispute with the licensee?
- Are you concerned about tax issues regarding income from your license agreement?

- Are you concerned about the licensee's possible breach of the agreement?
- Would you like information about patent misuse?

In this chapter, we provide you with information about monitoring your license arrangement after the agreement has been signed. We advise you to create a calendar that indicates the important dates in your license agreement (such as royalty payments and termination), and we help you interpret your royalty statements. We also suggest some strategies if you believe that the royalty reporting is inaccurate. Finally, we provide some advice on a subject called "patent misuse," which refers to situations in which a patent owner uses a valuable patent to coerce a licensee.

Treat Yourself!

One inventor told us that whenever he licenses a new invention, he uses some portion of the advance to buy something memorable for himself—a piece of artwork or some other special purchase. That way, long after the deal (as well as the income) has come and gone he still has the purchase to remind him that he successfully licensed an invention.

Create Your Contract Calendar

After you've celebrated the signing of your licensing agreement, you should take the following steps:

1. Make sure you have filed a clean copy of your license agreement (without any marks or scribbles) in your business file.
2. Make a list of all relevant due dates as established by the final, signed license agreement (explained below).
3. Make a list of relevant dates for intellectual property protection (explained below).

Your license agreement contains many dates and time periods. For example, the licensee must introduce the product to the market by a certain date. Or perhaps you have a certain time period to review samples and approve them. You may want to summarize these dates and time periods. Below is a chart with the common contract dates. Write the appropriate date on the left side.

> **TIP**
> **Your licensing calendar.** We suggest that you calendar (that is, write these dates on a calendar) or prepare a chronological list of these dates and keep it in your business file. Your computer, tablet, or smartphone should include methods of calendaring dates and offering pop-up reminders. You'll find these particularly handy in dealing with contract and intellectual property dates.

Rubber Vehicle Tire
No. 686,905

Intellectual Property Protection Dates

As a diligent protector of your patents, trademarks, and copyrights, remember to stay on top of important dates such as filing deadlines, patent expiration deadlines, and dates when you should pay maintenance fees. Because it's possible to search the patent office abstracts for free, you may also want to calendar periodic searches to check for new inventions that are similar to your own. If you have a federal trademark registration, remember to calendar filing dates for trademark renewal and incontestability.

License Dates	
1. Effective date	This is the date that the license agreement goes into effect. This date is in the introductory paragraph, the term section, or the exhibit attached to your agreement (which contains the essential business terms). Sometimes, the date is on the signature page.
2. Renewal dates	If you have an agreement that is renewable, the dates for renewal should be listed. These dates would be in the term section, the termination section, or the exhibit attached to your agreement. Locate and chart these dates. For example, if you signed the agreement on September 10, 2018 and the agreement could be renewed in two years, the renewal date would be September 10, 2020.
3. Renewal notice date	A renewal usually occurs when one side notifies the other of its intention to renew (or not to renew), depending on the agreement. Most often, the licensee has the choice to renew.
	This notice of renewal usually must be sent to the other side by a certain date, for example, 60 days prior to the renewal date. If the renewal date is September 10, then 60 days prior would be July 11 (counting backwards on a calendar and not counting the date of renewal). That's the date when you must be notified of the renewal decision. This information would be listed in the term section, the termination section, or the exhibit attached to your agreement.
4. Delivery dates	These are dates you have established for deliverables, which are items you must create and deliver to the licensee. (See Chapter 15 for more information on deliverables.) These dates would be in the deliverables section, the services section, or the exhibit attached to your agreement.
5. Service dates	These are dates you have established for performance of services. (See Chapter 15 regarding service provisions.) These dates would be listed in the deliverables section, the services section, or the exhibit attached to your agreement.
6. Advance or lump sum payment dates	Make a list of all dates when advances or lump sum payments are due. These dates are in either the payment section or the exhibit attached to your agreement.

License Dates (continued)	
7. Royalty payment dates	Royalty payments are commonly made 30, 60, or 90 days after the end of a calendar quarter. For example, if a calendar quarter ended March 31, 2020 and the licensee had 60 days to send you the payment, then the statement and payment would be due on May 30, 2020. These dates are in the payment section or the exhibit attached to your agreement.
8. Dates to complain about royalty statements	Generally, a licensor has a limited time to complain about the accuracy of a royalty statement. For example, if you establish a complaint time limit of one year, then you cannot complain after that date. Calculate the period of time based upon when you should receive each statement. The time period is usually in the audit or the payment section of the agreement.
9. Date for introduction of licensed products	This would be the date that the licensee has agreed to offer the licensed product for sale. This may also be the date that the licensee has agreed to show the licensed product at a certain trade show or exhibition. You can usually find this date in the exploitation section or in the exhibit attached to your agreement.
10. Termination date	If there is a fixed termination date, calendar it. This date would be in the term section, the termination section, or the exhibit attached to your agreement.
11. Delivery of insurance information	If applicable, this would be the date by which the licensee must give you proof of insurance. This date would be in the insurance section.

Dealing With Royalty Statements

Your first experience with a royalty statement might not be as you imagined. For example, you rip open the envelope, toss aside the statement and look at the check. *$687.00???* How can it be so small? You find the statement and pore over the columns trying to decipher the codes and numbers. If they make you feel dizzy, you're not alone. Royalty statements can be a confusing experience. This section offers some advice on how to handle them.

Here are some general tips that should help you stay on top of your royalty statements:

- First, save the envelope in which the statement was mailed and staple it to the document. This will verify the date of mailing.

- Second, examine the statement date and statement period for the payments. (The statement date is the date the royalty statement was completed—not necessarily the date it was mailed.) The statement period is the period covered by the statement, for example, 4th Quarter 2020. There may also be a period end date which indicates the final date of the period for which the statement is issued. Review your agreement to make sure that you are receiving a statement for the appropriate period. For example, if your quarterly report includes six months of activity, then there's a mistake.
- Third, compare the royalty rates in the statement with the rates that are established in your contract to make sure they are accurate.
- Fourth, look at the deductions and credits and compare them to what is permitted under the agreement. If you are confused about the size of a deduction, particularly if there is no explanation, request an itemized accounting for it.
- Fifth, find the sales figures (often titled "Units Sold"), or if you are paid per use, then look for the appropriate number (sometimes titled "Usage"). Locate the sublicensing revenue, if any.
- Finally, do the math. Prepare your own spreadsheet and verify that the statement is correct.

Common Royalty Problems

Most royalty statement errors are the results of negligence, not intentional acts of wrongdoing. The following are the types of errors that are commonly blamed on computer problems:
- incorrect royalty rates
- incorrect listing of deductions, and
- indecipherable statements.

If you have one of these problems or just don't understand the structure of the statement, call the licensee and ask for an explanation. Someone in the accounting department should be able to provide the information. If no one does, don't get mad. Ask for the supervisor or manager of the department. Keep trying to move up the chain of command. When you can't go any further and if you still aren't satisfied, get the name and position of the final person you have spoken with and confirm your conversation with a letter. Keep a copy. We don't advise using a strident or angry tone in your confirming letter. For what to do next, review the section below on resolving disputes.

What If the Sales Figures Appear Inaccurate?

If you believe the licensee is misstating sales figures, you can begin your inquiry informally, for example, with a phone conversation. Tell the licensee or your contact at the licensee company that the sales figures seem low. Is there any way to verify the numbers? You should avoid accusing the licensee of wrongdoing. First, you may be wrong. Second, the misstatement may be a result of negligence or a technical problem such as a computer error, not intentional wrongdoing.

You Have a Limited Period of Time to Complain

Most audit provisions establish a limited time period to challenge the accuracy of a royalty statement. Usually, this period is 12 or 24 months. Although we do not urge you to rush into a royalty dispute, you should be aware of these time limitations and make any necessary challenge in a timely manner. Otherwise, you may lose the right to question the statement.

If you don't find the licensee's explanation satisfactory and you still want to pursue the matter, you should have more than a hunch before proceeding. Do you have any other means of determining sales? Some trade magazines publish sales figures and charts. Some research companies can also obtain this information for you. It might also be available through company reports or online services such as Lexis/Nexis. (See Chapter 6 for information on business research.) You may want to consult with an accountant or a lawyer familiar with invention licensing.

(For more information on attorneys, see Chapter 18, "Help Beyond This Book.")

Bringing in the Auditors

If you've exhausted every other method of obtaining accurate information regarding your suspicions, you may have to audit the licensee. An audit should be performed *only* as a last resort. It's fairly expensive (you're paying an accountant's hourly rate), and will likely generate considerable ill will with the licensee. Because an audit can be expensive, you shouldn't begin it unless you have good reason to believe you'll recoup your expenses. Consult with an attorney or accountant knowledgeable in invention licensing and get an opinion as to the reasonableness of an audit. (See Chapter 18, "Help Beyond This Book.")

In the event you do hire an auditor, you should cap the costs. That is, you and the auditor should agree on the maximum to be spent on the audit. Under the model audit provision we provided in Chapter 9, the licensee pays your auditor's expenses in the event of a substantial discrepancy. In the model agreement, we suggested that the licensee pay expenses if the audit uncovers a difference of $1,000.

You will need to send an audit letter to the licensee as notification that you are seeking an audit. Below is an example.

Sample Audit Request Letter

Date: _____

Dear: _____

I have received your royalty statement dated [*date of statement*]. The amount of that statement, [*indicate amount, if any*], does not seem to reflect the sales success attributed to the licensed products. As our previous attempts at resolving this issue have failed, I have no other choice but to exercise my rights under the audit provision of our license agreement, dated [*date of agreement*].

I have contacted [*name of CPA or accountant who will perform the audit*] to perform the audit. My auditor will be in contact with you shortly, and I hope that you will provide all of the information requested and permitted under our agreement.

My auditor will need access to all company books and records that relate to the agreement and to sales of the licensed products, including work sheets, foreign and domestic ledgers, calculations and statements, and any other documents accessible to outside auditors of your company operating in accordance with the Generally Accepted Audit Standards (GAAS). In addition, the auditor will need access to company personnel who maintain the financial records and can answer questions that may arise.

Sincerely,

Licensor

Resolving Licensing Disputes

Licensing isn't always a smooth experience, and you might have disputes with your licensee. The key to resolving disputes is negotiation—the same type of negotiation you used to work out your license in the first place. (Review Chapter 10 for suggestions on negotiation.)

Creating a Paper Trail

Always start with informal attempts at resolving disputes. Use the telephone or meet in person. If these attempts fail, you need to create a paper trail. That is, you need to build a series of documents that demonstrate you have made every reasonable attempt to resolve your dispute.

Below is an example of a letter that could be used after informal methods to resolve the dispute have failed. Always set a date by which you would like to resolve the matter. You will also note that the letter does not threaten litigation. The letter states that the writer will "consider exercising rights" and hopes to resolve the dispute "amicably." The reason for this is explained in the section on declaratory actions, described below.

> Dear Tom:
>
> In recent conversations with Jim Smith at SportCo, I have been unable to resolve a dispute arising from our licensing agreement dated February 1, 2020. According to the agreement, I was to receive an advance payment of $10,000 on March 1, 2020. That payment was not made.
>
> I have suggested several solutions to resolve this problem, including a series of payments spread over three months. However, none of these suggestions have been accepted. As a result, we seem to have a serious problem affecting the license. I am hopeful that we can resolve this amicably within the next month. Unless we can resolve it, I must consider exercising my rights under the dispute resolution procedures in the agreement. Please contact me after you have reviewed this letter.
>
> Sincerely,
>
> *Licensor*

Avoiding Declaratory Actions

Normally, as the party that is wronged or injured, you bring the lawsuit in your state of residence (unless the jurisdiction provision in your agreement provides otherwise). However, sometimes the other party, anticipating the lawsuit, files what is known as a declaratory action in its state of residence. A declaratory action is when one party goes to court claiming a dispute exists and asks for a declaration of each party's rights.

In order to bring a declaratory action, there must be proof of an actual controversy. An actual controversy exists when there is an explicit threat of a lawsuit or, to use legal lingo, when one party has a "reasonable apprehension of litigation."

This brings us back to your letter to the licensee. If the letter threatens legal action—for example, "If you do not pay the money next week, I will sue you in federal court"—then the licensee may file a declaratory action in its state of residence claiming an actual controversy exists. That is, even though you're the one who has suffered, you will have to go to the licensee's home state to fight the lawsuit. To avoid this possibility, we suggest that you do not threaten litigation in your letter and always leave open an option to resolve the dispute amicably.

If your agreement has a mandatory arbitration clause, you can't threaten litigation. You must proceed to arbitration. See Chapter 14 for more on arbitration provisions.

When Letters Fail

If letters have failed to resolve the problem, it's probably time to consult with an attorney knowledgeable in licensing inventions. A lawyer will be able to help you determine whether you should exercise your dispute resolution rights under the agreement. That is, will you file a lawsuit? Or, if your license agreement includes an arbitration provision, will you instigate arbitration? It can be very difficult to judge the merits of your case and the likelihood of winning in litigation or arbitration. An experienced lawyer's advice is as important in deciding whether to sue as in representing you during the suit. If you need assistance in locating an attorney, see Chapter 18, "Help Beyond This Book."

One issue that may be important is attorneys' fees. If you have an attorneys' fees provision in your agreement, you'll recover fees if you prevail. However, if you lose the dispute, you may be obligated to pay the licensee's attorneys' fees. Review these provisions in your agreement.

No matter how strongly you believe that you are in the right and should win a lawsuit, it's possible that an attorney will disagree with your assessment. If that is the case and you still feel strongly, get a second opinion. If two attorneys disagree with your assessment of the problem, you might have to face the fact that you should drop the dispute.

Avoiding Patent Misuse and Illegal Agreements

Sometimes the parties to a license agreement unintentionally create an agreement that is illegal. In cases where the license agreement contains an illegal provision, a court may void the license agreement or terminate patent rights. For example, a grant back provision, as discussed in Chapter 15, could violate the law and create an illegal license agreement. Illegal grant backs, tying agreements, and similar problems are known as patent misuse. Below, we discuss misuse and related issues and how to avoid these problems.

Antitrust Laws and Patent Misuse

Patent misuse is a subcategory of the antitrust laws. Antitrust laws prevent powerful companies from using their market strength to stifle competition. For example, if all of the manufacturers of cold remedies joined together and conspired to fix prices, this would be unfair to consumers and would violate antitrust laws.

Tying Arrangements

Patent misuse occurs when a patent holder coerces a licensee into an unfair or unethical business arrangement. How can a patent owner coerce a licensee? The most common example is called tying. Under an illegal tying arrangement, a licensee of a patented device is forced to purchase an additional unpatented product. For example, the licensee is told that if it wants the patented doughnut-making machine, it must also buy the licensor's doughnut dough.

Because misuse laws are aimed at patent bullies, you might not feel they have much importance to you. After all, you haven't coerced anyone to license your invention. Unfortunately, even if you have acted properly, you could still be subject to these issues because a licensee may claim patent misuse as a basis to cancel the license agreement. Patent misuse is commonly pleaded as a defense to breach of a patent license agreement. So if you sued your licensee for breaching your agreement—say, for nonpayment of royalties—you might suddenly find yourself in the position of having to prove that you did not misuse your patent.

For example, say you licensed a method for measuring blood pressure that uses a patented monitor and an unpatented wristband. After two years, the licensee stops making payments. You sue, but the licensee defends itself claiming patent misuse. The licensee argues that you engaged in an unfair tying arrangement because you forced it to use your wristband when it could have bought a cheaper imitation from a competitor. You are suddenly on the defensive—forced to prove that the wristbands are protectable and that the law permits you to jointly license both these items.

Fortunately, in 1988, after lobbying by patent owners, Congress enacted the Patent Misuse Amendments, which helped patent owners by giving the

courts more leeway in determining if an arrangement is fair. In April 1995, the Federal Trade Commission and the Justice Department also announced new antitrust licensing guidelines that establish a safety zone for intellectual property licensing arrangements for licensors whose inventions account for less than 20% of a relevant market. For example, if your licensed product accounts for less than 20% of the market, your tying arrangement is presumed to be legal and not anticompetitive. This "safety zone" is only a presumption, not a hard-and-fast rule, but it helps to make litigation more predictable for smaller companies owning patents.

In addition, the Supreme Court has determined that it is permissible to require a licensee to purchase nonstaple goods from a patent holder. Nonstaple goods are goods designed to carry out the patented processes, with little or no use outside of the patented processes. For example, it was legal for the patent owners of a glucose-measuring device to require licensees to purchase their blood glucose test strips. The strips were separately patented and were nonstaple items in that they had little use outside of the glucose-measuring process.

In summary, if you are licensing a patented invention and you are linking the license to the sale or license of another device, you should be aware of rules regarding tying arrangements. Your agreement will be legal and enforceable if you can demonstrate any of the following:

- You did not coerce the arrangement based upon your marketing power.
- You offered the licensee reasonable alternative options to obtain the tied product.
- The tied product is a nonstaple—a product designed to carry out the patented processes that has little or no use outside of the patented process.

Tie-Ins and Tie-Outs

There are two types of tying arrangements. A tie-in requires that the licensee buy a separate product from the licensor. A tie-out prevents the licensee from purchasing or using a separate product made by a different company.

Illegal License Length and Hybrid Licenses

Throughout this book, we have advised against creating a license that lasts longer than the term of your patent. For example, if 15 years remain on your patent, you should not negotiate for a license of 20 years. Why not? Because the Supreme Court ruled in 1965 that it was a misuse of patent rights for a licensor to collect royalties on an expired patent and that

such agreements were invalid. (*Brulotte v. Thys*, 379 U.S. 29 (1965).) The Supreme Court's decision has been criticized for failing to recognize the realities of invention valuation, and many companies created a "workaround" by negotiating one royalty rate during the term of the patent and a lower rate for the period after expiration. However, such agreements were also found to be invalid under a 2002 case in which a court prohibited this two-tiered royalty. (*Scheiber v. Dolby Laboratories, Inc.*, 293 F.3d 1014 (7th Cir. 2002).) In short, a provision that provides for patent royalties after expiration of the patent will be unenforceable.

If you're not licensing a patent, this is not an issue. So, for copyrights, trademarks, and trade secrets, the license can extend for decades.

There are, however, two situations in which the license can last longer than the length of a particular patent. The first situation occurs if your license includes all patents that may issue during the term. As we explained in Chapter 13, this type of grant is terminated "upon the expiration of the last remaining patent."

The second situation occurs if you are licensing both patents and trade secrets, trademarks, or copyrights (known as a hybrid license). If you are licensing a package of intellectual property rights, the license can continue for as long as protection exists for any one of the properties. In the case of trade secrets and trademarks, that protection can be perpetual (forever). However, in a hybrid license, it might be patent misuse to continue to receive the same royalty rate after the expiration of the patent. Why? Basically, it's unfair to require the licensee to pay for a patent that is in the public domain. The royalty rate must decrease in relation to the value of the expired patent. This reduction can be done by allocating varying values for each item (such as patents and trademarks) licensed.

For example, say you created a peel-off formula for nail polish and sold it under the trademark Striptease. The formula is patented and the trademark is federally registered. You license the patent and trademark to a major cosmetic firm and your agreement contains two royalty rates: a fixed rate for licensed products, and a second rate in the event that the patent expires or is determined invalid. This second rate would apply only to use of the trademark Striptease. A sample hybrid royalty provision is provided in Chapter 9.

Dear Rich:
Can We License Individual Patent Claims?

Dear Rich: We recently received a CIP patent (continuation in part) patent with numerous claims pertaining to different industries. For example, one claim covers the invention as it relates to government. Another claim covers the invention as it relates to the medical industry, etc. Can the owner of a patent assign or license the rights to specific claims within the patent? For example, can we license or assign only the rights of the claims pertaining to the medical industry to a biochemical company? According to *Patent It Yourself* (Nolo) author David Pressman, the answer is "Generally yes, unless the licensing of less than all of the patent claims is in furtherance of a scheme to monopolize a certain industry beyond the monopoly conferred by the patent—for example, in one case when a company was willing to license a critical patent only if the licensee took licenses under some additional undesirable patents, that was held to be an illegal antitrust practice, since it extended the patent monopoly beyond its ordinary scope." Occasionally, a party that is being sued for patent infringement will raise this issue as a defense (known as "patent misuse"). Pressman reminds readers that when it comes to questions of antitrust law, things can get complicated (as the law is often vague on the subject). It's one of those areas where an attorney's consultation is probably necessary.

Preventing Development of Competitive Products

We advise against including a provision that bars the licensee from developing a similar invention. In other words, you should not forbid the licensee from independently creating a competing invention or technology. You can prohibit the licensee from any unauthorized use of your intellectual property rights in creating a competitive device. But you should not prohibit independent invention activity. A provision that bars development of competing products is likely to be challenged as patent misuse.

The Taxman Cometh

You might have already received tax advice regarding license payments. If not, you should consult with an accountant or a tax expert. Although detailed tax advice is beyond the scope of this book, below are some general tax concepts and principles.

Ordinary Income Versus Capital Gains

Generally, licensing income is taxed as an ordinary gain, just like ordinary business income. You may claim certain deductions or credits where applicable, but you must pay taxes on all of the income you receive during each year. However, when you assign your patented invention and give up all of your rights to it, your income from the assignment can be taxed as capital gains. Moreover, self-employment tax need not be paid on the earnings. In other words, your tax treatment is different if you permanently transfer your rights in the patented invention.

These rules can vary depending upon whether patent, trademark, trade secret, or copyright law protects the invention. You should also realize that the title of your agreement or the terms you use (that is, license, sale, or assignment) are not what governs tax treatment. For tax purposes, these terms are only "transactional labels." The IRS examines the substance of the agreement to determine if it transfers all of the assets. If you are concerned about how your income will be taxed, you should consult with a tax attorney or financial adviser before entering into a license agreement.

Combined Off-Board Device and Starter/Charging/Battery System Test
No. 6,988,053

Double Taxation and Foreign Licensing

In the event that you entered into a licensing agreement with a company in another country, you will want to avoid double taxation. What is double taxation? Let's say you had a licensing deal with a British company. The British government would withhold a portion of your British royalty check for British taxes. The U.S. government would also tax your income. As a result, you would have paid income tax both to Britain and the United States.

There are two ways that you can avoid double taxation. One way is to claim the foreign taxes paid as a deduction or credit against your U.S. taxes. A second method is sometimes available. A foreign tax authority may agree to refund taxes provided that U.S. tax authorities are notified of your income and of the tax payments to the foreign authority. The foreign tax authority will usually have a special tax form that you must complete in order to qualify for this refund.

Deductions

You should keep track of deductions to offset licensing income. An accountant or tax guide can advise you as to types of deductions available. For example, materials used for creating prototypes, as well as phone, fax, and travel expenses—to the extent that they are part of your inventing business—are all deductions. Most of these expenses can be deducted in the year in which they were incurred. However, large expenses must be depreciated. This means that the expense is spread out over several years—sometimes, the life of the patent—with a portion of it being deducted each year.

Quality Control

We advise you to review samples of the licensed product periodically. Your samples or quality control provision will explain the number of samples you can obtain and the period of time in which you may complain about licensee quality. See Chapter 12 for an explanation of samples and quality control.

Your product review should help you determine if your invention is being utilized properly and if something has been done to your invention that is not permitted under the agreement. For example, say you believe that additions made to your invention might infringe another invention. Notify the licensee in writing of your approval or disapproval, and keep a copy of the letter. Make sure that your letter is received within the time required under your samples or quality control provision and that it is sent in accordance with the notice provision.

Help Beyond This Book

Licensing and Intellectual Property Resources...398

Licensing and Inventor Organizations...398

Other Intellectual Property Resources...400

International Licensing Resources..401

Working With an Attorney 402

Intellectual Property Attorneys...402

Other Legal Specialties...402

Finding an Attorney 403

How to Keep Your Fees Down..403

For many of you, this book provides all the information you will need to license your invention. However, you might find yourself in a complicated situation that will require additional research or professional advice from an attorney or other expert. If you need to get outside help, don't fall into the trap of simply letting someone else control all the details of your situation. By educating yourself with this book and the other resources listed in this chapter, you'll be able to work with professionals more efficiently, keep your costs down, and be in a better position to evaluate their services.

Nolo's Online Provisional Patent Application

Nolo, the publisher of this book, offers Nolo's Online Provisional Patent Application (www.nolo.com) that assists applicants filing a provisional patent application with the U.S. Patent and Trademark Office.

Licensing and Intellectual Property Resources

If you're looking for more information on the licensing process, you may want to review some of the resources and publications listed below. We've grouped background materials into the following categories:

- licensing and inventor organizations
- international licensing resources, and
- other intellectual property resources.

Licensing and Inventor Organizations

There is a network of inventor organizations throughout the United States. Through the following organizations, you can obtain a wealth of information about the licensing process, including legal and business advice and referrals to prototype makers, product agents, and other professional contacts:

- PTO Independent Inventor Resources (www.uspto.gov). In 1999, the PTO established a new office aimed at providing services and support to independent inventors.
- United Inventors Association (UIA) (www.uiausa.org) is a national inventor's organization.
- Invention Convention (www.invention convention.com). The National Congress of Inventor Organizations (NCIO) maintains this invention website that includes links, trade show information, and advice for inventors.
- Ronald J. Riley's www.InventorEd. org has links and advice for inventors.

Legal Research and Law Libraries

For the nitty-gritty details of licensing and intellectual property law, you can conduct your own legal research. Especially if you find yourself in a dispute over your invention or if a lawsuit is threatened, you may want to find out exactly what the law says about your particular situation. Finding an answer to a specific legal question generally involves reading treatises for a general understanding of a particular legal area, finding applicable statutes, and reading the cases in which judges have interpreted these statutes.

Conducting legal research is not as difficult as it may seem. Nolo publishes a basic legal research guide, *Legal Research: How to Find & Understand the Law,* by Stephen Elias and the Editors of Nolo. It walks you through the various sources of law, explains how they fit together, and shows you how to use them to answer your legal question. Some legal research can be performed on the Internet. A good place to start your Internet research is Nolo (www.nolo.com).

For detailed legal research, however, you will probably have to visit a local law library. If there's a public law school in your area, it probably has a law library that's open to the public. Other public law libraries are often run by local bar associations or as adjuncts to the local courts. Law libraries associated with private law schools often allow only limited public access. Call to speak with the law librarian to determine your right to access. You can always call your local bar association to find out what public law libraries are in your area.

- Licensing Executives Society (U.S.A. and Canada) (www.lesusacanada.org) is an organization for attorneys and licensing executives from the United States and Canada. The organization publishes a directory listing specialties for licensing attorneys throughout the United States and Canada.
- Intellectual Property Owners (IPO) (www.ipo.org) is an association that serves owners of patents, trademarks, copyrights, and trade secrets. It is the sponsor of the National Inventor of the Year Award.
- Inventor Mentor (www.inventor-mentor.com) offers condensed reports and other guidance for inventors. The site is maintained by inventor Jack Lander.
- Patent License Exchanges such as Yet2.com offer—for a fee—the ability to post information about patented inventions for would-be licensees.

Other Intellectual Property Resources

Provided below are some additional sources of information on the various forms of intellectual property law. Many of these sources are accessible through the Internet.

Nolo's Legal Encyclopedia

Nolo's website (www.nolo.com) also offers an extensive Legal Encyclopedia which includes a section on intellectual property. You'll find answers to frequently asked questions about patents, copyrights, trademarks, and other related topics, as well as sample chapters of Nolo books and a wide range of articles. Under "Legal Articles," click on "Patent, Copyright & Trademark."

Patents

At its website (www.uspto.gov), the U.S. Patent & Trademark Office (USPTO) offers a number of informational electronic guides, including an introduction to patents ("Patent Basics") and an online search for patent attorneys registered to practice before the USPTO by name, city, state, and country ("Finding a patent practitioner"). The USPTO also has an online searchable database of patent abstracts (short summaries of patents). For purposes of patent searching, this database is an excellent and inexpensive first step in the searching procedure.

To visit the USPTO's website— where you'll also find its searchable database—go to www.uspto.gov/patent. Most patent forms can be downloaded from the website, as can many important publications including the *Manual of Patent Examining Procedures*.

Online patent searching. Online searching is ideal for locating a specific patent and performing preliminary research but, by itself, is not suitable for proving patentability or validity. The main reason being that the patents in most online databases usually go back only to 1971, and it's possible that a patent issued before that date might demonstrate the obviousness or lack of novelty for a new invention. (For most high-tech inventions, this limitation isn't a problem, since the relevant prior art is post-1960s.)

Online searching has some obvious advantages, such as cost and ease of use. In order to perform online searches, you must have access to certain databases. You can search using your own computer or via an existing terminal that is dedicated to patent searching, such as at a Patent Trademark Resource Center (PTRC), a large company or law firm, or in the USPTO. The following free databases are available:

- **The U.S. Patent & Trademark Office**
(www.uspto.gov). An online
searchable database of patents and
drawings that cover the period from
January 1976 to the most recent
weekly issue date (usually each
Tuesday).
- **Google Patent Search** (https://patents.
google.com). Google Patent Search
covers the entire collection of issued
patents and millions of patent
applications made available by the
USPTO from patents issued in the
1790s through those most recently
issued in the past few months. It also
includes international patents.

Copyright

The Copyright Office has numerous
circulars, kits, and other publications that
can help you, including one on searching
copyright records. These publications and
application forms can be downloaded
directly from www.copyright.gov.
Frequently requested Copyright Office
circulars and announcements are also
available via the Copyright Office's
Forms and Publications Hotline Number,
202-707-9100.

Trademarks

The Trademark Office is a division of
the USPTO. Information about the
operations of the Patent and Trademark
Office is available from the USPTO's
website at www.uspto.gov/trademark. This
site includes the relevant applications and
trademark office forms.

International Licensing Resources

The following resources can help you
analyze opportunities for international
licensing of your invention:

- **The U.S. Department of Commerce**
(DOC) (www.commerce.gov) and
the **U.S. Small Business Administration**
(SBA) (www.sba.gov) are interested
in helping the sales of U.S. goods
overseas. If an inventor has a track
record and the possibility of actually
placing a product in the market
(or already has a product and is
seeking to market it overseas), the
DOC and SBA offer assistance.
Also, check out the Department of
Commerce site at the International
Trade Administration (ITA) (www.
commerce.gov/bureaus-and-offices/
ita) or the DOC's export information
(www.export.gov).
- **European Patent Office** (www.epo.org)
provides links to patent licensing
exchanges, mailing lists, patent
information providers, registered
European patent agents, law offices,
and patent offices for member states.

Working With an Attorney

A number of situations may lead you to seek an attorney's advice: a complex license negotiation, a dispute over your invention, or a simple need for guidance. Attorneys have various specialties, and you will need to select a lawyer who is qualified to provide the advice you need.

Intellectual Property Attorneys

First, you should make sure your attorney is knowledgeable about intellectual property law. Most intellectual property attorneys are familiar with licensing and can negotiate a deal or prepare a license agreement. Don't make the mistake of hiring a lawyer whom you trust but who works in a different field—such as the lawyer who masterfully handled your friend's personal injury case. Intellectual property law should be handled by a specialist.

Second, you should find an attorney who has expertise in the particular type of intellectual property that applies to your invention. Some intellectual property attorneys specialize in one type of intellectual property—copyrights, trademarks, or patents. If, for example, you're concerned about ownership or licensing of a patented invention, you should seek an intellectual property attorney who specializes in patents.

The American Intellectual Property Law Association (www.aipla.org) may be able to assist you in locating attorneys in your area. The Intellectual Property Law Association of the American Bar Association also has a listing of intellectual property attorneys. You can reach it at 312-988-5000.

Other Legal Specialties

For certain tasks, you will need an attorney who specializes in a particular area other than intellectual property. If you have concerns about taxes or an IRS dispute, you will need a tax attorney; if you are overwhelmed by debt, you will need a bankruptcy attorney; if you are sorting out your business form (for example, forming a corporation), you will need a business attorney.

In addition to all these specialties, some lawyers focus on litigation. Not all intellectual property attorneys are litigators. If you have a license dispute and want to sue someone (or someone has threatened to sue you), you will need an intellectual property attorney who specializes in litigation. Litigators usually bill on an hourly basis, though sometimes they may take a case on contingency. Under a contingency arrangement, if you win, the attorney receives a percentage—usually one-third to one-half—of any money recovered in the lawsuit. If you lose, the attorney receives nothing.

Finding an Attorney

The best way to locate an attorney is by referrals through friends or other inventors. It's also possible to locate an attorney through a state bar association or through a local county or city bar association. Check the online yellow pages and ask the bar association if they have a lawyer referral service. When interviewing an attorney, ask questions about clientele, work performed, rates, and experience. If you speak with one of the attorney's clients (for example, another inventor), ask questions about the attorney's response time, billing practices, and temperament.

How to Keep Your Fees Down

Most attorneys bill on an hourly basis ($250 to $400 an hour) and send a bill at the end of each month. Some attorneys bill on a fixed-fee basis. That is, you pay a set fee for certain services—for example, $5,000 for a license negotiation.

Here are some tips to reduce the size of your bills.

Keep it short. If your attorney is being paid on an hourly basis, then keep your conversations short (the meter is always running) and avoid making several calls a day. Consolidate your questions so that you can ask them all in one conversation.

The same is true with emails. Keep them concise and consolidate them when possible.

Get a fee agreement. We recommend that you get a written fee agreement when dealing with an attorney. The fee agreement is a negotiated arrangement establishing fixed fees for certain work rather than hourly billings. Read it and understand your rights as a client. Make sure that your fee agreement includes provisions that require an itemized statement along with the bill detailing the work done and time spent, and that allow you to drop the attorney at any time. If you can't get fixed billings, ask your attorney to estimate fees for work and ask for an explanation if the bill exceeds the estimates.

Mad at Your Lawyer?

In many states, such as California, a client always has the right to fire an attorney (although this does not terminate the obligation to pay the attorney). If you don't respect and trust your attorney's professional abilities, you should switch and find a new attorney. Beware, though: Switching attorneys is a nuisance and you may lose time and money.

Review billings carefully. Your legal bill should be prompt and clear. Do not accept summary billings, such as the single phrase "litigation work" used to explain a block of time for which you are billed a great deal of money. Every item should be explained with the rate and hours billed. Late billings are not acceptable, especially in litigation. When you get bills you don't understand, ask the attorney for an explanation—and ask the attorney not to bill you for the explanation.

Be careful if you engage a law firm. If you sign a fee agreement with a law firm (rather than a single attorney), be careful to avoid a particular billing problem sometimes referred to as multiple or "bounced" billings. This occurs when the same work is performed by several attorneys. For example, two attorneys at the firm have a 15-minute discussion about your case. You are billed by both attorneys. To avoid this, make sure that your fee agreement does not bind you to this type of arrangement. If you are billed for these conferences, send a letter to your attorney at the firm explaining that you only want that attorney to work on your case and that you should be contacted before work is assigned to another attorney at the firm.

What Is a Retainer?

A retainer is an advance payment to an attorney. The attorney places the retainer in a bank account (in some states, this must be an interest-bearing account), and the attorney deducts money from the retainer at the end of each month to pay your bill. When the retainer is depleted, the attorney may ask for a new retainer. If the retainer is not used up at the end of the services, the attorney must return what's left. The amount of the retainer usually depends on the project. Retainers for litigation, for instance, are often between $2,000 and $5,000.

Watch out for hidden expenses. Find out what expenses you must cover. Watch out if your attorney wants to bill for services such as word processing or administrative services. This means you will be paying the assistant's salary. Also beware of copying charges. Some firms charge a per-page copy fee that surpasses any commercial copy center. Look out for these hidden expenses in your fee agreement.

Do your best to limit the attorney's services. It's common for a license to take one to two months or more to negotiate. These agreements go through many drafts.

You can help to limit the number of drafts by reaching a clear agreement with your attorney as to the goals of the negotiation. For example, if getting a $10,000 advance is most important, tell your lawyer that is your number one priority. Once you have achieved most or all of your goals, then be flexible on remaining issues so that you can save time.

Don't take litigation lightly. As a general rule, beware of litigation! If you are involved in a lawsuit, it may take months or years to resolve. Some go on for decades. It often costs $10,000 or more, and the only ones who profit are usually the lawyers. If you're in a dispute, ask your attorney about dispute resolution methods such as arbitration and mediation. Often, these procedures can save money, and they're faster than litigation. If those methods don't work or aren't available, ask your attorney for an assessment of your odds and the potential costs before filing a lawsuit. The assessment and underlying reasoning should be in plain English. A lawyer who can't explain your situation clearly to you probably won't be able to explain it clearly to a judge or jury.

What's a Conflict of Interest?

Lawyers are bound by ethical rules to disclose if a potential conflict of interest exists. A conflict of interest occurs whenever the lawyer represents adverse interests, for example, if your attorney also represents the licensee. When a conflict of interest exists, there is the potential that your attorney may not battle as forcefully for your position. For example, if the attorney represents you and a licensee, it is possible that the attorney will be apprehensive of endangering a lucrative relationship with the licensee for your sake. Another danger is that the attorney could use confidential information obtained from one party against the other party.

Always ask your attorney if there is a potential conflict. The attorney should disclose a conflict without being asked, but some attorneys do not. Although we recommend against retaining a lawyer with a potential conflict of interest, it is possible, in some cases, that an attorney can vigorously represent your interests nonetheless. This is a judgment call that should be made based upon your feeling for the attorney and any other information you have obtained, such as references from other clients. If you want to proceed, you can sign a waiver in which you relinquish any right to complain about the situation later. If you do not want to proceed, do not sign a waiver and find a different attorney.

How to Use the Downloadable Forms on the Nolo Website

Editing RTFs...408

List of Forms and Interviews..409

This book comes with forms and files that you can access online at: **www.nolo.com/back-of-book/LICE.html** To use the files, your computer must have specific software programs installed. Here is a list of types of files provided by this book, as well as the software programs you'll need to access them:

- **RTF.** You can open, edit, print, and save these form files with most word processing programs such as Microsoft *Word*, Windows *WordPad*, and recent versions of *WordPerfect*.
- **MP3.** You can listen to these audio files using your computer's sound system. Most computers come with a media player that plays MP3 files, or you may have installed one on your own.

Editing RTFs

Here are some general instructions about editing RTF forms in your word processing program. Refer to the book's instructions and sample agreements for help about what should go in each blank.

Underlines. Underlines indicate where to enter information. After filling in the needed text, delete the underline. In most word processing programs you can do this by highlighting the underlined portion and typing CTRL-U.

Bracketed and italicized text. Bracketed and italicized text indicates instructions. Be sure to remove all instructional text before you finalize your document.

Optional text. Optional text gives you the choice to include or exclude text. Delete any optional text you don't want to use. Renumber numbered items, if necessary.

Alternative text. Alternative text gives you the choice between two or more text options. Delete those options you don't want to use. Renumber numbered items, if necessary.

Signature lines. Signature lines should appear on a page with at least some text from the document itself.

Every word processing program uses different commands to open, format, save, and print documents, so refer to your software's help documents for help using your program. Nolo cannot provide technical support for questions about how to use your computer or your software.

CAUTION

In accordance with U.S. copyright laws, the forms provided by this book are for your personal use only.

List of Forms and Interviews

The following files are in Rich Text Format (RTF) and are available for download at **www.nolo.com/back-of-book/LICE.html**

Form Title	File Name
Agreement Worksheet	AgreeWorksheet.rtf
Letter Confirming Employee's Ownership of Intellectual Property Rights	EmployeeOwner.rtf
Joint Ownership Agreement	JointOwnership.rtf
Assignment of Rights: Patent	AssignPatent.rtf
Assignment of Rights: Patent Application	AssignPatentApp.rtf
Assignment of Rights: No Patent Issued or Application Filed	AssignNoPatent.rtf
Agent Letter Agreement	AgentLetter.rtf
One-Way Nondisclosure Agreement	OneWayNondisclose.rtf
Mutual Nondisclosure Agreement	MutualNondisclose.rtf
Contract Worksheet	ContractWorksheet.rtf
Sample Letter of Intent	LetterIntent.rtf
Option Agreement	OptionAgreement.rtf
Terms Sheet	TermsSheet.rtf
License Agreement	LicenseAgreement.rtf
Checklist for Reviewing a License Agreement	ReviewChecklist.rtf
Sample Audit Request Letter	AuditRequest.rtf
Escrow Agreement	EscrowAgreement.rtf
License Dates	LicenseDates.rtf

The following files are Audio (MP3).

Form Title	File Name
Secrets of Successful Licensing	LicenseSecrets.mp3
Common Licensing Provisions	LicenseProvisions.mp3
Contract Law Damages	ContractDamages.mp3
Ten Common Contract Problems	10CommonContract.mp3

Index

A

Accountants
    for audit process, 226–227, 387
    tax advice from, 394, 395
Act of God (force majeure provision), 290–291, 333, 344
Actual controversy, 389
Advance payments
    overview, 108
    agent commissions applied to, 116
    dates for, 384
    defined, 208
    evaluation of a license agreement presented to you, 371
    financial analysis determining royalty rates and, 218–219
    license agreement provision for, 261, 280
    licensing flexibility reduced by, 108
    nonrecoupable, 209
    nonrefundable, 208, 209
    option payments treated as, 246
    and the product pie, 219
    recoupable, 208
Advertising
    as deduction for net sales royalties, 215
    in trade magazines, 118, 138
Agent(s)
    overview, 116
    attorneys acting as, 126–127
    benefits of using, 116–117
    commercial potential, the "bag of parts" analysis to determine, 39
    commission for, 116, 120–121
    commission owed after termination of agreement with, 119, 121, 126

competing invention also represented by, 116
defined, 116
distinguished from employees, 116–117
distinguished from partnership, 23, 116–117
distinguished from scams, 130–131
evaluation of your invention by, 130
fiduciary duty of, 116
finding, 117–118
industry custom to use, 117
letter of intent identifying, 241
no guarantee of a license given by, 117, 121
nondisclosure agreements with, 119
as party to license agreement, 180
payments and statements to, in license agreement, 282
principal, defined, 116
prototypes for, 119
referrals to find, 117–118
royalty rate information from, 217
solicitation difficulties by inventor as reason to use, 117, 134, 136
solicited companies, list of, 119, 126
termination of agreement with, 119, 121, 126
    See also Agent agreements; Scams
Agent agreements
    overview, 120
    alternative dispute provisions, 126
    confidentiality provision, 121
    defined, 17
    disclaimer provision, 121
    escrow account for Properties Income, 121
    exclusive vs. nonexclusive, 120
    expenses of agent, 121
    general provisions, 126
    impact on licensing, 17
    indemnification, 121

introductory material, 120
obligations of agent, 120
obligations of inventor, 120
payments, 120–121
Properties Income, defined, 120
sample Agent Letter Agreement, 122–125
signatures, 126
termination of, royalties owed for licenses
  after, 119, 121, 126
Agent Letter Agreement, 122–125
Agreements that can affect licensing, avoiding
  conflicts among
  overview, 12, 13
  purpose of agreements, identifying, 15
  sample Agreement Worksheet, 19
  tracking, 18, 19
  types of, 15–17
Agreement Worksheet, 19
Alternative dispute resolution
  overview, 335
  evaluation of a license agreement presented to
    you, 374
  for license agreements, 271–272, 285–286,
    336, 337
  for option agreements, 245
  for oral licenses, 238, 252
  See also Arbitration; Mediation
American Intellectual Property Law Association,
  402
American Pet Products Association (APPA), 137
Angel investors, 100–102
Anticompetitive rules. See Patent misuse and
  illegal agreements
Antitrust laws
  and continuation in part (CIP) patent,
    licensing of, 393
  patent misuse as subcategory of, 390
  spin-off royalties and, 224
  See also Patent misuse and illegal agreements

Arbitration
  overview, 335
  advisory, 335
  agent agreements and, 126
  attorney consultation on likelihood of winning,
    390
  attorneys' fees and, 153
  binding, 335
  for employment-related ownership disputes, 84
  evaluation of a license agreement presented to
    you, 374
  following mediation, 337
  foreign license agreements, 153
  joint ownership agreement provision for, 110
  license agreements provision for, 271, 285–286,
    336
  licensee objections to, 335, 337
  option agreement provision for, 245, 251
  private arbitration, 336
  pros and cons of, 335
  resources on, 336
  See also Alternative dispute resolution;
    Mediation
Articles of manufacture, utility patents and, 48
Asia, marketplace share of, 147
"As provided herein," defined, 367
Assignment of rights
  attorney for, 25
  bankruptcy of the licensee and, 326–327
  caution against assignment for "promise" of
    future payments, 25
  consent not needed for licensee affiliates or
    new owners, 273, 288, 343
  consent not unreasonably withheld, 273, 288, 343
  defined, 9
  to employee, 84
  evaluation of a license agreement presented to
    you, 375
  joint ownership created by assignment for
    money, 104

joint ownership created by assignment to a partnership, 104

license agreement provisions for, 189, 273, 288, 333, 342–343

license agreements usually nonassignable/nontransferable, 189

licenses compared to, 9–10

lump sum payment for, 211

mandatory, provisions not applicable to, 343

with no patent or application, 30–31

with patent application, 25, 28–29

patent applied for by assignee, 313

with patent approved, 27

preinvention assignments (employment agreements), 73–75

recording patents with USPTO, 25

spouse signature, 25–26, 104

sublicensing distinguished from, 189

transferring ownership to your business, 21, 25–31

unlimited exclusive licenses as having the same effect as, 9

written, requirement for, 25

Attachments and exhibits provision, 273, 287, 333

evaluation of a license agreement presented to you, 376

"incorporated by reference," 341–342, 353

See also Exhibits

Attorney(s)

overview, 402

as agents, 126–127

conflicts of interest of, 127, 405

disclosures about patents made to, 33

disclosures made to, confidentiality of (attorney-client privilege), 175

finding and interviewing, 403

firing/switching, 403

foregoing a fee in exchange for percentage of licensing royalties, 127

intellectual property attorneys, about, 402

in law firms, 404

litigator specialists, 402

resources for finding, 399, 402

working with, 403–405

See also Attorney consultations; Attorneys' fees; Legal research

Attorney consultations

assignments, 25

attorney for, 360

challenges to ownership, 20

for employment-related ownership disputes, 73, 77, 84

for evaluation of a license agreement presented to you, 369

for likelihood of winning in a lawsuit or arbitration, 390

nonprofit corporations, transfer of ownership to, 24

patent applications, 52–53

patent infringements, 20, 316

patent search/written opinion, 302–303

second opinion on assessment of a lawsuit, 390

when letters fail to resolve a dispute, 389–390

Attorneys' fees

agreement for, 403, 404

American Rule on, 333

arbitration agreements awarding to the victor, 153

awarded to the winner in lawsuits, provision for, 270, 285, 332, 333–335, 374

caution on one-way provisions for, 334

contingency basis, 316, 402

cost for lawsuits, 333

evaluation of a license agreement presented to you, 374

as factor in disputes, 390

fixed-fee basis, 403

hourly, 402, 403

keeping fees down, 403–405

and litigation costs, 405

for patent applications, 53

patent search/written opinion, 302
retainers, 404
waived for percentage of licensing royalties, 127
Audits of license agreements
overview, 387
accountants authorized to conduct, 226–227
attorney or accountant consultation prior to, 387
company representative designated to assist, 227
confidentiality of, 227
contingency auditors, 227
cost of audit paid in disputes, 228, 229, 387
cost of, capping, 387
defined, 226
dispute resolution, 227–229
evaluation of a license agreement presented to you, 372
foreign licenses and, 153
frequency of audits, 226
interest rate for disputes, 227, 228
notice prior to, 226
notification of request for, 387–388
provision in license agreement, 228, 264
royalty statement disputes, 387–388
sample Audit Request Letter, 387–388
termination of license agreement and, 227

B

Bankruptcy
and credit-card borrowing for inventing expenses, 96
of licensee, termination cannot be claimed for, 326–327
of licensor, 327
mandatory assignments under, as not preventable by "nonassignable" provision in license agreement, 189
Bayliss, Trevor, 134
"Best efforts," defined as term used in contracts, 240–241

"Best of your knowledge," 303
Boilerplate (miscellaneous) provisions, 332–350
overview, 332–333
attorneys' fees, awarded to the prevailing party, 270, 285, 332, 333–335
evaluation of a license agreement presented to you, 376–377
force majeure, 290–291, 333, 344
headings, 333, 344
importance of, 332
integration (entire understanding), 272, 287, 332, 340–341, 376
for joint ownership agreement, 110, 114
for nondisclosure agreements, 163, 167
notice, 273, 287, 333, 341, 377
relationships (no joint venture), 273, 287, 333, 342, 377
severability, 332, 340
waiver, 272, 287, 332, 339–340, 376
See also Arbitration; Assignment of rights; Attachments and exhibits provision; Escrow; Governing law (choice of law); Jurisdiction; Mediation
Breaches of license agreements
commercialization requirement as, 316
cure period for, 325–326
incurable breaches, 326
material breaches, defined, 324–325
monitoring each other to determine adherence, 10
termination of agreements for, 10, 316, 324–325
Brokers, to find angel investors, and signs of a scam, 101–102
Building security, 61
Business Development Centers, 102
Business directories, 139
Business forms
overview, 20–21
See also Transferring ownership to your business

C

California
attorneys acting as agents, 126–127
incorporation costs, 24
independent contractors distinguished from employees, 87
preinvention assignments, limits on, 73, 75
Capital, and loan qualification, 99
Capital gains, 394
Challenges to ownership
attorney needed for, 20
former associate claims ownership, 20
licensee challenging validity of, 18
patent infringement, 20
See also Indemnity; Warranties
CIP (continuation in part) patent, licensing of, 393
Claims-made policies, 319
Clean room (independent development), 59
Coinventors, defined, 107
Collateral. *See* Secured loans
Combination inventions, 49
Commercialization. *See* Exploitation
"Commercially reasonable efforts," defined as term, 240–241
"Commercially reasonable quantities," defined as term, 317
Commercial potential, assessment of
overview, 36–37
avoidance of false hopes, 41
"bag of parts" analysis for price point, 39
caution about scam marketing firms, 41
crowdfunding as no guarantee of, 98
expert opinion, 41
for foreign licensees, 149–151
the funding process and, 91–93
Innovation Center (University of Oregon) factors to consider, 37–39, 92–93
Patent It Yourself factors, 39–40, 92
Small Business Administration tests for, 37
solicitation of your invention and, 136
testing the waters yourself, 40
test marketing, 94
Commercial success, myth that legal rights will guarantee, 58
Composition of matter, utility patents and, 48
Computers
security to maintain trade secrets, 61
semiconductor chip protections, 67
software created after hours, ownership of, 71
Confidentiality
attorney-client privilege, 175
of audits, 227
implied relationships, 170
of license agreement, 268, 284
most favored nations and, 362
signatures in your invention notebook as alternative to nondisclosure agreement, 158
waiver agreements specifically giving up, 156, 170–172
See also Nondisclosure agreements
Connecticut, state ownership of state employees' inventions, 81
"Considered," defined, 367
Contingency auditors, 227
Continuation in part (CIP) patent, licensing of, 393
Contract standards, good faith and best efforts, 239–241
Contract Worksheet, 179, 200–203
Co-ownership. *See* Joint ownership
Copyright Office
mask work registration, 67
as resource, 401
Copyrights
overview, 8, 65
aspects not protected by, 65, 66
business-owned copyrights, length of, 65
cost of registration deducted from royalties, 312–313
derivative works and, 65

emailing or mailing copies of works will not provide protection, 64

employees and, 60, 79

fees, 67

grant backs and, 362

independent contractors and, 79, 80

infringement of, burden of proof for, 68

length of protection, 65, 67

licensee challenging validity of, 18

licensee registers in its name, 313

of mask works (semiconductor chips), 67

nonfunctional features of invention and, 45–46, 65, 66

originality to author as priority in, 48, 65

registration not required, 65, 67

resources, 401

Corporations

angel investors and, 100–101

initial public offerings (IPOs), 100

for investment by family and friends, 99–100

investment via, 108

license agreement signature line for, 289–290

nondisclosure statement signature line for, 167–168

personal guarantees of loans to, 97

Corporations, transferring ownership to your

advantages of, 23–24

agreements for corporation and stock, impact on licensing, 16

assignment of rights, 21, 25–31

joint ownership agreements, authorized signatures, 110

legal requirements for formation of, 24

limited personal liability for business debts and, 21, 24

nonprofit corporations and, 24

piercing the corporate veil, 24

reasons for forming, 21

shareholders in, 23–24

Covenants, defined, 301

See also Warranties

Credit cards, self-financing with, 96

Credit risk modeling (CRM), 99

Credits and returns deduction from net sales, 214, 216

Cross-territory sales, limiting, 193, 259, 278

Crowdsourcing

overview, 97

crowdfunding, 98

crowdinvesting, 98

crowdlending, 98

disclosure as drawback to, 97

success rates of, 98

See also Internet; Online resources

Currency, provision for payment in U.S., 226, 263

D

Death of licensee, "nonassignable" provision in license agreement not applicable in case of, 189

Debts and uncollectible account deductions from net sales, 215

Declaratory action, avoiding, 389

Deductions. See Net sales royalty deductions

Defend Trade Secrets Act (DTSA), 56, 169, 174

Delaware, preinvention assignments, limits on, 74

Deliverables, 293–295

dates for, 384

definition of, 357

delivery and approval, 295, 358, 359

evaluation of a license agreement presented to you, 377

included in grant of rights, 359

new invention rights created during making of, 359–360

schedules and development services, 295, 358

See also Service agreements; Service provisions

Derivative works, copyright and, 65

Design patents
  overview, 8, 63
  fees for, 66
  filing deadline, 64
  infringement of, burden of proof for, 67–68
  length of protection, 64, 66
  length of time required to obtain, 66
  nonfunctional features of invention and,
    45–46, 63, 64, 66
  registration of, 65
  standard for obtaining, 64
Disclosure agreements. *See* Nondisclosure
  agreements
Disclosure of your invention
  overview, 12, 32
  to attorneys, 33, 175
  employment agreements and requirement for,
    72–73, 74
  to investors, 102–103
  nondisclosure agreements and, 33
  public disclosure as ending trade secret
    protection, 32, 55
  public disclosure, loss of patent rights due to,
    32, 34, 158
  public disclosure, patent rights and prior art
    requirement exception, 50
  of university-employee inventions, 82
  See also Confidentiality; Nondisclosure
    agreement(s)
Disputes
  attorney consultation when letters fail, 389–390
  attorneys' fees as factor in, 390
  date for resolution, inclusion of, 388
  declaratory actions, avoidance of, 389
  informal attempts (telephone calls or
    meetings), 388
  negotiation as key to resolving, 388
  paper trail, creation of, 388–389
  royalty statement errors, 385–388

  See also Alternative dispute resolution; Audits
    of license agreements; Breaches of license
    agreements; Lawsuits
Distribution chains, and solicitation, 135–136
Divorce, spouse signature to avoid disputes in
  event of, 104

E

Earnings
  as federal employee-inventor, 81
  as university employee-inventor, 82, 83
Edison, Thomas, inspiration/perspiration
  equation of, 42
Emotions, and product presentations, 147
Employment agreements
  assignment of innovations, 74
  breach by employee, 72
  defined, 16
  disclosure of inventions, 72–73, 74
  employee manual or other guidelines, as
    legally binding, 72
  holdover clause for preinvention assignments, 73
  impact on licensing, 16
  nondisclosure agreements (NDAs), 174–175
  power of attorney, 72, 74
  preinvention assignments, 71–75, 82, 83
  sample provisions of, 74
  See also Employment and invention ownership
Employment and invention ownership
  overview, 20, 70–71, 137
  attorney for disputes about, 73, 77, 84
  copyrights, 60, 79
  disputed ownership, resolution of, 84
  employed-to-invent doctrine, 75, 77–78
  employees distinguished from agents, 116
  employees distinguished from independent
    contractors, 86–87
  government employees, 79–81
  independent contractors and exceptions to
    rules for, 75, 79, 80, 81, 86–87

inventions created after hours, 71, 72, 73, 76–77

patentable inventions, 70, 71–79

patents claimed immediately after quitting a job, 73

shop rights (employer right to use without compensation), 70, 77, 78–79, 84

state laws limiting preinvention assignments, 73–75

trademarks, 70

trade secrets, 70, 71–79

transfer of rights to employee, 84–85

university employees, 81–83

See also Employment agreements; Independent contractors

Encyclopedia of Associations, 138

Entire understanding (integration), 272, 287, 332, 340–341, 376

Equipment and Tool Institute (ETI), 138

Escrow

overview, 345

for agents, 121

evaluation of a license agreement presented to you, 376

license agreement provision for, 291, 333, 345–346

miscellaneous (boilerplate) provisions for, 350

sample Escrow Agreement for release of trade secrets, 346–350

EUBusiness, 154

Europe

enforcement of foreign patent rights in, 150

GNP (gross national product), 151

marketplace share of, 147

resources for, 154, 401

time period for nondisclosure agreements, 166

See also Foreign licensees; International patent rights

European Patent Office, 154, 401

Evaluation agreements, and impact on licensing, 17

See also Option agreements

Evaluation of a license agreement presented to you

overview, 368–369

attorney for, 369

checklist for reviewing, 370–377

cover letter for, 379

key provisions, identifying, 369

modification chart, 378

preparation of electronic files for, 368–369

reviewing the provisions, 369–377

strategies for, 368–369

See also Modifications to your license agreement by licensee

Exclusive vs. nonexclusive agent agreements, 120

Exclusive vs. nonexclusive license agreement grant, 186–187, 258, 277

and duty of licensee to market/exploit, 311

unlimited exclusive licenses, 9

Exhibit A section of license agreement, 274, 290

Exhibits

fact sheet as, 236, 251, 252

license agreement as, for option agreement, 245

patent application as, 256

royalty rate as, 290

service agreement as, 353

See also Attachments and exhibits provision

Expenses

spreadsheet for tracking, 94, 95

start-up, 36

See also Fees and costs; Funding; Tax deductions of invention expenses

Exploitation

date of, 267, 283

duty to market, state law on, 311

evaluation of a license agreement presented to you, 373

license agreement provision requiring, 267, 283, 316–317

licensee warranty of, 310–311
refusal by licensee, in order to keep an invention off the market, 311
termination of license agreement for failure to bring to market, 269
territory not exploited, right to terminate due to, 152–153, 194, 270, 326
Export.gov, 154

F

Fact sheet summarizing negotiation, 235–238, 252
Family and friends
   investments from, 99–100
   loans from, 98–100
   for marketing opinion research, 40
Federal laws
   attorneys' fees, award of, 333–334
   Bayh-Dole Act (1980), 82
   Defend Trade Secrets Act (DTSA), 56, 169, 174
   federal contractors and ownership of inventions, 81
   federal employees and ownership of inventions, 80–81
   independent contractors distinguished from employees, 86–87
   Invention Developers law, 129–130
   Patent Misuse Amendments, 391
   Semiconductor Chip Act, 67
   See also Antitrust laws; Patent misuse and illegal agreements; U.S. Patent and Trademark Office (USPTO)
Federal Trade Commission, 129
Federation of International Trade Associations (FITA), 154
Fee deduction, from net sales, 215
Fees and costs
   agent representation, 120–121
   assignment of patents, 25

costs of producing the invention, importance to licensee, 39, 170
design patents, 66
of foreign patent rights, 148
incorporation, 24
overall patent costs, 148
for patent filing and maintenance, 47, 53, 58, 94, 148, 312–313
prototypes, 94, 119
scams, 128–129, 130
search for patentability, 93
spreadsheet for tracking, 94, 95
test marketing, 94
trade shows, 144, 145
See also Attorneys' fees
Fictitious business names, 21
Fiduciary duty, of agents, 116
Financial analysis, royalty rates based upon, 218–219
F.O.B. royalties, 225
Force majeure provision, 290–291, 333, 344
"Foregoing," defined, 367
Foreign licensees
   overview, 147–148
   cost of patent protections and, 148
   infringement, ability to sue for, 150
   license agreements with, 152–153
   marketability-per-nation analysis, 149–151
   no license at all is better than a bad license, 154
   prior experience of licensee with U.S. companies, 152
   reliability of the licensee, determining, 151–152
   resources for, 154, 401
   taxes and, 153, 395
   terminology, learning about, 154
   time limits triggered by U.S. patent filing, 154
   See also International patent rights; Territory, license agreement provisions for

Forms
downloads and updates of, 408
editing RTFs, 408
list of forms and interviews available, 409
types of files available, 408
See also specific forms including license agreement form
Forum selection. *See* Jurisdiction
France, as market, 151
FRANDS (Fair, Reasonable, and Non-Discriminatory terms) for SEP licenses, 190
Freight/shipping deduction from net sales, 216
Friends. *See* Family and friends
Functional vs. nonfunctional features of invention
overview, 45–47
copyrights and, 45–46, 65, 66
design patents and, 45–46, 63, 64, 66
nonfunctional features, comparison of forms of protection for, 66–68
trademarks and, 45–46, 62, 66
trade secrets and, 45–46, 56–57
utility patents and, 45–46
Fund an Idea, 98
Funding
overview, 91
define your invention in writing and drawings, 91
determining the amount you need, 91–95
miscellaneous expenses, 94
patentability/novelty search, 93
patent application, 94
prototypes, 93–94
spreadsheet for tracking expenses, 94, 95
start-ups and difficulty of getting conventional sources of, 91
test marketing, 94
See also Funding sources; Joint ownership; Tax deductions of invention expenses

Funding Circle, 98
Funding sources
overview, 94
angel investing, 100–102
bank loans, 97, 99
credit cards, 96
crowdsourcing, 97–98
due diligence of funders, 101
loans compared to investments, 95–96
loans from family and friends, 98–100
qualification for loans (the five "Cs" of credit), 99
SBA loans, 98
self-financing, 94
signature loans, 96–97
state SBA-style lending assistance, 102
venture capital, 102–103
See also Funding; Investments; Loans

G

General partnerships. *See* Partnerships
General provisions. *See* Boilerplate (miscellaneous) provisions
Germany, as market, 151
Gifts, joint ownership issues and, 106
GMAR (guaranteed minimum annual royalty), 209, 212–214, 219, 222–223, 262, 282
GNP (gross national product), 151
Good-faith and fair dealing, implied covenant of, 239
Google Patent Search, 42, 401
Governing law (choice of law)
distinguished from jurisdiction, 338, 339
evaluation of a license agreement presented to you, 375
for license agreements, 152, 272, 286, 332, 337–338
for nondisclosure agreements, 173
for option agreements, 251

Government
    contractors of, and ownership of inventions, 81
    employees of, and ownership of inventions, 79–81
    enforcement of intellectual property laws not pursued by, 53
Government regulation or review
    patent term extensions due to, 50–51
    safety tests, 51
Grant back (licensor ownership), 291, 362–363, 376
    illegal, 363, 390
    See also Improvements to invention
Grant of rights
    deliverables included in, 359
    evaluation of a license agreement presented to you, 370
    exclusive vs. nonexclusive rights, 186–187, 258, 277
    improvement ownership rights and, 187, 360
    "including but not limited to" language in, 188
    intellectual property rights, 186–188
    in letter of intent, 241
    nonassignable/nontransferable grant, 189
    overly broad grants, example of, 188
    sublicenses, 186, 189, 191–192, 225, 259, 263, 277, 370
    See also Reservation of rights in license agreements; Territory, license agreement provisions for
"Gray marketing" outside licensed territory, 193
Gross revenues, defined, 116
Gross sales, defined, 207
Guaranteed minimum annual royalty (GMAR), 209, 212–214, 219, 222–223, 262, 282

H

Hawaii, small business loans, 102
Headings provision, 333, 344

"Hereinafter referred to," defined, 367
"Heretofore granted," defined, 367
Hybrid license royalty, 212, 222, 262, 280–281, 392–393

I

Idaho, forum selection invalid in, 339
Ideas
    copyright not protecting, 65
    licensing of, 55
Illegal uses, patents not awarded for, 48–49
Illinois, preinvention assignments, limits on, 74, 75
Implied agreements, 34
Implied confidential relationship, 170
Improvements to invention
    overview, 357
    definition of, 182, 275
    evaluation of a license agreement presented to you, 375
    grant of rights to, 187, 360
    independently created, 360–362
    joint ownership agreement provisions for, 110
    license agreement language for, 257, 275
    licensee making, and ownership question, 187, 362–363
    most favored nations/licensee clause, 296, 361–362, 375
    new patentable invention created during requested improvements, 359–360
    right of first refusal, 296, 360–361, 375
    See also Deliverables; Grant back (licensor ownership)
Indemnity
    overview, 20, 303
    in agent agreements, 121
    avoiding provisions in licensee-provided agreements, 305–307
    evaluation of a license agreement presented to you, 372

license agreement provisions for, 264–266, 282–283, 305, 311

licensee indemnity, 266, 311

limited to third-party claims against the licensee, 304

in nondisclosure agreements, 172

not addressed in licensee's agreement, 310

paying for, 282–283, 307–310

qualification of, 304, 307

See also Warranties

Independent contractors

copyrights and, 79, 80

distinguished from employees, 86–87

government contractors, ownership of inventions, 81

nondisclosure agreements with, 174–175

preinvention assignments, state laws limiting are not applicable to, 75

written agreements with, 87

See also Employment and invention ownership

Independent development of inventions

and breach of NDAs, 165–166

and exclusions of confidential information in NDAs, 165–166

as legitimate means of obtaining trade secrets, 59

Independent inventors. *See* Inventors, independent

Indiegogo, 98

Industry customs and particulars

agents preferred to independent inventors, 117

learning about, prior to solicitation, 135–136

reservation of rights expressly excluding a particular market, 188–189, 259

royalty rates, 217, 219

Industry standards

FRANDS (Fair, Reasonable, and Non-Discriminatory terms) for SEP licenses, 190

standard-essential patents (SEPs), 190

standard-setting organizations (SSOs), 190

Injunctions, as nondisclosure agreement provision, 172–173

Innovation, ordinary, 49

Installation of equipment provision, 292, 355

Insurance

date for proof of, from licensee, 385

evaluation of a license agreement presented to you, 373

for infringement lawsuits, defensive, 315

for infringement lawsuits, offensive, 315, 316

product liability, 268, 283, 317–319, 326

Integration (entire understanding), 272, 287, 332, 340–341, 376

Intellectual Property Owners (IPO), 399

Intellectual property rights

overview, 6–7, 8

analysis of types of rights, prior to licensing, 45–47

attorney specialists in, about, 402

compliance with laws, provision in license agreement, 267, 283, 373

component approach to analysis of types of, 46–47

costs of registration deducted from royalties, 312–313

dates and time periods, tracking of, 383

defined, 45

evaluation of a license agreement presented to you, 372–373

"first to create" as myth in, 48

forms of, overview, 8

hybrid license agreements including, 212, 222, 262, 280–281, 392–393

infringement lawsuits, insurance against, 315, 316

infringement lawsuits, laws on attorneys' fees for, 333–334

infringement lawsuits, provision for, 314–315

as license agreement provision, generally, 153, 183, 184, 266, 312–315

license agreements made without protection of, 55

licensee registers in its name, 313

notification of, marking products with (e.g. symbols), 313–314

obtaining, resources for, 398–401

tying arrangements and, 391

See also Copyrights; Functional vs. nonfunctional features of invention; Ownership; Patent(s); Trademarks; Trade secrets

International patent rights

and compensation for pendency infringements, 52

cost of, as consideration in obtaining, 148

infringements on, ability to sue, 150

license agreement provision for, 153

Nonpublication Request if international rights not sought, 60

Provisional Patent Application (PPA) and, 54

resources on, 401

time limits for, triggered by U.S. patent filing, 154

See also Foreign licensees

International Trade Association (ITA), 154

International trademark rights, 62

Internet

caution about disclosures of patents on, 34

split territorial licenses as problematic for products sold on, 193

websites, trademarks and, 63

See also Crowdsourcing; Online resources

Introductory material

agent agreements, 120

evaluation of a license agreement presented to you, 370

joint ownership agreements, 109

license agreement provisions, 255–256

Invalidity, in license agreements, 272, 287, 376

Invention(s)

combination, and utility patents, 49

defined, 5

definition of, for letter of intent, 241

definition of, for license agreement, 180–184, 256, 257–258, 275–276

definition of, for option agreement, 246

independent development of, 59

name/nickname of, 256

pioneer, 218

reverse engineering and, 58–59, 167

See also Commercial potential, assessment of; Disclosure of your invention; Funding; Improvements to invention; Intellectual property rights; Inventors, independent; License(s); Nondisclosure agreements (NDAs); Prototypes

Invention Convention, 398

Invention marketing scams. *See* Scams

Invention promotion companies. *See* Scams

InventNet, 147

InventorEd.org, 399

Inventor Mentor, 399

Inventors' associations, 147, 398–399

Inventors, independent

associations for, 147, 398–399

bias/presumptions about, overcoming, 141

industries that prefer agent solicitations vs., 117

personal appearance of, and trade show attendance, 146

treat yourself for a successful license, 382

See also Agent(s); Agreements that can affect licensing, avoiding conflicts among; Inventor's notebook; Solicitation of potential licensees

Inventor's notebook
  overview of importance and use of, 34, 35
  confidentiality agreements created by
    signatures in, 158
  confidentiality agreements for personal
    market research, 40
  date of invention recorded in, 107
  tamperproof, 35
  tax deductions of invention expenses and, 36
Investments
  angel investors, 100–102
  crowdinvesting, 98
  defined, 95
  disclosures to investors (with nondisclosure
    agreement), 102–103
  due diligence of investors, 101
  from family and friends, 99–100
  joint ownership and, 108
  loans as form of, 108
  loans compared with, 95–96
  venture capitalists (VCs), 102–103
  See also Corporations
IRS, employees distinguished from independent
  contractors, 86–87

J

Joint ownership (co-ownership)
  overview, 20, 103–105
  acceptance of money, effects of, 106–108
  assignment of individual interests by, 104, 105
  created by assignment for money, 104
  created by assignment to a partnership, 104
  created by a will, 104
  and revenue splitting, 104, 105, 110
  spouse signatures and, 104
  See also Joint ownership agreements; Joint
    ownership created by patented joint invention
Joint ownership agreements
  overview, 15–16, 108

alternative dispute resolution, provisions for, 110
authority to sign if representing a partnership
  or corporation, 110
coinventors, defined, 107
decision making, provisions for, 109
defined, 15
impact on licensing, 16
improvements and revisions to invention,
  provisions for, 110
introduction section, 109
miscellaneous (boilerplate) provisions, 110, 114
ownership percentage interests, provisions for,
  109
revenue splitting law and need for, 105
right to manufacture and sell, provisions for,
  109
sample agreement, 111–114
separate agreements for each invention, 109
signatures, 104, 110
transferring ownership to a partnership and,
  21, 104, 110
Joint ownership created by patented joint invention
  overview, 103
  and need for joint ownership agreement, 105
  and revenue splitting, 105
  See also Joint ownership; Joint ownership
    agreements
Jurisdiction
  overview, 338–339
  determined by first person to file a suit, 174
  distinguished from governing law, 338, 339
  evaluation of a license agreement presented to
    you, 375
  for license agreements, 152, 272, 287, 332, 339
  modification by licensee of your agreement
    on, 367
  for nondisclosure agreements, 173–174
  for option agreements, 251
  states not honoring, 339
  strategies for selecting, 339

K

Kansas, preinvention assignments, limits on, 74, 75
Kickstarter, 98
Know-how
  defined, 57
  nondisclosure agreements and, 57
  services agreement for, 57, 355
  services provision in license agreement for training, 291–292, 354–355

L

Late payments, 229, 264
  evaluation of a license agreement presented to you, 372
Law libraries, and legal research, 399
Lawsuits
  attorney consultation on likelihood of winning, 389–390
  attorneys' fees, awarded to the winner in, 270, 285, 332, 333–335, 374
  avoidance of threats of, 389
  for breach of good faith, 239
  for consent to sublicense withheld, 192
  declaratory action in case of actual controversy, 389
  for false statements about another inventor or invention, 235
  FRAND disputes, 190
  insurance against, 315, 316
  for nondisclosure agreements, breach of, 157, 165–166
  for patent infringements, license agreement provision for, 267, 283, 314–315, 373
  for patent infringements, money earned via, 58, 315
  types the licensee may be involved in, 302–303
  See also Alternative dispute resolution; Disputes; Governing law (choice of law); Indemnity; Jurisdiction

Lawyers. See Attorneys
Legal research and law libraries, 399
Legal rights. See Intellectual property rights
Letter Confirming Employee's Ownership of Intellectual Property Rights, 84–85
Letter of intent
  overview, 238
  as binding/not binding, 238, 244
  date for executing a written contract, 244
  fact sheet summarizing negotiations incorporated into, 236
  and good faith/best efforts, 244
  provisions of, 238, 241, 244
  sample, 242–243
  See also License agreement(s); Option agreements
Lexis/Nexis database, 140
Liability insurance (product), 268, 283, 317–319, 326
License(s)
  overview, 5–6
  assignments compared to, 9–10
  challenges to ownership that could affect, 18, 20
  defined, 5
  flexibility of, 7
  terminology of, 6
  See also Agent(s); Agreements that can affect licensing, avoiding conflicts among; Commercial potential, assessment of; Disclosure of your invention; Intellectual property rights; License agreement(s); Records and record keeping; Solicitation of potential licensees; Transferring ownership to your business
License agreement(s)
  overview, 178–179
  amendments and modifications of, 179
  "business terms" and "term sheet," defined, 178
  caution on promises to fix the agreement later, 341

Contract Worksheet, 179, 200–203
fact sheet as exhibit attached to, 236
fact sheet summarizing negotiations for, 235–238, 252
flexibility of, 7
for foreign licensees, 152–153
"good faith" and "best efforts," defined as terms, 239–241
hybrid, 212, 222
implied, 34
prior to patent issuance, 54
term (length) of the agreement, defined, 178
without intellectual property protection, 55
written, as strongly recommended, 9
written, licensee wants to proceed without, 236, 238, 252
See also Audits of license agreements; Breaches of license agreements; Disputes; Evaluation of a license agreement presented to you; Letter of intent; License agreement form; License agreement provisions; Modifications to your license agreement by licensee; Negotiation of licenses; Option agreements; Oral license agreements; Patent misuse and illegal agreements; Process of licensing; Records and record keeping; Termination of license agreements
License agreement form, 255–298
definitions of contract terms listed at beginning, 255
editing the RTF, 408
Exhibit A, 274, 290
handwritten modifications, 298
initialing of handwritten changes, 298
language use in modifications, 297
modifications to, 297–298
new sections, adding, 298
online source for, 408
ordering of sections, 298
sample License Agreement, 257–274

signatures, 274, 288–290
word processor, modifications with, 297
See also License agreement provisions
License agreement provisions
advance payments, 261, 280
agent as party to, 180
alternative dispute resolution, 271–272, 285–286
approval of licensed goods, 153
assignability, 189, 273, 288, 333, 342–343
attorneys' fees and expenses, award of, 270, 285, 332, 333–335, 374
audits, 228
commercialization (exploitation) requirement, 267, 283, 316–317
confidentiality, 268, 284
copyright registration, 183, 257–258, 275–276
date of execution/effective date, 195, 384
definition of the invention, 180–184, 256, 257–258, 275–276
definition of the licensed process, 185, 256, 258, 275–276, 277
definition of the licensed product, 180–181, 184–185, 258, 276
deliverables, 293–295
fee to licensor, nonrefundable and nonrecoupable, 263
force majeure provision (natural disasters), 290–291, 333, 344
governing law (choice of law), 152, 272, 286, 332, 337–338
headings, 333, 344
infringement lawsuits against third parties, 267, 283, 373
installation of equipment, 292, 355
insurance, product liability, 268, 283, 317–319
integration (entire understanding), 272, 287, 332, 340–341, 376
intellectual property laws, compliance with, 267, 283, 373

intellectual property protection, generally, 153, 183, 184, 266, 312–315
intentions of the parties, 256
introduction, 255–256
invalidity, 272, 287, 376
jurisdiction, 152, 272, 287, 332, 339
liability of licensor, limitation of, 266
name/nickname of invention, 256
no patent, 183
notices, 273, 287, 333, 341, 377
parties, identification of, 179–180
patented and nonpatented (but protectable) features, 184, 258, 276
patent is issued, 181–182, 257
patent is pending, 181, 182, 256, 257, 275
payments and statements to licensor, 263, 282, 371
reissues, extensions, continuations, divisions, substitutions to patent, 182, 275
relationships (no joint venture), 273, 287, 333, 342, 377
severability, 332, 340
tech support, 292–293, 356–357
trademark registration, 183–184, 257–258, 275–276
trade secrets, 257–258, 275–276
training of licensee employees, 291–292, 354–355
waiver, 272, 287, 332, 339–340, 376
"whereas" provisions, 256
See also Attachments and exhibits provision; Escrow; Evaluation of a license agreement presented to you; Grant of rights; Improvements to invention; Indemnity; Quality control and samples; Royalty provisions in license agreements; Term (length) of license agreements; Termination of license agreements; Warranties
Licensed process, definition in the license agreement, 185, 256, 258, 275–276, 277

Licensed products
combination products, 185
dates for introduction of, 385
defined, 184
definition in the license agreement, 180–181, 184–185, 258, 276
definition in the option agreement, 246
evaluation of a license agreement presented to you, 370
Licensees
challenging validity of your intellectual property, 18
death of, and assignment of license agreements, 189
defined, 6
purchased by another company, and assignment of license agreements, 189
as the right partner for your endeavor, 136
subsidiary creation by, and assignment of license agreements, 189
See also Licensee's license agreement; Profits by licensee; Reputation of licensee company; Solicitation of potential licensees
Licensee's license agreement, overview, 366
Licensing calendar, 383–385
Licensing Executives Society, 399
Licensing Journal, finding an agent through, 118
Licensing memorandums, 142
Licensor, defined, 6
Limited liability
corporations and, 21, 24
limited partnerships and, 23
piercing the corporate veil, 24
Limited partnerships, 23, 25
LLCs (limited liability companies)
assignment of rights to, 25–31
for investment by family and friends, 99–100
license agreement signature line for, 289–290
nondisclosure statement signature line for, 167–168
personal guarantees of loans to, 97

Loans
    bank loans, 97, 99
    credit cards, 96
    crowdlending, 98
    defined, 16, 95
    due diligence of lenders, 101
    from family and friends, 98–100
    as form of investment, 108
    impact on licensing, 16
    investments compared with, 95–96
    joint ownership and effects of, 106–108
    personal guarantees of, 97
    qualification for (credit risk modeling), 99
    qualification for (five "Cs" of credit), 99
    signature loans, 96–97
    Small Business Administration (SBA) loans, 98
    written form of, state law requiring, 106
    See also Promissory notes; Secured loans
Local governments, development funding
    through, 102
Lump sum payment for a license (as alternative
    to royalties), 208–209, 210, 211, 384
Lump sum payment for an assignment, 211

M

Machines, utility patents and, 48
Manual of Patent Examining Procedure (MPEP,
    USPTO), 55, 400
Manufacturing or outsourcing agreements, and
    impact on licensing, 16
March-in rights (federal rules for university-
    owned inventions), 82
Marketability-per-nation analysis, 149–151
Marketability. See Commercial potential,
    assessment of
Marketing costs as net sales royalty deduction, 215
Marketing scams. See Scams
Mask works, 67
Material breach
    commercialization requirement and, 316
    defined, 324–325

Mediation
    overview, 335, 336
    agent agreements and, 126
    arbitration following, 337
    for employment-related ownership disputes, 84
    evaluation of a license agreement presented to
        you, 374
    joint ownership agreement provision for, 110
    license agreement provision for, 271, 285–286,
        337
    option agreement provision for, 245
    pros and cons of, 336
    See also Alternative dispute resolution;
        Arbitration
Minimum annual royalty payments, guaranteed
    (GMAR), 209, 212–214, 219, 222–223, 262, 282
Minnesota, preinvention assignments, limits on,
    74, 75
Miscellaneous provisions. See Boilerplate
    (miscellaneous) provisions
Modifications to your license agreement by
    licensee
    overview, 366
    legalese you might encounter in, 367
    "most important" approach to, 368
    redline/strikeout revisions, 368
    stylistic changes, 366
    substantive changes, 366
    weighing the consequences, 366–367
    "yes, no, maybe" approach to, 367
    See also Evaluation of a license agreement
        presented to you
Monitoring license agreements
    overview, 12, 382
    for breaches of agreement, 10
    dates and time periods, tracking of, 383,
        384–385
    quality control, 395
    See also Disputes
Montana, forum selection invalid in, 339
Most favored nations/licensee clause, 296,
    361–362, 375

N

National Congress of Inventor Organizations (NCIO), 147, 398
National Inventor Fraud Center, 131
Natural disasters (force majeure) provision, 290–291, 333, 344
NDAs. *See* Nondisclosure agreement(s)
Negotiation of licenses
  overview, 12, 178–179, 232
  asking questions vs. making demands, 232
  avoiding costly mistakes: the list of "don'ts," 232, 234
  competing inventors, making statements about, 235
  Contract Worksheet, 179, 200–203
  of disputes, 388
  fact sheet summarizing results of, 235–238
  personal conduct during, 232, 234
  personal meetings as preferable for, 232
  real-world example of, 14
  record keeping for, 207
  reminding the licensee that any deal is subject to approval of the final contract, 207
  resources for, 235
  "take it or leave it" deal, 234
  "turning it over to the lawyers" phase (for drafting/revising), 178
  two distinct stages of, 233
  the written license contains objectionable items, 233
  written license not forthcoming, 236, 238, 252
  See also Letter of intent; License agreement(s); Option agreements
Net sales, defined, 207, 214
Net sales royalty
  overview, 209–210, 280
  defined, 208, 261, 280
  generally recommended over lump sum payment, 210

  license agreement provisions for, 214, 216, 220–221, 261
  net sales, defined, 207, 214, 216
  promotional items included in, 220–221, 261
  See also Advance payments; Net sales royalty deductions
Net sales royalty deductions
  overview, 214–215, 216
  cap on, 216
  credits and returns, 216
  debts and uncollectible accounts, 215
  fees, 215
  freight/shipping, 216
  limit placed on amount of, 216
  local taxes, 216
  as percentage vs. actual amounts, 216
  promotion/marketing/advertising, 215
  quantity discounts, 215
  sales commission, 215
Newsletters, 138
No joint venture provision, 273, 287, 333, 342, 377
Nondisclosure agreement(s) (NDAs)
  overview, 34, 156
  for audits, 227
  authority to bind the company, checking the signing person for, 158
  caution about waiver agreements, 156
  company-provided NDA, review of, 159
  company unwilling to sign, 158, 168
  compare yours with sample agreements in text, 34
  defined, 16
  and disclosure of inventions, 33
  for employees and independent contractors, 174–175
  for evaluation agreements, 17
  evaluation of a license agreement presented to you, 373

immunity from liability (whistleblower
protection for employee/contractors), 174
impact on licensing, 16
implied confidential relationships, 170
with investors, potential, 102
and joint ownership, 107
for know-how, 57
lawsuits claiming damages for breach of, 157,
165–166
licensing memorandums containing, 142
option agreements and, 251
for outsourcing or manufacturing agreements,
17
for personal market research evaluators
(logbook approach), 40
prior to product presentations, 140, 146
proceeding without, and methods of guarding
rights, 168–170
protection of confidential information a
requirement of, 157, 166
record keeping of disclosures, 161
trade secrets protected via, 57, 157–158, 165
for trade-show on-the-spot product
presentations, 146
waiver agreements, 156, 170–172
See also Nondisclosure agreement provisions
Nondisclosure agreement provisions
overview, 157, 160
certification of confidentiality of disclosure, 161
company-provided agreements, checking for
basic elements of, 159
definition of confidential information, 161,
162
exclusions from confidential information,
162, 165–166
indemnification, 172
injunctions, 172–173
jurisdiction and choice of law, 173–174
miscellaneous (boilerplate), 163, 167

mutual NDA (optional), 160, 166
obligations of the receiving party, 163, 166
one-way NDA, 160–168
One-Way Nondisclosure Agreement (sample),
162–164
oral disclosures not permitted, 161
oral disclosures to be protected by follow-up
letter to confirm, 161
parties, 160, 162
signatures, 167–168
summary, 160, 162
time periods, 163, 166–167
Nonfunctional features. *See* Functional vs.
nonfunctional features of invention
Nonobviousness requirement for utility patents,
49–50
Nonprofit corporations, transferring ownership
to, 24
Nonrecoupable, defined, 209
Nonrefundable, defined, 209
North Carolina
forum selection invalid in, 339
preinvention assignments, limits on, 74
Notice provisions, 273, 287, 333, 341, 377
Notification of intellectual property on products
(e.g. symbols), 313–314
"Notwithstanding," defined, 367
Novelty requirement for utility patents, 49, 50

O

Occurrence policies, 318
Online resources
agent, finding, 118
angel investors, 101
arbitration, 336
attorneys, finding, 399, 402
business directories, 139
companion page for book, 2
crowdsourcing sites, 98

foreign licensees, 154

form downloads, 408, 409

insurance for pursuit of infringement lawsuits, 315

inventors' associations, 147

legal research, 399

license exchanges, 138

Nolo's Legal Encyclopedia, 400

patent searching, 400–401

Provisional Patent Application (PPA) filing, 53

on scams, 131

Small Business Administration (SBA), 98

specific company information on, 140

trade associations, 137–138

trade magazines, 138

trademark applications, 63

trade newsletters, 138

trade shows, 144

updates of book, 2

U.S. Securities and Exchange Commission (SEC), 102–103

See also Crowdsourcing; Internet

Operations provisions, in letter of intent, 241

Option agreements

overview, 236, 244–245

arbitration/dispute resolution, 251

attachment of license agreement to, 246

confidentiality and, 251

defined, 16

definitions of the invention and the licensed products, 246

as exclusive, 246

fact sheet summarizing negotiations incorporated into, 236, 251

and good faith/best efforts, 246

impact on licensing, 16

jurisdiction and choice of law, 251

license agreement attached as exhibit to, 245

licensee does not proceed ("does not exercise its option"), 246, 251

licensee proceeds ("exercises its option"), 245

negotiation of the license agreement following, 245

nonrecoupability and nonrefundability of option payment, 246

option period, 245

payments for option, 246

renewals of, 251

reservation of rights and, 251

and royalties, deduction from, 246

sample Option Agreement, 246–251

See also Evaluation agreements

Oral disclosures, 161

Oral license agreements

overview, 9

alternative dispute resolution provisions for, 238, 252

fact sheet summarizing negotiations as basis of, 236, 252

proof of, as difficult, 9

state laws limiting to one year term, 9

and written agreement not forthcoming, 236, 238, 252

written agreements as preferable to, 9, 34, 252

Ordinary innovation, 49

Ornamentality, defined, 64

Outsourcing or manufacturing agreements, and impact on licensing, 16

P

Partnerships

agreements for, and impact on licensing, 17

defined, 17

license agreement signature line for, 289

nondisclosure statement signature line for, 167–168

Partnerships, transferring ownership to
  agent representation distinguished from, 23,
    116–117
  assignment of rights, 25–31
  authorized signatures, 110
  creation of, by actions of the parties, 22–23
  joint ownership created via, 21, 104, 110
  limited partnerships, 23, 25
  and personal liability for business debts, 22, 23
  tax consequences of, 22
  See also Assignment of rights
Patent(s)
  continuation in part (CIP), licensing of, 393
  "first to file" as priority in, 48, 50
  grant backs and, 363
  license agreements and, 181–182, 184, 257,
    258, 275, 276
  licensee challenging validity of, 18
  mailing a copy of invention specs to yourself
    will not provide protection, 64
  resources, 400–401
  same result accomplished by different/novel
    method, 42
  search for new inventions similar to yours, 383
  search for novelty/patentability, 93
  search for warranty purposes, 302–303
  search patent databases, 42, 53, 400–401
  See also Assignment of rights; Design patents;
    Joint ownership created by patented
    joint invention; Patent misuse and illegal
    agreements; Patent pending period; U.S.
    Patent and Trademark Office (USPTO);
    Utility patents
Patent infringements
  overview, 20, 58
  attorney for, 20, 316
  insurance for, offensive and defensive, 315, 316
  lawsuits against, license agreement provision
    for, 314–315

money earned via lawsuits for, 58, 315
  as ownership challenge, 20
  pendency (patent pending) period and, 51–52
  and publication of pending application by
    USPTO, 52, 60
  same invention, 20
  same invention, licensed without patent
    protection, 55
  similar or equivalent invention, 20
Patent License Exchanges, 399
Patent misuse and illegal agreements
  overview, 390
  antitrust laws and, 390
  grant backs as, 363, 390
  hybrid licenses and royalty rate after patent
    expiration, 212, 392–393
  illegal license length, 392
  Patent Misuse Amendments, 391
  preventing development of competitive
    products, 394
  tie-ins and tie-outs, 392
  tying arrangements, 390–392
Patent pending period
  hybrid license agreements during, 212, 222
  infringement activity not preventable during,
    51–52
  license agreements during, 54, 181, 182, 256,
    257, 275
  and Nonpublication Request, 60
  and publication of pending patents by the
    USPTO, 52, 60
  and trade secrets, importance of, 32, 34, 60,
    171–172
  and waiver agreements, 171–172
Payments
  of agents, 120–121, 282
  caution against assignments for "promise" of
    future payments, 25
  evaluation of a license agreement presented to
    you, 371

execution of agreements accompanied by, 12

implied confidential relationships depend on expectation of, 170

license agreement provision, 282

lump sum, for a license, 208–209, 210, 211, 384

lump sum, for assignment, 211

for option agreement, 246

in U.S. currency, 226, 263

See also Advance payments; Late payments; Revenues; Royalties

Payment statements, 263, 282, 371

Personal jurisdiction. *See* Jurisdiction

Per-unit royalty, 208, 210, 262

Per-use royalty, 208

Phone calls for solicitation, 143–144

Pioneer inventions, 218

Pitches. *See* Product presentations; Solicitation of potential licensees

PPA. *See* Provisional Patent Application

Principal, defined, 116

See also Agent(s)

Prior art

and public domain as defense against NDA breach, 165–166

and utility patents, 49, 50, 53, 54

Processes, utility patents and, 48

Process of licensing

overview, 10

evaluation of prospective licensees, 12

example of, 13–15

execution (signing) of agreements, 12

meeting prospective licensees, 10, 12

schematic overview of, 11

See also Commercial potential, assessment of; Disclosure of your invention; License agreement(s); Monitoring license agreements; Negotiation of licenses; Records and record keeping; Solicitation of potential licensees; Termination of license agreements

Product pie, 219

Product presentations

advice from a successful inventor, 13–14

agent as performing duties of, 117

appointment for, as goal of solicitation, 142

emotions and, 147

nondisclosure agreements prior to, 140, 146

preparation for, 146–147

prototypes for, and alternatives, 135

Provisional Patent Applications and protection during, 54

at trade shows, on-the-spot, 145–146

written materials as supplement to, 147

See also Solicitation of potential licensees

Product reps. *See* Agent(s)

Profits by licensee

and deficiency in guaranteed minimum annual royalty, 214

and financial analysis to determine royalty rate, 218–219

25/75 split of, as starting point for royalty rate, 218

Promissory notes

forms for, 100

for loans from family and friends, 100

Promotional items, including in net sales, 220–221, 261

Property

evaluation of a license agreement presented to you, 370

as term in license agreement, 255, 256, 257–258

Proprietary rights. *See* Intellectual property rights

Prototypes

for agent representation, 119

alternatives to, 135

benefits of developing, 93

as cost in licensing, 93–94, 119, 135

finding a company to build, 135

for product presentations, 135

Provisional Patent Application (PPA)
  overview, 53–54
  coinventors and, 107
  expiration of, 54
  and filing date for patent, 50, 53, 54
  international patents and, 54
  joint ownership and, 107
  online filing of, 53
PTO Independent Inventor Resources, 398
Public domain
  copyright law not protecting works in, 65
  as defense to lawsuit for breach of NDA,
    165–166
  defined, 45
  expired patents as entering, 51

Q

Quality control and samples
  evaluation of a license agreement presented to
    you, 373
  monitoring of, 395
  provision for, 267, 283, 317
Quantity discount deduction from net sales, 215

R

"Reasonable best efforts," defined as term, 241
"Reasonable efforts," defined as term, 240–241
Records and record keeping
  agreements that could affect licensing, 18, 19
  business notebook and files, 34–35
  clean copy of completed license agreement, 383
  Contract Worksheet for license agreement,
    200–203
  date of execution/effective date of license
    agreements, 195, 384
  dates and time periods, tracking of (calendar),
    383–385
  of disclosures, 161
  of negotiation of license agreements, 207
  review of signed documents to avoid conflicts,
    15, 18

  for tax deduction of inventing expenses, 94, 95
  written agreements essential, 34, 35
  See also Inventor's notebook; Nondisclosure
    agreements
Relationships (no joint venture) provision, 273,
  287, 333, 342, 377
Renewal of agreements
  dates for, 384
  initial term with, 198, 260, 323
  notice date, 384
  option agreements, 251
  record keeping of, 18, 19, 384
  short term with, based upon sales, 197, 198,
    260, 279
Renewal of trademark registration, 62, 383
Representations, defined, 300
  See also Warranties
Representation. *See* Agent(s)
Reputation of licensee company
  licensor investigation of, 12
  scams and rule enabling evaluation of, 130
  and "take it or leave it" deal, 234
  and trade secret disclosure without an NDA,
    168, 169
Reservation of rights in license agreements, 186,
  191, 277–278
  evaluation of a license agreement presented to
    you, 371
  expressly excluding a particular market,
    188–189, 259
  and multiple licensees of same invention, 189,
    191
Revenues
  gross revenues, defined, 116
  joint ownership and splitting of, 104, 105, 110
  joint ownership created by acceptance of
    money, 106–108
  from lawsuits for patent infringements,
    58, 315
  See also Advance payments; Fees and costs;
    Payments; Royalties; Taxes

Reverse engineering
 patents as protected from, 58–59
 trade secrets not protected from, 59, 167
Reversion/reversionary rights, 9
Right of first refusal
 of invention improvements, 296, 360–361, 375
 of new inventions, 361
Royalties
 overview, 207, 280
 dates for payment of, 385
 dates to complain about accuracy of
  statements, 385
 defined, 208
 definition of terms used in discussions of,
  207–209
 evaluation of a license agreement presented to
  you, 371
 fluctuating/sliding rate, 211, 220
 FRANDS and "reasonable," 190
 hybrid license royalty, 212, 222, 262, 280–281,
  392–393
 in letter of intent, 244
 lump sum payment as alternative to, 208–209,
  210, 211, 384
 minimum annual royalty payments,
  guaranteed (GMAR), 209, 212–214, 219,
  222–223, 262, 282
 option payments deducted against, 246
 per-unit royalty, 208, 210, 262
 per-use royalty, 208, 210–211
 reduced if patent not issued, 54
 spreadsheets for tracking and computing, 207
 See also Advance payments; Audits of license
  agreements; Net sales royalty; Royalty
  provisions in license agreements; Royalty
  rates; Royalty statements
Royalty provisions in license agreements
 advance payment, 221–222, 280
 date for recording sales, 220, 221, 261
 in Exhibit A, 290

F.O.B. royalties, 225, 263, 282
guaranteed minimum annual royalty
 payments, 222–223, 282
hybrid royalty payments, 222
indemnity and fund from, 265–266, 282–283,
 308–310
intellectual property registration costs, 312–313
late payments, 229, 264, 372
license fee, 263
net sales, 214, 221, 261
net sales deduction cap, 216
net sales with percentage deduction (vs. actual
 amount), 216
payment acceptance does not preclude
 disputes, 226
payment "cure" provision, 225
payment in U.S. currency, 226, 263
payment period, 225–226
promotional items included in net sales,
 220–221, 261
royalty rate, 222
for spin-offs, 223, 224, 263, 281
sublicensing revenues, 225, 263
third-party license royalty, 223, 225, 263, 281
See also Royalty rates
Royalty rates
 overview, 216–217
 based on financial analysis, 218–219
 help to obtain basic rate information, 217
 industry "standard" (customary), 217, 219
 inventor dissatisfaction with, 219–220
 license agreement provision for, 222
 and term of agreement, shortening of, 220
 25/75 split of profits as starting point for, 218
Royalty statements
 overview, 385
 analysis of, 385–386
 attorney or accountant consult about, 387
 audits and, 387–388
 common problems, 386

confirmation letter to licensee, 386

contact licensee for explanation, 386–387

dates for complaints about, 385, 387

outside references to validate sales numbers, 387

sales figures inaccurate, 386–387

See also Audits

S

Samples and quality control. *See* Quality control

Savings analysis, royalty rates based on, 218

Scams

overview, 128

angel investors, 101–102

distinguished between an agent and scam artist, 130–131

federal Invention Developer laws against, 129–130, 131

fees and costs, 128–129, 130

Internet attempts to find an agent and probability of encountering, 118

marketing firms, 41

operation of, 128–129

resources on, 131

Secured loans

collateral requirements, 99

defined, 97, 107

rights to your invention as collateral for, as limiting license rights, 107–108

written agreement for, 107

Securities laws, compliance with, 102–103

Security agreements, 107

Semiconductor Chip Act, 67

SEPs (standard-essential patents), 190

Service agreements

overview, 12

determining the need for, vs. service provisions in the license agreement, 352–353

incorporated into the license agreement, 353

for know-how (training), 57, 355

resource for, 353

for tech support, 356

See also Deliverables

Service provisions

overview, 352

dates for, 384

evaluation of a license agreement presented to you, 377

if separate service agreement needed instead of, 352–353

installation of equipment, 292, 355

technical support, 292–293, 356–357

training the licensee's personnel, 291–292, 354–355

See also Deliverables

Severability, 332, 340

Shareholders, 23–24

Shop rights, 70, 77, 78–79, 84

Signature loans, 96–97

Signatures

agent agreements, 126

assignments, spouse signature, 25–26, 104

authority to bind the company, 110, 158, 167–168, 288–290

editing RTFs, 408

effective date as dependent on, 195

initialing of handwritten changes, 298

in inventor's notebook, as confidentiality agreement, 158

joint ownership, spouse signatures, 104

license agreements, 274, 288–290

nondisclosure agreements, 167–168

Silva, David, 13–15

Small Business Administration (SBA) loans, 98

Software created after hours, ownership of, 71

Solar Energy Industries Association, 139

Sole proprietorships
  license agreement signature line for, 288–289
  nondisclosure statement signature line for, 167
Sole proprietorships, transferring ownership to
  advantages of, 21–22
  name/fictitious business name of, 21–22
  no actions required to transfer, 25
  personal liability for all debts of, 21
Solicitation of potential licensees
  overview, 134, 142
  agreement to protect confidentiality required
    prior to, 140
  appointment for formal presentation as goal
    of, 142
  biases of companies against outside
    submissions, 140–142
  commercial potential, realistic assessment of,
    136
  company, gaining knowledge of specific, 135,
    139–140
  difficulties with performing, as reason to use
    an agent, 117, 134, 136
  finding companies, 137–139
  industry, gaining knowledge of, 135–136
  inside contacts within companies, 141, 142
  inventors' associations and, 147
  letter writing, 143
  licensing memorandums not recommended
    for independent inventors, 142
  methods of making contact, 142–146
  no license at all is better than a bad license,
    136, 154
  phone calls, 143–144
  sample letter, 143
  trade shows, 144–146
  and working within your industry, 137
  See also Agent(s); Foreign licensees; Product
    presentations
South Carolina, forum selection invalid in, 339

Spain, as market, 151
Spin-offs, royalties on, 223, 224
Spouses
  assignment signature by, 25–26, 104
  joint ownership signature by, 104
Standard-essential patents (SEPs), 190
Standard Industrial Classification (SIC) Code,
  139
Standards. See Industry standards
Start-up expenses, tax deductability of, 36
  See also Tax deductions of invention expenses
State laws
  for attorneys acting as agents, 126–127
  attorneys' fees, award of, 333–334
  implied duty of licensee to market/exploit the
    invention, 311
  incorporation, 24
  independent contractors distinguished from
    employees, 87
  jurisdiction/forum selection invalid in, 339
  limited partnerships, 23
  loans required to be in writing, 106
  oral agreements, 9
  preinvention assignments, limits on, 73–75
  state employees and ownership of inventions, 81
  trade secrets, 56, 169
  usury, 227
  See also Governing law (choice of law);
    Jurisdiction
State lending assistance, 102
Strickler, Yancy, 98
Sublicensing, 186, 189, 191–192, 225, 259, 263,
  277
  evaluation of a license agreement presented to
    you, 370
SuperPages.com, 139
Survival of license agreement provisions
  following termination, 270, 285, 319, 329
  evaluation of a license agreement presented to
    you, 374

T

Tax deductions of invention expenses
overview, 395
business requirement, 103
depreciated expenses, 36, 395
IRS legal basis for, 103
record keeping for, 36, 103
start-up expenses, 36
when the deduction begins, 36
See also Taxes
Taxes
attorney or accountant consultation for, 394, 395
capital gains vs. ordinary income, 394
as deduction against net sales, 216
foreign license agreements and, 153, 395
limited partnerships and, 23
partnerships and, 22
separate service agreements and consequences for, 353
See also Tax deductions of invention expenses
Tech support provision, 292–293, 356–357
Telephone security, 61
Tennessee Valley Authority, as exception to employee-inventor rules, 81
Term (length) of license agreements
overview, 260–261, 278
commencement of (date of execution/effective date), 195, 384
evaluation of a license agreement presented to you, 371
factors to consider in setting length of, 194–195
fixed term without renewal, 197–198, 261, 280, 323
hybrid license royalties and, 212, 392–393
illegal license length, 392
indefinite term, 197, 261, 279

initial term with renewals, 198, 260, 323
in letter of intent, 241
as long as the licensee continues to sell the products, 198–199, 261, 280
for patent term, 196–197, 212, 260, 278–279, 323
renewal date, 384
renewal notice date, 384
shortening, with a view toward renegotiating royalties, 220
short term with renewal rights based upon sales (and exhibit for sales requirement), 197, 198, 260, 279
termination rights as working in conjunction with, 196, 197, 268–269, 284, 323
Termination of license agreements
overview, 196, 284, 322
at-will (licensee option), 269, 285, 324
audit provision following, 227
bankruptcy and, 326–327
for breaches, caution against overbroad provisions, 325
for breaches of agreements, 10, 316, 324–325
cure period to fix breaches, 325–326
date of, 385
effects of (posttermination provision), 270, 285, 327–328, 374
evaluation of a license agreement presented to you, 374
for failure to bring to market (exploit), 269
for fixed term, 323
licensor's right to, 269–270, 326
record keeping of, 18, 19
return of molds, plans, and related materials, 328, 374
reversion/reversionary rights, 9
sales of products following, 327
sample License Agreement, 268–270

survival of provisions following, 270, 285, 319, 329, 374

term (length) of agreement works in conjunction with, 196, 197, 268–269, 284, 323

for territory not exploited, 152–153, 194, 270, 326

upon the expiration of the last remaining patent, 392

Territory, license agreement provisions for

overview, 192–194, 278

cross-territory sales, limiting, 193, 259, 278

evaluation of a license agreement presented to you, 371

"gray marketing" outside, 193

statement of, 259

territory not exploited, right to terminate as to, 152–153, 194, 270, 326

worldwide territory, 178, 192, 194

Test marketing, 94

Third-party license royalty, 223, 225

Trade associations

defined, 137

foreign, 154

as source of potential licensees for solicitation, 137–138

Trade directories, 139

Trade magazines

advertisements, and finding an agent, 118

advertisements, and finding solicitation sources, 138

for basic royalty rate information, 217

sales figures and charts as reference in, 387

for solicitation sources, 138

Trademark Office. *See* U.S. Patent and Trademark Office (USPTO)

Trademarks

overview, 8, 61–62

cost of registration deducted from royalties, 312–313

"date of first use" as establishing, 62–63

defined, 61

federal registration, 62–63

fees, 67

first to use in commerce as qualifying for, 48, 62

grant backs and, 362

hybrid licenses and, 393

infringement of, burden of proof for, 68

intent-to-use registrations (reserving), 63

international, 62

length of protection, 62, 67

licensee challenging validity of, 18

licensee registers in its name, 313

monitoring, 383

nonfunctional features of invention and, 45–46, 62, 66

product configuration protected by, 61–62

quality controls in license agreement and maintenance of, 283

registration not required, 62

renewals of registrations, 62, 383

resources on, 63, 401

state registration, 63

symbol for, 62

trade dress protected by, 61

waiver agreements as threat to, 171

websites and, 63

Trade newsletters, 138

Trade secrets

overview, 8, 55–56, 156–157

active management required for, 60–61

companies generally will not steal, 169

company reputation, and disclosures made without an NDA, 168, 169

defined, 55–56

disclosing "around" the secret, 170

disclosures as terminating protection of, 32, 55

disclosures made without an NDA, methods
to help guard rights, 168–170
federal law (DTSA) protecting, 56, 169, 174
functional features of invention and, 45–46,
56–57
grant backs and, 362
improper means of obtaining, defined, 56, 169
independent development as legitimate means
of obtaining, 59
independent development resulting from
disclosure of, 165–166
infringements, proving, 58
know-how as, 57
legitimate means of obtaining, 58–60
length of protection (confidentiality), 58
misappropriation of, defined, 169
nondisclosure agreements to protect, 57,
157–158, 165
nonfunctional features of invention and, 57
patented inventions also protected by, 32, 60
patents compared to, 57–60
pendency (patent pending) period and need
for protection of, 32, 34, 60, 171–172
publication of the pending patent by USPTO
and loss of protection for, 60
reverse engineering as legitimate means of
obtaining, 59, 167
sample escrow agreement for release of,
346–350
security systems and protection of, 61
stamps and signs to mark, 61
state laws and, 56, 169
See also Nondisclosure agreement(s)
Trade shows, 118, 144–146
Training of licensee employees
service agreement for, 57, 355
service provision for, 291–292, 354–355

Transferring ownership to your business
overview, 20–21
assigning rights, 21
nonprofit corporations, 24
See also Corporations, transferring ownership
to your; Joint ownership (co-ownership);
Partnerships, transferring ownership to; Sole
proprietorships, transferring ownership to
Tying arrangements, 390–392

U

Underlying inventions, utility patents and, 48
Uniform Trade Secrets Act (UTSA), 169
United Inventors Association (UIA), 398
University employees, ownership of inventions,
81–83
University of Oregon, Innovation Center factors
for commercial potential, 37–39
Unlimited exclusive license, 9
U.S. Department of Commerce
and foreign licensees, 154, 401
SIC Code, 139
website, 154
U.S. Department of Energy, as exception to
employee-inventor rules, 81
Usefulness requirement for utility patents, 48–49
U.S. Patent and Trademark Office (USPTO)
address and contact information, 54–55
assignment of patents, recording of, 25
categories of inventions qualifying for utility
patent, 48
design patents, 65
patent application, 47
patent searching online, 401
patents legally required to be issued or
rejected within 3 years, 51
PTO Independent Inventor Resources, 398

publication of pending applications, Nonpublication Request, 60

publication of pending applications, request for early, 60

publication of pending patent applications, 52, 60

requirements for utility patent, 48–50

resources available, 400

rules and regulations governing, 55

scam complaints and responses must be publicized by, 130

trademark intent-to-use applications, 63

trademark registrations, 63

trademark resources, 401

website, 400

U.S. Postal Service, as exception to employee-inventor rules, 81

USPTO. *See* U.S. Patent and Trademark Office

U.S. Securities and Exchange Commission (SEC), 102–103

U.S. Small Business Administration (SBA)

foreign licensee assistance by, 154, 401

test for commercial potential of inventions, 37–38

website, 401

U.S. Supreme Court

employed-to-invent doctrine, 75

illegal license lengths for patents, 392

licensees may challenge validity of intellectual property ownership, 18

licensees required to purchase nonstaple goods, 291

and obviousness requirement for utility patents, 49

Utah, preinvention assignments, limits on, 75

Utility patents

overview, 8, 47

application process (prosecution of the patent application), 52–53

applications, assignment of rights sent with, 25, 28–29

applications, licensing prior to issuance of, 54

attorney for, 52–53

categories of inventions qualifying for, 48

claims of, drafting, 51

continuation application, 51

defined, 47

expiration of, and entrance into the public domain, 51

fees and costs, 47, 53, 58, 94, 148, 312–313

filing an application, 47

filing date, expiration of provisional application and, 54

filing date, provisional application's effect on, 50, 53, 54

"first to file" as priority in, 48, 50

functional features of invention and, 45–46

as "hunting license" to stop infringers, 47

legal deadlines for filing, 53

length of time required to obtain, 53

maintenance fees, 47, 58

name of invention, 256

nonobviousness requirement, 49–50

novelty requirement, 49, 50

prior art as factor in, 49, 50, 53, 54

publication of pending applications by USPTO, 52, 60

resources for, 52, 53

term extensions due to government regulations or review, 50–51

term of, 50–51

trade secrets compared to, 57–60

usefulness requirement, 48–49

See also Patent pending period; Provisional Patent Application (PPA); U.S. Patent and Trademark Office (USPTO)

V

Venture capitalists (VCs), 102–103

W

Waiver, in license agreements, 272, 287, 332, 339–340, 376

Waiver agreements (of confidentiality), 156, 170–172

Warranties
overview, 20, 300–301
"best of your knowledge," 303
defined, 300–301
evaluation of a license agreement presented to you, 372
guaranteeing ownership, 301
as license agreement provision, 264, 266, 282, 310
noninfringement (without qualification), 302–303
noninfringement (with qualification), 302
not addressed in licensee's agreement, 310
power and authority (ownership), 301
See also Indemnity; Warranties by licensee

Warranties by licensee
overview, 310
as license agreement provision, 266, 310
to obey the laws, 311
to sell the invention, 310–311

Washington, preinvention assignments, limits on, 75

Websites. *See* Internet; Online resources

Whistleblower protections in NDAs, 174

Wikipedia, and finding trade associations, 137

Wills, joint ownership created by, 104

Y

Yet2.com, 138, 399 ⬤